Ethics and Trauma in Contemporary British Fiction

48 DQR STUDIES IN LITERATURE

Series Editors

C.C. Barfoot - A.J. Hoenselaars
W.M. Verhoeven

Ethics and Trauma in Contemporary British Fiction

Edited by
Susana Onega and
Jean-Michel Ganteau

Amsterdam - New York, NY 2011

Cover photo: Jessica Aliaga Lavrijsen, 2009

Cover design: Aart Jan Bergshoeff

The paper on which this book is printed meets the requirements of
'ISO 9706: 1994, Information and documentation - Paper for documents -
Requirements for permanence'.

ISBN: 978-90-420-3326-9
E-Book ISBN: 978-94-012-0008-0
©Editions Rodopi B.V., Amsterdam - New York, NY 2011
Printed in The Netherlands

TABLE OF CONTENTS

INTRODUCTION

JEAN-MICHEL GANTEAU AND SUSANA ONEGA

The rise of trauma theory in the critical field is a recent phenomenon associated with the revival of interest in the ethical component of literature that took place in the 1980s as a reaction of academia against the scepticism and relativism propounded by extreme postmodernist thinkers and certain uses of deconstruction, especially in the wake of the controversy surrounding the discovery of Paul de Man's pro-Nazi writings in 1987 and Jean Baudrillard's publication of a series of short polemics denying the reality of the Gulf War.[1]

In an earlier study,[2] we traced the evolution of this ethical turn and its branching out into two main, antagonistic trends: a neo-humanist

The co-authorship of this Introduction and the co-editing of the book by Susana Onega is part of a research project funded by the Spanish Ministry of Science and Innovation (MICINN) and the European Regional Development Fund (ERDF) (code HUM2007-60135) while those of Jean-Michel Ganteau are part of a project funded by the French Ministry of Education through the laboratory to which he belongs (EA 741).

[1] Jean Baudrillard, "La Guerre du Golfe n'aura pas eu lieu", *Libération*, 4 January 1991, 5; "The Reality Gulf", *The Guardian*, 11 January 1991, 25; "La Guerre du Golfe a-t-elle vraiment lieu?" *Libération*, 6 February 1991, 10 ; "La Guerre du golfe n'a pas eu lieu", *Libération*, 29 March 1991, 6 ; *La Guerre du Golfe n'a pas eu lieu*, Paris: Galilée, 1991; *The Gulf War Did Not Take Place*, trans. and intro., Paul Patton, Bloomington and Indianapolis: Indiana University Press; Sydney: Power Publications, 1991.

[2] Jean-Michel Ganteau and Susana Onega, Introduction, in *The Ethical Component in Experimental British Fiction since the 1960's*, eds Susana Onega and Jean-Michel Ganteau, Newcastle: Cambridge Scholars Publishing, 2007, 1-9. See also Geoffrey Galt Harpham, *Getting It Right: Language, Literature, and Ethics*, Chicago: University of Chicago Press, 1992; Michael Eskin, "Introduction: The Double 'Turn' to Ethics and Literature?", *Poetics Today*, XXV/4 (Winter 2004), 557-72; *"On the Turn": The Ethics of Fiction in Contemporary Narrative in English*, eds Bárbara Arizti and Silvia Martínez-Falquina, Newcastle: Cambridge Scholars Publishing,

ethics, of a rather normative, deontic type, implying an overall moral dimension, generally associated with the stable ego of the character as present in classic realist texts based on linguistic transparency; and a newer, Levinasian and post-Levinasian ethics, of a non-deontic, non-foundational, non-cognitive, and above all non-ontological type, expounded by critics like Zygmunt Bauman,[3] Andrew Gibson,[4] Robert Eaglestone,[5] or Drucilla Cornell,[6] very much at home with experimentalism, that has come to be identified with the practice of postmodernism. Within this second trend, a variety of more specific and context-sensitive branches have appeared under the wider banners of the ethics of truths (highly compatible with literature's powers of defamiliarisation) and the ethics of alterity, or the ethics of affects, place, spectrality and pleasure, among many others, all of them oriented towards some wider opening, some greater sensibility and a surrender of "the same" in favour of "the other/the infinite", that which is "otherwise than being",[7] that which is not here, with correlative notions like vulnerability and disinterestedness.

Trauma theory as it is applied in the essays contained in this book belongs in the sphere of this non-deontic, post-Levinasian ethics. The concrete origins of the theory are traceable to the Yale School of deconstruction, where former pupils or colleagues of Paul de Man, like Cathy Caruth, Shoshana Felman and Geoffrey H. Hartman moved from deconstruction to trauma studies, as they felt the need to develop new critical tools capable of accounting for the assessment of Holocaust fiction and the testimonies of survivors. Their work combines resources from a number of critical schools, including

---

2007; Susana Onega, "The Ethics of Fiction: Writing, Reading and Representation in Contemporary Narrative in English: A Research Project", in *Literatures in English: Priorities of Research*, eds Wolfgang Zach and Michael Kenneally, Tübingen: Stauffenburg Publishers, 2008, 57-64.

[3] Zygmunt Bauman, *Postmodern Ethics*, Oxford: Blackwell, 1993.

[4] Andrew Gibson, *Towards a Postmodern Theory of Narrative*, Edinburgh: Edinburgh University Press, 1996; *Postmodernity, Ethics and the Novel: From Leavis to Levinas*, London: Routledge, 1999.

[5] Robert Eaglestone, *Ethical Criticism: Reading After Levinas*, Edinburgh: Edinburgh University Press, 1997.

[6] Drucilla Cornell, *The Philosophy of the Limit*, London and New York: Routledge, 1992.

[7] Emmanuel Levinas, *Otherwise than Being: or, Beyond Essence* (1974), trans. Alphonso Lingis, The Hague: Martinus Nijhoff, 1981.

Freudian psychoanalysis, feminism, New Historicism and deconstruction.

It is a commonplace of trauma studies that the pioneer of trauma research in the medical field was Pierre Janet, a contemporary of Freud's, who collaborated with Jean-Martin Charcot at the Pitié Salpêtrière in Paris and worked on memory impairment and dissociation in the case of traumatised patients. However, it is Freud's name that, inevitably, crops up most often in the literature on the subject, with "Moses and Monotheism" (1939) as the most often quoted of his texts. Earlier essays like "Thoughts for the Time on War and Death" (1915), and "Beyond the Pleasure Principle" (1920), are also widely recognised as having played an essential part in the definition of psychic trauma as different from and, in principle, unrelated to, physical trauma. As Roger Luckhurst notes in his useful introduction to the rise of trauma theory,[8] in the transition from the early to the late nineteenth century, the meaning of "trauma" and related terms like "traumatic", "traumatism", or "traumatise" underwent a significant "transfer of meaning from the physical to the psychical [as a result] not just of emerging mental sciences but also of Victorian modernity". The turning point in this transfer of meaning was the recognition by medics "that [railway] accident victims could escape physical injury completely, yet suffer persistent forms of mental distress long after the event". As Luckhurst explains, in "On the Psychical Mechanism of Hysterical Phenomena", published as early as 1883, Freud and Joseph Breuer made a path-breaking observation when they contended that "the strange physical symptoms of the hysteric – the trance states, violent mood swings, amnesia, partial paralysis of the body, and so on – could be modelled on the traumatic effects of accidents".[9] From this insight, Freud and Breuer went on to define psychical trauma as the inability to assimilate an unprecedented or overwhelming event by the usual mental mechanisms:

---

[8] Roger Luckhurst, "Mixing Memory and Desire: Psychoanalysis, Psychology, and Trauma Theory", in *Literary Theory and Criticism*, ed. Patricia Waugh, Oxford and New York: Oxford University Press, 2006, 497-507.
[9] *Ibid.,* 498.

> ... a psychical trauma is something that enters the psyche that is so unprecedented or overwhelming that it cannot be processed or assimilated by usual mental processes. We have, as it were, nowhere to put it and so it falls out of our conscious memory, yet is still present in the mind like an intruder or a ghost.[10]

After his distancing from Breuer, Freud's flagging interest in traumatic neurosis was revived by confrontation with massive shell-shock neurosis during World War I. At the time, physically sound soldiers who broke down and refused to return to the front were systematically treated as malingerers or deserters. However, they suffered not only from "memory gaps, but also repeatedly re-experienced extreme events in flashbacks, nightmares, and hallucinations months or even years afterwards".[11] As Anne Whitehead points out in her useful study, *Trauma Fiction*, Freud approached this phenomenon in a series of essays beginning with "Thoughts for the Times on War and Death" (1915) and "On Transcience" (1916), continuing with "Mourning and Melancholia" (1917) and culminating in "The Uncanny" and "Beyond the Pleasure Principle" (1920).[12] In these shorter, earlier texts, Freud works on the persistence of primitive, or anterior psychic states and elaborates on the movement of trauma as ceaseless return to the traumatic moment of fixation. From the crucial perception that trauma goes along with a failure of memory, he goes on to establish an opposition between the sane person's ability to memorise dates and the traumatised patient's compulsion to repeat the traumatic event, and to relive the past, obliterating the distinction between past and present and disrupting the linear model of temporality. Characteristically, the compulsive repetition of the traumatic event or episode does not take place immediately after it has occurred. On the contrary, there is usually a chronological gap, what Freud describes in *Moses and Monotheism* as the "incubus period", or period of "latency", sometimes of many years, between the traumatic event and the appearance of its

---

[10] *Ibid.*, 499.
[11] *Ibid.*, 500.
[12] Anne Whitehead, *Trauma Fiction*, Edinburgh: Edinburgh University Press, 2004, 133.

symptoms, so that the memories are theoretically subject to retrospective transformation and open to endless reinterpretation.

As is well known, Freud thought that the earliest form of trauma is sexual trauma, which he situates in childhood. As Whitehead recalls, already in "Project for a Scientific Psychology", published in 1895, Freud had contended that the crucial element in the workings of sexual trauma is its "belatedness", the fact that the event is not registered as traumatic until much later, when the child has reached sexual maturity and only after a second event in adult life produces a jolt to transform the meaningless fragments from childhood into significant memories. It is only after this second event that the symptoms of the trauma are expressed in the form of nightmares or flashbacks. Characteristically, the event is experienced again with full force but perceived as incomprehensible and belonging in the present. As Whitehead points out, to Freud, the neurotics' "compulsion to repeat" traumatic experiences over and over again, constitutes "an attempt to achieve a retrospective mastery over the shocking or unexpected event that has breached the defensive walls surrounding the psyche". However, the repetition is not in itself a guarantee of cure, since "Although the event returns in a vivid and precise form in the traumatic nightmare or flashback, it is simultaneously accompanied by amnesia".[13]

The notions of "belatedness" and "repetition compulsion" honed out by Freud were elaborated on by psychoanalysts like Pierre Janet, Carl G. Jung and Sandor Ferenczi.[14] One of Janet's most useful contributions in this respect was his distinction between "traumatic memory" and "narrative memory" and his contention that the neurotic's cure is achieved only after the patient manages to integrate the fragmentary contents of nightmares or flashbacks, arranging them chronologically and situating them in the past of the individual's life history.[15] This insight was reinforced by Carl C. Jung's observation, after working in the Burgholzli Psychiatric Hospital in Zurich from

---

[13] *Ibid.*, 119, 140.
[14] See especially, Sandor Ferenczi, *Le traumatisme* (1982), Paris: Payot, 2006. See also Marc Amfreville, *Écrits en souffrance: Figures du trauma dans la littérature nord-américaine*, Paris: Michel Houdiard Éditeur, 2009, for a masterful application of Ferenczi's ideas to the analysis of trauma in US literature.
[15] Whitehead, *Trauma Fiction*, 140.

1900 to 1910, that in many cases in psychiatry, the patient has a secret story no one knows of. To Jung, therapy only really begins after the investigation of that wholly personal story, what he describes as "the patient's secret, the rock against which he is shattered. If I know his secret story, I have a key to the treatment."[16] It is this narrative aspect of trauma that makes the findings of trauma studies so relevant for creative writers and critics alike.

The pioneering work on traumatic neurosis and shell shock carried out by Freud, Janet, Jung and other early psychoanalysts continued in the first two thirds of the twentieth century. However, trauma studies did not surface as a distinct medical branch until 1980, "when post-traumatic stress disorder (PTSD) was first included in the diagnostic canon of the medical and psychiatric professions ... [as a] result of sustained political campaigning by Vietnam veterans". Only after conclusive evidence of the impact of wartime experience on combatants was gathered by the research commissioned by these veterans, did the American Psychiatric Association acknowledge for the first time that "a psychiatric disorder could be wholly environmentally determined and that a traumatic event occurring in adulthood could have lasting psychological consequences".[17] It is at this point that, as Whitehead notes, the concept of trauma is transferred from medical and scientific discourse to the field of literary studies, thus providing the basis for the development of a critical theory seeking to elaborate on the cultural and ethical implications of trauma. As was pointed out earlier, this transference took place at the University of Yale in the mid-1990s.

The earliest evidence of this transference was the publication, in 1991, in two issues of *American Imago*, of a series of essays reprinted in 1995 in a volume edited and introduced by Carthy Caruth, entitled *Trauma: Explorations in Memory*. As Caruth explains in the Introduction, the aim of the volume was to "examine the impact of the experience, and the notion, of trauma on psychoanalytic practice and theory, as well as on other aspects of culture such as literature and pedagogy, the construction of history in writing and film, and social or

---

[16] Carl G. Jung, *Memories, Dreams,* Reflections, New York: G. P. Putnam's Sons, 1965, 117.

[17] Whitehead, *Trauma Fiction*, 4.

political activism".[18] In other words, the approach to trauma was wholly interdisciplinary, with contributions by clinical psychologists, psychiatrists, sociologists, pedagogues, creative writers, film-makers and literary critics. This interdisciplinarity is a defining characteristic of trauma studies at large, addressing, as it does "both public and private questions that are relevant for psychology, philosophy, ethics and aesthetics".[19]

In the Introduction, Caruth rereads the Freudian notions of belatedness and repetition-compulsion from a Lacanian perspective and defines the traumatic experience as "the inability fully to witness the event as it occurs, or the ability to witness the event fully only at the cost of witnessing oneself". Central to the traumatic event, then, are its unaccountability and immediacy, that is, the impossibility of understanding and placing it in time and memory, so that "The force of this experience would appear to arise precisely ... in the collapse of its understanding". [20] Drawing on Freud's contention that, in the case of trauma, belatedness is not caused by "repression" but "latency", Caruth goes on to argue that "its blankness – the space of unconsciousness – is paradoxically what precisely preserves the event in its literality". To Caruth, this means that "what trauma has to tell us – the historical and personal truth it transmits – is intrinsically bound up with its refusal of historical boundaries; ... its truth is bound up with its crisis of truth".[21]

In Chapter 5 of her later book, *Unclaimed Experience: Trauma, Narrative, and History*, Cathy Caruth returns to the question of memory and truth, building on Lacan's rereading of Freud's interpretation of dreams as the fulfilment of a wish. As she explains, whereas Freud interprets the dream of a father traumatised by the accidental burning of his child as the story of a sleeping consciousness unable to face the traumatic fact, Lacan focuses his interpretation on the awakening forced on the father by the voice of the child appealing to him from inside the dream itself: "Father, don't you see I am

---

[18] Cathy Caruth, Introduction, in *Trauma: Explorations in Memory*, ed. Cathy Caruth, Baltimore, MD and London: Johns Hopkins University Press, 1995, 4.

[19] Luckhurst, "Mixing Memory and Desire", 497.

[20] Caruth, Introduction, in *Trauma*, 7.

[21] *Ibid.*, 8.

burning?"[22] In Lacan's reading, the awakening represents a paradox about the necessity and impossibility of confronting death: "Waking up in order to see, the father discovers that he has once again *seen too late* to prevent the burning."[23] The dream, then, is neither a fiction (as in Freud's interpretation) nor a direct representation, but a repetition that reveals, in its temporal contradiction, how father and child are inextricably bound together, how the very consciousness of the father as father is linked inextricably to the impossibility of adequately responding to the plea of the child at its death.[24] As Caruth explains, "it is this bond that the dream reveals, exemplarily as the real, as an encounter with a real established around an inherent impossibility".[25] Thus, "Lacan resituates the psyche's relation to the real not as a simple matter of seeing or of knowing the nature of empirical events, not as what can be known or what cannot be known about reality, but as the story of an urgent responsibility, or what Lacan defines, in this conjunction, as an *ethical* relation to the real".[26]

Therefore, if for Freud, the compulsion to repeat the traumatic experience over and over again constitutes an attempt to achieve a retrospective mastery over this experience, from a Lacanian perspective, it offers a glimpse into the true nature of the survivor's plea: his compulsion to define himself in relation to the traumatic event, and to respond adequately to it, and his inability to do so.

In his contribution to *Trauma: Explorations in Memory*, entitled "Truth and Testimony: The Process and the Struggle",[27] Dori Laub describes the need of Holocaust survivors in similar terms as "an imperative need to *tell* and thus to come to *know* one's story, unimpeded by ghosts from the past against which one has to protect oneself", undermined by the realisation that

---

[22] Cathy Caruth, *Unclaimed Experience: Trauma, Narrative, and History*, Baltimore, MD: John Hopkins University Press, 1999, 99-102.

[23] *Ibid.*, 100 (emphasis in the original).

[24] *Ibid.*, 100-103.

[25] *Ibid.*, 103.

[26] *Ibid.*, 102.

[27] Dori Laub, "Truth and Testimony: The Process and the Struggle", in *Trauma*, 61-75. See also Geoffrey H. Hartman, *The Longest Shadow: In the Aftermath of the Holocaust*, Bloomington and Indianapolis, IN: Indiana University Press, 1996.

> ... no amount of telling seems ever to do justice to this inner
> compulsion. There are never enough words or the right words. There
> is never enough time or the right time, and never enough listening or
> the right listening to articulate the story that cannot be fully captured
> in *thought, memory* and *speech*.[28]

Trapped in this vital paradox, survivors characteristically structure
their whole life as a substitute for the mourned past and often have
resort to silence, even though the silencing of truth does not bring
about peace but rather provokes an endless struggle over delusion:
"The 'not-telling' of the story serves as a perpetuation of the tyranny
.... The longer the story remains untold the more distorted it becomes
in the survivor's conception of it, so much so that the survivor doubts
the reality of the actual events."[29] Paradoxically, however, according
to Laub, it is precisely the witnesses' failure to tell the traumatic
events without distortions, gaps and misconstructions about
themselves that is central to the Holocaust experience.[30]

   In "Trauma within the Limits of Literature", Geoffrey H. Hartman
extends the symptoms of trauma to our contemporary society at large,
which he sees as deeply wounded and ethically compliant, struggling
under "the impact of specific historical shocks like the Holocaust and
other genocides, but also [under] the impact of electronic media on the
feelings of viewers, especially the transmission of what Luc Boltanski
has named 'distance suffering' (*souffrance à distance*)".[31]
Traumatised by collective shocks of an unprecedented magnitude and
anaesthetised by the media, contemporary society has become
incapable of assimilating and expressing pain. Refusing witnessing
and mourning, contemporary society opts for silencing the truth, even
though, as Harman explains, "If there is a failure of language,
resulting in silence or mutism, then no working through, no catharsis,
is possible". Echoing Janet and Jung, Hartman contends that the value
of literature lies precisely in its ability to give voice to trauma:

---

[28] Laub, "Truth and Testimony", 63 (emphasis in the original).
[29] *Ibid.*, 64.
[30] *Ibid.*, 65.
[31] Geoffrey H. Hartman, "Trauma within the Limits of Literature", *European Journal of English Studies*, VII/3 (December 2003), 258.

"Literary verbalization ... still remains a basis for making the wound perceivable and the silence audible."[32]

Concurring with Hartman, Caruth and Dominick LaCapra,[33] among others, Stef Craps, in the Introduction to his monograph *Trauma and Ethics in the Novels of Graham Swift*, points to history as a key element in the analysis of collective trauma.[34] Indeed, concern for the victims of PTSD, or of other collective traumas like the Holocaust, the atomic bomb, the genocides in Cambodia, Croatia and Iraq, the terrorist attacks by fundamentalists, the "middle passage" and other racially induced massacres, or natural and man-made catastrophes like typhoons and Chernobyl cannot be envisaged apart from the general historical and socio-cultural context in which they took place and contributed to the rethinking of political and ethical values. As we have seen, a key feature in this rethinking of values is the unprecedented interest in the Otherness of the Other (a defining feature of trauma theory) that is constitutive of the all-encompassing cultural moment described earlier as the ethical turn in moral philosophy and criticism that emerged at the end of the twentieth century, after Europe had gone through the excruciating experience of two World Wars and the whole process of decolonisation and, largely under the influence of historical materialism, had learnt to give voice to the vanquished, losers and victims of history seen as catastrophe.

In the field with which we are more specifically interested here, this ethical and traumatic moment is both represented and actualised in a number of genres and subgenres, like the Holocaust novel (a sub-genre addressed by Gerd Bayer in his reading of three contemporary novels representative of the "postmemory" category),[35] the First

---

[32] *Ibid.*, 259.

[33] Dominick LaCapra, *History and Memory after Auschwitz*, Ithaca, NY and London: Cornell University Press, 1998; *Writing History, Writing Trauma*, Baltimore, MD and London: Johns Hopkins University Press, 2001.

[34] Stef Craps, *Trauma and Ethics in the Novels of Graham Swift: No Short-Cuts to Salvation*, Brighton and Portland: Sussex Academic Press, 2005. See also Susana Onega, "The Nightmare of History, the Value of Art and the Ethics of Love in Julian Barnes' *A History of the World in 10½ Chapters*", in *Ethics in Culture: The Dissemination of Values through Literature and Other Media*, eds Astrid Erll, Herbert Grabes and Ansgar Nünning, Berlin: Walter de Gruyter, 2008, 335-37.

[35] See Andrea Reiter, *Narrating the Holocaust*, London and New York: Continuum, 2000, for a taxonomy of generic and rhetorical devices used in Holocaust survivor narratives.

World War novel (Pat Barker's trilogy necessarily comes to mind here), but also the whole constellation of narratives constituting, for example, the various post-colonial canons (an example of which the reader is presented with in Anne Whitehead's reading of Delia Jarrett-Macauley's *Moses, Citizen and Me*), women's studies, and gay and lesbian literature (as made clear in José M. Yebra's analysis of the trauma of gayness in Alan Hollinghurst's *The Line of Beauty*). Indeed, these labellings must necessarily remain provisional since in most cases there appears to be a high degree of porosity between the categories and tags used to describe the literary corpus itself, on the one hand, and the critical/theoretical corpus, on the other, as the two seem to work hand in hand, having been constructed simultaneously. More precisely, in the field of poetics, there seems to be some consensus around the definition of what various critics, from Luckhurst to Whitehead have called "traumatic realism",[36] a category relying on such traits as: heavy resort to intertextuality; emphasis on repetition (in various guises, including anachronism, hence haunting and uncanny effects); fragmentation (in the extreme case of J.G. Ballard's *Atrocity Exhibition,* as Jakob Winnberg's essay makes clear); or also the representation of psychological de-doubling – confirmed, for instance, by the permanence of the Jekyll-and-Hyde motif in novels like Martin Amis' *Time's Arrow*, analysed by María Jesús Martínez-Alfaro. (Similarly, affective doubling and the creation of anxious modes as a means of anticipating and attempting to pre-empt or displace traumatic events or memories is an important formal influence on Amis and McEwan, amongst others.)

Even though these are the poetic traits most often referred to by trauma critics, we might as well add another, all-encompassing feature which corresponds to the process of intensification (through hyperbolical soliciting of affects) that crops up from the early definitions of trauma and which must be numbered among the most characteristic and efficient ways in which the text becomes rhetorically, thus pragmatically, iconic of PTSD, by relying not only on the representation but also on the performance of its affects, as shown in Susana Onega's evocation of the ethics of extreme troping in

---

[36] Michael Rothberg, *Traumatic Realism: The Demands of Holocaust Representation*, Minneapolis, MN and London: University of Minnesota Press, 2000.

Jeanette Winterson's *The Stone Gods*. Moreover, this overview of the narrative poetics of trauma cannot be complete without alluding to that hybrid form which seems to emblematise it best, that is, testimony, [37] a genre in its own terms, whose specificity is to be at the crossroads of the poetical, the historical, the clinical and the ethical, acting as the textual nexus of the relation to the Other and eschewing all vision of totality to promote openness and the refusal to reduce and stabilise meaning. [38]

What emerges from the above is some invariant common to most manifestations of trauma and particularly germane to literary expression and poetic investigation, that is, relation. For, in fact, the absence of relation (between various fragments of the traumatised victim, in Freud's and Ferenczi's analyses, for instance), or the inherent positing of relation are foremost in both the fictional and critical literature on the subject. This is evidenced by the repetitive nature of trauma which implies an inherent connexion to another place and another time, and another psychological state, that of the pre-trauma stage, most obviously (Otherness in its most basic parameters). And it also implies, as forcefully analysed by Caruth among others, the relation to other traumas, individual and collective, and to other people, as she makes clear when describing "the way in which our own trauma is tied up with the trauma of another, the way in which trauma may lead, therefore, to the encounter with another, through the very possibility and surprise of listening to another's word". [39] This commentary leads her to sketch a trauma-based, alterity-oriented definition of history: "To put it somewhat differently, we could say that the traumatic routine of history means that events are only historical to the extent that they implicate others"; [40] or else, "history is precisely the way in which we are implicated in each others' traumas". [41] The essays by Angela Locatelli, María Jesús Martinez-Alfaro, Silvia Pellicer-Ortín and Lena Steveker, and most of the

---

[37] See Shoshana Felman and Dori Laub, *Testimony: Crises of Witnessing in Literature, Psychoanalysis and History*, New York and London: Routledge, 1992.

[38] See Emmanuel Levinas, *Totality and Infinity: An Essay on Exteriority* (1961), trans. Alphonso Lingis, London: Kluwer Academic Publishers, 1991.

[39] Caruth, Introduction, *Trauma*, 8.

[40] *Ibid.*, 18.

[41] *Ibid.*, 24.

articles in the collection, address the question of the historicity of trauma from various perspectives.

Another notion that should be borne in mind is the quasi-natural association between trauma and an ethics of the deconstructionist (as opposed to the neo-humanist) type, whether it taps the power of defamiliarisation (as shown by Charley Baker's, Angela Locatelli's and Jakob Winnberg's readings), or is more concerned with what, in the wake of Drucilla Cornell, might be called an ethics of the limits, or a liminal ethics (the type of ethics that Georges Letissier sees in Ian McEwan's *Atonement* and that Jean-Michel Ganteau argues is at the heart of Michael Moorcock's *Mother London*). This leads us back full circle to Caruth's considerations on the link between trauma and ethics, for, as we have seen, the most characteristic feature of the relations between trauma and ethics is a waning or collapse of understanding that is concomitant with a waxing of violent affect, a crisis of understanding and history that goes along with the dominance of a paradox according to which trauma is known/expressed in the very impossibility of knowing/expressing itself, history is told in the impossibility of telling itself, testimony exists in the impossibility of telling itself totally. The observation of the paradoxical nature of trauma and its effects may lead us, ultimately, to introduce a third element in the trauma-ethics dyad, namely, the fact that the very openness of trauma (its temporal openness, the cognitive hole that it implies, the impossibility for the subject to conceive of its totality) may display some affinity with that time-honoured aesthetic category, the sublime which, in the Kantian definition, acts through surprise and the soliciting of paroxysmal affects, and entails a failure of faculties (more specifically of the imagination) to figure out a whole/the totality of an object of magnitude, thus producing a spasm in the subject. As with the sublime, then, literary trauma, concerned as it is with the experience of limits and the destabilisation of the accepted, might be considered as an emotional experience that strikes at the roots of identity and durably displaces certainties. Trauma would, thus, be compatible with a conjectural mode that would throw us subjects, in our capacity as readers and critics, into a complex ethical state of disquieted "negative capability".

READING TRAUMA IN PAT BARKER'S
REGENERATION TRILOGY

LENA STEVEKER

The First World War – "*the* great seminal catastrophe" of the twentieth century[1] – claims a prominent position in British cultural memory.[2] As Paul Fussell points out in his study *The Great War and Modern Memory*, the idea of this war, which the British have remembered and mythologised as the "Great War",[3] "derives primarily from the images of the trenches in France and Belgium".[4] These trenches have become a symbol not only of the murderous atrocities of the first modern war, but also of the countless soldiers who were severely traumatised by their experiences on the Western front. Servicemen on all sides broke down on a large scale once they were faced with the horrors of industrialised warfare. Tens of thousands of British officers and members of other ranks were

---

[1] George F. Kennan, *The Decline of Bismarck's European Order*, Princeton, NJ: Princeton University Press, 1979, 3.

[2] In his groundbreaking study, *The Great War and Modern Memory* (1975), Paul Fussell underlines the eminent importance of the First World War within British cultural memory when he argues that "the dynamics and the iconography of the Great War have proved crucial political, rhetorical, and artistic determinants of subsequent life" (Paul Fussell, *The Great War and Modern Memory*, Oxford: Oxford University Press, 2000, 315). For a detailed analysis of the First World War and the discourses of British cultural memory, see Chapter IX, 310-35, of Fussell's study.

[3] The exhibition "In Memoriam: Remembering the Great War", hosted by the Imperial War Museum London from 30 September 2008 to 6 September 2009, bore witness to the central role that the myth of the "Great War" still claims in official discourses of British cultural memory. See Imperial War Museum London, "In Memoriam: Remembering the Great War" (30 September 2008 – 6 September 2009): http://london.iwm.org.uk/server/show/conEvent.2495 (accessed 23/01/2009).

[4] Fusell, *The Great War*, ix.

diagnosed with diverse combat neuroses, which were subsumed under
the term "shell shock".[5]

It is this scene of traumatised soldiers of the First World War that
provides both context and thematic focus for Pat Barker's
Regeneration Trilogy, which investigates the impact of the First
World War on British society and culture. As I will argue in this
chapter, Barker approaches the aspect of trauma from three different
socio-cultural perspectives. In *Regeneration* (1991) and *The Ghost
Road* (1995), trauma is set in relation to aspects of gender, while *The
Eye in the Door* (1993) explores the psychological dimension of
trauma and provides ethical comments on the traumatised subject and
society.[6]

Trauma and gender

In the Author's Note to *Regeneration*, Barker acknowledges Elaine
Showalter's *The Female Malady* as one of the sources she used for
writing her novel.[7] In her study, Showalter elaborates on the
phenomenon once described as shell shock, arguing that "it was
related to social expectations of the masculine role in the war".[8]
Wartime notions of masculinity celebrated emotional repression and
self-control as the epitome of manly behaviour. As Showalter
explains:

> Chief among the values promoted within the male community of the
> war was the ability to tolerate the appalling filth and stink of the

---

[5] According to Elaine Showalter, 80,000 soldiers were diagnosed with shell shock by
the end of the war and from 1919 to 1929 114,600 ex-servicemen applied for pensions
on grounds of disorders related to shell shock (Elaine Showalter, "Male Hysteria:
W.H.R. Rivers and the Lessons of Shell Shock", in *The Female Malady: Women,
Madness, and English Culture, 1830-1980* [1985], London: Virago, 1987, 168, 190).
As Showalter explains, the term "shell shock" was a medical misnomer since the
symptoms the term was used to describe neither resulted from being shelled nor were
related to cases of shock (*ibid.*, 168). For a detailed analysis of shell shock as a cultural
concept, see Peter Leese, *Shell Shock: Traumatic Neurosis and the British Soldiers of
the First World War*, Basingstoke: Palgrave, 2002.
[6] Pat Barker, *The Regeneration Trilogy*, London: Viking, 1995, which includes the
three novels *Regeneration* (1-221), *The Eye in the Door* (222-424) and *The Ghost
Road* (425-459). All subsequent references are to this edition.
[7] *Ibid.*, 220.
[8] Showalter, "Male Hysteria", 171.

trenches, the relentless noise, and the constant threat of death with stoic good humor, and to allude to it in phlegmatic understatement. Indeed, emotional repression was an essential aspect of the British masculine ideal.

However, many British soldiers failed to live up to this "heightened code of masculinity",[9] since once they had been exposed to the intolerable circumstances of the trenches, they inevitably experienced intense emotions such as fear of death, grief and horror. The following eyewitness account gives an impression of what soldiers had to endure:

> I lost count of the shells and all count of time. There was no past to remember, and no future to think about. Only the present agony of waiting, waiting for the shell that was going to destroy us. Waiting to die.[10]

Caught between the atrocious reality of trench warfare and the social norms of gendered behaviour, many soldiers broke down with symptoms of hysteria including paralysis, blindness, deafness and muteness.[11] They thus showed a complaint that had until then been primarily known in women.[12] In his study *Shell Shock*, Peter Leese asserts:

> Before the war, hysterical women collapsed and retired to the bedroom there to find a private space away from the pressure and expectations of

---

[9] *Ibid.*, 169, 172.

[10] P.J. Campbell, *In the Cannon's Mouth*, London: Hamish Hamilton, 1979, quoted in Leese, *Shell Shock*, 26.

[11] According to Showalter, the term "shell shock" referred both to symptoms of hysteria and to neurasthenic disorders such as insomnia, nightmares, disorientation, dizziness, heart palpitations, and depression. Since "Symptoms of hysteria ... appeared primarily among the regular soldiers, while neurasthenic symptoms ... were common among officers", social class was a marker of difference among soldiers suffering from shell shock-related disorders (Showalter, "Male Hysteria", 174). For wartime discussions of the reasons for such class differences, see *ibid.*, 174-75.

[12] Leese points out that, although cases of male hysteria had already been discussed at the end of the nineteenth century, hysteria "was still a condition most widely associated with women" when the First World War broke out (Leese, *Shell Shock*, 17).

the male gaze, their collapse matching expectations of femininity and accepted within those limits. Male traumatic neurosis follows a similar pattern.[13]

According to Showalter, the reasons for epidemic hysteria among British soldiers are similar to those for female hysteria. Being forced into the constricted space of the trenches, men found themselves in a situation of confinement that in many ways was analogous to that of women in the nineteenth and early twentieth centuries.[14] Like Victorian women, many British soldiers suffered from powerlessness and the loss of autonomous control over their own lives.[15] Since hysteria was regarded as a female malady, "shell-shocked", that is, hysterical soldiers were accused of effeminate behaviour. Not only were they often stigmatised as malingerers and cowards, but many men also experienced their own emotional and physical reactions to the war as signs of emasculating weakness. The First World War, that was mythologised as the "most masculine of enterprises", ironically turned out to trigger a "crisis of masculinity" that expressed itself in shell shock: "If the essence of manliness was not to complain, then shell shock was the body language of masculine complaint, a disguised male protest not only against the war but against the concept of 'manliness' itself."[16]

Regeneration can indeed be read as a literary reworking of Showalter's argument since it functions as a "commentary on wartime constructions of masculinity".[17] Set in Craiglockhart War Hospital, the actual medical institution where many traumatised soldiers were sent during the First World War, *Regeneration* is populated by soldiers who have been sent to Craiglockhart in order to undergo treatment for shell shock. One of their therapists is Dr Rivers, who is modelled on the neurologist, anthropologist and psychiatrist W.H.R. Rivers who

---

[13] *Ibid.*, 39.

[14] Showalter "Male Hysteria", 172-73.

[15] *Ibid.*, 173-74.

[16] *Ibid.*, 172, 173, 171, 172.

[17] Greg Harris, "Compulsory Masculinity, Britain, and the Great War: The Literary-Historical Work of Pat Barker", *Critique*, XXXIX/4 (1998), 295. See also Leese, who argues that "Barker follows ... the feminist critic Elaine Showalter ... who believed shell shock to be an epidemic of male hysteria that helped redefine the gender roles of men ... in wartime and postwar British society" (*Shell Shock*, 174).

treated traumatised soldiers at Craiglockhart during the war.[18] As the novel's main voice of medical authority, Rivers contends that the First World War destabilises generally accepted constructions of gender because it forces men into roles which have traditionally been ascribed to women: "One of the paradoxes of the war ... was that this most brutal of conflicts should set up a relationship between officers and men that was ... domestic. Caring ... maternal."[19] According to Rivers, many soldiers break down, since they have been feminised by the war:

> They [the soldiers] had been *mobilized* into holes in the ground so constricted they could hardly move .... The war that has promised so much in the way of 'manly' activity had actually delivered 'feminine' passivity, and on a scale that their mothers and sisters had hardly known. No wonder they broke down .... Any explanation of war neurosis must account for the fact that this apparently intensely masculine life of war and danger and hardship produced in men the same disorders that women suffered from in peace.[20]

This statement is clearly reminiscent of Showalter, who argues that British First World War soldiers "were silenced and immobilized and forced, like women, to express their conflicts through their body".[21] Repeatedly contemplating the effects the war has on male self-perception, Rivers provides a running commentary that links his patients' war traumas to the notion of emasculation and, therefore, to questions of gender identity.

The Ghost Road, which is the third novel in Barker's trilogy, most explicitly links trauma and gender with the help of Rivers' treatment of a soldier named Ian Moffet, who suffers from a paralysis of his legs.[22] Rivers identifies Moffet's paralysis as "pure hysteria",[23] and

---

[18] For an account of Rivers' approach to male hysteria, see W.H.R. Rivers, "The Repression of War Experience", *The Lancet*, 2 February 1918: http://net. lib.byu.edu/~rdh7/wwi/comment/rivers.htm (accessed 30/01/2009). See also W.H.R. Rivers, *Conflict and Dream* (1932), London: Routledge, 1999. For a short overview of his therapeutic methods, see Showalter, "Male Hysteria", 181-89.

[19] Barker, *Regeneration*, 97.

[20] *Ibid.*, 98, 196 (emphasis in the original).

[21] Showalter, "Male Hysteria", 171.

[22] Barker, *The Ghost Road*, 440.

[23] *Ibid.*, 456.

Moffet makes it very clear that he is deeply troubled by the implications of emasculation in the diagnosis.[24] By way of treatment, Rivers draws stocking tops on Moffet's thighs, which he then gradually "lowers" until eventually "as the stockings are *unrolled*, so to speak, the ... paralysis .... Retreat[s]."[25] Getting rid of the feminine garments drawn onto his skin, Moffet quite literally gets rid of the signs of alleged femininity that undermine his male self-respect.[26] Therefore Rivers' treatment constitutes a strategy of re-masculinisation,[27] since it helps the patient to identify his symptoms as an expression of feminine behaviour, which he rejects because of the conflict this behaviour inflicts on his male identity.

In *Regeneration*, Rivers first realises that his patients have "been trained to identify emotional repression as the essence of manliness".[28] He knows that traumatised soldiers who show signs of hysteria violate the culturally coded norms of masculine behaviour: "Men who broke down, or cried, or admitted to feeling fear, were [regarded as] sissies, weakling, failures. Not *men*." Although Rivers is convinced that his patients have to acknowledge their emotions if they want their therapies to be successful, he is also fully aware of the socio-cultural implications of such acceptance:

> In leading his patients to understand ... that horror and fear were inevitable responses to the trauma of war and were better acknowledged than suppressed, ... that tears were an acceptable and helpful part of grieving, he [Rivers] was setting himself against the whole tenor of their upbringing.[29]

Wanting his patients to accept their reactions to the traumatic events they experienced at the Western front, Rivers not only criticises, but deconstructs traditional notions of masculinity:

> The change he demanded of them ... was not trivial. Fear, tenderness –
> these emotions were so despised that they could be admitted into

---

[24] *Ibid.*, 456-57.
[25] *Ibid.*, 441.
[26] *Ibid.*, 256-57, 459.
[27] Harris, "Compulsory Masculinity", 297.
[28] Barker, *Regeneration*, 44.
[29] *Ibid.*, 44 (emphasis in the original).

consciousness only at the cost of redefining what it meant to be a man.[30]

It is thus through Rivers that Barker links the discussion of trauma to the aspect of gender. Having Rivers realise that the construction of gender roles has to be re-negotiated because of his patients' traumatic experiences and their reactions to them, Barker presents trauma as the decisive trigger of the crisis of masculinity during the First World War.

Traumatic splits: selfhood and otherness
The second novel in Barker's trilogy, *The Eye in the Door*, also revolves around the topic of trauma. The novel explores questions of mental stability and the psychological possibilities of surviving trauma. It also negotiates ethical questions pertaining to the relationship between self and other. In her study *Unclaimed Experience: Trauma, Narrative, and History*, Cathy Caruth defines trauma as a "wound inflicted ... upon the mind".[31] Barker's protagonist Billy Prior, a severely traumatised officer sent to Rivers for treatment, suffers from such a wound of the mind. When he first arrives at Craiglockhart (in *Regeneration*), he has lost both his memory and his ability to speak, because he has suffered from "a traumatic experience by any standards",[32] as Rivers puts it. Although he is able to regain both speech and memory with Rivers' help, [33] it turns out (in *The Eye in the Door*) that his trauma has caused him to develop a split personality. Within certain situations, another personality controls his consciousness. Billy created this second personality in order to protect himself from both physical and psychological harm while serving in the French trenches. This other personality describes the moment of his creation as follows:

---

[30] *Ibid.*, 45.
[31] Cathy Caruth, *Unclaimed Experience: Trauma, Narrative, and History*, Baltimore and London: The Johns Hopkins University Press, 1996, 3.
[32] Barker, *Regeneration*, 95.
[33] *Ibid.*, 92-94.

"I was born ... in a shell-hole in France .... He [Billy] was wounded. Not badly, but it hurt. He knew he had to go on. And he couldn't. So I came."[34]

Both Rivers and Billy refer to this second personality as his "other state".[35] Since the second personality does not identify with Billy and even refuses to refer to him as "I",[36] he clearly represents an internal other who differs from Billy's self.

In order to depict this other, who represents the wound inflicted upon Billy's mind, Barker makes use of an image fed into the British cultural imaginary by Robert Louis Stevenson's novella *The Strange Case of Dr Jekyll and Mr Hyde* (1886). Stevenson's protagonist Dr Jekyll, who claims that his ability to create an internal other "sh[akes] the very fortress of identity",[37] embodies a late Victorian "paranoid terror of involution or the unravelling of a multiformed ego".[38] Barker takes up the image of Jekyll and Hyde in order to express an individual's fear of losing his autonomous identity. Both Billy and Rivers repeatedly refer to Stevenson's protagonist when they discuss Billy's state of dissociation. Having told Rivers about his internal other, Billy, for example, asks him: "You've read Jekyll and Hyde?"[39] Rivers in turn notices how Billy "spoke of looking at his hands to make sure they had not been transformed into the hairy hands of Hyde", and he contemplates that "It was odd how the term 'Jekyll and Hyde' had passed into the language, so that even people who had never read Stevenson's story used the names as a shorthand for internal divisions".[40]

Barker follows Stevenson's strategy of conceptualising Mr Hyde as Dr Jekyll's dangerous mirror image since Billy's internal other is constructed as an unfeeling and potentially violent personality. When

---

[34] Barker, *The Eye in the Door*, 395, 396.

[35] *Ibid.*, 321, 397.

[36] *Ibid.*, 394.

[37] Robert Louis Stevenson, *The Strange Case of Dr Jekyll and Mr Hyde* (1886), project Gutenberg, 1992, 86: http://www.gutenberg.org/dirs/etext92/hyde10.txt (accessed 20/01/2009).

[38] Judith Halberstan, *Skin Shows: Gothic Horror and the Technology of Monsters*, Durham, NC: Duke University Press, 1995, 55.

[39] Barker, *The Eye in the Door*, 322.

[40] *Ibid.*, 328.

Billy first tells Rivers about his split personality, he confesses that he is afraid that the other might live out – Hyde-like – his sadistic inclinations:

> I [Billy] have certain impulses which I do not give way to except in strict moderation and at *the other person's request*. At least, in *this* state I don't .... in the the the the other state I might not be so *fucking* scrupulous .... I'm frightened.[41]

Indeed, Billy's fear is justified because his other unscrupulously inflicts physical harm upon him.[42] However, in contrast to Stevenson's novella, in which Hyde is described as "pure evil",[43] Barker's novel does not characterise the figure of the other as the epitome of evil as I will argue in the following.

Billy is not the only character in *The Eye in the Door* who experiences moments of dissociation. Although Billy is the only one who develops a split personality, almost all traumatised soldiers who appear in Barker's novel come to see their fighting selves as personalities different from themselves.[44] It is through these characters that Barker presents the "Jekyll and Hyde performance" as a suitable method of coping with trauma and, therefore, as a positive phenomenon.[45] The poet Siegfried Sassoon, who features as one of Rivers' patients in *Regeneration* and *The Eye in the Door*,[46] explains that he has "always coped with the situation [at the Western front] by blocking out the killing side, cutting it off".[47] Another of Barker's traumatised characters argues along similar lines when he describes

---

[41] *Ibid.*, 321, 326 (emphasis in the original).

[42] *Ibid.*, 396-97.

[43] Stevenson, *Dr Jekyll and Mr Hyde*, 88.

[44] Even the non-combatant Rivers has experienced "an attempt at dissociation of personality", which leaves him "a deeply divided man". A traumatic event witnessed during his childhood "had occasioned a deep split between the rational, analytical cast of his [Rivers'] mind and his emotions" (Barker, *The Eye in the Door*, 330, 327).

[45] *Ibid.*, 388.

[46] The poet and novelist Siegfried Sassoon was indeed one of Dr Rivers' patients at Craiglockhart. For a short survey of Sassoon's medical history, see Showalter, "Male Hysteria", 178-80.

[47] Barker, *The Eye in the Door*, 389.

dissociation – which he defines as the ability to "switch off" – as an absolute necessity for fighting. In this officer's opinion, one of his men died because:

> "He couldn't switch off .... I'm quite certain when he finally got the bayonet in, he saw it bleed. And that's the opposite of what should be happening. You know I saw men once ... in close combat, as the manuals say, and one man was reciting the instructions. *Lunge*, one two: *twist*, one, two, *out*, one, two .... Literally killing by the numbers. And that's the way it has to be."[48]

Even Billy, who has begun to fear his internal other as a Hyde-like "malignant double",[49] comes to realise that this other fulfils a useful function. With the help of Rivers, Billy is eventually able to remember that his second personality, who claims to have been born in the French trenches, is not the only internal other he has created in his life. In fact, he experienced his first dissociation during his childhood in reaction to his parents' repeated marital conflicts. Rivers interprets this split as follows:

> "I think when you were quite small you discovered a way of dealing with a very unpleasant situation. I think you found out how to put yourself into a ... dissociated state. And then in France, under that *intolerable* pressure, you rediscovered it .... you rediscovered a method of coping."[50]

All of Barker's characters who comment on the "Jekyll and Hyde performance" characterise dissociation as their only means of surviving trauma. In *The Eye in the Door*, the "Jekyll and Hyde" state symbolises both a threat to and a necessity for the human mind. As Barker outlines the internal other not only as the harmful result of trauma, but also as a prerequisite for surviving it, she eventually undermines Stevenson's strategy of equating otherness with evil.

What is more, it is not the internal division into self and other as such that *The Eye in the Door* depicts as dangerous. Following contemporary psychoanalytical theory, Barker applies a concept of

---

[48] *Ibid.*, 346 (emphasis in the original).

[49] *Ibid.*, 328.

[50] *Ibid.*, 401 (emphasis in the original).

selfhood that is based on difference instead of identity. In her study *Shadow of the Other* (1998), psychoanalyst Jessica Benjamin points out that "Many contemporary relational analysts have begun to consider the importance of conceiving of a multiple rather than a unified self".[51] Within this context of multiple selfhood, Benjamin claims that self and other always co-exist within one and the same subject: "the *position* of the other is internal to the self."[52] She argues that:

> Tolerating ambivalence, being able to feel both love and hate toward the same object, does not mean that love and hate are synthesized so that love triumphs over hate. Rather, it means that hate can be borne. Difference, hate, failure of love can be surmounted not because the self is unified, but because *it can tolerate being divided.*[53]

According to Benjamin, the multiple self can sustain difference and contradiction, because it is able to recognise its others.[54] An individual experiences the co-existence of self and other as problematic only if the self cannot connect to its other(s), if it does not recognise its multiplicity:

> In dissociation, the awareness of transition or discrepancy between different self states is blocked. In this case we understand that *the self has lost contact with its multiplicity* because of dissociation ... and not because of a repression of conflict by a unified self.[55]

The concept of selfhood outlined in the second novel in Barker's trilogy bears a striking resemblance to theories such as Benjamin's. Once again acting as the novel's voice of authority, Rivers hypothesises that the internal other does not have to be integrated into the self, since both necessarily co-exist within a single subject: "Perhaps, contrary to what was usually supposed, duality was a stable

---

[51] Jessica Benjamin, *Shadow of the Other: Intersubjectivity and Gender in Psychoanalysis,* New York and London: Routledge, 1998, 105.
[52] Benjamin, *Shadow of the Other,* 102 (emphasis in the original).
[53] *Ibid.,* 105 (emphasis added).
[54] *Ibid.,* 100-108.
[55] *Ibid.,* 106 (emphasis added).

state; the attempt at integration, dangerous."[56] Rivers contends that
difference created by duality only destabilises the subject if self and
other are not linked to each other. For example, he believes his
colleague Head is able to cope with difference because his self and his
internal others have access to each other: "Head's dissociation was
healthy because the researcher and the physician each had instant
access to the experience of the other, and both had access to Head's
experience in all other areas of his life." In contrast, "[Billy] Prior's
[dissociation] was pathological because areas of his conscious
experience had become inaccessible to memory".[57] Billy is cut off
from his internal other. Neither can he remember anything he did in
"the other state",[58] nor can he control the actions of this other who
shares his body, but not his mind. When his internal other seizes
control over his body, Billy is completely at his mercy.

Although Billy fears and rejects his internal other, Rivers
encourages him to acknowledge "the other state" as part of his
identity:

> There has to be a moment of ... recognition. Acceptance. There has to
> be a moment when you look into the mirror and say, yes, this too is
> myself.[59]

Once again, this is reminiscent of *Dr Jekyll and Mr Hyde.* Rivers'
words echo those of Jekyll, who sees Hyde in a mirror and states:
"This, too, was myself."[60] But unlike Stevenson's protagonist, Billy
succeeds in accepting his internal other. While Jekyll commits suicide
once his initial acceptance of Hyde has turned into complete and utter
rejection, Billy is able to acknowledge the difference within himself.
He eventually "heal[s] the split" his traumas have caused,[61] because he
is able to recognise the other as part of himself. "Recognition" thus
turns out to be the key element of the concept of selfhood outlined in
Barker's novel since it constitutes a strategy of establishing and re-

---

[56] Barker, *The Eye in the Door*, 392 (emphasis added).
[57] *Ibid.*, 330.
[58] *Ibid.*, 321.
[59] *Ibid.*, 402.
[60] Stevenson, *Dr Jekyll and Mr Hyde*, 89.
[61] Barker, *The Eye in the Door*, 402.

establishing the link between self and internal other which trauma has severed.

An ethics of recognition

Like contemporary psychoanalysts who argue that self and other(s) necessarily co-exist within one and the same subject, philosophers such as Emmanuel Levinas and Paul Ricœur have also taken a keen interest in selfhood and otherness. Conceptual differences notwithstanding, both Ricœur and Levinas argue that the relationship between self and other is determined by ethical questions. In *Oneself as Another*, Ricœur not only states that otherness is "constitutive of selfhood as such",[62] but also emphasises that his concept of selfhood foregrounds "the ethical primacy" of the relationship between self and other.[63] According to Levinas, the other is linked to the self since its total otherness not only questions the self in its own existence, but also forces the self to enter into a relationship of responsibility from which it cannot withdraw.[64] As Simon Critchley puts it his Introduction to *The Cambridge Companion to Levinas*, it is the "event of being in relation with the other as an act or a practice ... that Levinas describes as 'ethical'".[65]

Within this context of ethics, the concept of selfhood that Barker's novel *The Eye in the Door* outlines can be seen to include an ethical dimension, too. When Rivers wants Billy to recognise his internal other, he not only recommends a psychological treatment meant to heal Billy's split personality. Asking his traumatised patient to acknowledge and accept the other within himself, Rivers also argues for an ethical strategy that allows the self to recognise the internal other instead of assimilating or silencing it. Recognition thus becomes

---

[62] Paul Ricœur, *Oneself as Another*, trans. Kathleen Blamey, Chicago: University of Chicago Press, 1992, 3.

[63] *Ibid.*, 168.

[64] Emmanuel Levinas, *Die Spur des Anderen. Untersuchungen zur Phänomenologie und zur Sozialphilosophie*, ed., trans. and foreword Nikolaus Krewani, Freiburg: Alber, 1983, 218-21.

[65] Simon Critchley, *The Cambridge Companion to Levinas*, Cambridge: Cambridge University Press, 2002, 12.

an ethical act that enables the self to accept the other as an entity in its own right.

However, in *The Eye in the Door*, it is not only the traumatised officer Billy who needs to recognise his internal other, but also British wartime society in general, which Barker repeatedly describes as incapable of acknowledging the traumatic experiences of those who fought in the First World War. Rivers has a dream in which he finds himself in the trenches:

> France. Craters, a waste of mud, splintered trees. This was a dreadful place .... He was entirely alone, until, with a puckering of the surface ... the mud began to move ... to rise and stand before him in the shape of a man. A man who turned and began striding towards England .... again the mud gathered itself into the shape of a man, faster and faster until it seemed that the whole night was full of such creatures, creatures composed of Flanders mud and nothing else, moving their grotesque limbs in the direction of home.[66]

As these mud men are clearly reminiscent of Billy's internal other, who was also born in a muddy hole in France, they symbolise the traumas of British soldiers. Rivers' dream further implies that England is confronted with traumatised soldiers returning home from the war just as Billy is confronted with his internal other.

Analogous to Billy's internal other, the mud creatures Rivers dreams of represent the Other of British wartime society. In several of her novels, Barker criticises the way in which British society treated these others. In *Another World*, in which she approaches the First World War through the memories of the dying ex-servicemen Geordie, Barker describes British postwar society as being engaged in a process of collective repression. Through Geordie, she illustrates how soldiers were obliged to repress their war traumas:

> I [Geordie] suppose the truth is I was shell-shocked, but they didn't seem to talk about that in them days. You just had to shut up and get on with it. You know, you were alive, you had the same number of arms and legs you set off with so what the bloody hell were you

---

[66] Barker, *The Eye in the Door*, 398.

moaning on about? That was the attitude, and for all you were supposed to be heroes .... You just had to snap back.[67]

The Eye in the Door explicitly accuses British society of having turned its back on those who fought in the war.

Billy's fiancée-to-be Sarah happens to come across a group of severely injured soldiers when she visits a war hospital:

> ... she saw ... a row of figures in wheelchairs, but figures that were no longer the size and shape of adult men. Trouser legs sewn short; empty sleeves pinned to jackets .... They'd been pushed out here to get the sun, but not right outside, and not at the front of the hospital where their mutilations might have been seen by passers-by.[68]

The soldiers, Sarah realises, are hidden away so that civilians do not have to face the atrocious reality of war that has been inscribed on these mutilated bodies.[69] In this scene, Barker exposes the hypocrisy of a society that marginalises those men for whose sufferings it is responsible. As these two examples show, Barker criticises British post-war society for rejecting its others. When Sarah furiously points out that "the country ... should bloody well be prepared to look at the result" of the war which manifests itself in the mutilated men hidden away from the public,[70] she does indeed call for an act of recognition. Through Sarah, Barker seems to argue that British society should have accepted its others instead of excluding and silencing them. Recognising them would have constituted an ethical act of acknowledging that these men and their traumas too were part of British society during and after the First World War.

As we have seen, Pat Barker's *Regeneration Trilogy* is intricately engaged in exploring the aspect of trauma. First, Barker argues that the traumas caused by the First World War served as the decisive trigger of the crisis of masculinity which British society was faced with during the war. Second, her novels present trauma as a wound of the mind that can only be healed if the self is able to sustain the

---

[67] Pat Barker, *Another World* (1992), *A Novel*, New York: Picador, 2000, 402.
[68] Barker, *The Eye in the Door*, 142-43.
[69] *Ibid.*, 145.
[70] *Ibid.*, 143.

difference between itself and its internal others to which it has relegated its traumatic experiences. Therefore, the novels can be seen as privileging a concept of selfhood that is based on difference instead of identity. And last, but not least, Barker's trilogy suggests that the process of healing the traumatised self has to undergo is based on recognition. The moment of recognition the novels call for constitutes an ethical act that not only allows the self to accept the other within itself caused by trauma, but also urges society to welcome the traumatised self back into its midst.

THE ETHICAL CLOCK OF TRAUMA IN
EVA FIGES' *WINTER JOURNEY*

SILVIA PELLICER-ORTÍN

The socio-historical events that shaped the last century have challenged our world-view and our perception of time in relation to history and the individual. Trauma studies have brought this fact to the fore and, consequently, their importance in the critical field has grown since its birth in the mid 1990s, while at the same time literary works have increasingly become privileged sites for the representation of the effects of individual and collective traumas in our contemporary age. However, the appearance of trauma studies should not be considered as an isolated phenomenon, since it is closely linked to the ethical turn in literary criticism and philosophy that took place in the 1980s. This ethical turn manifested itself in the critical field as a revival of interest in the ethical potential of literature, an issue that had come to a dead end in the previous decades with the demise of humanism. As David Parker, among others, has explained, the turn to ethics in the critical field ran parallel to "a turn to the literary within ethics, in the field of moral philosophy".[1] There is a clear connection, then, between the targets of moral philosophy, ethical criticism and the study of trauma in literature. What is more, ethical criticism and trauma studies are both centrally concerned with the individual. As Stef Craps has pointed out, "an important sub-strand of the ethical turn [characterised by] an intense preoccupation with the demands of otherness ... is also

The research carried out for the writing of this article is part of a research project financed by the Spanish Ministry of Science and Innovation (MICINN) and the European Regional Development Fund (ERDF) (code HUM2007-61035). The author is also grateful for the support of the Aragon Government and of her institution, the University of Zaragoza.

[1] *Renegotiating Ethics in Literature, Philosophy and Theory*, eds Jane Adamson, Richard Freadman and David Parker, Cambridge: Cambridge University Press, 1999, 14.

a defining feature of trauma theory".[2] In this respect, the study of trauma in literature may be regarded as a branch of the study of ethics in its different artistic manifestations.

Some literary texts more clearly require an ethical analysis than others, and this is the case of the works of Eva Figes. Born in Berlin in 1932 into an assimilated German-Jewish family, with the outbreak of the Second World War, Figes had to emigrate to Britain. Her father was able to escape from the Dachau concentration camp, but her grandparents were not, and they died in Poland. The traumatic memories triggered off by these family events and by the experience of war she endured as a child, her feelings of inadequacy and otherness due to her position as a German-Jew living in a foreign country, and her later attempts to assimilate and understand British culture and society as an adult are some of the facts that shape her literary production, especially her fictional work, which so far consists of sixteen novels.

Throughout her fiction, from the first novel, *Equinox* (1966), to the latest one, *A Journey to Nowhere: A Woman Looks for the Promised Land* (2008), Eva Figes invariably creates fragmented and deeply disturbed characters who strive for self identity and wholeness in the course of the narration. Most of these characters have endured some kind of traumatic experience that keeps them attached to the past, incapable of progressing towards the future. Consequently, all her novels share a number of recurrent motifs, such as the failure of human communication and relationships; the search for psychological identity and wholeness; the self-fragmentation and alienation of individuals; the complicated relationship between past and present; a background of war; the Holocaust; and the experience of being a Jew, among others. Most of her novels also have in common the use of Modernist techniques associated with stream-of-consciousness fiction, such as direct "interior monologue",[3] to represent the fluidity and fragmentariness of the characters' inner world.

Besides these common characteristics, the novels also show differences that allow us to classify them into three main groups:

---

[2] Stef Craps, *Trauma and Ethics in the Novels of Graham Swift: No Short-Cuts to Salvation*, Brighton: Sussex Academic Press, 2005, 9.
[3] Brian Gerard McLaughlin, *Structures of Identity: A Reading of the Self-Provoking Fiction of Christine Brooke-Rose, Bryan Stanley Johnson, Eva Figes, and Paul West*, Michigan: UMI Dissertation Services, 1981, 158.

feminist novels about the experience of women in a patriarchal world; novels about Postmodernist issues such as the instability of identity and the relativity of reality; and novels about the traumas caused by armed conflicts in general and the effects of the Holocaust and the experience of Jewishness in particular. *Winter Journey* is the first novel in this third group. Published in 1967, it was awarded the "Guardian Fiction Prize" the same year. On the whole, reviewers agreed that in this novel Figes had managed to portray in an admirable way the inner world of suffering and pain endured by the protagonist. When W.L. Webb, literary editor of *The Guardian*, gave her the award, he praised the depiction of the novel's main character in these terms: "we [readers] feel the stammer of that old heart, hear the grinding of that pack ice in his brain, and come to know, as if we had inherited it, the pain of his experience and the pulse of the will which keeps him going."[4] He also referred to the fact that Figes had been able to add "something" to our sense of what we are and what the novel can tell us. The need to find out what this "something" might be justifies my intention to carry out an analysis of the novel from the perspective of trauma studies.

Janus' story from the perspective of trauma studies

Winter Journey tells the story of Janus, an old and decrepit war veteran suffering from Post Traumatic Stress Disorder. In Greek mythology, Janus, the god of beginnings, gateways and doors, was usually depicted with two heads, looking in opposite directions, one to the past and the other to the future. The name, then, provides an accurate iconic image of the self fragmentation of the protagonist and of his traumatic conception of time for, unlike the Greek god, Figes' Janus is caught in an stagnant present associated with the phase of repetition-compulsion, in Freud's understanding of the term.[5]

According to Freudian psychoanalysis, one of the first symptoms of trauma is the distorted perception of time experienced by individuals or groups that have gone through some traumatic experience. Thus, in her book *Trauma. Explorations in Memory*, Cathy Caruth offers a definition of trauma as a pathology consisting

---

[4] Peter Conradi, "Eva Figes", in *British Novelists since 1960: Part 1: A-G. Dictionary of Literary Biography*, XIV/1, ed. Jay L. Halio, Detroit, MI: Gale, 1982, 300.

[5] Sigmund Freud, *Beyond the Pleasure Principle* (1920), ed. and trans. James Strachey, New York: W.W. Norton, 1989, 19-20.

> ... solely in the *structure of its experience* or reception: the [traumatic] event is not assimilated or experienced fully at the time, but only belatedly, in its repeated *possession* of the one who experiences it. To be traumatised is precisely to be possessed by an image or event.[6]

Also using Freudian terminology, Caruth employs the term "latency" to designate "the period during which the effects of the experience are not apparent, ... the successive movement from an event to its repression to its return".[7] And, in keeping with her allegiance to the Yale School of deconstruction, she defines the belatedness of trauma as an "aporia" in Derrida's use of the term, since: "the traumatic event is not experienced as it occurs, it is fully evident only in connection with another place, and in another time."[8] Belatedness, latency and the unspeakability of trauma implicit in its aporetic nature are, then, essential concepts for the understanding of the representation of trauma in literature.

The critics Ronald Granofsky (1995) and Sean McAlister (2006), in an attempt to adapt psychological terminology to the analysis of trauma in literature, have tried to identify the specific narrative devices employed in fiction to depict traumatic events. Both signal as most frequent the abandonment of realistic categories of "time, space, causality and number".[9] Granofsky argues that "the trauma novel depicts the state of mind after those categories have broken down in the face of the monstrously irrational",[10] while, according to Sean McAlister, the blend of past and present plays a crucial role in representing identities fragmented by traumatic events.[11]

Echoing this, *Winter Journey* presents Janus as an old man, but still possessed by the horrible events of war he experienced as a young soldier, and still unable to assimilate them by transforming his traumatic memories into narrative memories. In keeping with this,

---

[6] *Trauma: Explorations in Memory*, ed. Cathy Caruth, Baltimore, MD and London: Johns Hopkins University Press, 1995, 4-5 (emphasis in the original).

[7] *Ibid.*, 7.

[8] Cathy Caruth, "Introduction to Psychoanalysis, Culture and Trauma I", *American Imago* (Spring 1991), 7.

[9] Ronald Granofsky, *The Trauma Novel: Contemporary Symbolic Depictions of Collective Disaster*, New York: Peter Lang, 1995, 17.

[10] *Ibid.*, 22.

[11] Sean McAlister, "'The Explosive Devices of Memory': Trauma and the Construction of Identity in Narrative", *Language and Literature*, XV/1 (February 2006), 104.

most of the novel consists of Janus' stream of thoughts as they are being formed in his mind through free association of ideas, even though the narrative is controlled at a higher narrative level by an omniscient narrator who depicts the events happening around Janus and offers readers access to his and the other characters' minds (for instance, his neighbours). In order to understand Janus' life story, readers would have to impose a chronological pattern on Janus' subjective flux of perceptions and thoughts, separating present from past events, current actions from memories of the war, with the scanty help of the external narrator's comments.

This chronological arrangement of events, whose true nature only becomes clear at the end of the novel, eventually allows readers to build up the story of a man who was a soldier in an unspecified armed conflict, and who in the course of it went deaf in a train accident.[12] His name was Janus Stobbs, he was married to Nora and they had two children, Nan and Ted. Their common and uneventful life changed dramatically with the outbreak of the war. After his return from the front, he was rejected by every member of his family. The action is situated in London at the time when Janus is a very old man, Nora has died and he is incapable of living on his own, so Nan, now a widow and the mother of Dan, has to take care of him.

Eva Figes' novel shares, then, striking traits with Modernist fiction and also with the ideas on time and memory of the French philosopher Henri Bergson (1859-1941), especially his concept of *durée*. As I will attempt to show, Figes gives this category a further turn by presenting it as disrupted by the processes of repetition-compulsion and acting out characteristic of trauma.[13] The analysis will also attempt to determine whether this Modernist outlook on time may be considered as a feature of the traumatic process itself and of its representation in fiction. Once the relationships of time and trauma in *Winter Journey* have been analysed, I will address the ethical implications of representing this special dimension of time: is *durée* a limbo for the mentally imbalanced, or an ethical space where soldiers can live after having participated in the war? And, in more general terms, is this

---

[12] Peter Conradi describes the effects of this lack of chronological sequencing as follows: "Without a continuous narrative, plot, or the character development which we think of as Victorian, the novel can become almost nebulous" ("Eva Figes", 300).

[13] Dominick LaCapra, *Writing History, Writing Trauma*, Baltimore and London: The Johns Hopkins University Press, 2001.

timeless narrativisation of the traumatic experience together with the Modernist impulse towards experimentation that dominates the novel the only ethical way of representing the aporetic phenomenon of trauma? Was Eva Figes' *Winter Journey* anticipating the turn to ethics experienced by literary criticism and moral philosophy in the 1980s? What is the role the novel demands of readers when it comes to interpreting the timeless world of the main character? These are the main questions I will try to answer in the following pages.

Trauma breaks the clock: *durée* and the narrativisation of traumatic experience
The question of the possibility or impossibility of narrating traumatic events in time is a key issue for trauma critics and writers alike, bringing to the fore the existence of a "narrative/anti-narrative tension at the core of trauma". Indeed, as Roger Luckhurst notes:

> Of late, an array of visual and written stories involving trauma have ostentatiously played around with narrative time, disrupting linearity, suspending logical causation, running out of temporal sequence, working backwards towards the inaugurating traumatic event, or playing with belated revelations that retrospectively rewrite narrative significance.

Jean-François Lyotard held an even more radical outlook on the relationship of time and trauma, since he believed that "trauma freezes time, and therefore any possibility of narrative".[14] This led Lyotard to argue that, confronted with trauma, the only thing art can do is to record its unrepresentability, what he describes in Derridean terms as "the aporia of art and its pain. It [art] does not say the unsayable, but says that it cannot say it."[15] In keeping with this, he concluded that "any narrative temporalization is an unethical act".[16] Other critics, however, believe the opposite, as they think that narrative has the power to help humans understand the world and its aporias. For example Paul Ricœur, in *Time and Narrative*,[17] held the view that

---

[14] Roger Luckhurst, *The Trauma Question*, London: Routledge, 2008, 80 (where Lyotard is quoted).
[15] *Ibid.*, 47.
[16] *Ibid.*, 81.
[17] Paul Ricœur, *Time and Narrative*, vols. I-III, trans. K. McLaughlin and D. Pellauer, Chicago: Chicago University Press, 1984-1988.

"narrative heals aporia",[18] because "humans can comprehend time only as narrative".[19] Thus, Ricœur contended that narrative offers the means to reconsider our human condition, and so, placing trauma in narrative time is a good way of orienting our existence in the world.

These two strikingly divergent positions with regard to the relationship of narrative time and trauma may help us understand the complexity of Eva Figes' conception of time in *Winter Journey*. The events that make up Janus' life are not portrayed in an ordered way. There are no clear spatial or temporal references and the scarce interventions of the external narrative instance are limited to the recording of the opinions of the neighbours,[20] and the reporting of a few events, such as Janus and Dan's conversations.[21] In sharp contrast to this, the events experienced by Janus are rendered as they are being produced in his psyche at the time of ideation. The first words of the novel are a clear example of this:

> Numm bll num mun ssoo sss tck. I dreamt, that was it. Not a soul about. Came to the house, that was it, the key fitted, no mistake there. Everything strangely quiet, only I didn't think it strange. Just went up the stairs as usual, except no, not as usual, quicker, not stopping for breath. And the tread didn't creak. No voices on the ground floor either. And then suddenly, round the bend of the landing: sky .... But it's there, all here as usual, the dark humps. Only that queer feeling. Where to go.[22]

All the action that takes place in *Winter Journey* develops in one single day and is structured according to the parts of the day: *Early Morning, Mid-Morning, Noon, Afternoon and Night*. This brings to mind Modernist works like Virginia Woolf's *Mrs Dalloway* (1925) or James Joyce's *Ulysses* (1922). These writers broke new literary ground by introducing a new conception of narrative time that promoted the subjective time of the mind over the external time of the clock. Their turn inward showed the influence of, among others, Henri Bergson's path-breaking theories of time and duration. The

---

conception of time in *Winter Journey* belongs in this Modernist tradition, which Eva Figes seems to be very well aware of.

One of Bergson's main arguments was that human beings can be sure only of their own existence, that is, the sensations, feelings, desires and representations that produce some sort of change in the inner state of the individual.[23] From this, Bergson moved on to underline the importance of the subjective perception of time and reality. He explained that the perception of time varies according to the perceiver's state of mind.[24] Therefore he formulated the concept of *durée* or duration. He distinguished two kinds of *durée*: *réelle* and *interne*. *Durée réelle*, or chronological time, is defined as "the present only, or, if we prefer the expression, simultaneity".[25] D*urée réelle* refers to the heterogeneous and exterior events that take place at the very present moment. It is defined as "the intersection of time and space",[26] and it is represented as the juxtaposition of events.[27] By contrast, *durée interne*, or psychological time, is identified as:

> ... a qualitative multiplicity, with no likeness to number; an organic evolution which is not yet an increasing quantity; a pure heterogeneity within which there are no distinct qualities. In a word, the moments of inner duration are not external to one another.[28]

Pure duration could be visualized as a continuous line where events appear as a flow in which the present is affected by the past and the future. Duration thus implies movement and heterogeneity and is indivisible, that is, one moment cannot be separated from another because all of them form part of the continuous flow.[29] Pure duration is seen as a life force, a never-ending flux that continuously reinterprets itself. In *Time and Free Will*, the French philosopher gives an image of duration as an elastic band being stretched. This band is contracted to a point, the present, and then it expands progressively,

---

[23] Henry Bergson, *Memoria y vida: Textos escogidos por Gilles Deleuze* (1977), trans. Mauro Armiño, Madrid: Alianza Editorial, 1987, 7.

[24] *Ibid.*, 12.

[25] Henri Bergson, *Time and Free Will: An Essay on the Immediate Data of Consciousness* (1910), trans. R.L. Pogson, New York: Dover Publications, 2001, 227.

[26] *Ibid.*, 110.

[27] Bergson, *Memoria y vida*, 36.

[28] Bergson, *Time and Free Will*, 226.

[29] Bergson, *Memoria y vida*, 20-21.

making a longer line. The important thing is not the line itself but the action that traces the line: that movement is duration.[30]

Applying these ideas to Figes' novel, it can be observed that the only references to time in *Winter Journey* are not related to clock-time but to the internal rhythms of the main character's mind. From the start, it is easy to see that Janus distrusts the rational perspective of clock-time. He thinks of the mechanical perspective of chronological time as unreal and treacherous, for example, when he tells his grandson: "You can spend your life on clocks and still not know all about them, my lad. Just remember that."[31] For Janus, chronological time is something that cannot be apprehended in an objective way. Further, throughout the novel, the ticking of clocks constantly interrupts the flow of his thoughts as a kind of reminder that mechanical time elapses while the time in his mind struggles for progression, as is suggested when he remarks: "Skin stays slack, nothing renews. And yet the clock goes on ticking"[32] or, "Fish are one flesh, fowl are one flesh. Man too. Tick tock went the clock, and the striking mechanism."[33]

Furthermore, Bergson's belief in a subjective perception of reality is made apparent throughout Janus' narration in comments such as:

> The mechanism of a clock is a delicate thing. As I used to tell Nora, no two clocks are alike .... Anyone would think that clocks have a soul.[34]

Here, the clock is personified and time has a different dimension for each individual, since the only access human beings have to time is subjective. Indeed, Bergson's definition of *durée interne* is made explicit in *Winter Journey* in the sense that life is understood as a continuous flux, as Janus' words illustrate: "I know where I am there, one thing leads to, there's a thread like a railway track which leads on and it all follows."[35] Here, Janus proposes the image of a thread or a railway track, instead of Bergson's elastic band, to express the extension of the present into the past and the future in terms of

---

[30] Bergson, *Time and Free Will*, 110.
[31] Figes, *Winter Journey*, 61.
[32] *Ibid.*, 10.
[33] *Ibid.*, 117.
[34] *Ibid.*, 61.
[35] *Ibid.*, 71.

duration. The image reinforces Janus' traumatised condition, since the first attempts by Victorian medics to characterise trauma was aimed at the treatment of victims of railway accidents and we know that Janus himself had a train accident in which he became deaf.

In an essay entitled "Internal Clocks and the Representation of Time", J.H. Wearden contends that the conception of a psychological category of time as based on the idea of an "internal clock" has been "central to recent conceptions of psychological time".[36] If this is so, then Eva Figes may be credited with the inauguration of an even more productive image, since what Wearden defines in his article is what Figes had illustrated in her novel many years earlier: the way in which the length of a tick can be perceived in very different ways depending on the individual,[37] or rather, on the different internal clock-times of each individual. In Wearden's definition, time acquires a circular trajectory instead of being a continuous flow advancing towards the future. In the novel, time also seems to move in circles that travel between Janus' past and present while he tries to advance in order to "keep moving".[38] As the reader will eventually realise, the reason why he is stuck in the past has to do with his traumatic war memories.

Janus' wars
Readers are allowed access to Janus' mental world thanks to the use of various narrative techniques associated with Modernist fiction, such as the free association of ideas, direct and indirect interior monologues, ellipses, anachronisms, anaphora, anacoluthon, the figurative use of images and other rhetorical devices meant to enhance the impression of fluidity and subjectivity of Janus' stream of consciousness. Out of his troubled and disarranged thoughts the reader can extract the basic facts they constantly turn around: that he went to the front; that when

---

[36] J.H. Wearden, "Internal Clocks and the Representation of Time", in *Time and Memory: Issues in Philosophy and Psychology*, eds Christoph Hoerl and Teresa McCormack, Oxford: Oxford University Press, 2006, 37.

[37] *Ibid.*, 39.

[38] Figes, *Winter Journey*, 59. In a review of the novel, Juliette Wells highlights Janus' efforts to keep moving as a key fact to understand his suffering and his immersion in the traumatic memories of the past throughout the novel: "Making efforts to 'keep moving' in spite of physical pain, he tends to drift into impressionistic, wide-ranging memories of earlier episodes in his life" (Juliette Wells, "Eva Figes", in *British and Irish Novelists since 1960*, ed. Merrit Moseley, Detroit, MI: Thomson Gale, 2003, 133).

he came back he was unable to integrate in society; and that he was rejected by his children, his wife Nora and even his neighbours. Nora's resentment against him is registered by Janus in a characteristic way: "Sometimes I'd pretend not to hear the words: pig, boor, bore, grunt, fucking cunt grunt or noises to that effect."[39] The war affected society as a whole, especially the soldiers' families. Nora is no exception: in Janus' description of her, she also seems to suffer from some sort of psychosomatic disorder or war trauma:

> Nora vomiting into the sink, strands of sticky hair falling over her face, skin shining with yellow lustre. It's all in her mind, the quack said, psycho-something, she doesn't like war.[40]

Moreover, readers eventually come to know that Nora had a miscarriage after Janus' return, so that both events are linked in her mind: "Didn't like the war, or childbirth, afraid of both, draw your own conclusions, who starts both?"[41] The obvious answer is "men": men start wars and men are blamed for making women pregnant without caring for them. In Nora's words:

> But then who is to blame for hard times? Men, she'd say in her rock bottom voice, all you can do is kill each other and then come home and give us more kids to fill the gap. Women.[42]

Nora's trauma not only evinces the negative consequences of war for women but also a deep mistrust of males. Thus, the family situation Janus encountered after the war increases his sense of alienation: "Nobody missed me, nobody knows."[43] This sort of mutually alienating relationship was a common experience among soldiers returning from war who, like Janus, would develop shell shock neurosis.

Shell shock was first studied by Breuer and Freud[44] and, after the First World War by Freud and other psychiatrists like the British

---

[39] Figes, *Winter Journey*, 12-13.
[40] *Ibid.*, 14.
[41] *Ibid.*, 24-25.
[42] *Ibid.*, 25.
[43] *Ibid.*, 95.
[44] Josef Breuer and Sigmund Freud, *Studies on Hysteria* (1892-93), eds and trans. J. and A. Strachey, Harmondsworth: Penguin, 1991.

Charles S. Myers.[45] By insisting on the psychological, rather than
physical causes and consequences of trauma, psychoanalysis
reinvented the terms of the already heated dispute between rival
theories on its aetiology.[46] However, as early as 1919, the neurologist
F.W. Mott described the symptoms of a shell-shocked soldier as both
physical and psychological:

> He [the patient] has little or no idea of time and place, and his power
> of recognition and comprehension are greatly impaired. He may be
> deaf or mute or a deaf-mute.[47]

This description perfectly matches that of Janus, since he became
deaf due to an accident that took place during the war. These early
studies on shell shock (also termed battle shock or battle fatigue)
forerun the definition, in 1980, of Post Traumatic Stress Disorder
(PTSD) by the American Psychiatric Association. The syndrome,
which emerged from the treatment of Vietnam veterans, was
characterised in terms of "intrusive symptoms (such as nightmares,
flashbacks and persistent memories), avoidance symptoms (such as
emotional numbing, withdrawal from the world and avoidance of
reminders) and symptoms of overarousal (such as insomnia and

---

[45] Sigmund Freud, "Thoughts for the Time on War and Death" (1915), in *Civilisation,
Society and Religion*, ed. Albert Dixon, Penguin Freud Library XIV, London and New
York: Penguin, 1991, 57-90; C.S. Myers, *Shell Shock in France 1914-1918*,
Cambridge: Cambridge University Press, 1940. See also Freud, *Beyond the Pleasure
Principle.*

[46] Luckhurst, *The Trauma Question*, 34. The psychiatrist Judith Lewis Herman offers
a useful description of the evolution in the understanding of shell shock in the
following description: "Under the conditions of unremitting exposure to the horrors of
trench warfare, men began to break down in shocking numbers. Confined and
rendered helpless, subjected to constant threat of annihilation, and forced to witness
the mutilation and death of their comrades without any hope of reprieve, many
soldiers began to act like hysterical women. They screamed and wept uncontrollably.
They froze and could not move. They became mute and unresponsive. They lost their
memory and their capacity to feel .... Initially, the symptoms of mental breakdown
were attributed to a physical cause. The British psychologist Charles Myers, who
examined some of the first cases, attributed their symptoms to the concussive effects
of exploding shells and called the resulting nervous disorder 'shell-shock' ....
Gradually military psychiatrists were forced to acknowledge that the symptoms of
shell shock were due to psychological trauma" (*Trauma and Recovery: From
Domestic Abuse to Political Terror* [1992], London: Pandora, 2001, 20).

[47] F.W. Mott, *War Neuroses and Shell Shock*, London: Hodder and Stoughton, 1919,
quoted in Luckhurst, *The Trauma Question*, 80-81.

irritability)".[48] As with shell shock, PTSD was suffered by "those confronted with an experience involving actual or threatened death or serious injury, or a physical threat to the physical integrity of the self considered to be outside the range of normal experience".[49] In a recent study, Solomon, Shklar and Mikulincer also explicitly relate PTSD to battle shock and underline its physical and psychological effects:

> Acute combat stress reaction, previously termed battle shock or battle fatigue, encompasses an array of reversible psychiatric and somatic symptoms and impaired functioning. Although persons with combat stress reaction may recover, combat stress reaction often crystallizes into chronic posttraumatic stress disorder (PTSD) and places casualties at risk for chronic PTSD.[50]

The figure of the shell-shocked soldier has become a kind of icon among trauma victims in the twentieth century,[51] and Janus is a clear representative of it. This alienated and deaf war veteran has clear symptoms of having suffered battle fatigue or PTSD, but, a better understanding of his condition might be had by considering Dominick LaCapra's distinction between two main stages in the process of overcoming trauma. The first is the process of "acting out", characterised by the compulsive repetition of the traumatic event. During this phase, time and again the subject is compelled to relive the traumatic event in an unconscious way. This process is manifested in nightmares, the repetition of past events, anxiety, unknown fears, and even auto-mutilation. As LaCapra explains:

> In acting out tenses implode, and it is as if one were back there in the past reliving the traumatic scene. Any duality (or double inscription) of time (past and present or future) is experientially collapsed.[52]

The second is the stage of "working through", or the healing process based on the understanding and structuring of the traumatic

---

[48] Patrick J. Bracken, "Post-modernity and post-traumatic stress disorder", *Social Science and Medicine*, LIII/3 (September 2001), 733.
[49] Luckhurst, *The Trauma Question*, 1.
[50] Shklar Solomon and Mikulincer, "Frontline Treatment of Combat Stress Reaction: A 20-Year Longitudinal Evaluation Study", *The American Journal of Psychiatry*, CLXII (12 December 2005), 2309.
[51] Luckhurst, *The Trauma Question*, 50.
[52] LaCapra, *Writing History*, 21-22.

event in an ordered and logical way. As this description suggests, this
process involves the subject's capacity to transform aporetic or
unspeakable traumatic memories into narrative memories. The first
psychiatrist to distinguish between traumatic memory and narrative
memory was Pierre Janet, a contemporary of Freud's. His path-
breaking contention was that the cure is achieved when the patient
manages to integrate the fragmentary contents of nightmares or
flashbacks, situating them in the past of his or her own life story.[53]
Once the traumatised subject is able to integrate and arrange
chronologically the fragmentary elements of the shocking event that
come to the conscious mind in the form of nightmares or flashbacks,
the healing or "working through" of the trauma begins: the subject is
then able to grasp what happened to him or her and to place it in the
past, thus coming to terms with it. In LaCapra's own words: "Working
through is an articulatory practice: to the extent one works through
trauma, one is able to distinguish between past and present and to
recall in memory that something happened to one."[54]

Janus' process of acting out is represented in various ways. The
war veteran suffers from nightmares that bring the horrors of war to
the present, as in the following anguishing dream:

> There's no end to the tunnel, air is getting short, a downward motion, I
> can feel it, I can't breathe, there must be another end .... And then, a
> long breath and silence. It's over. The tin alarm clock glowing in the
> dark.[55]

On some occasions, the terrifying memories of the war take the
form of ghostly visitations, as Janus explains: "Nights are too long,
what I am to do with them, watching ghosts come to the silent
window, fighting the cold."[56] At other times an image brings the past
into the present, as when Janus looks at his daughter Nan and is
reminded of his dead wife Nora.[57] Moreover, the atmosphere that
characterises the novel is one of decadence and pessimism, as can be

---

[53] Anne Whitehead, *Trauma Fiction*, Edinburgh: Edinburgh University Press, 2004, 140.
[54] LaCapra, *Writing History*, 21-22.
[55] Figes, *Winter Journey*, 11.
[56] *Ibid.*, 12.
[57] *Ibid.*, 83.

seen in sentences like "It is no use, nothing will grow",[58] an allusion to Janus' lack of faith in the possibility of post-war regeneration. Figes' return to the paradigm of Modernist literature brings to mind the images of sprouting corpses, frozen landscapes, and dirty settings of *The Waste Land*;[59] Eliot's reference to the lack of belief in future regeneration in Britain in the second part of the poem;[60] and the images of desolation and decadence of London in the aftermath of the First World War,[61] which Eva Figes reproduces in her novel. Another link between Figes' novel written at the end of the 1960s and Eliot' poem published in 1922 is Figes' seeming endorsement of Eliot's pessimistic conception of the world as a desolate and empty waste land harbouring no future for the post-war generations.

In "Beyond the Pleasure Principle", Freud defined repetition-compulsion as the neurotic patient's need to repeat compulsively the shocking event that had caused the trauma. This compulsion is experienced by Janus when he relives the sound of the train that caused his deafness:

> Four-thirty. That train, I couldn't have heard that train, not without my aid on. And yet I always hear it, I always have heard it, every night in the dark of the small hours, ever since ... ever since this house, ever since the war ....[62]

The sound has remained in his head physically and also psychically, as a re-enactment of the accident. Indeed, besides the physical injury, Janus evinces a psychological wound in the compulsive repetition of the moment of the accident whenever the sounds come to his head. He is an irrecoverable chronic patient, unable till the end of the novel to move on to the phase of working through his trauma.

---

[58] *Ibid.*, 42.

[59] T.S. Eliot, *The Waste Land*, I, ll. 60-76; II, ll. 115-16; III, ll. 188-195, in *The Waste Land and Other Poems* (1940), London: Faber and Faber, 1990, 21-49.

[60] "You ought to be ashamed, I said, to look so antique / .... / Well, if Albert won't leave you alone, there it is, I said. / What you get married for if you don't want children?" (II, ll. 156-64, in *ibid.*, 29).

[61] "Sweet Thames, run softly, for I speak not loud or long. / But at my back in a cold blast I hear / The rattle of the bones, and chuckle spread from ear to ear" (III, ll. 184-86, in *ibid.*, 30).

[62] Figes, *Winter Journey*, 11.

The psychiatrist Judith Lewis Herman distinguishes three main PTSD symptoms: "hyperarousal", "intrusion" and "constriction".[63] Intrusion is similar to repetition-compulsion, as it consists of the belated reliving of a traumatic event:

> Long after the danger is past, traumatized people relive the event as though it were continually recurring in the present .... It is as if time stops at the moment of trauma.[64]

Constriction refers to a person's paralysis when he or she feels utterly powerless and incapable of resistance. Janus also experiences this incapacitating feeling of paralysis and numbing: throughout the novel he keeps affirming his intention to "keep moving" but he never succeeds in doing so.[65] Herman also distinguishes three main stages in the recovery from trauma – "safety", "remembrance" and "mourning"[66] – and, echoing Pierre Janet, points out that the last two can be represented in literature by showing characters that fight to transform their traumatic memories into narrative memories. This is precisely what Janus attempts to do, but fails. Herman argues that traumatic memory is "wordless and static",[67] and she explains that

> The second stage of recovery has a *timeless* quality that is frightening. The reconstruction of the trauma requires immersion in a past experience of frozen time; the descent into mourning feels like surrender to tears that are endless.[68]

Janus seems to live in this timeless traumatic sphere ruled by the subjective rhythm of psychological time: "a day [is] as long as a year and all the stars circle overhead. It takes time, learning how clocks work, geraniums grow."[69] Thus, although objectively he finds himself in a state of post-war safety, his immersion in his own traumatic duration makes it impossible for him to distinguish between past and present and so to provide his traumatic memories with a narrative

---

[63] Herman, *Trauma and Recovery*, 35.
[64] *Ibid.*, 37.
[65] Figes, *Winter Journey*, 15, 45.
[66] Herman, *Trauma and Recovery*, 155.
[67] *Ibid.*, 175.
[68] *Ibid.*, 195 (emphasis added).
[69] Figes, *Winter Journey*, 66.

pattern that would initiate his healing process. Janus' experience of timelessness and his abnormal representation of time are symptoms of his disturbed mental processes. His experience of war has been so horrible that it cannot be coped with in rational terms and cannot be arranged according to chronological paradigms. Janus himself provides an explanation of how the war ruined his chronological conception of time in one of his direct interior monologues:

> Time was when you could have a three course lunch and tea after for that, or see a show and have the bus fare home after. But now. What to do now? Time was when the day went like clockwork, never a minute to spare, every part fitting in with every other part, striking on the hour, set for a week. What happened? Where? What day is it?[70]

Bergson explained that, in duration, memory projects the past into the present, since "we are our past",[71] that is, our present is made of remembering past moments. However, in *Winter Journey* the main character cannot distinguish the past from the present: stuck in the process of acting out his war trauma, he is unable to move beyond his own duration. As Janus' last reflections illustrate:

> And there, where a day is as long as a year and the year is as long as a century and eternity splits into a second and only one direction remains whichever way you turn, I will sit down.[72]

At the end of the novel, Janus is in hospital, he knows that his attempts to keep moving have failed and that his only possibility is to stay in the timeless dimension he has inhabited throughout the novel. So, it is in this timeless world, where the only thing he can be sure of is his own existence, that Janus is expected to remain forever.

From Janus' monologues and the few narrator's interventions it is impossible to know if the war he participated in was the First World War, the Second World War or both of them, since in his digressions he mentions events from the two, such as "the Battle of the Somme" (World War I);[73] or "Stalingrad, D-day and VE-day" (World War II).[74]

---

[70] *Ibid.*, 46.
[71] Bergson, *Memoria y vida*, 48.
[72] Figes, *Winter Journey*, 118-19.
[73] *Ibid.*, 47.
[74] *Ibid.*, 24. The mention of Stalingrad adds to the unreliability of the narrator's digressive musings, since a British soldier could not have participated in what was a confrontation between the Germans and the Russians.

Further, as we have seen, in what may be described as both an ironic metacomment and an attempt to emphasise the atemporality of trauma, Eva Figes associates Janus' deafness with a train accident, the sort of accident that gave rise to the study of trauma in the late nineteenth century. Further still, Figes has constant recourse to the imagery and symptomatology both of shell shock neurosis (the mental illness associated with the First World War), and of PTSD (the syndrome of veterans of the Vietnam War and of other post-World War II armed conflicts).

In his analysis of the genealogy of the concept of trauma, Roger Luckhurst mentions the Battle of the Somme as the turning point in the First World War, the first time that soldiers suffering from shell shock were not branded as cowards and condemned to death.[75] This is one of the few battles mentioned in the novel and one in which Janus seems to have taken part:

> Morris lost two fingers on his left hand at the battle of the Somme (one of them) .... Not only fingers. Wet sheets flapping in alleys between high walls of sooty brick and a clatter of small hard boots down the iron stairs.[76]

This is the only clear reference that would allow us to set Janus' past in a concrete time in history; however, he also mentions events of the Second World War, for example, when he says:

> Only sometimes I turn events over, pick out the odd item, like Stalingrad, that was a cold place, the abdication, coronation, D-day, VE-day, any day. The year that girl got murdered in the signal box.[77]

As the quotation suggests, here Janus is making reference to key battles in the Second World War as well as to other key historical events (the abdication of Edward VIII and the coronation of Queen Elizabeth II), and to traumatic events that he has not lived directly, but might have read about or learnt through the media ("the year that girl

---

[75] Luckhurst, *The Trauma Question*, 52.
[76] Figes, *Winter Journey*, 47.
[77] *Ibid.*, 24.

got murdered in the signal box"), all of which have somehow entered his conscious mind and coexist with his own traumatic war memories in the timeless sphere of his subjective duration. The fact that, in this list of unlived experiences he includes "any day" adds to the impression of the self-fragmentation and alienation of a character capable of looking at his life from the outside as the repetition of a single day.

The difficulty in establishing the armed conflict Janus is referring to,[78] and the general scarcity of specific historical and temporal references, confer a representative character on Figes' fictionalisation of the ills of war. It does not really matter whether it was the First or the Second World War that caused Janus' trauma, for both were extremely destructive armed conflicts that brought unprecedented suffering on humanity. Further, the scarcity of spatio-temporal and historical referents parallels the timeless dimension designed for the main character, reinforcing the traumatic atmosphere of the inner reality where he lives and where there is no distinction between past and present and between the lived, the witnessed, and the imagined. In any case, the blurring of times and settings, the theme of war and the Modernist techniques employed in the novel are all mechanisms for the fictional representation of trauma.

Modernism and the representation of trauma

A key feature of *Winter Journey* is its intertextual connection with Virginia Woolf's *Mrs Dalloway*.[79] Both novels employ stream-of-consciousness techniques to access the main characters' minds, both are set in the aftermath of war and both portray shell-shocked characters immersed in the process of acting out their traumas. However, whereas Woolf presents Septimus Warren Smith's condition without entering his consciousness, his suffering being mediated through Clarissa's perspective, Figes offers the reader direct access to Janus' mind through direct and indirect interior monologue.

---

[78] For instance, Brian Gerald McLaughlin analyses related aspects of *Winter Journey* but he does not address the question of which armed conflict is represented in the novel (*Structures of Identity*).

[79] Eva Figes' indebtedness to Virginia Woolf is a salient feature of her literary production as a whole. See Anna Maria Stuby, "Eva Figes's Novels", in *Engendering Realism and Postmodernism. Contemporary Women Writers in Britain*, ed. Beate Neumeier, Amsterdam and New York: Rodopi, 2001, 105-16; Wells, "Eva Figes"; Conradi, "Eva Figes"; or McLaughlin, *Structures of Identity*.

Thus, Figes takes Woolf's novel only as a starting point for her own investigation of trauma. She acknowledges the influence of Woolf by choosing a similar theme, a similar style, and a similar shell-shocked character, but gives the plot a further turn by giving centrality to what in the earlier novel is a subsidiary plot-line and by granting Janus the possibility Woolf had denied Septimus of expressing his feelings and thoughts. Virginia Woolf depicted Septimus as a deeply wounded and alienated character, who was incapable of working through his feelings of guilt and pain and of integrating in society. Incapable of communicating his feelings to his doctor and wife, he is finally bound to commit suicide. Eva Figes changes this outcome, as she does not condemn Janus to self-slaughter. Although Janus has not worked through his trauma at the end of the novel, the ending is rather ambiguous: the only thing readers know is that he will remain for ever in the timeless sphere the author has designed for him. A remote possibility of recuperation is hinted at in the bond Janus manages to establish with his grandson Dan. This can be observed in episodes like the one quoted below, in which Dan asks Janus questions and the old man tries to respond by telling him a story. However, Janus always fails in his attempts at storytelling and, unable to verbalise his trauma, he remains stuck in the repetition-compulsion process:

> Janus took the rough-gloved small hand and Dan did not try to pull it away.
> "Do the fish know about that then, the sky and everything moving?"
> "The sun doesn't move"
> … Tell me a story ….
> "I can't remember, it's difficult to start. I must try".[80]

The creation of affective bonds between first-generation survivors and family members of the third generation is a recurrent strategy in Figes' fiction in general, meant to suggest the possibility of regeneration and renewal. For example, in *Tales of Innocence and Experience*[81] the relationship through storytelling established between a German-Jewish grandmother and her English granddaughter is the

---

[80] Figes, *Winter Journey*, 89-91.
[81] Eva Figes, *Tales of Innocence and Experience*, London: Bloomsbury, 2003.

only possibility the old woman has to verbalise and work through the trauma caused by her childhood experience of the Holocaust.

In the case of *Winter Journey*, Figes' acknowledgment of *Mrs Dalloway* and her use of stream-of-consciousness techniques reinforce the current critical view that Modernity and Modernism have shaped the trauma paradigm in which we live nowadays. As Roger Luckhurst points out, the critic Tim Armstrong has gone so far as to argue that the formal innovations associated with Modernist aesthetics, such as temporal dislocation and anamnesis (memory loss), are directly linked with the traumatic effect of the First World War on Western consciousness.[82] Consequently, if we follow this line of argumentation, it is easy to see why the Modernist techniques employed in *Winter Journey* are most appropriate for the representation of trauma in fiction. The question that remains to be answered is whether Figes' use of experimental techniques and themes in *Winter Journey* is an ethical way of depicting trauma.

Trauma and the ethical dimension of timelessness
The last point I would like to address in this study is concerned with the ethical implications of Figes' choice of subject matter, since the task she set herself raises one of the most difficult ethical issues with regard to our socio-political and cultural structures: the degree of responsibility society has towards soldiers and other human beings involved in armed conflicts. This issue has been widely argued in relation to the Holocaust and the Vietnam War,[83] and does not seem to have a clear-cut, easy answer. Considering all the elements analysed in *Winter Journey*, it can be stated that the response that the novel begs for is one which makes readers conscious in a non-sensationalist way of the fatal consequences of war on everybody, soldiers and civilians alike.

The ethical complexity of the situation is reproduced in the novel by the fact that, as a war veteran, Janus is both a victim of the war and an active agent of destruction and murder. The ambiguity of his

---

[82] Luckhurst, *The Trauma Question*, 53.
[83] For example, the work done by the psychologist Emmett Early in *The Raven's Return: The Influence of Psychological Trauma on Individuals and Culture*, Illinois: Chiron Publications, 1993, where he illustrates the results of his therapy with Vietnam veterans; or also, in relation to the treatment of child soldiers in Sierra Leone, Anne Whitehead's analysis of Delia Jarrett-Macauley's novel *Moses, Citizen and Me* in this present volume.

position is enhanced by the timeless dimension in which he is condemned to live, that may be read both as a symptom of his trauma and as the only space where he can assuage his feelings of pain and guilt. These feelings are evident in reflections like this one:

> Only I have to listen to the spirit walking, confess in church on Sunday, I have sinned, only I have to choose, wanting nothing, walk through the snow in thin boots, wanting only to hibernate. Only I am shut out.[84]

Here he illustrates how he is not able to work through his past traumatic memories and his choice is not to face the past but to "hibernate", to live in this timeless "acting out" sphere.

As we have seen, Figes gives Janus' consciousness the opportunity to express the fragmentation of his post-war self, how physically and spiritually ill he is, how guilty, lonely and neglected he feels, yet readers do not feel sorry for him in any sort of sentimental way; rather, they are struck by the detached and deeply disturbing way in which the destructive effects of the war are portrayed. Therefore, Figes' novel seems to follow LaCapra's notion of "empathy" and "empathic unsettlement" as regards the reactions that readers are expected to experience when reading trauma literature. In his dealing with the ethical issues arisen by trauma writing, LaCapra explains that the most appropriate emotion a work of art addressing the question of trauma should arouse in readers is that of empathy, which he defines as "a form of virtual, not vicarious, experience … in which emotional response comes with respect for the other and the realization that the experience of the other is not one's own".[85] In fact, this describes the effects of the style and techniques used in *Winter Journey*. The author does not judge any of the characters' actions but simply depicts the disturbed workings of the main character's mind from a neutral perspective. Consequently, readers come to respect Janus' acts while at the same time they detach themselves from the events narrated and do not identify with him. Indeed, Eva Figes does not seek the readers' identification with the main character, but rather tries to awake in them a feeling described by LaCapra in the following terms:

---

[84] Figes, *Winter Journey*, 97.
[85] LaCapra, *Writing* History, 40.

Being responsive to the traumatic experience of others, notably of victims, implies not the appropriation of their experience but what I would called empathic unsettlement, which should have stylistic effects or, more broadly, effects in writing which cannot be reduced to formulas or rules of method.[86]

In contrast to reader identification, which raises serious doubts from an ethical perspective in that it seeks to situate readers in the place of the victim, LaCapra's concept of empathic unsettlement has a clear ethical dimension as it begs readers to put themselves "in the other's position while recognizing the difference of that position and hence not taking the other's place".[87] In this sense, LaCapra's notion of empathic unsettlement can be related to Levinas' ethics of alterity, which demands of the reader an attitude of responsibility towards the Other and its emphasis on the individual's capacity to feel with the Other, especially the Other's suffering, while recognising his or her utter Otherness.[88]

Winter Journey may be said to meet these ethical criteria. The war has condemned Janus to isolation, alienation and endless pain, yet suffering is not the exclusive territory of soldiers like him: readers also have access to the pain lived by women like Nora and children like Ted and Nan, so they are constantly situated in the position of making their own divergent demands for an ethical and empathic response from readers. In this respect, it could be stated that Eva Figes establishes a Levinasian "face-to-face relationship" between readers and characters, especially Janus. This relationship is defined as the way the Self must get outside itself to put itself in the Other's place in order to understand his or her feelings, as the only ethical mode humans have of living in society and of "feeling responsible for" the Other's pain.[89] Thus, we are asked to look at Janus in the face and feel his pain beneath his utter Otherness, while at the same time we are also asked to contemplate and empathise with the pain of his wife and children, who blame Janus (as a member of the armed forces) for their own pain.

---

[86] *Ibid.*, 41.
[87] *Ibid.*, 78.
[88] Emmanuel Levinas, *Basic Philosophical Writings*, eds Adriaan T. Peperzak *et al.*, Indiana: Indiana University Press, 1996.
[89] Levinas, *Basic Philosophical Writings,* 19, 90.

As the analysis has shown, the novel creates a complex emotional atmosphere in the aporetic terms described by Lyotard, by expressing the unrepresentable and unutterable nature of Janus' trauma in strictly narrative terms, through the restriction of factual information, the limitation of narrative perspective to the workings of Janus' mind and the drastic reduction of authorial interventions, thus forcing readers to participate actively in the unravelling of the drama and judge for themselves. As we have seen, the sheer difficulty in unravelling the plot, which brings to the fore Janus' utter Otherness, makes it impossible for readers to identify with him, while at the same time the extreme emotionality of the events narrated beg for the readers' empathic unsettlement. It may be concluded, therefore, that Figes' work succeeds in the endeavour of approaching traumatic events ethically and of conveying an empathic understanding of the pain and suffering of human beings who have gone through the traumatic experience of war.

In this respect, the frozen sphere of time that has been the main target of this study may be read not only as the traumatic space of Janus' inner world, but also, in more general terms, as an aesthetic attitude towards the representation of trauma in narratives. From the perspective of Lyotard's notion of the unrepresentability of trauma and Derrida's concept of the aporia of meaning, it could be stated that, by imagining into being the timeless and extremely subjective mental dimension where Janus finds himself, Figes has found a liminal space from which she can give voice to feelings of suffering and guilt too horrible for representation by traditional means, a space from which she can challenge official notions of warfare that present soldiers as heroes, treat mental illnesses as symptoms of effeminacy and cowardice, and justify manslaughter with historical, political and racist arguments. The ambiguity and sheer difficulty in representing Janus' condition is strictly ethical: it shatters received notions of good and evil and opens up new possibilities of representing and, consequently, of working through the collective trauma that gives paradigmatic entity to our contemporary age.

"Nobody's Meat": Revisiting Rape and Sexual Trauma through Angela Carter

Charley Baker

In the Introduction to this volume, Susana Onega and Jean-Michel Ganteau suggest that "literary trauma, concerned as it is with the experience of limits and the destabilisation of the accepted, might be considered as an emotional experience that strikes at the roots of identity and durably displaces certainties".[1] The most notable feature of Carter's speculative fictions – *The Magic Toyshop* (1967), *Heroes and Villains* (1969), *The Infernal Desire Machines of Doctor Hoffman* (1972) and *The Passion of New Eve* (1977) – is the repeated presence, and experienced by the majority of her female and male protagonists, of rape and sexual assault. None of Carter's victims are entirely unaffected by their assaults and experiences – but they do demonstrate a range of very different yet equally valid responses to their experiences, responses which often differ from social expectations of victims proposed through dominant medical, legal and psychological discourses. In this respect Carter displaces the myths, defined as "certainties", which are held about rape and rape victims.

Carter emphasises difference and individuality in traumatic responses, and is a deeply ethical writer in this sense. Through a process of defamiliarisation – both in examining male rape as a phenomenon and the allegedly atypical reactions of females who are assaulted – Carter exposes and explores the ethical lacuna between assumed (through traditionally white, middle-class, masculine medico-legal discourses) responses and actual experiences. In discussing male rape, Carter was – and remains – way ahead of her time. This again adds to the deeply committed ethical component of her work. The unsettling, disruptive element of Carter's fiction leaves

---

[1] See page 19 of this present volume.

her readers in the position of witnesses to another's trauma and in a relatively incommensurate position between their expectations and actuality represented.

Revisiting rape

Before discussing Carter's fictions in detail, some observations about sexual trauma and the sociohistorical context and importance of Carter's work need elucidation. In defining trauma, we may return to its historical, psychoanalytical roots or turn to contemporary conceptions in the sense of the modern diagnosis of Post-Traumatic Stress Disorder as detailed in the American Psychiatric Association's *Diagnostic and Statistical Manual of Mental Disorders.*[2] Laura S. Brown questions the slightly earlier version of the psychiatry bible – the *DSM-III-R* – definition of trauma as being the experience of an event outside of the range of human occurrence and experience, rightly pointing out that rape and sexual assault are experiences that fall:

> ... well within the "range of human experience." They are the experiences of most of the women who come into my office every day. They are experiences that could happen in the life of any girl or woman in North America today. They are experiences to which women accommodate; potentials for which women make room in their lives and their psyches. They are private events, sometimes known only to the victim and perpetrator.

In the most recent edition of the *DSM*, these issues have been partially addressed with less emphasis placed on the unusualness of an experience and more on individual response as defining a trauma. It should not need to be pointed out that, no matter how common an occurrence and no matter how the individual reacts, rape is undeniably a trauma inflicted upon an individual. However, as Brown points out in the epilogue to her paper, the redefinitions in the *DSM* "continue to beg the question of whether all of the interpersonal and intrapsychic

---

[2] American Psychiatric Association, *Diagnostic and Statistical Manual of Mental Disorders* (1952), Arlington: American Psychiatric Press, 2000 (revised text).

effects of trauma can be adequately described within one diagnosis".[3] Bearing this in mind, this essay follows Carter's own purpose in avoiding diagnostic labelling because the very real experiences of those who do not respond – or who refuse to respond – in a manner that is either socially expected or meets the diagnostic criteria for Post Traumatic Stress Disorder may be excluded from analysis. Indeed, as Frazier *et al.* suggest,

> [a] growing body of research demonstrates that traumatic experiences are not followed by unmitigated distress. Survivors of even quite horrific events also report positive life changes as a result of struggling to come to terms with those events ... survivors who report positive life change are also at less risk for developing trauma-related disorders, including posttraumatic stress disorder.[4]

Again, it should be unnecessary here to point out that the potential for positive life-changing effects following trauma does suggest that trauma may be a life-enhancing experience.

Rape and sexual trauma in Carter's fiction induce a unique, highly individualised form of madness that not only resists categorisation within clinical discourse but often actively refutes it through the allegedly atypical reactions of those who have undergone trauma. In a concisely non-diagnostic fashion, Cathy Caruth defines the word "trauma" as describing "a response, sometimes delayed, to an overwhelming event or events, which takes the form of repeated, intrusive hallucinations, dreams, thoughts or behaviours stemming from the event, along with numbing that may have begun during or after the event, and possibly also increased arousal to (and avoidance of) stimuli recalling the event".[5] One feature of trauma, explicated through Carter's portrayal of Melanie and her metaphorical rape in

---

[3] Laura S. Brown, "Not Outside the Range: One Feminist Perspective on Psychic Trauma", in *Trauma: Explorations in Memory*, ed. Cathy Caruth, Baltimore: The Johns Hopkins University Press, 1995, 101.

[4] Patricia Frazier, Ty Tashiro, Margit Berman, Michael Steger and Jeffery Long, "Correlates of Levels and Patterns of Positive Life Changes Following Sexual Assault", *Journal of Consulting and Clinical Psychology*, LXXII/1 (February 2004), 19.

[5] Caruth, Introduction, in *Trauma: Explorations in Memory*, 4.

The Magic Toyshop,[6] is psychical dissociation during, and sometimes after, the traumatic event. As Bessel A. van der Kolk and Onno van der Hart eloquently summarise it:

> There is little evidence for an active pushing away of the overwhelming experience; the uncoupling seems to have other mechanisms. Many trauma survivors report that they automatically are removed from the scene; they look down at it from a distance or disappear altogether, leaving other parts of their personality to suffer and store the overwhelming experience.[7]

In one sense, this psychological cutting off from the experience, in the loosest understanding of madness, is akin to the loss of touch with reality that occurs with severe mental illnesses. In clinical literature, dissociation is seen as a necessary psychic defence mechanism but one which is, paradoxically, potentially damaging in the longer term.[8] Trauma does not only encompass the experience but also the survival of the experience, as Caruth suggests: "The problem of survival, in trauma, thus emerges specifically as the question: What does it mean for *consciousness* to survive?"[9] The struggle for survival of post-trauma consciousness necessarily implies that the body has survived: "the term *trauma* is understood as a wound inflicted not upon the body but upon the mind."[10] As will be examined, if we compare Carter's Melanie and Marianne's very different levels of dissociation from their traumas, we can see that non-dissociation leads to a greater sense of control during and after the assault and so to a better psychological integration of, and recovery from, the traumatic occurrence. Survival of consciousness and thus survival as coherent being is a key message to both Carter's and Kathy Acker's texts. A contemporary of Carter's, Acker was at times deemed anti-feminist, for example, in *Empire of*

---

[6] Angela Carter, *The Magic Toyshop* (1967), London: Virago, 2001.

[7] Bessel A. van der Kolk and Onno van der Hart, "The Intrusive Past: The Flexibility of Memory and the Engraving of Trauma", in *Trauma: Explorations in Memory*, 168.

[8] David A. Sandberg and Steven J. Lynn, "Dissociative Experiences, Pathology and Adjustment, and Child and Adolescent Maltreatment in Female College Students", *Journal of Abnormal Psychology*, CI/4 (November 1992), 717.

[9] Cathy Caruth, *Unclaimed Experience: Trauma, Narrative and History*, Baltimore: The Johns Hopkins University Press, 1996, 61 (emphasis in the original).

[10] *Ibid.*, 3 (emphasis in the original).

the Senseless, where she provides a rousing message through Abhor, the heroine, who is raped and abused repeatedly in the text. This message seems particularly apt in relation to dissociation as a unique, but variably successful, form of post-trauma madness: "Let our madness turn from insanity into anger."[11]

It has been demonstrated clinically that a number of psychosocial factors affect psychological survival and recovery, as suggested by Sarah E. Ullman *et al.* when they write: "few demographic or assault characteristics predicted symptoms, whereas trauma histories, perceived life threat during the assault, postassault characterological self blame, avoidance coping, and negative social reactions from others were all related to greater PTSD symptoms severity."[12] Bodily damage – "assault characteristics" – does not correlate to psychical damage in life or in Carter's fictions, as evidenced through Melanie's lack of physical injury but catastrophic psychic damage, or also as compared to the extreme physical injury yet relative coherency of psyche experienced by Albertina in *The Infernal Desire Machines of Doctor Hoffman*. Bodily damage is a crucial part of the judicial process and of rape victim's experience – the emphasis on the severity of the rape is evidenced by the correspondent severity of physical injury in many courtrooms – yet women are trained to be passive in order to potentially save their lives. As Abhor in Acker's *Empire of the Senseless* states, when faced with rape: "I quickly chose a raped body over a mutilated or dead one."[13] Furthermore, if an individual dissociates during an attack, fighting back and potentially receiving the judicially necessary body damage is impossible.

Rape began to be viewed during the late 1960s and 1970s, when Carter produced her most speculative fictions, as being less about the sexual act itself and more about power and control – male expression of dominance over females in a degrading and humiliating way – a view supported and solidified by Groth's influential 1979 study. Groth

---

[11] Kathy Acker, *Empire of the Senseless* (1988), London: Picador, 1989, 169.
[12] Sarah E. Ullman, Henrietta H. Filipas, Stephanie M. Townsend and Laura L. Starzynski, "Psychosocial Correlates of PTSD Symptom Severity in Sexual Assault Survivors", *Journal of Traumatic Stress*, XX/5 (October 2007), 821.
[13] Angela Carter, *The Infernal Desire Machines of Doctor Hoffman* (1972), London: Penguin, 1982, 64.

identified three patterns of rape: anger, power and sadism.[14] All three patterns contain elements of the expression of male dominance over females through sexual means. Caruth writes that PTSD "reflects the direct imposition on the mind of the unavoidable reality of horrific events, the taking over of the mind, psychically and neurobiologically, *by an event that it cannot control* ... trauma is not simply an effect of destruction but also, fundamentally, an enigma of survival".[15]

As suggested by Gillian C. Mezey and Pamela J. Taylor, victims "themselves tend to emphasise their sense of helplessness and loss of control, during and after the attack, as more damaging than the sexual aspect of the encounter *per se*".[16] Susan Brownmiller, in her seminal and highly influential 1975 text *Against Our Will: Men, Women and Rape*, went so far as to state that rape "is nothing more or less than a conscious process of intimidation by which all men keep all women in a state of fear".[17] Brownmiller also suggests that, alongside women being physiologically the natural victims of rape, their status as rape victims is taught to daughters from a young age:

> Women are trained to be rape victims. To simply learn the word "rape" is to take instruction in the power relationship between males and females .... Rape has something to do with our sex. Rape is something awful that happens to females.[18]

Brownmiller goes on to detail "rape myths" – "ALL WOMEN WANT TO BE RAPED. NO WOMAN CAN BE RAPED AGAINST HER WILL, SHE WAS ASKING FOR IT, IF YOU'RE GOING TO BE RAPED YOU MIGHT AS WELL RELAX AND ENJOY IT"[19] – that serve to keep men in the paradoxical position of dominant, potential aggressors and necessary protectors of women, who are passive victims in need of protection. Examining the rape situation, Brownmiller states that women cannot "win" –

---

[14] A. Nicholas Groth, *Men Who Rape: The Psychology of the Offender*, New York: Plenum Press, 1979, 13.

[15] Caruth, *Unclaimed Experience*, 58 (emphasis added).

[16] Gillian C. Mezey and Pamela J. Taylor, "Psychological Reactions of Women Who Have Been Raped", *British Journal of Psychiatry*, CLII/3 (March 1988), 330.

[17] Susan Brownmiller, *Against Our Will: Men, Women and Rape*, Harmondsworth: Penguin, 1975, 15.

[18] *Ibid.*, 309.

[19] *Ibid.*, 311.

struggling and risking further violence or remaining passive and reaffirming the myths of rape:

> Her position, at once, is unprepared and defensive. She cannot win; at best she can escape defeat .... Femininity has trained her to lose.[20]

What Carter suggests is that psychological power can be retained by victims, even within situations where physical control is lost, and that the discourse of femininity which trains women to be passive victims can indeed be refuted. Of note: the issue of male rape is barely mentioned in these discussions, often passed over as a feature of war or penal institutions. Perhaps understandably, the social climate that had only just begun to allow an open discourse about female sexual assault was not ready for acceptance or discussion about male rape. As Irina Anderson writes, discussion about male rape is a recent discoursal phenomenon and hence, "current conceptualizations about male rape lag behind those of female rape, that is, current male rape perception is at the stage that female rape perception was several years ago in terms of individuals' knowledge, beliefs and attitudes".[21]

Reinforcing the perspective of women-as-victim, Stevi Jackson asserts that during "the course of their psychosexual development, men and women learn the typical vocabularies of motive of rapist and victim respectively .... Sexual behaviour is social behaviour", leaving rape conceptualised as "simply an extreme manifestation of our culturally accepted patterns of male-female relationships".[22] This perspective, alongside the commonly held rape myths detailed by Brownmiller, lead to negative and damaging social attitudes and behaviours towards victims. Issues such as the degree of bodily damage being indicative of degree of resistance (saying "no" is not enough apparently), allegations of victim blame through erroneous elements, such as dress, behaviour and use of alcohol or drugs, designation of individual as victim rather than individual, and

---

[20] *Ibid.*, 360.

[21] Irina Anderson, "What is a Typical Rape? Effects of Victim and Participant Gender in Female and Male Rape Perception", *British Journal of Social Psychology*, XLVI/1 (March 2007), 228.

[22] Stevi Jackson, "The Social Context of Rape: Sexual Scripts and Motivation", in *Rape and Society: Readings on the Problem of Sexual Assault*, eds Patricia Searles and Ronald J. Berger, Oxford: Westview Press, 1995, 26-27.

expectations of how individuals should feel and respond post-assault can in fact be as damaging as experience of rape itself, leading to underreporting and re-traumatization. These extrinsic psychosocial factors all impact upon psychological recovery from sexual trauma, as is well documented in clinical literature examining gender roles, stereotypes, assumptions, beliefs and myths around both male and female rape victims.[23] Furthermore, work focusing on the correlated notions of victim self-blame and poor psychosocial adjustments post-rape,[24] and on victim's social support and its relationship to victim self-blame[25] confirm the view that societal attitudes deeply affect traumatised individuals.

More recent fiction demonstrates the lack of social change regarding rape in the years since Carter first exposed and subverted these issues. In her 2003 novel, *Rape: A Love Story*, Joyce Carol Oates explores, explicitly and bravely, precisely the assumptions made by society about rape victims and the subsequent use of such myths to manipulate and deny her protagonist, Teena, access to legal retribution following a brutal gang rape that leaves her near dead and permanently disabled.[26] In Sophie Hannah's 2007 novel, *Hurting Distance*, rape victim Naomi does not disclose her trauma verbally, only testifying through a webpage for rape survivors. Yet she herself

---

[23] Ruth Graham, "Male Rape and the Careful Construction of the Male Victim", *Social and Legal Studies*, XV/2 (June 2006), 187-208; Kelly Simonson and Linda Mezydlo Subich, "Rape Perception as a Function of Gender-Role Traditionality and Victim-Perpetrator Association", *Sex Roles: A Journal of Reseach*, XL/7-8 (April 1999), 617-34; Kathy Doherty and Irina Anderson, "Making Sense of Male Rape: Constructions of Gender, Sexuality and Experience of Rape Victims", *Journal of Community and Applied Social Psychology*, XIV/2 (20 February 2004), 85-103; Anderson, "What is a Typical Rape?, 225-45; Michelle Davis and Paul Rogers, "Perceptions of Male Victims in Depicted Sexual Assaults: A Review of the Literature, *Aggression and Violent Behaviour*, XI/4 (July-August 2006), 367-77; Tendayi Viki G. and Dominic Abrahams, "But She Was Unfaithful: Benevolent Sexism and Reactions to Rape Victims Who Violate Traditional Gender Role Expectations", *Sex Roles: A Journal of Research*, XLVII/5-6 (September 2002), 289-93.
[24] Patricia A. Frazier, "Victim Attributions and Post-Rape Trauma", *Journal of Personality and Social Psychology*, LIX/2 (August 1990), 298-304.
[25] Irina Anderson and Antonia Lyons, "The Effect of Victims' Social Support on Attributions of Blame in Male and Female Rape", *Journal of Applied Social Psychology*, XXXV/7 (July 2005), 1400-17.
[26] Joyce Carol Oates, *Rape: A Love Story* (2003), London: Atlantic Books, 2006.

must acknowledge the anger that her letter will cause because she conceives her experience outside of the socially ascribed and accepted boundaries of the other victims on the site:

> I will never tell anybody my so-called story, which means there will be no justice, no punishment for those who deserve it. Sometimes that thought is pretty hard to take. Still, it's a small price to pay for not having to spend the rest of my life being thought of as a victim ....
> On the "What Is Rape" page of your site, you list a number of definitions, the last of which is 'any sexually intimidating behaviour'. You go on to say, "No physical contact needs to have taken place – sometimes an inappropriate look or comment is enough to make a woman feel violated." When I read that, I wanted to hit whoever wrote it.
>
> I know you'll disapprove of this letter and me and everything I've said, but I'm sending it anyway. I think it's important to point out that not all rape victims have the same mindset, vocabulary and attitudes.[27]

Carter, in many senses reacting against the discourses of the 1970s that re-inscribed men and women as diametrically opposed oppressor-victim, replicates the suggestion from Hannah that victims – many of whom may well not want to be defined as victims – do not all react in the same way or conceptualise their rapes in a precisely defined manner.

In her 1979 polemic *The Sadeian Woman*, Carter does not hold much sympathy with de Sade's Justine, who, devout in an ideologically-perfect victim status, learns "not self-preservation but self-pity" from her experiences.[28] Indeed, Sarah Gamble suggests that one of Carter's "primary purposes in the book is to urge women to repudiate the dubious status of passive, suffering martyr".[29] This, combined with her subversive representations of rape, has led to some critics insinuating that in some ways she condones sexual violence against women. This issue has been considered by Sally Keenan, who writes:

---

[27] Sophie Hannah, *Hurting Distance*, London: Hodder and Stoughton, 2007, 1-2.

[28] Angela Carter, *The Sadeian Woman* (1979), London: Virago, 2000, 51.

[29] Sarah Gamble, *Angela Carter: Writing From the Front Line*, Edinburgh: Edinburgh University Press, 1997, 100.

... radical feminist critics in the decade following the publication of *The Sadeian Woman* took Carter to task, accusing her of reinforcing patriarchal representations of women that degraded them .... In the context of those debates, Carter was seen by these critics to be running with the enemy.[30]

This strident critique of Carter is clearly demonstrated by the radical feminist Andrea Dworkin, who dismisses Carter as a "pseudofeminist" who enters "the realm of literary affectation heretofore reserved for the boys" with her "endemic contempt" of de Sade's actual victims.[31] Carter's brutal representation of sexual violence can be viewed more subversively through examination of her representations of rape as necessarily demythologising issues of patriarchal power that serve to reinforce the binary of male aggressor and female victim, deconstructing the myth that only women can be raped and examining the highly individual psychological responses of characters who undergo sexual trauma.

Carter's fiction

In a timely manner, as resonant today as thirty years ago, Carter suggests through the notable absence in her fiction of any legal recourse following rape that women must begin to deconstruct their socially ascribed victim status in order to have any chance of survival as autonomous, coherent individuals. She explores the notion of women winning, retaining power and refusing to be victims within the male denotation of victim despite atrocious experiences. This is most apparent in her 1979 short story "The Company of Wolves", a reworking of the Little Red Riding Hood fairy tale. The girl refuses to be the wolf's victim: "her fear did her no good, she ceased to be afraid .... The girl burst out laughing; she knew she was nobody's meat."[32]

---

[30] Sally Keenan, "Angela Carter's *The Sadeian* Woman: Feminism as Treason", in *The Infernal Desires of Angela Carter: Fiction, Femininity, Feminism*, eds Joseph Bristow and Trev Lynn Broughton, London: Longman, 1997, 139. Sarah Gamble also details what she views as misinterpretations of *The Sadeian Woman*, in particular Andrea Dworkin's and Susanne Kappeler's (*Angela Carter*, 99-104).

[31] Andrea Dworkin, *Pornography: Men Possessing Women*, London: The Women's Press, 1981, 84-85.

[32] Angela Carter, "The Company of Wolves" (1979), in *The Bloody Chamber*, London: Vintage, 1995, 117-18.

Carter's overarching metaphor suggests that while society may be full of wolves, women need not lie down and be their "meat" but can retain their sense of autonomous self. As Margaret Atwood writes, the girl "wins the herbivore-carnivore contest by refusing fear, by taking matters into her own hands, by refusing to allow herself to be defined as somebody's meat".[33] Earlier critics did not react to the short story in such a positive way: Patricia Duncker, for example, was highly critical of what she saw as Carter's mere reproduction of the patriarchal system as shrouded by fairy tale.[34] These opposing views mimic the social climate in which the story was published, with debates raging around censorship, pornography and freedom of expression. The feminist perspectives were in opposition themselves, and it is little wonder that Carter taps in to this debate with such frank narratives.

Melanie, in Carter's *The Magic Toyshop*, is a far more conventional victim during her metaphorical rape by the swan in Uncle Philip's production of *Leda and the Swan*. She suffers from the classic symptoms earlier described by Caruth, both during and after her trauma:

> She was hallucinated: she felt herself not herself, wrenched from her own personality, watching this whole fantasy from another place; and, in this staged fantasy, anything was possible ....
> The swan made a lumpish jump forward and settled on her loins. She thrust with all her force to get rid of it but the wings came down all around her like a tent and its head fell forward and nestled in her neck. The gilded beak dug deeply into the soft flesh. She screamed, hardly realising she was screaming. She was covered completely by the swan but for her kicking feet and her screaming face. The obscene swan had mounted her. She screamed again. There were feathers in her mouth .... After a gap of consciousness, she found that Finn was kneeling beside her, pulling her skirt decently down for her. The passionate swan had dragged her dress half off.[35]

---

[33] Margaret Atwood, "Running with the Tigers", in *Flesh and the Mirror: Essays on the Art of Angela Carter*, ed. Lorna Sage, London: Longman, 1994, 130.

[34] Patricia Duncker, "Re-imagining the Fairy Tales: Angela Carter's Bloody Chambers", *Literature and History* X/1 (April 1984), 6-7.

[35] Angela Carter, *The Magic Toyshop* (1967), London: Virago, 2001, 166-67.

Melanie dissociates from the event, loses her self, and her metaphorical rape is more of a psychical violation than an actual physical one, though no less traumatic. The description of the "obscene swan" is described in the physical language of rape, Melanie is fully and classically traumatised, experiencing an ontological, rather than physical assault. As Jean Wyatt puts it, Melanie's metaphorical rape "retains the psychological effect that theorists and survivors of rape report: that is, women experience rape not only as a physical violation, but as a denial of their humanity, of their agency and self-determination".[36]

Unlike Melanie, Carter's heroine in *Heroes and Villains*, Marianne, is subversive in retaining psychological power both during and after her attack. As Elisabeth Mahoney says,[37] Carter first subverts the traditional defining character of male-mind-rational, female-body-beautiful by describing Marianne as the "only rational woman left in the whole world",[38] while Jewel is "probably the most beautiful man left in the world".[39] Marianne's primary response to Jewel's impending attack is anger, as was the case of threatened gang rape earlier, when she "discovered she was not in the least frightened, only very angry indeed".[40] She is "determined to maintain her superior status at all costs", despite her physical pain – "scalding, she felt split to the core but she did not make a sound for her only strength was her impassivity and she never closed her eyes". Crucially, Marianne stays fully involved in the attack, not allowing Jewel to control her, to assert his power over her, or induce fear, maintaining a cold and unaffected front. In keeping her eyes open, she also refuses to dissociate from the attack – Jewel may have raped her body but he has not raped her mind. The conversation between the two, both before and after the attack, is a definitive struggle for power. She calmly asks: "Why did you do it to me?",[41] not with a tone of bewilderment but indignation.

---

[36] Jean Wyatt, "The Violence of Gendering: Castration Images in Angela Carter's *The Magic Toyshop, The Passion of New Eve*, and 'Peter and The Wolf'", in *Angela Carter*, ed. Alice Easton, Basingstoke: Macmillan, 2000, 66.
[37] Elisabeth Mahoney, "'But elsewhere?': The Future of Fantasy in *Heroes and Villains*", in *The Infernal Desires of Angela Carter*, 79.
[38] Angela Carter, *Heroes and Villains* (1969), London: Virago, 1988, 55.
[39] *Ibid.*, 61.
[40] *Ibid.*, 49.
[41] *Ibid.*, 55.

She retains her intellect while Jewel struggles between the world of the body and his quasi-intellectual teachings by experimental puppet-master Donally, forcing him to admit: "I'm very frightened of you", giving her "the advantage".

In comparison to Marianne's uncharacteristic response, Jewel's motives are less complex, mirroring Groth's psychodynamics of the power rape: rape is used as a tool to demote Marianne from her superior status, to teach her a lesson, to consume her intellect and her body, almost a necessary act in which Jewel has "nailed" her "on necessity".[42] Carter uses an interesting phallic and colloquial metaphor, reminiscent of slang phraseology – man screws woman – literally nailing her in penetration. Their enforced marriage is far more traumatic and disempowering for Marianne, who in direct contrast to her psychological response to rape, attempts to "force herself into a condition of detachment"[43] at the thought of it. "There's no choice in being a wife", Marianne states, and while women's choice is removed by the very nature of rape, there is a choice for her in not being consumed by rape.[44] Donally's desire that Jewel "swallow ... and incorporate"[45] her for the purposes of his social experimentation by raping her provides a metaphoric chain from "nailing" to "consumption" – and Marianne refuses to be consumed. Jewel and Marianne's subsequently consenting sexual relationship remains antagonistic, with the metaphoric chain moving to "annihilation" – "as soon as she and the young man found out how to annihilate one another, she was unable to think about anything else for long".[46] It is Jewel's intellect, represented in particular through his eyes, that frightens Marianne as she simultaneously discovers the power of her own body and desire through her sexual autonomy and pleasure, and in the power she wields to annihilate Jewel through the sexual act. The tables of power have turned.

Carter makes continual references to Marianne and Jewel gazing upon and into one another, questioning both what they see and what they fantasise about seeing. Jewel sees the "firing squad" when

---

[42] *Ibid.*, 56.
[43] *Ibid.*, 69.
[44] *Ibid.*, 114.
[45] *Ibid.*, 56.
[46] *Ibid.*, 87.

looking at Marianne, visualising his death through the fact that he exists in her eyes only "by virtue of the extravagance of [his] metaphors".[47] Elizabeth Mahoney points out that Marianne's objectification of Jewel allows her "the possibility of new narratives of sexual subjectivity which are not grounded in the victim/master dyad".[48] In this respect, Marianne is a dangerous opposition for Jewel. As rape did not achieve the desired re-evaluation of his power over Marianne, he turns to impregnating her for

> Revenge .... Shoving a little me up you, a little me all furred, plaited and bristling with knifes. Then I should have some status in relation to myself.

Pregnancy, described in terms of infection and violence, is more of an abuse of her body and her mind than the rape was, his "spurt of seed a terrible violation of her privacy".[49] Ultimately, neither of these attempts to disempower and oppress Marianne works, even after he begins to beat her. She crucially retains her consciousness and, once he has been destroyed through his inability to gain power over her, she will take over the tribe in her autonomous self, "be the tiger lady and rule them with a rod of iron".[50]

Albertina, the daughter of Dr Hoffman in Carter's 1972 novel, *The Infernal Desire Machines of Doctor Hoffman*, suffers a very different kind of attack. One potential difficulty in reading her non-traumatised response to her attack lies in the fact that Carter does not allow access to Albertina's voice or her emotions after her rape, giving only Desiderio's witnessing, interpretation and memories. Albertina is placed in the category of victim by Desiderio, who kisses her "forlorn hair",[51] and due to her injuries she needs complete physical care after her gang rape by the Centaurs. Yet again, it appears that only her body is damaged; she retains her intellect and is able to theorise her rape (as being the projection of her desires) rather than being dissociated from the trauma. Desiderio states:

---

[47] *Ibid.*, 120.
[48] Mahoney, "But elsewhere?", 85.
[49] Carter, *Heroes and Villains*, 90.
[50] *Ibid.*, 150.
[51] Carter, *Doctor Hoffman*, 181.

I admired her ruthless empiricism for she was convinced that even though every male in the village had obtained carnal knowledge of her, the beasts were still only emanations of her own desires, dredged up and objectively reified from the dark abysses of her unconscious. And she told me that, according to her father's theory, all the subjects and objects we had encountered in the loose grammar of the Nebulous Time were derived from a similar source – my desires; or hers; or the Count's. At first, especially, the Count's, for he had lived on closer terms with his own unconscious than we. But now our desires, perhaps, had achieved their day of independence.[52]

Her physical loss of consciousness during the attack can be seen as a form of bodily dissociation from the situation that allows her to retain her conscious self intact.

As Aidan Day remarks, in "the state of universal abandon it is most frequently the female that suffers the severest depredations",[53] and this is made evident in Carter's simultaneous placing of Desiderio's and Albertina's assaults. Albertina's repeated rapes by the Centaur's "tumescent" organs are marked by "a hideous struggle" during which she becomes "mired by blood".[54] Pitted against this is Desiderio's knowledge that he "would not be left out of the savage game", admitting that he will be treated with "far less severity because they respected the virile principle and reviled the female one". In comparison, he is "caressed" by the female Centaurs, cannot "help but quicken with pleasure", and experiences the "subtlest of tortures ... bathed in a series of the most exquisite sensations on the very table where they cruelly abused the flesh of the one I loved best".[55] The lead Centaur later apologises to him "because she was my mate, therefore my property, and so he must apologise to me".[56] The reader is given a male perspective on both ownership of the female and on the Centaurs' motives:

---

[52] *Ibid.*, 186.
[53] Aidan Day, *Angela Carter: The Rational Glass*, Manchester: Manchester University Press, 1998, 90.
[54] Carter, *Doctor Hoffman*, 179.
[55] *Ibid.*, 180.
[56] *Ibid.*, 182.

> ... the males clearly did not know it was a rape. They showed neither enthusiasm nor gratification ... the rape had had elements of the kind of punishment said to hurt the giver more than the receiver though I do not know what they were punishing her for, unless it was for being female to a degree unprecedented among them.[57]

By only giving a male perspective on the event, a male denotation of Albertina as victim when she clearly does not view herself within this definition, the polarisation of the two attacks and the misogynistic apology to Desiderio – which he notably fails to question as being a little skewed – Carter can be interpreted as commenting on the masculine appropriation of rape through medical and legal discourses. Alternatively, Sally Robinson asserts, from the perspective of postmodernism, that the "overt masculinisation of the narrative ... serves to subvert the mechanisms of identification that support the successful narrativisation of violence against women ... placing the woman reader in an impossible position".[58] From either perspective, the reader cannot help but find such a violent scene uncomfortable, forcing either ethical questioning or deliberate ignorance. Furthermore, the deliberate turning away from the trauma through ignoring the scene is in itself unethical, and strikes at the heart of the debate around ethics and trauma. If we turn away from the difficult but essential witnessing of trauma, or secondary witnessing through testimony, then the risk of trauma continuing, not only for the individual but for legions of future individuals, remains high. It is through ignorance of the brutal actuality of rape and sexual trauma that the phenomenon continues without serious examination.

Carter explores ways in which women can retain control and defy the systems of oppression that attempt to place them in the role of passive victim. Carter also examines the idea that women can be actively complicit in their status as victim, though I strongly disagree with Sarah Gamble's suggestion that Marianne "brings much of the violence she suffers at the hands of Jewel upon herself".[59] In fact, for Carter, complicity and collusion with the patriarchal system of

---

[57] *Ibid.*, 180-81.
[58] Sally, Robinson, "The Anti-hero as Oedipus: Gender and the Postmodern Narrative in *The Infernal Desire Machines of Doctor Hoffman*", in *Angela Carter*, ed. Easton, 115.
[59] Gamble, *Angela Carter*, 77.

oppression is in no way the same as victim blame, nor does it lead to man having the right to rape women in any way, shape or form.

Indeed for many of Carter's female victims, such as Melanie, complicity is an inescapable, life-saving necessity because of the systems in which they are confined. Carter's most extreme example is her portrayal of the girls kidnapped and brutalised by Zero in *The Passion of New Eve* (1977). Zero is the ultimate personification of misogyny, almost to the extent of becoming a caricature, as Roz Kaveney proposes, suggesting that life in

> Zero's melange is a nightmare representation of male desire and the sort of complicity in one's own oppression .... What stops Carter ever looking like a radical feminist, rather than a radical and a feminist, is a sense of irony and perspective.[60]

Yet while Carter turns Zero into a parodic figure, the violence and degradation he inflicts is very real – for example, in order to "illustrate the humility he demanded" of his seven wives, he "would smear his excrement and that of the dog upon their breasts".[61] The girls are so brutalised by Zero, who "believed women were fashioned of a different soul substance from men, a more primitive, animal stuff, and so did not need the paraphernalia of a civilised society such as cutlery, meat, soap, shoes", that they become entirely complicit in their victim status. They are grateful to him for allowing them "the sophistication of cups and plates",[62] subservient in the extreme as "they loved him and did not think they were fit to pick up the crumbs from his table".[63] Despite his sexual demands and the viciousness with which he exacts them, they argue defensively and jealously over where Eve(lyn) will fit into the "matrimonial rota" that "absolutely regulated their lives".[64]

It is difficult to read these girls in a sympathetic light as they provoke an uncomfortable sensation in the reader, who can see their brutalisation but also their complicity in this regime of degradation. Their one potential redeeming feature lies in the manner in which they

---

[60] Roz Kaveney, "New New World Dreams: Angela Carter and Science Fiction", in *Flesh and the Mirror*, 182.
[61] Angela Carter, *The Passion of New Eve* (1977), London: Virago, 1998, 85.
[62] *Ibid.*, 87.
[63] *Ibid.*, 85.
[64] *Ibid.*, 88.

form a community of their own, defying his authority and venomous hatred of lesbianism by communicating and embracing sexual relationships with one another. Yet even these small acts of rebellion are not particularly insubordinate, as Eve(lyn) states: "These practices were an inevitable concomitant of harem life and the wives excused them to themselves by, when the sun came up and they were themselves again, pretending nothing whatsoever had happened."[65] In comparison to these women, Marianne refuses to be complicit in the system – "I'll do as I want"[66] – and is by far the most subversive heroine, the one who finally wins through.

Women can be, or can become, complicit not only in their own oppression but in other women's oppression. Sue Lees, for example, looks at the manner in which the language of the "discourse of female reputation", perpetuated by both males and females in denoting girls as either frigid or sluttish, "acts as a material practice with its own determinate effects, acting as a form of control over their emotions and passions and steering girls into subordinate relationships with men".[67] In Carter, this lack of female solidarity between the girls in Zero's harem can be attributed to their own fear and oppression, as in the case of the female Centaurs, who do not protect Albertina because they are themselves intended as victims of humiliation.[68] Mrs Green, the Barbarian's matriarchal surrogate mother in *Heroes and Villains*, reacts to Marianne's threatened gang rape in a "sad, coaxing voice", ineffectually and "pathetically" attempting to dissuade the brothers with an air of jaded resignation.[69] Marianne, "more cruelly wounded in her pride than in her body", is told by Mrs Green that it is "the way of the world .... Young men will always take advantage, dear .... And we all have to take what we can get." Yet while Mrs Green appears to be attempting misguidedly to instruct Marianne to accept her fate as a woman – she must "learn to reconcile herself to everything from rape to mortality" – she is paradoxically "smug and comfortable" with a sense of "pleasure and revenge" at Marianne's alleged fall from

---

[65] *Ibid.*, 106.
[66] Carter, *Heroes and Villains*, 97.
[67] Sue Lees, *Ruling Passions: Sexual Violence, Reputation and the Law*, Buckingham: Open University Press, 1997, 4.
[68] Carter, *Doctor Hoffman*, 180.
[69] Carter, *Heroes and Villains*, 48.

superiority.[70] Denied a female confidant and support against her enforced marriage, Marianne enters into denial, temporarily left vulnerable with little of the strength that stood her so well during the attack.

Carter uses the character of Eve(lyn) in *The Passion of New Eve* to explore the positions of violated and violator. Raped once as a man by Mother, and repeatedly as a woman by Zero, he makes an interesting correlation between his previous sexual life as a man and his new, abused position as a woman. It is only from within this new position as a violated female that he can appreciate the "crucial lack of self" as violated, which

> ... forced me to know myself as a former violator at the moment of my own violation. When he entered me, the act seemed to me one of seppuku, a ritual disembowelment I committed upon myself, although I was only watching him and only felt my pain and unpleasure in his joy at my pain and pleasure at my distress.[71]

In spite of, or perhaps because of his new insights into the experience of the victim, Eve(lyn) is so overcome by desire upon meeting the iconic Tristessa (who is a male transvestite) that he rapes him. Tristessa theorises – "I thought ... I was immune to rape"[72] – as a biological male, and he perceives himself as being raped not by being penetrated but in being forced to penetrate. Carter creates a situation that is extremely subversive and not acknowledged legally: a female raping a male – one which is mirrored by Mother's raping of Eve(lyn) prior to his gender reassignment surgery.

Desiderio's rape by the Acrobats of Desire is represented as such an immense trauma that a natural disaster ensues, wreaking havoc and destroying the landscape. The rape of a male by another male is presented here as much more symbolically traumatic in the eyes of Desiderio – arguably due to a masculine fear of being penetrated, being placed in the category of Other, as lack and hole, as the one to be penetrated. This assertion is supported by clinical literature on male rape, as suggested by Ruth Graham who, using Judith Butler's 1993

---

[70] *Ibid.*, 59.
[71] Carter, *The Passion of New Eve*, 101-102.
[72] *Ibid.*, 137.

text *Bodies that Matter: On the Discursive Limits of Sex*, states in her excellent essay on the construction and experience of male victims of rape:

> Returning to Butler's (1993) theory that heterosexuality is based on an understanding of whether bodies penetrate or are penetrated, the male rape discourse supports a definition of sexuality as one in which men desire women to penetrate, and women desire penetration by men, despite the problem that male rape poses for such a theorization. Perhaps this too helps explain why male rape is often conceptualized as a particularly abhorrent form of sexual assault: if heterosexual men are defined by their desire to penetrate 'the other' (the woman/feminine) and also by their resistance to being penetrated by 'the same' (the man/masculine), the conceptualization of male rape as particularly devastating and horrific makes sense.[73]

Desiderio states, using the blunt tone Carter deploys when introducing rape scenes, "in this holy city, I was fucked in the anus, against my will",[74] going on:

> I was trapped. I could not move. I was filled with impotent rage .... The pain was terrible. I was most intimately ravaged I do not know how many times. I wept, bled, slobbered and pleaded but nothing would appease a rapacity as remorseless and indifferent as the storm which raged outside and now reached a nightmarish hurricane.

Desiderio withdraws into a cave after being raped, a symbolic re-entering of a space as opposed to being entered, that may be interpreted in Freudian terms as a regression to the maternal womb and a yielding to the death drive. The male disbelief at being raped, rape being a specifically female experience, leads to a similarly traumatic dissociation from the consciousness and selfhood as Melanie experiences – "I was so far outside myself they might just as well have cut me up and juggled with me and, for all I know, they did".[75] Yet his psychological dissociation is specifically different, being from the masculine self. As Sue Lees writes, drawing on male

---

[73] Graham, "Male Rape", 199.
[74] Carter, *The Passion of New Eve*, 115.
[75] *Ibid.*, 117.

victim statements: "It is the victims who are stigmatised as gay, soft, cripples, or 'not real men' or who by the nature of the act are rendered effeminate."[76] Desiderio retreats due to "a great need to leave humanity behind for a while", [77] the humanity that rapes and the humanity that constructs the masculine male as immune to rape.

Yet if all that happens to Desiderio and Albertina in Dr Hoffman's world is a projection of unconscious desires and, as Desiderio states, his experience is only against his will "as far, that is, as I was conscious of my desires",[78] the inescapable question here is whether Carter is exploring rape as a male fantasy – both to be inflicted and have inflicted? Similarly, is Carter examining the idea of rape as a female fantasy, or deconstructing the myth that women want to be raped? Albertina theorises that her rape must have been the product of her desires, while Zero's women are subject to horrific tortures and abuses by him, but come to believe this is their life-giving force. Marianne states that Jewel is "nothing more than the furious inventions of my virgin nights".[79]

Carter is on extremely controversial ground here, as Aidan Day writes: "The ideological dodginess of the rape scene in *Heroes and Villains* resides in the fact that the rape might be read as the fulfilment of Marianne's repressed desire."[80] As discussed by Brownmiller, notions of unconscious female fantasies of rape stem from psychoanalysts Karen Horney and Helene Deutsch, who looked upon masochism as "an essential element of femininity", before arguing, damagingly, that young girls have fantasies of rape.[81] Brownmiller argues that even conscious rape fantasies are "the product of male conditioning" given "the pervasive male ideology of rape (the mass psychology of the conqueror)" and subsequent "mirror-image female victim psychology".[82] Carter explores the myth that women may fantasise about rape, but it is clear from the violence of her depictions of rape that the reality is never the same as any naïve fantasy, and the

---

[76] Lees, *Ruling Passions*, 106.
[77] Carter, *Doctor Hoffman*, 118.
[78] *Ibid.*, 115.
[79] Carter, *Heroes and Villains*, 137.
[80] Day, *Angela Carter*, 44.
[81] Brownmiller, *Against Our Will*, 316.
[82] *Ibid.*, 324.

two should not in any way be equated. Furthermore, as previously explored, neither Albertina nor Marianne allow themselves to be seduced by the notion of conquering male and passive rescued female, determining instead to retain their own autonomous power.

There are no easy analyses of Carter's representations of rape, and it is easy to see why critics find Carter a difficult writer when she explores topics as sensitive as this. Paulina Palmer comments on the problems that writers can have with the representation of rape and sexual violence, asking:

> ... how can the writer, while emphasising the horror of the crime, avoid sensationalising and glamorising it? How can she succeed in depicting the complex response of the victim – her feelings of terror, humiliation and isolation during the act and her contradictory feelings of guilt and anger afterwards?[83]

Through a process of defamiliarisation and head-on confrontation – both in examining male rape as a phenomenon and the atypical reactions of females who are assaulted – Carter successfully represents rape by provoking a response in readers and thus opening a textual and social space for discussion about the ethical lacuna between dictated or assumed responses and actual experiences, and for the excavation and subversion of rape myths – in particular, the myth that men cannot be raped. This confrontation with the brutal reality of rape as opposed to shrouding the topic is deeply ethical. Literature that discusses sexual assault and rape gives voice to victims who in other discourses are often silenced, accused, blamed and judged. When rape victims are given voice their testimony is often questioned and doubted – as indeed happened with Carter's work. Carter provides fictionalised testimonies that explore the extent to which victims can retain psychological control during sexual trauma and after. As Elaine Jordan also asserts, narratives in which women – though in Carter's case it also refers to male victims – demonstrate the possibility "of carrying on unhumiliated under the greatest possible threat to your

---

[83] Paulina Palmer, *Contemporary Women's Fiction: Narrative Practice and Feminist Theory*, Jackson: University of Mississippi Press, 1989, 85.

surviving integrity as an agent not an object"[84] are crucial for the project of making rape visible – a project that remains as vital now as thirty years ago.

---

[84] Elaine Jordan, "Enthralment: Angela Carter's Speculative Fictions", in *Plotting Change: Contemporary Women's Fiction*, ed. Linda Anderson, London: Edward Arnold, 1990, 30.

"A New Algebra": The Poetics and Ethics of Trauma in J.G. Ballard's *The Atrocity Exhibition*

Jakob Winnberg

> Art ... is loyal to humanity only through inhumanity toward it.[1]

Doubling the wound

Some seven years before J.G. Ballard's *The Atrocity Exhibition* was published, Andy Warhol produced a particularly haunting work called *Ambulance Disaster*.[2] The work consists of the doubling of a photograph depicting a crashed ambulance with an apparently dead woman slumped out of one of the windows. This doubling of the image reflects a doubling of trauma – not only are we confronted with a more or less traumatic event, requiring the assistance of an ambulance: what was supposed to be the vehicle of relief has, in a cruel instance of irony, exacerbated the trauma. The instrument of help and healing has failed, is out of order. As if to underline this doubled trauma, in the most famous print of the work, the bottom image repeats the top image with a clear difference: bleaches, lines and tears, the most conspicuous of which effaces the woman's face in a way that may be accidental, but seems callously calculated.

---

[1] Theodor Adorno, *Aesthetic Theory* (1997), ed., trans., and intro. Robert Hullot-Kentor, London: Continuum, 2004, 257.
[2] See reproduction below. This is the print on display in the Andy Warhol Museum, Pittsburgh.

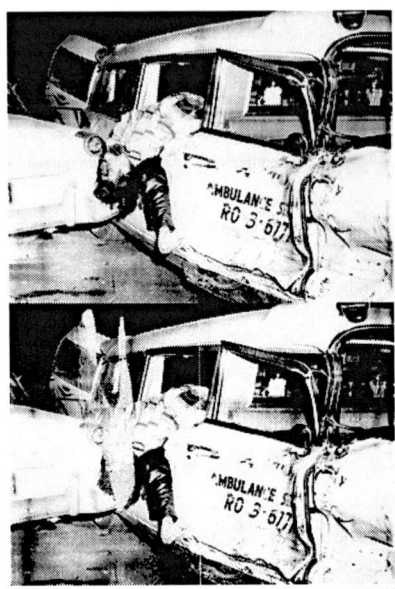

Andy Warhol, *Ambulance Disaster* (1963)
© The Andy Warhol Foundation for the Visual Arts, Inc. c/o Pictoright Amsterdam
2009

In all these aspects, *Ambulance Disaster* may serve as a pretty much perfect visual equivalent and forerunner of Ballard's novel, one of the main motifs of which notably is car crashes and their victims, as well as other forms of disasters, staged in "Serial Deaths".[3] Moreover, the protagonist is a psychiatrist who suffers from a continual trauma that he actively participates in by incessantly repeating a few key scenarios with minor variations that amount to an exacerbation and proliferation of the trauma: the psychiatrist, the instrument of help and healing, is out of order. Thus, in effect, to play on Derrida's words, there is no outside-trauma. Indeed, the narrative as a whole offers no real outside position, for although there is a character called Dr Nathan who functions as a representative of analytical rationality, he too is engulfed in what the narrator calls the "spinal landscape" of trauma, depicted in the novel through half-connected, obscure fragments, which clash and blend with an ultimate effect of radical

---

[3] J.G. Ballard, "Serial Deaths", in *The Atrocity Exhibition* (1970), London: Flamingo, 2001, 4.

defamiliarisation. Nor does the narrative itself progress so much as repeat and recombine.

Yet, there is an alternative way of reading this doubling of trauma in both Warhol and Ballard. As Cathy Caruth argues, trauma is always "a double wound",[4] in the sense that it is "experienced too soon, too unexpectedly, to be fully known and is therefore not available to consciousness until it imposes itself again, repeatedly, in the nightmares and repetitive actions of the survivor".[5] Caruth reads further significance into this doubling by relating it, by way of Freud, to Tasso's *Jerusalem Liberated*, in which Tancred kills his beloved Clorinda unwittingly, only to subsequently slash at a tree in which, again unbeknown to him, Clorinda's soul is imprisoned – with this second wound, however, Clorinda's voice is released, making it cruelly known to Tancred that he has wounded his beloved, again.[6] It is the doubling of the wound, then, of trauma, that makes possible its acknowledgement as a wound, as affectively, which is to say existentially, significant. Reading Warhol in accordance with Caruth's understanding of the doubling of the wound, we may say that it is precisely the obscene tear of the repetition that brings out the full force of the disaster, of the trauma, which in the first instance may remain hidden. Arguably, Ballard's novel may be read similarly, as concerned with a repetition-compulsion geared towards the restitution of lost significances.

It is this possibility that I wish to pursue in this essay, as I consider what I propose to call the novel's poetics of trauma.[7] And it is indeed the repetition-compulsion located on both the diegetic and the formal levels of the novel that most obviously manifests this poetics. Now, it has already been the subject of much debate what sort of poetics would be the poetics of trauma, and that debate has also immediately been framed in terms of ethical adequacy. According to a prominent notion of such ethical adequacy, decidedly influenced by such thinkers as Emmanuel Levinas and Jean-François Lyotard, the representational

---

[4] Cathy Caruth, *Unclaimed Experience: Trauma, Narrative, and History*, Baltimore, MD: John Hopkins University Press, 1996, 3.

[5] *Ibid.*, 4.

[6] *Ibid.*, 2.

[7] I use the word "poetics" here in the double, mingled sense of a theory of literary discourse and a specific practice of literary composition – the latter is usually guided by the former.

aspects of Ballard's poetics of trauma would evidence a fidelity to trauma that is in itself profoundly ethical.

However, I wish to immediately problematise any such congratulatory formalist ethical reading of the novel's poetics by focusing not so much on the ethics of the representation of trauma, as on the ethics of being in trauma and the ethics of the post-traumatic, as they emerge in the more diegetic dimension of the novel. Moreover, I am focusing here on collective, cultural trauma, rather than on individual trauma. In this way, I also approach the question of the novel's ethico-political resonance. This is an especially pertinent issue in the case of Ballard's novel, since the diverse aspects of trauma suffusing it would seem to eclipse not just most ethical, but seemingly all political, openings. Yet, as it turns out, some aspects of the novel's sustained poetics of trauma might in fact herald such openings.

This poetics of trauma resides most obviously in the narrative's concern with the accumulated cultural trauma of Western civilisation in the wake of modernity, or of what is possibly a subsequent postmodernity: a brutal consumer society and an increasingly technologised and mass-medialised world tending towards a hyperreal and inhuman state, in which the subject is bombarded with images and events impossible to assimilate and structure.[8] As Mark Fisher argues:

> Unlike Ballard's earlier novels, *The Atrocity Exhibition* adds nothing: the traumatic events which are its concern are simply those which took place in the 1960s. There is no need to postulate some additional environmental transmutation on the order of a natural disaster, the

---

[8] As Elaine Showalter similarly observes, what she calls "hystories", "multiply rapidly and uncontrollably in the era of mass media, telecommunications, and e-mail" (Elaine Showalter, *Hystories: Hysterical Epidemics and Modern Media*, New York: Columbia University Press, 1998, 3-5). See also Kirby Farrell, who conceives of cultural "modernism as a cumulative series of upheavals that are spikes in a rising baseline of stress: markers for massive, disorienting storms of new information and technology" (*Post-Traumatic Culture: Injury and Interpretation in the Nineties*, Baltimore: The Johns Hopkins University Press, 1998, 27); and Mark Fisher, who proposes that we "understand 'postmodernity' as an essentially material phenomenon, describing its effects primarily in terms of the impact that new telecommercial configurations have on the human nervous system" (*Flatline Constructs: Gothic Materialism and Cybernetic Theory-Fiction. Transmat: Resources in Transcendental Materialism* (2005), FC1s1.htm: http://www.cinestatic.com/trans-mat/Fisher/ [accessed 08/07/2008]). See also Ballard's note on the novel (*The Atrocity Exhibition*, 145).

novel implies: contemporary culture is itself a disaster-in-progress, an unnatural disaster, an atrocity exhibition.[9]

Indeed, according to Ballard himself in the annotated edition of the novel, *The Atrocity Exhibition*

> ... is directly inspired by [Kennedy's] death, and represents a desperate attempt to make sense of the tragedy, with its huge hidden agenda. The mass media created the Kennedy we know, and his death represented a tectonic shift in the communications landscape, sending fissures deep into the popular landscape that have not yet closed.[10]

Like Warhol, then, Ballard is concerned with the traumatic impact of the society of the spectacle, and just like Warhol does in Hal Foster's reading, Ballard "selects moments when [the] spectacle cracks (the JFK assassination, the Monroe suicide, ... car wrecks), but cracks only to expand".[11] This expansion of the spectacle is evident in the novel's representation of a cityscape in which "The billboards multiplied around them, walling the streets with giant replicas of napalm bombings in Vietnam, the serial deaths of Elizabeth Taylor and Marilyn Monroe terraced in the landscapes of Dien Bien Phu and the Mekong Delta".[12] The crack, the wound, in the spectacle, which might have had some subversive, liberating force, becomes immediately swallowed up in the perpetuation of the spectacle as doubling of trauma. The novel makes clear that "media (paradoxically) immediatize trauma, making it instantly available even as they prepackage it into what will become increasingly preprogrammed stimulus-response circuitries".[13] Importantly, "Trauma is not only the 'content' of this experience, but the very mode of experience itself". Rather than serving any therapeutic, sense-making function, by "Compulsively repeating particular audio-visual sequences, the media itself functions like a trauma victim".[14]

---

[9] Fisher, *Flatline*, FC2s9.htm. The index page of Fisher's online-book is FCcontents.htm.

[10] Ballard, *The Atrocity Exhibition*, 33-34.

[11] Hal Foster, *The Return of the Real: The Avant-Garde at the End of the Century*, Cambridge: The MIT Press, 1996, 136. In many respects, Debord's *Society of the Spectacle* may be read as a gloss on Ballard's novel.

[12] Ballard, *The Atrocity Exhibition*, 4.

[13] Fisher, *Flatline*, FCcontents.htm.

[14] *Ibid.*, FC2s10.htm.

The form of Ballard's novel reflects the breakdown of cognitive and affective faculties as we know them (or think we know them) in the wake of this traumatic spectacle, and therefore it itself emerges as a symptom of trauma. At the same time, this formal breakdown is also an example of the "dissolution of the novel" that has been accorded ethical significance by postmodern critics such as Andrew Gibson.[15] More significantly, though, the novel gains an ethico-political force in defying the representational consensus and "happy consciousness" (as understood by Herbert Marcuse in *One-Dimensional Man* and, after him, by Stjepan Meštrović in *Postemotional Society*) that relegate the inhumanity, the fundamental trauma, of modernity – or postmodernity – to the realm of the un(re)presentable. In these aspects, the novel comes across as supremely ethico-politically responsive and responsible rather than unapologetically nihilistic, even if the latter easily becomes one's immediate impression of the novel. Indeed, like Warhol's works, novels by Ballard such as *The Atrocity Exhibition* and *Crash* have been read as affectless, apolitical, and lacking in ethical responsivity. As Maylis Rospide points out, not only do these novels imply "the impossibility of an experimental posthuman ethics that nevertheless delivers an ethical message", but "the meld between flesh and steel" that is depicted in them "destroys the bodily possibility of Levinasian ethics".[16]

However, such readings might be questioned both in the case of Warhol and of Ballard, if we consider them in terms of what Foster calls "traumatic realism", that is, "as referential *and* simulacral, connected *and* disconnected, affective *and* affectless, critical *and* complacent".[17] For instance, as a relatively unfiltered record of what appears to be, not just mental, but general social and ontological disorder, *The Atrocity Exhibition* avoids neutralising the otherness of this disorder in the name of a hegemonic normality. Thus, the novel becomes itself a potentially traumatic experience, putting the reader in contact with the unacknowledged underside of society, with an unacknowledged cultural trauma.

---

[15] See Andrew Gibson, *Postmodernity, Ethics and the Novel: From Leavis to Levinas*, London: Routledge, 1999, 85-108.

[16] Maylis Rospide, "When Experimentation Becomes Ethics: 'A Duty Dance' with Literature in Will Self's Work", in *The Ethical Component in Experimental British Fiction Since the 1960s*, eds Susana Onega and Jean-Michel Ganteau, Newcastle: Cambridge Scholars Publishing, 2007, 177.

[17] Foster, *The Return of the Real*, 130 (original emphasis).

In this manner, the novel might be taken as an instance of the negative aesthetics theorised most thoroughly by Theodor Adorno.[18] Andrzej Gasiorek's description of *The Atrocity Exhibition* and its sibling novel, *Crash*, as "apocalyptic renderings of the hidden and possibly deviant logics of the technological age",[19] points in this direction too. However, the most disturbing, indeed somewhat traumatic, question the novel may give rise to is that of whether its representation is simply one of negative mimesis – a negative mirror image that magnifies the underside of society – or whether it is ultimately a perfect mimesis of the actual condition of society and the human mind, a condition that would become apparent were we but to bracket our natural attitude. If the latter is the case, *The Atrocity Exhibition* may be read as a phenomenology of being – but of being in a world in which "being" and "nothingness" (to borrow Sartre's terms) have become indistinguishable, have become one and the same: interiority and exteriority, fiction and actuality, model and reality, inauthentic and authentic have all bled into each other, creating the "spinal landscape" of Ballard's novel, in which a total conflation of everything on the same plane eradicates all difference and critical distance – and if this landscape would appear to us as incommensurably other, it somewhat paradoxically eradicates alterity too, thus pulling the rug from under "ethics as first philosophy" in Levinas' understanding.[20]

Moreover, this conflation is both the cause of trauma and its effect, the trauma of conflation resulting in a repetition-compulsion through which conflation proliferates virally. In staying true to this landscape, the novel calls upon us to ponder whether, as Fisher puts it, "breakdown behaviour becomes the only conceivable 'rational' response to a world that is itself breaking down".[21] Indeed, the rational itself is in question here, as Fisher's inverted commas indicate. The world is not simply breaking down, but is being reconfigured according to a new (il)logic with attendant new "truth"-"values". We are, to speak with Jean Baudrillard, passing into the third order of

---

[18] Theodor Adorno, *Aesthetic Theory* (1997), ed., trans., and intro. Robert Hullot-Kentor, London: Continuum, 2004.

[19] Andrzej Gasiorek, *J.G. Ballard*, Manchester: Manchester University Press, 2005, 16.

[20] Fisher similarly notes the novel's "treatment of technical, organic and geological features as elements belonging to a single plane".

[21] *Ibid.*, FC2s9.htm.

simulacra, into the transparency of Evil, and thus into the realm of fatal strategies, where upping the ante becomes the only possible route of subversion: breaking down not just as response, but as challenge to breakdown, on its own terms.[22]

Therefore – and this is my main focus here – the novel invites a reading in terms of Alain Badiou's ethics of fidelity to the truths of events, as that fidelity involves "the determination to think a world according to the principle of what has come to change it, to make it new".[23] This fidelity would be the task both of the character Travis on the diegetic plane of the novel, and of the reader confronted with the novel as event. For the novel may be seen as a trauma to ethics itself – an event, a disruption, a dissolution which challenges us to rethink ethics, to reconsider the limits of what it is possible to conceive of as ethical. In other words, this essay is fuelled by my conviction that it is an important task for ethical criticism to find works that befuddle received ethical understandings, be they humanist or post-humanist, deontological or non-deontological, so that the limits of ethics may be reinvestigated and rethought.[24] I move towards such a rethinking here, through discussions of the novel as response to and (re)presentation of trauma, that is, the novel's poetics of trauma; and of the novel's ethical dimension, residing in its fidelity to trauma – in its (re)presentation of trauma, and, at the same time, in its offering of trauma as event and challenge.

Yet, even as I seek here to go beyond the limitations of both foundational and non-foundational ethics by turning to Badiou's alternative for an ethical understanding of Ballard's novel, I find Ballard revealing the limitations, or aporias, of Badiou's ethics as well. In Badiou, to be ethical is to maintain one's fidelity to a truth

---

[22] On the three orders of simulacra, Jean Baudrillard, *Symbolic Exchange and Death*, trans. Iain Hamilton Grant, London: Sage, 1993, 50; on the transparency of evil, see Jean Baudrillard, *The Transparency of Evil: Essays on Extreme Phenomena*, trans. James Benedict, London: Verso, 1993, 33-36; and on fatal strategies, see Jean Baudrillard, *Fatal Strategies* (1990), trans. Philip Beitchman and W.G.J. Niesluchowski, London: Pluto, 1999.

[23] Gibson, *Postmodernity*, 147-48.

[24] See Jakob Winnberg, "On the Limits of the Ethical: Experimentalism and the Emotional Attitude in *The Infernal Desire Machines of Doctor Hoffman* and *Hawksmoor*", in *The Ethical Component in Experimental British Fiction*, 71-90.

arising from an incommensurable event.[25] Trauma could be seen as the figure for such events, insofar as "Trauma is a 'mind-blowing' experience that destroys a conventional mind-set and compels (or makes possible) a new worldview",[26] and is "always the story of a wound that cries out, that addresses us in the attempt to tell us of a reality or truth that is not otherwise available".[27] Evil, in Badiou, is an effect of the truth-processes emerging out of such events, and resides either in the refusal of fidelity, entailing the betrayal of a truth, or in a corrupted fidelity, in the form of fidelity to the simulacrum of a truth, or in the form of the maintenance of fidelity to a truth to the point of disaster.[28] In the final analysis, the total trauma of Ballard's novel is impossible to gauge ethically even in these terms, as the simulacrum and disaster are the truths of this event.

Yet, in order to reach this conclusion (or lack of a conclusion), this doubling of the wound in ethics, we must unravel the various levels of trauma in the novel.

"The Optimum Wound Profile": a poetics of trauma

Most immediately, *The Atrocity Exhibition* constitutes, at least figuratively speaking, a trauma to the reader's conception of novelistic narrative and to his/her interpretive faculties, notwithstanding the reader's possible familiarity with, for instance, *The Making of Americans* and *Finnegans Wake*. Indeed, the novel has all the marks of the "trauma aesthetic" that Roger Luckhurst enumerates in his discussion of the "trauma novel": "temporal disruption ... disorders of emplotment ... refusal of easy readerly identification, disarming play with narrative framing, disjunct movements in style, tense, focalization or discourse, and a resistance to closure that is demonstrated in compulsive telling and retelling",[29] all of which would be geared towards representing the aporia of trauma, and which constitute not just a poetics of trauma, but also, as it were, a traumatic poetics. As Andrzej Gasiorek suggests, the novel

---

[25] Alain Badiou, *Ethics: An Essay on the Understanding of Evil*, trans. and intro. Peter Hallward, London: Verso, 2002, 58-89.
[26] Farrell, *Post-Traumatic Culture*, 19.
[27] Caruth, *Unclaimed Experience*, 4.
[28] Badiou, *Ethics*, 40-57.
[29] Roger Luckhurst, *The Trauma Question*, London: Routledge, 2008, 88.

> ... demands an alternative practice of reading. One cannot make sense
> of it, if indeed making sense is the point here, by trying to construe it
> within the parameters it rejects; a paradigm shift of sorts is enacted in
> its pages, and it is incumbent upon the reader to work in terms of the
> new perspective thereby laid out.[30]

That is, ultimately, the novel allows only an immanent reading, casting the reader in the same situation of foreclosed critical distance as that of the characters in the novel. One does not so much read *The Atrocity Exhibition* as enter it, encountering "a new algebra".[31]

If, nonetheless, one were to attempt an explicatory synopsis of Ballard's fragmentary and oblique novel, it could run as follows: the novel focuses on, and is mainly focalised through, the character Travis (whose name, however, changes slightly with each chapter).[32] Through this focalisation, we are brought directly into Travis' mind, which seems to be preoccupied with discerning the geometries of all possible situations and phenomena, including human beings, in an attempt to stage a perfect disaster scenario involving the semblances of a host of celebrities – thereby acting out a trauma apparently caused by a culture of mass mediated celebrity cults and deaths, often in conjunction with each other, but also searching for the optimal scenario that will somehow make sense of and redeem this traumatic world. Before dissolving completely into this project together with his lover, Karen Novotny, Travis has managed to involve a number of his students and patients in it. Travis is also pursued by Dr Nathan, his colleague, who serves as the rational counterpart to Travis' ostensible irrationalism. However, in his analyses and explanations of Travis' behaviour, Dr Nathan is eerily conversant, almost complicit, with Travis' conceptions – and thus what is allegedly psychosis rather gradually appears to be an accurate cognitive adaptation to phenomenal reality. At any rate, towards the end of the novel, Travis' world becomes *the* world, as "his central nervous system is acting as a powerful transmitter".[33] The final six chapters simply consist of reports on scientific studies conducted on this world and its

---

[30] Gasiorek, *J.G. Ballard*, 60.
[31] Ballard, *The Atrocity Exhibition*, 109.
[32] For the sake of clarity, I generally refer to the main character as "Travis" in this essay; the reader should, however, keep in mind that this constitutes an infidelity to Ballard's text.
[33] Ballard, *The Atrocity Exhibition*, 136.

inhabitants, matter-of-factly describing, for instance, how there is "an increasing incidence of sexual climaxes among persons cleaning automobiles",[34] or how "suburban housewives expressed a marked preoccupation with severe genital wounds of an obscene character".[35]

Through its fragmentary presentation of this plot, the novel depicts, as Fisher puts it, "a mediamatic repetition-compulsion culture in which trauma and mass communication have become indivisible". The novel is moreover marked by "a refusal to distinguish figure from (back)ground", with "no framing narrative that will attribute the perception to a disordered mind. Instead, Ballard replaces psychology ... with what is, in effect, a *geo-traumatics.*"[36] The novel's shorthand for this geo-traumatics is the "spinal landscape":

> The spinal landscape ... is that of the porous rock towers of Tenerife
> .... The inhospitality of this mineral world, with its inorganic growths,
> is relieved only by the balloons flying in the clear sky. They are
> painted with names: Jackie, Lee Harvey, Malcolm.[37]

The spine, carrying and protecting the *medulla spinalis* or spinal cord, may be read as a metonym for the nervous system, as in the nineteenth-century phenomenon of "railway spine", much referenced in the literature on trauma. With the advent of mass transport disasters, "Psychological reactions that seemed out of scale with the actual accident were explained as the effects of direct damage to the spine and central nervous system, and so the concept of 'railway spine' was born".[38] In modernity it was the victim of trauma who developed "railway spine". In postmodernity, as presented in Ballard's novel, it is the world around the victim that becomes a "spinal landscape", interiority and exteriority having merged. As Dr Nathan half explains, the war that Travis is staging "will be fought out on the

---

[34] *Ibid.*, 142.

[35] *Ibid.*, 155.

[36] Fisher, *Flatline*, FC2s9.htm (original emphasis).

[37] Ballard, *The Atrocity Exhibition*, 41.

[38] William Yule, *et al.*, "Post-Traumatic Stress Disorders in Adults", in *Post-Traumatic Stress Disorders: Concepts and Therapy*, ed. William Yule, Chichester: Wiley, 1999, 1. See also, for instance, Farrell, *Post-Traumatic Culture*, 9; and Luckhurst, *The Trauma Question*, 20-26.

spinal battlefields, in terms of the postures we assume, of our traumas mimetized in the angle of a wall or balcony".[39]

Therefore, we encounter a break here with the typical situation in which "in its response to trauma 'we see the psyche operating not to link but to de-link – to split or dissociate'".[40] In *The Atrocity Exhibition*, the trauma itself is an incessant linking of disparate elements through the dromo-logic of the mass media, and acting it out thus involves some sort of hyper-linking.[41] So the novel evinces the same logic as *Crash*, where, "far from leading to a repetition compulsion attributable to repression of the unconscious, the trauma of road accidents is a stimulus to a conscious exploration of all their parameters".[42]

Travis' obsession with linking events and beings through geometric aspects might seem to constitute a simply superficial form of engagement masking what is in fact a profound dissociation, especially given Dr Nathan's claim that Travis is tormented mainly by the very facts of time and space and by the human body[43] – Travis would hence seem to be the classical psychopathology of the traumatised subject dissociating him-/herself from all that is tangible (and consequently suggests both force and vulnerability) and the temporal dimension of being that allows traumatic events (which may have become equated with change *qua* change, space-time itself). As Dr Nathan speculates, Travis' repetition-compulsion might constitute "an attempt to render time and events meaningless by replication".[44] However, if one considers the novel in full, this attribution of a personal trauma with concomitant dissociative responses to Travis does not hold water. The title of one of the very first fragments, "Dissociation: Who Laughed at Nagasaki?",[45] turns out be a red herring, belying the main logic of the narrative. To read the narrative as concerning one man's melancholic and psychotic response to

---

[39] Ballard, *The Atrocity Exhibition*, 7.

[40] Gasiorek, *J.G. Ballard*, 155, quoted in Donald Kalsched, *The Inner World of Trauma: Archetypal Defences of the Personal Spirit*, London: Routledge, 1999, 66.

[41] I am playing here on Paul Virilio's notion of "dromology" (Paul Virilio, *Speed and Politics: An Essay on Dromology*, trans. Mark Polizzotti, New York: Semiotext(e), 1986).

[42] Gasiorek, *J.G. Ballard*, 89.

[43] Ballard, *The Atrocity Exhibition*, 8-9, 46.

[44] *Ibid.*, 46.

[45] *Ibid.*, 3.

trauma is to bracket the sociological and ontological context it establishes for its main protagonist.[46]

To recapitulate and clarify further: Travis finds himself in a media landscape that is itself traumatising and traumatic, itself repetition-compulsively replaying traumatic events, and that conflates everything on a single plane, thus neutralising traditional forms of sense-making and also heralding "the death of affect",[47] an "abstraction of emotion and intent".[48] In such a context – in a world of speed, of accessibility – time and space become abominations, as one is conditioned to instantaneousness; and in a world of screens, of films, of images, the flesh too becomes an abomination. Coupled with these processes, but adding up with them uneasily, is modernity's scientistic ethos of quantification, measurement and ultimate sense-making, which may be taken as partly responsible for the traumatic effect of this new world, since this ethos precludes Keats' "negative capability", which lets us rest in mysteries and uncertainties. Indeed, as Baudrillard would have it, in our witnessing of the murder of the real we are also witnessing the murder of the secret.[49] Travis' response to this situation is indeed a conscious exploration of the ontology of this traumatic new world, and an incessant quantification and measurement of events and phenomena, in search of their new underlying logic and ultimate configuration – the perfect disaster, which will redeem the world somehow. As Dr Nathan puts it, "He wants to kill Kennedy again, but in a way that makes sense".[50]

Travis is at least partly, as Brian McHale observes, "obsessed with the problem of isolating a 'modulus,' a single abstract form which is repeated in a series of unrelated and apparently formless or irregular phenomena",[51] as exemplified by Travis' question: "What code would

---

[46] As Gasiorek puts it, Dr Nathan is "a symbol of the detached scientist who thinks that he can explain everything, whereas Traven articulates social and psychological anxieties that cannot so easily be foreclosed" (*J.G. Ballard*, 60). Indeed, as Ballard points out about the spinal landscape in his notes, "the nervous systems of the characters [not simply that of Travis] have been externalized" (*ibid.*, 76).

[47] Ballard, *The Atrocity Exhibition*, 116.

[48] *Ibid.*, 109.

[49] Jean Baudrillard, *Passwords*, trans. Chris Turner, London: Verso, 2003, 33-36.

[50] Ballard, *The Atrocity Exhibition*, 50.

[51] Brian McHale, *Postmodernist Fiction*, London: Routledge, 1987, 70.

fit both this face and body and Karen Novotny's apartment?"[52] As McHale further points out,

> This theme of the 'modulus' at the level of story-content in *The Atrocity Exhibition* exactly duplicates the formal organization of the stories, in which a fixed repertoire of modules, many of them repeated from the earlier apocalyptic novels, are differently recombined and manipulated from story to story.[53]

The novel also repeats and recombines intratextual elements throughout, so that what at first appears to be fragmented and randomised turns into a metastasation of key significances throughout the body of the text. This metastasation does not simply occur on the properly narrative level, but to a large extent occurs in the more or less free-floating phrases that entitle the chapters and the numerous sub-fragments of each chapter, and which often find correspondences in other such titles or in narrative passages located elsewhere. So, for instance, the fragment entitled "The Death of Affect" does not in any direct way illustrate or refer to that phenomenon, which is instead diagnosed by Dr Nathan in a fragment entitled "Biomorphic Horror".[54] In this way, the novel's form illustrates the viral nature of the cultural trauma it depicts. For, as Fisher argues:

> Rather than treating trauma as something with which the organism is affected only contingently, Ballard implies that trauma is a general condition ... distributing particular tics – swarms of repetition-compulsions – across a culture that is indistinguishable from nature. Culture, like the organism, is composed of tics, compulsions and looped behaviours, rather than simply afflicted by them. The 'abstract patterns' that Dr Nathan and his supposedly psychotic patients discover repeated across architectural, biological and geological assemblages are the vectors through which this trauma spreads. Trauma is ... a distributed event, not merely echoed or referenced in the repetition-compulsions, but continued, prolonged, propagated.[55]

---

[52] Ballard, *The Atrocity Exhibition*, 58.
[53] McHale, *Postmodernist*, 70.
[54] Ballard, *The Atrocity Exhibition*, 116.
[55] Fisher, *Flatline*, FC2s9.htm.

Indeed, if "media, in [the novel], function ... as conduits through which trauma can propagate itself",[56] the novel itself is another such medium. In this conflation of the presented and the mode of presentation there is some complicity. If, as Gasiorek contends, "this text suggests that to exhibit [horrific events] for the delectation of the public is to perpetuate atrocity",[57] the novel is still itself partly such a perpetuating atrocity exhibition. At the same time, though, as Farrell suggests in his discussion of literary expressions of cultural trauma,

> ... efforts to objectify and express distress require the renewal or even the escalation of narrative conventions because overfamiliarity may dull the perception – and reception – of an injury, even though its pain persists", and so, "imagination keeps trying to devise a more forceful and convincing vocabulary. Today's horror is tomorrow's cliché – in life as well as art.[58]

If Ballard's exposition of cultural trauma may seem questionably complicit, it may also be seen as required in order to drive the point home. What may be seen as unethical is, accordingly, at the same time ethical in its fidelity.

Even so, the fact remains that the novel's geo-traumatics constitutes a waning of otherness and may be read as a new sort of imperialism of the ego, which here seeks to order and possess the world in accordance with a logic of pervading trauma. We are witnessing, not the defensive extension of interiority to fend off trauma, or a traumatic invasion of interiority, but "the folding out of interiority into a pure exteriority, registered by the subject as shock or trauma".[59] We are witnessing again, with Baudrillard, the murder of the secret. It is also important to note that the ensuing conflation of the sex drive and the death drive in fact neutralises both: there is no desire involved in Travis' scenarios, but rather a melancholic arrangement of geometries. As Gasiorek remarks, "the experiential subject described here is, as Deleuze would have it, 'no more a desiring self than the Other is, for him, a desired object endowed with real existence'" and, significantly, "for Deleuze, a world peopled by such subjects is simply 'a world without Others, and thus a world without the possible. The

---

[56] *Ibid.*, FC2s10.htm.
[57] Gasiorek, *J.G. Ballard*, 66.
[58] Farrell, *Post-Traumatic Culture*, 33.
[59] Fisher, *Flatline*, FC1s1.htm.

Other is that which renders possible'."[60] So how, with the death of affect – the ground of ethics from the "moral sense" school to Levinas – as well as of alterity, can there be an ethical opening in this text? Or how can the text be seen to be doing any kind of ethical work?

"The Yes or No of the Borderzone": an ethics of trauma

In fact, as already suggested, a significant ethical dimension of the novel resides in its very fidelity to the traumatics that would seem to short-circuit ethics as such. It is also in this regard that the novel's negative aesthetics assumes an ethico-political force. As I mentioned earlier, the novel follows the aesthetic strategies that allow for maintaining trauma as aporia. As Luckhurst notes, in the context of postmodern theories of trauma narrative following thinkers such as Lyotard, "other formal choices that do not find ways of figuring this aporia become unethical".[61] In accordance with this ethics of trauma narrative, the novel does not seek to frame or contain the trauma, and so heeds its alterity, letting it break up sameness and becoming hostage to it.

Yet, if what one becomes hostage to is, on a general level, the death of alterity, this ethical opening is surely a trap-door: a trauma to ethics itself. But what if this is the only way, and to do otherwise would be tantamount to a betrayal of the world? It is here that Badiou's notion of "an ethics of truths" might lead us further than a Levinasian ethics, especially in conjunction with Baudrillard's notion of "fatal strategies". If there is no outside-trauma, no Other of this total conflation, then any ethical, and indeed ethico-political, work must be immanent, must remain faithful to the truth of this situation. As Fisher points out,

> Ballard's fiction suggests that the position of transcendent social critic assumed by [Fredric] Jameson and [Christopher] Lasch itself marks a failure to adequately register the immanentizing processes capitalism's cyber-socius is undergoing. These processes, Ballard insists, can only be tracked homeopathically, using techniques that are flat with them.[62]

---

[60] Gasiorek, *J.G. Ballard*, 69. The quotations are from Gilles Deleuze, *The Logic of Sense*, trans. Mark Lester and Charles Stivale, London: Athlone, 1990, 69.

[61] Luckhurst, *The Trauma Question*, 89.

[62] Fisher, *Flatline*, FC2s9.htm.

In this way, *The Atrocity Exhibition* seems to follow Baudrillard's argument for the obsolescence of all existing value systems and modes of analysis in the face of "the third order of simulacra".[63] The conflation of everything on one plane may also be read as a figure for the liquidation of "two-dimensional culture" into "one-dimensional culture" detected by Marcuse.[64] This one-dimensional culture now reigns supreme – at least in Ballard's novel – and critical theory is simply a useless illusion, the light of a dead star.[65]

Ethical work must take some turns to avoid becoming similarly useless. My reason for turning to Badiou here is not that I accept his refutation of Levinas, which I think is wrong-headed, but because Levinas' phenomenology simply cannot account for the world we enter through *The Atrocity Exhibition*.[66] It is as if one had passed the event horizon of a black hole, moving into a singularity where the laws of physics as we know them do not apply. It is here that Badiou's conception of ethics takes hold, as it is an ethics of universal truths that appear with the force of a radical event: "the becoming of a truth, the becoming of a subject, depend entirely on a pure event, which is itself beyond all the predictions and calculations that our understanding is capable of."[67] The significance of such an event is hinted at in Ballard's novel: "A unique event would take place here .... He had witnessed the annunciation of a unique event."[68] The unethical act for Badiou consists in breaking the fidelity to a truth, ceasing "to be the active part of that subject of a truth that you have happened to become".

"Keep going!" is Badiou's ethical motto.[69] And as we have seen, Travis indeed keeps going. And there is no question in *The Atrocity Exhibition* of an ethics of human rights, of victimhood, or of difference, all of which Badiou critiques as "'ethical' ideology"[70]

---

[63] Baudrillard, *Symbolic*, 50-86.

[64] Herbert Marcuse, *One-Dimensional Man: Studies in the Ideology of Advanced Industrial Society* (1964), intro. Douglas Kellner, London: Routledge, 2002, 59-86.

[65] As Gasiorek puts it, "There is, in short, no longer any totality to be grasped here any more than there is a critical vantage-point outside the system of representations within which the critique is offered" (*J.G. Ballard*, 209).

[66] For Badiou's discussion of Levinas, see *Ethics*, 18-29.

[67] *Ibid.*, 123.

[68] *Ibid.*, 3, 26.

[69] *Ibid.*, 91.

[70] *Ibid.*, 90.

which stands in the way of the radical equality of truths that are the same for all. There is only an ethics of fidelity to the truth of geo-traumatics.

Moreover, there is an allegiance in Travis' *modus operandi* to the political truth expounded by Badiou when he argues that "we are rivals to capital, rather than merely reacting against it".[71] One must enter the system on its terms: in fact, one is in the system, and must act accordingly. Foster's analysis of traumatic realism in Warhol may illuminate this point. Foster argues that Warhol's statement, "I want to be a machine",

> ... may point less to a blank subject than to a shocked one, who takes on the nature of what shocks him as a mimetic defence against this shock: I am a machine too, I make (or consume) serial product-images too, I give as good (or as bad) as I get.[72]

This, indeed, is in Baudrillardian terms a "fatal strategy", an attempt to challenge the system on its own terms by upping the ante and forcing the system's logic into hyper-logic; as Baudrillard puts it, "there is no liberation but this one: in the deepening of negative conditions".[73] Much like Warhol, Travis exemplifies "a preemptive embrace of the compulsion to repeat put into play by a society of serial production and consumption", in the belief that "if you enter it totally you might expose it".[74] Travis tries to decode everything, make everything add up, make everything reveal itself ultimately and optimally – a kind of fatal strategy in accordance with modernity's rationalism, its murder of secrecy. All of Travis' scenarios are fatal strategies, in pursuit of the more repetitive than repetition, the more conflated than conflation, the more abstracted than abstraction, the more spectacular than spectacle, and the more scandalous than scandal. There is no subversion in this, but rivalry; challenge: "This was chess in which every move was a counter-gambit."[75] Repetition-compulsion, or acting out, typically seen as a dead end in terms of therapy, is here a means of attaining a redemption denied by the system's logic, by pursuing that logic into hyperlogic – like Warhol,

---

[71] *Ibid.*, 114.
[72] Foster, *The Return of the Real*, 130-131.
[73] Baudrillard, *Fatal Strategies*, 184.
[74] Foster, *The Return of the Real*, 131.
[75] Ballard, *The Atrocity Exhibition*, 48.

repeating until you get the desired tear.[76] The novel only hints at what that desired tear would be, but the most pervasive hint one gets is that it involves "an attempt to surmount this death of affect".[77]

At any rate, as Gasiorek notes of the novel, there is a "strain between its fragmented evocation of apocalyptic psychosis and Traven's attempts to build bridges between seemingly unrelated phenomena and to redeem a tragic present through an act of restitution".[78] What Gasiorek says of *Crash* would hence be equally true of *The Atrocity Exhibition*: it houses "a kind of counter-narrative that tries to conceive the wound as the source of redemption, tries to imagine how, out of this disaster, the world might be recreated".[79] Indeed, "On this reading, the text's collage structure would be oriented less towards indeterminacy and more towards epiphany".[80] The messianic imagery of the narrative, especially of the last properly narrative chapter, does suggest that Travis is a figure of redemption, some sort of saviour of this fallen world, but a saviour of the fatal, ironic type.[81]

Yet, Travis' ultimate fate is, if not tragic, then ambiguous, putting the redemptive reading in question:

> *Undisturbed, the universe would continue on its round*, the unrequited ghosts of Malcolm X, Lee Harvey Oswald and Claude Eatherly raised on the shoulders of the galaxy. As his own identity faded, its last fragments glimmered across the darkening landscape, lost integers in a hundred computer codes, sand-grains on a thousand beaches, fillings in a million mouths.[82]

---

[76] For instance, as Farrell points out, "Most theorists speculate that the repetitive reliving of the traumatic experience must represent a spontaneous, unsuccessful attempt at healing" (*Post-Traumatic Culture*, 6, quoted in Judith Herman, *Trauma and Recovery: The Aftermath of Violence – From Domestic Abuse to Political Terror*, New York: Basic, 1997, 44).

[77] *Ibid.*, 91.

[78] Gasiorek, *J.G. Ballard*, 79.

[79] *Ibid.*, 120.

[80] *Ibid.*, 79.

[81] See Ballard, *The Atrocity Exhibition*, 138. As Farrell notes, cultural trauma, or a traumatic culture, typically awakens the need for such a messianic, redemptive figure (*Post-Traumatic Culture*, 20-23). Incidentally, this would couple Travis with Alain Badiou's prime example of fidelity to a truth: Saint Paul (*Saint Paul: The Foundation of Universalism*, trans. Ray Brassier, Stanford: Stanford University Press, 2003).

[82] Ballard, *The Atrocity Exhibition*, 137-38 (emphasis added).

Such ambiguities notwithstanding, the ethicality of the novel seems ultimately indeterminable, doubled with a tear. For how are we to gauge the ethicality of the truth that the novel maintains its fidelity to?

This problem appears to me to be inherent in Badiou's formulation of the ethics of truths. There seems to be no distinction between truths, no call for the evaluation of each truth, in Badiou, save the necessity of avoiding, besides the betrayal of a truth (Badiou's first form of evil), the evil of the simulacrum of a truth. The simulacral truth is a truth which is not ultimately universalisable, which would only hold for certain subjects and situations; Badiou's prime example is Nazism.[83] Yet, can one easily distinguish simulacral truth from truth proper, in all cases? It seems to me that one shortcoming of Badiou's ethics as it has so far been formulated is its failure to imagine the truly radical, overturning event that would throw the subject into a quantum state, ontologically, existentially, politically, ethically – the total trauma, geo- and pan-traumatics. In Badiou, the event always resides in a relatively local, particular situation, whereas in Ballard's novel, it is a total event, encompassing all. Indeed, as Nancy Glazener observes, Badiou's examples of events "are remarkably conventional",[84] and "dovetail unsurprisingly with dominant historical narratives", as they "similarly reinforce familiar understandings of what counts as an event".[85] Among Badiou's examples of events and the truths emerging from them are "the appearance, with Aeschylus, of theatrical Tragedy; the irruption, with Galileo, of mathematical physics; an amorous encounter which changes a whole life; the French Revolution of 1792".[86]

---

[83] Badiou, *Ethics*, 72-77.

[84] Nancy Glazener, "The Novel, the Social and the Event: An International Ethical Encounter", in *Textual Ethos Studies, or, Locating Ethics*, eds Anna Fahreaus and AnnKatrin Jonsson, Amsterdam: Rodopi, 2005, 39.

[85] Glazener also implicitly questions the presuppositions of Badiou's stance, as she notes that "Badiou's insistence that an event must proceed on the basis of the unnameable void of a situation seems likely to derive from an unelaborated belief that true thinking must serve the mobility of (social/political) power relations rather than their consolidation", and that the "doctrine of the event presumes that any established truth is ripe for supplanting" (*ibid.*, 40).

[86] Alain Badiou, *Infinite Thought: Truth and the Return to Philosophy*, ed. and trans. Oliver Feltham and Justin Clement, London: Continuum, 2005, 46. Here, one also wonders how precisely theatrical tragedy and the French Revolution constitute truths that are the same for all. As for the amorous encounter, how could it even potentially produce a truth that could transcend the particular situation and be universalised?

But what about the total traumatic event represented in Ballard's novel? Is there a truth to maintain one's fidelity to in that event? And if there is a truth, but it is precisely the truth of the precession of simulacra, then how does one gauge it as a truth? In the end, my discussion here too must hover in a quantum state: *The Atrocity Exhibition* is both profoundly ethical in promoting the disinterested persistence of someone who is the subject of a truth that is surely the same for all and ethically problematic in promoting the imperialism of one subject pursuing only its truth to the point of eradicating all others. We come up against Badiou's third form of evil: disaster, the objectification of a truth and its imposition as total and unqualified. Yet, it seems an ethics of truths must be an ethics of risks – it is with the fidelity to a truth that the risk of evil emerges, not vice versa.

It is thus that the reading of the ethico-political dimension of the novel is doubled with a tear. The logic of Warhol's *Ambulance Disaster* is also, in a manner, the logic of the argument as it finally stands here. A trauma to any humanist ethical perspective, including that profounder humanist perspective which is the ethics of alterity, *The Atrocity Exhibition* invites the post-humanist ethical perspective of the ethics of truths, only to rob it of its certitudes as well. The ethics of truths reveals itself as an ethics of the unexpected, an ethics that we do not know what to expect from – in a manner, a fatal strategy. If Ballard's novel represents a fatal strategy, in the double sense of depicting one and constituting one, it has a certain finality, but one which is uncertain: "We invent all these strategies in the hope of having them result in the unexpected event."[87] Could this be the basis of an ethics, in any conceivable sense of the word?

Still, the sort of challenge to ethics itself constituted by *The Atrocity Exhibition* is perhaps, as I have argued elsewhere, in and of itself profoundly ethical, as it returns us to the question of the very conditions of the ethical.[88] Through its poetics of cultural trauma, the novel seems to place itself beyond the limits of the ethical, and occasions a reconsideration of those limits, a reconsideration of precisely how liminal an ethics can be.

---

[87] Baudrillard, *Fatal Strategies*, 189.
[88] Winnberg, "On the Limits of the Ethical", 88-89.

Trauma as the Negation of Autonomy: Michael Moorcock's *Mother London*

Jean-Michel Ganteau

Focusing on one of the most original representatives of the subgenre known as "the London novel", in the context of a discussion of the ethics of trauma, may not immediately appear as a relevant choice.[1] This is all the more so since Michael Moorcock, even though his *Mother London* (1988) was acclaimed as a major contribution to the subgenre, has received scant critical attention and is generally discussed in relation with the works of Iain Sinclair or Peter Ackroyd – both more prolific authors who have contributed extensively to the literary representation of the metropolis. From a distance, it would appear that the evocation of London as traumatised space applies more specifically to the works of, say, Martin Amis (*London Fields* or *The Information*) or Ian McEwan and his intimations of vulnerability in his post-9/11 evocation of immanent and imminent trauma.[2] However, such texts as Sinclair's *White Chappell, Scarlett Tracings* or Ackroyd's *Hawksmoor* and *The Plato Papers*, to quote a few evident examples, come up as unmistakable representatives of a writing of space in response to the materialistic onslaught on a *genius loci* characterised by its visionary dimension. The arch representative of such an inflection may be the Blake of *Jerusalem*, as famously made clear by Ackroyd himself in his seminal evocation of Cockney

---

[1] For a working definition of the subgenre, see the Introduction to *London in Literature: Visionary Mappings of the Metropolis*, eds Susana Onega and John A Stotesbury, Heidelberg: Carl Winter, 2002, 9-17.

[2] For a reading of *Saturday* as the locus of trauma yet to come, thus presenting the reader with a temporal inversion of the usual vision of trauma (always referring back to an initial effraction), see Jean-Michel Ganteau, "Disquieted Negative Capability: The Ethics of Trauma in Contemporary Literature", paper given at the International Conference *Between the "Urge to Know" and the "Need to Deny": Ethics and Trauma in Contemporary Narrative in English* (forthcoming in the published conference proceedings).

visionaries.[3] That such narratives were written in reaction against an era dominated by materialism, the logics of profit and the havoc wreaked on the identity of the city brooks little doubt. Such narratives, by tapping the powers of a sublimely eternal London without limits are meant as committed texts that put economic and cultural responsibility high on their ethical agenda. The traumatic realism of such narratives is evocative of the effraction of loss, the difficulty of coming to terms with the widening gaps left by the disappearing *genius loci*, the acting out of repetition the better to achieve some measure of working through by drawing lines of continuity.

Such novels are rarely content with observing individual trauma, but are very much concerned with the collective, impersonal dimension of trauma, paradoxical as it may seem, and far from the original psychological definition of the pathology. They also mix the exceptional, extraordinary nature of trauma and more subdued, ordinary manifestations, thus extracting the theme from its most widely exploited contexts, that is, war (essentially the two World Wars), terrorism and psychiatry. Moorcock's all-embracing homage to the visionary, eternal city is devoted to the evocation of the effects of the Second World War – the effects that are confined to the civilian population, those ordinary citizens who had to bear the brunt of the Blitz and the later "doodlebug" (V1 and V2) attacks, the many who suffered terrible shocks that were to be reactivated by later violent events, the multitudes represented by a handful of characters called "The Patients", "citizens" or "celebrants" in the titles of various chapters or parts of the novel. Therefore *Mother London* relies on the evocation of the ordinariness and ubiquity of trauma through an emblematic method of representation, and resorts to synecdoche the better to probe at wider, unknown, inaccessible truths or realities. In so groping at that which is not directly presentable, in generally favouring exteriority over totality and a vision of completeness, in preferring the medium of the unlimited sublime to the more

---

[3] Peter Ackroyd, "London Luminaries and Cockney Visionaries", in *The Collection: Journalism, Reviews, Essays, Short Stories, Lectures* (2001), ed. Thomas Wright, London: Vintage, 2002, 341-51. For an analysis of *The Plato Papers* as a Blakean offshoot, see Susana Onega, "*The Plato Papers*: Peter Ackroyd's 'Contrary' to Blake's *Jerusalem*", in *London in Literature: Visionary Mappings of the Metropolis*, 183-209.

comfortable rules of the beautiful, the novel seems to evince an ethical preference for the effects of trauma and their literary representation.

My take in this article will be that what *Mother London* achieves is a high degree of collaboration between what Cathy Caruth has envisaged as "crisis of truth" or "collapse of ... understanding",[4] very much at home in our poststructuralist, deconstruction-prone age, and a deconstructive ethics of the limits of the type expounded by Drucilla Cornell (1992). Put differently, what the present study aims at is to work on the notion of relation, understood in various ways, be it the relation between the two critical and theoretical fields of trauma and ethics, or the relation between an image of the same and possibilities of otherness that trauma and ethics systematically posit and perform, in psychological, temporal or spatial terms. In so doing, I shall be led to argue that what is at stake in Moorcock's ethical treatment of trauma is the refusal of autonomy (of the subject and of the text) and the commitment to various versions of alterity. This will be done by focusing on the evocation of individual trauma, before moving on to an evocation of the collective. I shall finally concentrate on myth and romance as ethical, performative event.

Of bombs and doodlebugs
Mother London thematises the immanence of crisis. The first of the six parts, "Entrance to the City", introduces the reader to the tentacular metropolis through a sample of its inhabitants, disturbingly called "The Patients". They all suffer from various states of psychological or psychiatric disarray, and they meet in a clinic, a place not unlike the Tavistock Clinic, known for its specialising in treatment of post-traumatic states, perhaps, to undergo group therapy. Through the pages, a common pathological map appears, dominated by vulnerability, from mere depression to what at times cannot be far from psychosis. Above all, those patients, and more especially the three main protagonists, Mary Gasalee, Joseph Kiss and David Mummery, are characterised by the fact that they are survivors, a notion that extends to most of the city dwellers, as is suggested in David Mummery's evocation of Londoners, taken from his historical study of the city:

---

[4] *Trauma: Explorations in Memory*, ed. Cathy Caruth, Baltimore and London: Johns Hopkins University Press, 1995, 6-7.

By means of certain myths which cannot easily be damaged or
debased the majority of us survive. All old great cities possess their
special myths. Amongst London's in recent years is the story of the
Blitz, of our endurance.[5]

From the start, the story of the Londoners is sited in some "after", in
that it takes place after an individual, but also collective and historical,
traumatic shock and has to be contextualised within the wider
problematic of testimony. The sample of characters that the narrative
pores over and whose destinies it attempts to retrace in chaotic,
fragmented fashion is, according to the terminology used at the
Tavistock Clinic, a mixture of Adversity Groups – meaning groups of
traumatised patients whose coming together was crystallised by the
sharing of a common experience and Given Groups, whose links
predate the advent of the traumatic event, in so far as they share
traumatic experiences and a very specific common, Cockney culture.[6]
Interestingly, it is as members of both types of groups that their fate is
emblematic of post-war, contemporary London.

The text is rife with motifs taken from the field of trauma-related
pathologies, thereby providing a stable realistic anchoring. The
psychiatric component is explicitly thematised in the discourse of
patients, clinicians and narrator, which transforms the characters into
both survivors and direct witnesses of extreme events that took place
during those specific episodes of World War II. This is the case of
Mary Gasalee, whose husband died during one of the Luftwaffe raids
over London in 1940, while on leave and visiting his wife and
newborn child. The house that collapsed on the three of them and
burnt down allowed Mary Gasalee and her baby daughter escape into
the streets of the city in miraculous fashion, but she fell into a long
period of coma from which she was only to emerge in 1956. As a
child David Mummery was the victim of a V2 falling on the street
when he was on his way to the baker's. Even though he survived, the
visions of mangled flesh that he had to witness are shown to have
caused a great deal of psychological havoc, ultimately leading to his
suicide. Joseph Kiss, who was a warden during the war, made a

---

[5] Michael Moorcock, *Mother London: A Novel* (1988), London: Pocket Books, 1997,
5.
[6] Caroline Garland, *Understanding Trauma: A Psychoanalytical Approach*, London:
Duckworth, 1998, 196.

reputation for courage and efficiency for himself in saving people and neutralising unexploded bombs throughout the Blitz, several characters and the narrator attributing his ensuing unbalance to his wartime experiences. Such diegetic content, which gives pride of place to individual and historical trauma, is conveyed in a characteristic fashion through the means of what has been called "traumatic realism" by specialists of the literary representation of trauma[7] and is dominated by poetic modalities such as hyperbole, intensification, saturation, anachronism and fragmentation – devices that are supposed to be mimetic of traumatic effects and that problematise the conventions of transparent mimesis in a hyperbolical fashion.

It was Pierre Janet who raised the hypothesis of trauma as predicated on the dissociation of memory, and discriminated between two types of memory, that is, narrative memory and the inaccessible (to be envisaged in terms of what is inassimilable by Freud) traumatic memory.[8] And Freud's discoveries, particularly in "Beyond the Pleasure Principle", led to the confirmation of the problem of dissociation in traumatic neuroses, and the observation of a dissociation between repeating and remembering, as encapsulated in the seminal statement:

> The patient cannot remember the whole of what is repressed in him, and what he cannot remember may be precisely the essential part of it. Thus he acquires no sense of conviction of the correctness of the construction that has been communicated to him. He is obliged to *repeat* the repressed material as a contemporary experience instead of, as the physician would prefer to see, *remembering* it as something belonging to the past.[9]

---

[7] Anne Whitehead, *Trauma Fiction*, Edinburgh: Edinburgh University Press, 2004, 84; Michael Rothberg, *Traumatic Realism: The Demands of Holocaust Representation*, Minneapolis and London: University of Minnesota Press, 2000, 9; Dominick LaCapra, *Writing History, Writing Trauma*, Baltimore and London: Johns Hopkins University Press, 2001, 186.

[8] Bessel A. Van der Kolk and Onno Van der Hart, "The Intrusive Past: The Flexibility of Memory and the Engraving of Trauma", in *Trauma: Explorations in Memory*, 160-63.

[9] Sigmund Freud, "Beyond the Pleasure Principle" (1920), in *The Standard Edition of the Complete Psychological Works of Sigmund Freud*, XVIII, ed. James Strachey, London: Vintage, 2001, 18 (emphasis in the original).

However, it seems to me that, among the founding fathers of trauma theory, Sandor Ferenczi should be hailed for his analysis of fragmentation as protection. In a note to be found in his diary, dated 21 February 1932, he suggests that in extreme conditions of unpreparedness, when the traumatic event takes the patient unawares and produces maximum damage, the fright provoked by the external effraction produces a self-protective response leading to the separation of the self into several fragments, so that the whole may not be destroyed.[10] This analysis is corroborated and further developed in a later entry, dated 10 May 1932, in which Ferenczi states that the violent effraction or breaking through of the type analysed above triggers off a separation between pure reason and affects, conducive to what he calls and internal guardian angel of the self,[11] an analysis to be found in the works of contemporary psychologists and psycho-analysts among them Jacques Press, who offers the image of the internal foreign body, or grain of sand leading to the constitution of a pearl.[12] This leads him to provide an explanation for the prolonged dissociation between psychic components in the case of severe traumatic neurosis when separation and fragmentation are made total and permanent.[13] Now, such are extreme examples of trauma and, as Freud remarks, trauma may act in a radical way (total separation and amnesia) or in a more subdued one (partial separation and memory recall). And this is precisely what seems to characterise the evocation of trauma in Moorcock's novel, for in fact the clinical ingredient that

---

[10] Sandor Ferenczi, *The Clinical Diary of Sandor Ferenczi* (1988), ed. Judith Dupont, Cambridge, MA: Harvard University Press, 1995, 38-40.

[11] *Ibid.*, 102-106.

[12] Jacques Press, *La perle et le grain de sable: Traumatisme et fonctionnement mental*, Lausanne: Delachaux et Niestlé, 1999, 69. This notion is used by many contemporary critics and commentators, such as clinicians like Caroline Garland, in *Understanding Trauma: A Psychoanalytical Approach*, 23, and most famously, in their analysis of trans-generational trauma, Nicolas Abraham and Maria Torok, *The Crypt and the Kernel: Renewals of Psychoanalysis*, Chicago: University of Chicago Press, 1994. The image of the internal foreign body has many other equivalents, like that of the void or hole, the ghost or spectre, which has led psychoanalysts, historians and literary critics to insist on a failure not only of cognition (as evidenced by Caruth) but also of the faculty to archive, to inscribe and to represent (Press, *La perle et le grain de sable*, 62; Daniel Destombes, "Vos corps gonflent la terre comme les corps des monstres gonflent la mer", in *Actualité du trauma*, ed. Patrick Chemla, Ramonville: eres, 2002, 25-37).

[13] Press, *La perle et le grain de sable*, 202-204.

is signposted throughout is fragmentation, as opposed to other classical symptoms such as the compulsion to repeat and the manifestations of belatedness which, though thematised, are evoked in a much more discreet way.

The affinity between the dissociation induced by traumatic states and the ethics of alterity, based on the readiness to surrender the self to privilege the non-violent relation to the Other, in post-Levinasian models, cannot be overlooked in a study of the literary representation of trauma. I have pointed out elsewhere the inherent collaboration between the extreme experiences of trauma, the sublimity that they are associated with, and the way in which they open up towards the unknown, the other of the rational, the limits of imagination.[14] Bearing these ideas in mind, I would argue that, in *Mother London*, such a coming together of the traumatic and the ethical is equally at work. Without dealing with all characters whose post-traumatic symptoms are evoked in the narrative, I shall concentrate on the case of Mary Gasalee, the survivor from the hell of her burning house, during the Blitz. For one thing, her life, like that of her friends and fellow sufferers is never evoked in linear fashion, under the form of a biographical sketch. On the contrary, a great deal of chronological dislocation is resorted to the better to imitate the effects of trauma and to approximate to a structural performance of the symptoms. The sense of continuity is whittled away, and full direct knowledge is precluded, the fragmented narrative (fragmented to an extent that is graspable at first glance, when considering the table of contents and chronological markers appearing on it) introducing zones of darkness and wondering, narrative and descriptive gaps, within each one of the characters who always remain partial strangers to each other and to the reader. Such narrative choices point at the effects of fragmentation and help construct characterisation as a relation of partially obliterated selves, whose contours remain porous or ragged, displaying an image of permanent, ungraspable exteriority and a halo of mystery around each individual and the whole group. In the end, what this strategy amounts to privileging is an incomplete evocation that posits that one of the essential symptoms of trauma consists in coming to terms with a hole or lacuna, accepting a model of the self as frayed or fraying, and refusing to conceive of the self as totality and closure. Put differently, traumatic realism goes hand in hand with the idea of a

---

[14] Ganteau, "Disquieted Negative Capability", 13-15.

sensibility to the Other[15] or a being for the Other[16] that has been argued to constitute the fundamentals of the ethical relation.[17]

To return to Mary Gasalee, who confesses to suffering from survivor's guilt[18] as she escaped from the flames of wartime hell while her husband was burnt to death (he had waived the right to sleep in the Morrison shelter in their living room, believing it should be occupied by the young mother and the new-born child), she is plunged into deep narcolepsy as soon as she hands over her baby to the rescue team, on walking out of the blazing house. This coma lasts for sixteen years and preserves her, Sleeping Beauty-wise, as young as when she fell into it, a state characterised by a great deal of psychic activity at which the reader is allowed more than a glimpse through the internal focalisation on the dreaming or reminiscing character. The narrative, departing from the stricter conventions of the realistic idiom, chooses to introduce a powerful element of fantasy in the evocation of the Land of Dreams in which the comatose character lives, so as to present the reader with a hyperbolic figure of extreme dissociation, in which physical symptoms cannot be but expressed and relayed by textual ones as the mimetic regime is jarred to accommodate the disturbing idiom of romance. I would tend to see the eruption of romance as an ethical event performed on readers who have to let themselves be performed by the text,[19] and it is in such circumstances that the traumatic and the ethical are seen to converge to a potent, vertiginous effect.

More especially, the recurrence of the motif of fire (from fire-eating to oven, through burning houses) colonises the narrative, becomes the synecdoche of the war and war-inflicted trauma, and zooms in on the character of Mary Gasalee as a case study. At times, the impersonal narrator may choose to decontextualise some of her fits

---

[15] Emmanuel Levinas, *Autrement qu'être, ou au-delà de l'essence*, Paris: Le Livre de Poche, 1978, 100-16.

[16] Zygmunt Bauman, *Postmodern Ethics*, Oxford: Blackwell, 1993, 72-76.

[17] For a full-scale analysis for the relationship between postmodern aesthetics and ethics in the contemporary British novel, see *The Ethical Component in Experimental British Fiction since the 1960s*, eds Susana Onega and Jean-Michel Ganteau, Newcastle: Cambridge Scholars Publishing, 2007.

[18] Moorcock, *Mother London*, 439.

[19] Derek Attridge, *The Singularity of Literature*, London and New York: Routledge, 2004, 95-98.

of daydreaming to defamiliarising effect so as to destabilise the reader and plunge him/her into hellish visions:

> MRS GASALLEE came out of the flames. Trembling, she sat on a bench beside Brooke Green, Hammersmith, watching the pupils swaggering through the gates of St Paul's Girls School. She had a burn scar on her back, the exact imprint of a hobnail foot, perhaps where she was stepped on by a would-be rescuer during the Blitz.[20]

The recurrence of such passages or motifs acts as an efficient instance of realism of effect (as opposed to a more conventionally mimetic realism of aspect) in rhythmically performing the fixation to the moment of effraction, and therefore providing a sensorial image of the compulsion to return to the moment of fixation originally described by both Freud and Ferenczi. Such structural stammering comes to saturate the narrative, lending it an obsessive, haunted quality disrupting the transparency of mimetic representation and, in imitation of the effects of trauma, performing the symptoms of post-traumatic intensification, when the subject becomes his or her own trauma, the structural symptoms become the narrative spine, and the novel morphs into performed hyperbole. Interestingly, such a soliciting of an overwhelming affect goes along with a failure of memory, as suggested by the adverb "perhaps" in the above quotation, indicating a state of uncertainty shared by both the character and the narrator, as made clear by the resort to stable internal focalisation.

The victim's memory, though partially available, remains fragmentary, partly supplied by the reports of external witnesses and the legendary status of her rescue, and it is only towards the end of the narrative, as Mary Gasalee and her adult daughter come to meet a member of the rescue team that witnessed her walking out of the flames, that the following testimony is to be found:

> "We couldn't believe it. We were convinced you were dead even while we watched it happening. You just came walking out of that house. There was hardly a brick or a stick of it left that wasn't roaring flame. You just came walking out of it, your baby in your arms. A slight little thing you were, hardly any different than now. A girl yourself. But your dress was hardly touched, except for that one place

---

[20] Moorcock, *Mother London*, 29.

> where it was on fire. Like the shape of a boot. It was as if the fire
> couldn't harm you."[21]

Between report and legend the text hovers, unwilling to decide,
thematising the problematic nature and essence of testimony as
"speaking beyond understanding", in Anne Whitehead's terms,[22] as
evidencing the impossibility of bearing witness to oneself,[23] in the
sheer impossibility of witnessing that both prevents witnessing and
constitutes the very nature of witnessing.[24] In probing the limits of
understanding and imagination, the evocation of trauma privileges
openness to alterity – alterity not as the other man in Levinas' terms,
but as a structure of alterity in the perceptual field, as defined by
Gilles Deleuze,[25] applying to both the patient and other characters or,
at a distinct level, to the reader.

Dissociation and amnesia remain prevalent till very late in the
narrative, when the character, during one of her moments of
introspection, seems to cringe on the brink of reviving a submerged
piece of memory, in a passage hinting at the possibility of working
through:

> There was another crash, probably a second bomb, and the walls
> began to fall inwards as a fire blossomed pink, yellow and red like a
> vast rose so that she thought it was just gas at first, with no fierce
> flames, but then it was roaring all around the Morrison and she began
> trying to crawl from the shelter as debris drummed on its steel roof
> and one side of it fell in. Her memory is mixed up. Shortly afterwards,
> Olivia de Haviland dressed like a bird of paradise in her exotically
> feathered cowled cloak had arrived; though it might have been Merle
> Oberon … [26]

---

[21] *Ibid.*, 428.

[22] Whitehead, *Trauma Fiction*, 7.

[23] Dori Laub, "Truth and Testimony: The Process and the Struggle", in *Trauma*, ed.
Caruth, 65.

[24] *Ibid*, 64.

[25] Gilles Deleuze, *Logique du sens*, Paris: Minuit, 1969, 351-62. For further details on
the Deleuzian take on alterity as applied to trauma theory, see Anne Durand,
"'Trauma' et 'Autre'", in *Trauma et texte*, ed. Peter Kuon, Frankfurt: Peter Lang,
2003, 40.

[26] Moorcock, *Mother London*, 477.

Such a passage, hinting at what happens in a Land of Dreams peopled with the actresses and actors of the 1940s, comes as close as possible to the evocation of the utter violence of the moment of fixation. Interestingly, once again, the contribution of the literary text to the evocation of and delving into the nature of trauma is performed through a change in regime (from realism to fantasy), which makes the novel move along towards romance. By crafting such powerful narrative and aesthetic events, the narrative reminds us that the experience of literary texts "constantly exceeds the limits of rational accounting"[27] and comes asymptotically close to an iconic (in Peircian terms) evocation of trauma while multiplying the ethical reverberations inherent in the confrontation and acceptance of alterity.

Enter chorus
As suggested earlier, *Mother London* is a choral narrative. This means that, from the beginning, it is interested in a sample of London residents, that its primary concern is the relations among the group and that, through such a device, it is a novel about individual as much as collective trauma. But "choral" has a more specific sense, referring to the chanting of multiple voices, and by extension to some echoic quality. The trio of main protagonists share the experience of wartime trauma wreaked on helpless civilian populations. Young Mummery (whose name is evocative of the mummers or actors performing traditional plays especially in the Christmas period), a writer, seems to emblematise in many respects the figure of the primary witness of some violent event affecting himself and the community. It is also the case of Joseph Kiss, who saved innumerable civilians during the dark months of the Blitz, which makes him the arch emblem of the secondary witness, even though he is a victim himself. All three share yet another specific attribute: they can hear and keep hearing voices.

There is less evidence of such symptoms in David Mummery, even though he admits in one of the confessional chapters of the novels to being haunted by the voices of Londoners,[28] but the hallucinatory dimension of the protagonists' condition is foregrounded in the other two main characters, Joseph Kiss and Mary Gasalee. The former, a thespian of the visionary Cockney school, earned his living for a fairly long time through the mind-reading stunts he performs on the stages

---

[27] Attridge, *The Singularity of Literature*, 3.
[28] Moorcock, *Mother London*, 340.

of various small theatres, essentially in the metropolis since he soon discovers that his gift simply disappears when touring the provinces. He shares this knack for telepathy with Mary Gasalee, to the extent that each member of the trio is a medium, with the ability to connect with other people, to open him- or herself to the alterity, individual or collective, of other Londoners, as neatly encapsulated in the following statement: "Little currents of electricity in the air carrying the voices of all our times. People like me are individually tuned, not two the same."[29] The evocation of the telepathic disposition of the central characters has a decisive effect on the nature of the textual medium and disrupts realistic conventions by means of fragmented, italicised passages in free direct discourse in which the fragments of voices of Londoners are seen to haunt the consciousness of the protagonist and waft across the pages: the echoic quality of the narrative, articulated upon the structural figures of juxtaposition and fragmentation, contributes to the haunting atmosphere reminiscent of the symptoms of trauma.

What is different here, though, is the fact that the snatches of discourse do not necessarily come from the past but are the indices of the characters' connection with – or, more particularly, openness to – their contemporaries' thoughts and spoken words, thereby presenting the reader with a figure of alterity made immediately graspable through the textual layout. The chorus, in fact, is that of Londoners, and it obviously stands as an image of alterity (individual, collective, and also alterity as structure in the perceptual field).

In thus staging alterity as diffuse, permanent, all-pervasive forces to which the protagonists are naturally attuned, what the novel does is conflate the evocation of trauma and a textual image of what looks very much like vulnerability, sensibility or proximity to the other, in Levinasian terms: what the protagonists as haunted media, ceaselessly and naturally drawn to the others, are made to represent is the traditional ethical category of *excendance*.[30] Telepathy as naturalised through traumatic neurosis (or psychosis) is exploited as a means to perform an ethical statement. Both diegetic trauma and traumatic realism are instrumentalised to promote the ethical relation as

---

[29] *Ibid*, 279.
[30] Emmanuel Levinas, *De l'Evasion* (1935), Montpellier: Fata Morgana, 1982, 73. On *excendance* and the literary, see also Andrew Gibson, *Postmodernity, Ethics and the Novel: From Leavis to Levinas*, London and New York: Routledge, 1999, 36-42.

spontaneous, non violent, irresistible move out of the Self towards the Other so as to preclude autonomy and isolation and affirm the supremacy of the relation to the Other. The solitude of the traumatised subject as ethical being is thus transformed into the rejection of solitude. Separation may well be necessary for the same to enter in an ethical relation with the Other, but what *Mother London* chooses to stress is an ethics of generosity and solidarity based on the essence of relation. Such an idea is perhaps not so remote from the notion of empathic unsettlement that Dominick LaCapra develops in his discussion of trauma and history as a discipline, an attitude that should not degenerate into identification (Levinas' influence may be perceptible here), and in which cognitive processes are minimised to the advantage of affects. Such destabilising opening to the otherness of trauma LaCapra defines in the following terms:

> Being responsive to the traumatic experience of others, notably of victims, implies not the appropriation of their experience but what I would call empathic unsettlement .... At the very least, empathic unsettlement poses a barrier to closure in discourse and places in jeopardy harmonizing or spiritually uplifting accounts of extreme events from which we attempt to derive reassurance.[31]

Ultimately, what the choral, echoic dimension underlines is the idea of vulnerability to otherness in a novel whose take on historical trauma is that, even though it is made to appear in extraordinary circumstances, it is shared collectively in an ethical relation envisaged as ordinary.

We seem to be confronted here with what French psychoanalyst Emile Lumbroso analyses in his evocation of historical trauma, and more concretely the trauma of history, when he specifies that, in the case of trauma, one of the four main modalities of inscription corresponds to the case in which structural trauma enters in connection with historical trauma. In such instances, the subject is no longer able to discriminate between what concerns him particularly and what obtains for the more collective dimension of suffering. In such circumstances, individual trauma is activated by collective trauma.[32] Even though such a statement might be taken with a pinch of

---

[31] LaCapra, *Writing History*, 41.
[32] Emile Lumbroso, "Les lieux du trauma", in *Actualité du trauma*, ed. Peter Kuon, Frankfurt: Peter Lang, 2002, 20-21.

salt when addressing the question of the treatment of individual patients, the interconnectedness of individual and collective trauma is at the heart of the ethical relation as exemplified in *Mother London* in that, being couched in terms of sensibility and generosity towards the other, it presents the reader with a model of social and cultural organisation based on the virtues of solidarity and selflessness. This is a spirit that seems to be disappearing under the onslaught of economic liberalism and the ubiquitous logic of profit-making that the protagonists see at work in the mid-1980s – the diegetic present contaminated by the consequences of Thatcherite politics.

In some passages, Joseph Kiss becomes the spokesman of the Cockney tradition and passes strictures on new urban and economic policies that are transforming the face of the metropolis, sounding the theme of loss against which the novel as a whole, steeped in the ethics of alterity and intent in bearing witness to a disappearing world, is built.[33] The ethics of alterity and those of political commitment are given pride of place throughout. The trauma of loss cannot pass unnoticed, which makes testimony necessary. The faithfulness to an earlier version of social relations and of Cockney culture must be voiced. The main trauma that affects the metropolis is predicated on a sense of loss that seems to be the *primum mobile* of a narrative resorting to traumatic realism so as to evoke traumatised space.

In *Mother London*, the eponymous city clearly signposts, from the title on, the novel's priority, the writing of place, and more especially of traumatised space. Far from being presented as memory site, let alone commemoration site, the illimited city never lets itself be circumscribed and doxified, and nowhere in the novel is there room for an official history of the city to be privileged. Quite on the contrary, what appears throughout is a vision of mutable London, whether this refers to the images of the Blitz, where the ruinous landscapes are endowed with the intrinsic power of ruins to point to the illimited, that which is not there, the Other of place. This is clearly thematised in passages where the effects of the V2s are precisely documented, as is the case in David Mummery's vision:

> Walking through the rubble to where the baker's had been I discovered more lumps of bone and flesh, most of it nameless meat, but no loaves .... Past the back alleys of the shops, the houses beyond

---

[33] Moorcock, *Mother London*, 379-80.

had their windows blown out, their roofs broken. There was still a storm of dust coming from the crater and I could hear people screaming from within the piles of rubble.[34]

The hole or missing part of the landscape becomes the source of energy around which the evocation of traumatised space in seen to gravitate, foregrounding the sense of effraction and loss, and pointing at absence, some figurative evocation of the spatial Other. Many years after the events, the image comes back to haunt the protagonist, half memory, half repetition, refusing to let memory become stabilised, making room for ragged, frayed memories only, turning its back on total, clearly delineated history to promote the tentative, partial recall and understanding of testimony.

In such evocations, traumatised space becomes a modality of traumatised time, when strata upon strata accumulate to give temporal depth to the traumatised geography, connecting the present with some occurrence of the recent or remote past. In fact, there appears a singular sense of temporal depth in the narrative that is concerned with evoking a trauma's consequences for the present. The lives of the protagonists are dominated by the recurrent, haunting images of fire and the frequent, nagging return to scenes of original effraction, or moment of fixation. This implies that what is at the heart of the text's use of trauma is the return to a moment of origin. And clearly, such obsession with origins may be interpreted as allowing for the evocation of trauma, individual and collective, as if the trauma of the Thatcher years were a secondary moment in which the original effraction, that of wartime trauma, were re-activated, according to the most basic laws of *Nachträgligkeit* (understood as the influence of the second event on the first).

However, one step further, I would argue that what is at stake in harping on the Blitz as the origin is the indication that this moment of historical trauma itself reactivates a first traumatic event, as suggested by one of the recurring motifs – or at least references. This is indicated, namely, in the epigraph of Part Four, a fragment from James Pope-Hennessy's *History under Fire*, in which the German bombings of 1940 are compared to the damage wreaked by the Great Plague of 1665 and the Great Fire of the following year, both moments of intense insecurity and vulnerability. In such passages, the

---

[34] *Ibid.*, 347.

Blitz is seen as the reactivating agent of another historical moment of fixation that displaces the treatment of trauma from the individual to the collective, trans-historical sphere. In so doing, what Moorcock foregrounds is what has been analysed by Caruth in terms of the inherent connection of trauma that always refers to another time and another place.[35] Such thematic and aesthetic choices unmistakably point towards the intrinsically ethical dimension of the literary evocation of trauma, in which the reader's empathic unsettlement is solicited through the paradox of a representation where loss is evoked the better to be thwarted, orienting the narrative towards mourning rather than melancholia, hence working through.

Performing romance

Among the many critics who have commented on the nature of traumatic realism in contemporary literature (among whom LaCapra who, even though operating within the field of historiography, is very much aware of the subversion of mimesis inherent in the writing of trauma),[36] Anne Whitehead provides the best in-depth analysis of how contemporary fiction is problematised so as to articulate a new form of reality. For her, the main traits of traumatic realism are based on "the intensification of conventional narrative modes",[37] the signal characteristics of which are repetition, fragmentation, intertextuality and other means of performing the effects of trauma.[38] The disruption of mimetic transparency seems to take on board the various techniques honed out by the experimentalist brand of the Modernist and Postmodernist novels,[39] but I would argue that traumatic realism is

---

[35] Caruth, *Trauma*, 8.

[36] LaCapra, *Writing History*, 186.

[37] Whitehead, *Trauma Fiction*, 84.

[38] Roger Luckhurst gives a similar list, among which are to be found: temporal dislocation, some reluctance to comfortable identification, the rejection of closure, various type of enunciative and grammatical heterogeneity, compulsive repetition, etc. (Roger Luckhurst, *The Trauma Question*, London and New York: Routledge, 2008, 88). When dealing with *Moby Dick*, a monument of the American tradition and a contemporary classic that he sees as responding to the same traumatic paradigm, Marc Amfreville resorts to the notion of the rhyme that he borrows from Agamben, a device which illuminating encapsulates most of the traits of traumatic realism, both in spatial and temporal terms, and in relation to the motifs of fragmentation, doubling and surfacing. See Chapter VI of his monograph aptly entitled "Rimes et mises en abyme" (Marc Amfreville, *Écrits en souffrance*, Paris: Michel Houdiard, 2009, 139-63).

[39] Whitehead, *Trauma Fiction*, 87.

also geared on the resort to genres or modal inflections that are imported into what used to be the domain of realistic fiction. This is what appears clearly when concentrating on the corpus of primary texts that Anne Whitehead focuses on, novels from the 1980s to the present, which borrow from such tonal and generic ingredients as fantasy, the fantastic, the uncanny, the ghost story (to which could be added, in some cases, an unmistakably sublime colouring) whose importation mars the more transparent realistic idiom. Such choices, in turn, thwart the reader's expectations and trigger off destabilisation or, in LaCapra's terms, unsettlement. Interestingly, all generic or tonal ingredients mentioned above also belong to the wider, all-encompassing category of romance, and I would tend to see traumatic realism as evidenced in the above-mentioned corpus and in *Mother London* as yet another stage in the secular dialogue between the novel and romance and a resurgence of an earlier mode of fictional representation.

All such ingredients are present in *Mother London*, a narrative that boasts a realistic basis while multiplying coincidences, alluding to sundry miraculous occurrences, staging implausible characters endowed with telepathy and paranormal gifts, straining the reader's belief through the casting of Mary Gasalee as an avatar of Sleeping Beauty and the vision of David Mummery's saviour as a flying man, and multiplying instances of ontological migration through the means of the Land of Dreams (even though the latter is naturalised through the means of psychological unbalance). These are but a few elements that contribute to the introduction of an uncanny atmosphere at times relayed by a foray into pure fantasy, so much so that the realism seems installed to be seen all the better bursting at the seams, not unlike what is to be found in some of the more canonical instances of magical realism. This is an experience that Michael Rothberg captures when commenting on traumatic realism as applied to Holocaust fiction, an observation that applies to other works. For in fact, Rothberg conceives of traumatic realism as a doubly-oriented idiom in which a vestigial faithfulness to the tenets of realism goes along in unending tension with an anti-realist approach that insists on bearing witness to that which is not directly knowable.[40] This seems to me to encapsulate what is at work in Moorcock's novel, where the problematising of mimesis is a way of rejecting limits and of pointing towards external

---

[40] Rothberg, *Traumatic Realism*, 140.

heterogeneity, exteriority and alterity. For in fact what romance does in the context of this narrative is to specify that there are more memories, thoughts and affects than can be represented or simply presented.

Traumatic realism, in its collaboration with romance, is an apt tool to come to terms with the evocation of literary trauma in that they signal the void, hole or silence, partial or complete, that accompanies trauma. By renouncing the exhaustive obsession of the realistic idiom, what the tentative mode of romance does is eschew limits by showing that there are limits to what can be voiced, presented or represented – and, presumably, known. The intensification and hyperbole that characterise traumatic realism help point at the limits of representation and colonise the zone around the void, remaining on the verge of it, content with designating it, occupying through paroxystic affect the margins of the hole and ceaselessly probing at it. What romance does, in such instances, is solicit affects that show that there is something that cannot be shown or understood, or archived, or represented – or only partially so.[41] In the literary evocation of trauma in general and in *Mother London* in particular, what obtains is that romance is summoned as an ethical operator which presents that there is alterity, in some sort of negative presentation not unlike that characterising the nature of the Kantian or Lyotardian sublime.

In *Mother London* (and many other contemporary texts) what appears as characteristic of traumatic realism as accommodated by romance is the flaunting of trauma as the site of alterity or, more precisely, as the site of the ethical relation to the other *par excellence*. The harbouring of disruptive modes of representation effects some faltering of reading that is oriented towards and accountable to alterity.[42] One step further, I would argue that traumatic romance is an operator that prises open totality so as to let the reader experience the literary work happening as event,[43] in its singularity and in a present that disrupts habit and rejects any comfortable return towards sameness and identity. The miraculous, fantasy-strained, uncanny,

---

[41] The idea that trauma is predicated on alterity, in so far as it shows that one can only remain on the verge, speak from the brink, or speak around the void is developed by French psychologist Blandine Ponet (Blandine Ponet, "Au bord de l'autre", in *Actualité du trauma*, 52).

[42] Attridge, *The Singularity of Literature*, 80.

[43] *Ibid.*, 95.

marvellous events recounted in the narrative, and the attendant fragmented, disrupting poetic choices introduce the event of alterity, in which the reader has to relinquish his/her claims to activity and, instead of acting, must let him- or herself be performed by the text,[44] which implies accepting the failure of cognition inherent in trauma correlated on the rise of intensified, paroxystic affect. In the end, what I see as characteristic of this representative of the London novel that is also a representative of trauma fiction, is a narrative whose fundamental energy lies in its re-inscribing the powers of romance as a mode of disruption and identification that naturally accommodates traumatic realism and interestingly turns towards radical alterity. This means that it lets the reader be performed by the text in a new version of Levinasian sensibility or vulnerability. Romance would then be the crucible of literary trauma and ethical commitment to the Other – commitment in so far as performance both presents and transmits responsibility.

---

[44] *Ibid.*, 98.

WHERE MADNESS LIES: HOLOCAUST REPRESENTATION AND THE ETHICS OF FORM IN MARTIN AMIS' *TIME'S ARROW*

MARÍA JESÚS MARTÍNEZ-ALFARO

> Ends must not be permitted to precede beginnings and middles ... that way madness lies.[1]

> Style, of course, is not something grappled on to regular prose; it is intrinsic to perception. We are fond of separating form and content (for the purpose of analysis and so on), but they aren't separable. They come from the same place. And style is morality. Style judges.[2]

The representation of the Holocaust and the focus on the perpetrators

Martin Amis has often referred to the Holocaust as the crucial event of the twentieth century.[3] In an interview with Jonathan Noakes,[4] he admits to the Holocaust being a theme he had long been interested in,

The research carried out for the writing of this article is part of a research project financed by the Spanish Ministry of Science and Innovation (MICINN) and the European Regional Development Fund (ERDF) (code HUM2007-61035). The author is also thankful for the support of the Aragon Government and the University of Zaragoza.

[1] Salman Rushdie, *Shame*, London: Vintage, 1995, 22.
[2] Martin Amis, "The American Eagle: The Adventures of *Augie March* by Saul Bellow", in *The War Against Cliché: Essays and Reviews 1971-2000* (2001), New York: Vintage, 2002, 467.
[3] See, for instance, Carl and John Bellante, "Unlike Father, Like Son: An Interview with Martin Amis", *Bloomsbury Review*, XII/2 (December 1992), 16.
[4] Jonathan Noakes, "Interview with Martin Amis", in *Martin Amis: The Essential Guide* (Vintage Living Texts Series), eds Margaret Reynolds and Jonathan Noakes, London: Vintage, 2003, 20.

although he never really considered the possibility of writing a novel on it, that is, until the inception of *Times' Arrow*. When Noakes raises the issue of Amis juxtaposing "something which is tricksy and witty from a literary point of view" with the "huge tragedy" that the Holocaust was, the author replies that he still thought he had something to add to the subject. He respects those who think that the Holocaust should not be written about, but he does not agree with those who automatically reject the use of "sophisticated or witty ironic means for writing about something serious".[5] Technical and verbal virtuosity are second nature to Amis. In his view, one cannot become a different kind of writer because of the subject, and there is no subject literature is barred from. As he explains in another interview,

> I felt I was in a forest of taboos throughout writing this book [*Time's Arrow*]. This is the most difficult and sensitive subject ever, I think, but I do believe, as a writer, that there are no No Entry signs.[6]

Many of the questions posed to the author when interviewed as well as some of the negative criticism that *Time's Arrow* received point to the issue of who should or should not speak of the Holocaust, or write about it: who owns the Holocaust? Who has the right to speak for its victims? Nations? Individuals? Survivors? Descendants of victims or survivors? Competing over the ownership of any world calamity may seem inappropriate, even obscene. And yet the question of to whom the Holocaust belongs comes up repeatedly in public debates. As Marianne Hirsch and Irene Kakandes have pointed out:

> ... one could say that the Holocaust has remained poignantly present in very different areas of social and cultural life. Should a monastery be built on the grounds of Auschwitz? Should there be a monument to the murdered Jews of Europe in Berlin, the capital of the perpetrator nation? What should that monument look like? What stories should and should not be told? Is it legitimate for Steven Spielberg to tell the story of one good German, Oskar Schindler, when there were very few such rescuers? Can the Holocaust be funny, the subject of imaginative play, as it is for Roberto Benigni in *Life Is Beautiful*? What is the status of historical truth versus interpretation? These

---

[5] *Ibid.*, 20.
[6] Eleanor Wachtel, "Eleanor Wachtel with Martin Amis: *Interview*", *The Malahat Review*, CXIV (March 1996), 17.

debates and other recent ones … are carried out in the public media. For teachers and students in the humanities, the Holocaust has become a limit case, a prime site for testing aesthetic and ethical theories about mediation and representability.[7]

In his memoir *Literature or Life*, Jorge Semprún describes the days between his liberation from Buchenwald and his repatriation: "Can the story be told? Can anyone tell it?", he wonders. And, even if language is able to "contain everything", "can people hear everything? Will they be able to understand?"[8] Semprún's misgivings are a *topos* of Holocaust memoirs. What seemed to be at issue in the decades after World War II was not only Holocaust literature but literature itself. Theodor W. Adorno's famous assertion that it was "barbaric to write poetry after Auschwitz"[9] pointed to silence as the only possible ethical response in the aftermath of the massacre. To Adorno, it was impossible to represent the Holocaust in aesthetic terms: aestheticising it was as unacceptable as a reader gaining pleasure from a work of art that deals with it. Moreover, his words suggest that literature as a whole (and not only Holocaust literature) has become impossible after such an unspeakable crime. As is well known, Adorno later modified his views, arguing that: "Perennial suffering has as much a right to expression as a tortured man has to scream; hence it may have been wrong to say that after Auschwitz you could no longer write poems."[10]

Victims, their descendants, the Jewish people have a right to speak. Their testimonies have also shown their commitment to a duty: that of bearing witness. Survivors' narratives made for a new genre and they also created another: fictionalised accounts of the Holocaust, which have been thoroughly questioned, or at least questioned in a way that survivors' narratives have not. As Sue Vice points out, "critical preference for testimony over fiction has become such a truism that it

[7] Marianne Hirsch and Irene Kakandes, Introduction, in *Teaching the Representation of the Holocaust*, eds Marianne Hirsch and Irene Kakandes, New York: The Modern Language Association of America, 2004, 2.

[8] Jorge Semprún, *Literature and Life*, trans. Linda Coverdale, New York: Penguin, 1997, 13-14.

[9] Theodor W. Adorno, *Prisms*, trans. Samuel and Shierry Weber, Cambridge, MA: MIT Press, 1981, 34.

[10] Theodor W. Adorno, *Negative Dialectics*, trans. E.B. Ashton, London: Routledge and Kegan Paul, 1973, 362.

is hard to find any voices dissenting from it".[11] The bias towards testimony is often couched in formal terms, but the arguments adduced only masquerade, more often than not, as a formal issue. What one sees time and again in the area of the reception of Holocaust fiction is that "apparently literary criteria slide without warning into, or cover over, moral and moralistic issues".[12]

As if in answer to those who may feel that Holocaust literature belongs to the victims (and their descendants), Amis remarks:

> People say, legitimately in a way, what am I as an Aryan doing with this subject? But I'm writing about the perpetrators and they are my brothers, if you like. I feel a kind of responsibility in my Aryanness for what happened. This is my racial link with these events, not with the sufferers but with the perpetrators.[13]

The Holocaust happened to all. As Pilar Hidalgo explains, to "a generation of British novelists born after the Second World War, the Holocaust has come to epitomise not something alien in its enormity, perpetrated in faraway places, but something that is linked to what it is to be human".[14] I agree with Hidalgo when she argues that Holocaust novels fulfil the function of imaginary witnesses, though I would emphasise Martin Amis' point that bearing witness requires that we consider not only those to whom the Holocaust happened, in the strictest sense of the term – Holocaust victims – but also those who

---

[11] Sue Vice, *Holocaust Fiction*, London: Routledge, 2000, 5.

[12] *Ibid.*, 6.

[13] Wachtel, *Interview*, 47.

[14] Pilar Hidalgo, "Representing the Holocaust in Martin Amis's *Time's Arrow* and Caryl Phillips's *The Nature of Blood*", in *Towards an Understanding of the English Language, Past, Present and Future: Studies in Honour of Fernando Serrano*, eds José Luis Martínez-Dueñas Espejo *et al.*, Granada: Universidad de Granada, 2005, 250. See also Marianne Hirsch's notion of "postmemory", in *Photography, Narrative and Postmemory*, Cambridge, MA: Harvard University Press, 1997; "Surviving Images: Holocaust Photographs and the Role of Post-memory", in *The Holocaust and Visual Culture*, ed. Barbie Zelizer, New Brunswick, NJ: Rutgers University Press, 2001, 214-46; and Geoffrey Hartman's concept of "witnesses by adoption" (Geoffrey Hartman, *The Longest Shadow: In the Aftermath of the Holocaust*, Bloomington: Indiana University Press, 1996). Hirsch's postmemory points to an intersubjective space of remembrance, connected with a cultural or collective trauma that is not strictly based on identity or family connections. Hartman's coinage also suggests an enlargement of the family framework to encompass broader spaces of empathy and identification.

made it happen – the perpetrators. If those who suffered and died, or suffered and survived, were average people, the victimisers were equally ordinary.

It is hard to try and put oneself in the place of a victim, but it is also an ethical exercise to open one's eyes to the terrifying commonality of the perpetrators. If the Holocaust is, in Hidalgo's words above, linked to what it is to be human, it is also because it makes us face the fact that the most ordinary human beings can be capable of the most inhuman acts. The monstrous face of Nazism was all the more monstrous because of its terrible ordinariness. Thus, it is a key decision on Amis' part to focus on a perpetrator rather than a victim. Odilo Unverdorben, a Nazi doctor who installed the pellets of Zyklon B with which prisoners were gassed at Auschwitz, is also, as the narrator points out, "absolutely unexceptional, liable to do what everybody else does, good or bad, with no limit, once over the cover of numbers".[15]

Narrated in reverse chronological order, *Time's Arrow* ends in Odilo Unverdorben's birthplace: Solingen. The narrator refers to it as "a modest town" that "harbours a proud secret. It is this: Solingen is the birthplace of Adolf Eichmann".[16] Used by now to interpreting things against the unreliable narrator's words, the reader should see the pride referred to ("proud secret") as nothing but shame: the shame of a town forever associated with the Gestapo overseer directly responsible for the Final Solution. Hannah Arendt attended the Eichmann trial as a reporter for *The New Yorker* and she was struck by the fact that he lacked all the demonic qualities that the prosecution had attributed to him. Against the traditional concept of evil seen as ultimate depravity, corruption or sinfulness, she argued that the shocking truth that the trial revealed had to do, rather, with "the fearsome, word-and-thought-defying *banality of evil*".[17] While it would have been very comforting indeed to see that Eichmann was a monster, the trouble with him "was precisely that so many were like

---

[15] Martin Amis, *Time's Arrow or the Nature of the Offence* (1991), London: Vintage, 2003, 164.
[16] *Ibid.*, 170.
[17] Hannah Arendt, *Eichmann in Jerusalem: A Report on the Banality of Evil* (revised and enlarged edition), Harmondsworth: Penguin, 1984, 287 (emphasis in the original).

him, and that the many were neither perverted nor sadistic, that they were, and still are, terribly and terrifyingly normal".[18]

If the Holocaust does not belong only to victims and their descendants, the same can be said of Holocaust trauma, and of trauma in general. The novel's focus on a perpetrator who has managed to become someone else in the States but who is still traumatised by his past, as shall be argued in what follows, also hinders the impulse to link trauma with victimisation, excluding other possibilities. Victims of certain events may or may not be traumatised by them. Likewise, traumatised people may or may not be victims. There is perpetrator trauma, and with it comes the need to acknowledge that trauma does not entail the identification of the perpetrator and the victim. As Dominick LaCapra points out, "'victim' is not a psychological category", and so, the fact that "Himmler suffered from chronic stomach cramps or that his associate Erich von dem Bach Zelewski experienced nocturnal fits of screaming does not make them victims of the Holocaust".[19] Holocaust perpetrators were also "ordinary men"[20] in this: they lacked the demonic dimension that could have made them immune to trauma.

The ethical dimension of Amis' formal choices and their role in the narration of trauma

Earlier I quoted Jorge Semprún wondering whether people can hear and understand everything. As *Time's Arrow* shows, this "everything" also includes the fact that there can be such a thing as "routine atrocity". "Casual killing" is difficult to understand and so people tend to push it to the borders of the mind. Nothing is more cathartic than the translation of fact into fable, the fable of seeing the Nazis as devilish arch-villains or of reducing the Holocaust to a number of commonplaces. Amis plays with this impulse to reduce fact to fable precisely by having the narrator tell a fable that has to be decoded into fact by the reader. Amis' artistry in *Time's Arrow* is in tune with the Russian Formalist concept of "defamiliarisation". In Shklovsky's terms, the familiar way of telling something is not the artistic way,

---

[18] *Ibid.*, 257.
[19] Dominick LaCapra, *Writing History, Writing Trauma*, Baltimore and London: The Johns Hopkins University Press, 2001, 79.
[20] Christopher R. Browning, *Ordinary Men: Reserve Batallion 101 and the Final Solution in Poland*, New York: HarperCollins, 1992.

since artistry requires both defamiliarisation and a display of the devices by which the familiar is made strange. This view accounts for Shklovsky's well-known assertion that: "*Tristram Shandy* is the most typical novel of world literature." As he claims, the purpose of art is not to imitate the world, but to make it strange, which means that "the forms of art are justified by the laws of art [rather than] by their realism".[21]

Amis' literary wit does indeed defamiliarise the world in *Time's Arrow*, and it does so in a way that shows narrative virtuosity not to be devoid of ethical significance. Berel Lang made the point that the moral enormity of the Holocaust could not fail to affect the act of writing about it and the strategies used to represent it.[22] But even these strategies can become familiar, as much as evil or mass violence can. The narrative world of *Time's Arrow* breaks the most basic rules of mimesis and constantly calls attention to its own fictionality. However, it is precisely for this reason that the formal devices used to deal with the Holocaust in the novel may be seen as conveying a truth, in Alan Badiou's sense: a truth that should be distinguished from knowledge. Knowledge repeats, while truth is "first of all something new .... A truth appears in its newness because an eventful supplement interrupts repetition."[23] The novel shakes us out of familiarity with our own history, end even out of familiarity with Holocaust representation. By defamiliarising the familiar, by making it strange, the author adopts a more ethical perspective on the Holocaust, since he forces us to rework our ways of looking at it. As Andrew Gibson points out:

> The important, formal distinctions between narratives, or modes of narrative are not merely formalistic. They do not describe a given narrative form as simply a reflection or embodiment of an ethics primarily found elsewhere in the narrative text, though this was how a whole Anglo-American tradition of novel criticism as represented by

---

[21] Victor Shklovsky, "Sterne's *Tristram Shandy*: Stylistic Commentary", in *Russian Formalist Criticism*, eds Lee T. Lemon and Marion J. Reis, Lincoln and London: University of Nebraska Press, 1965, 57.
[22] *Writing and the Holocaust*, ed. Berel Lang, New York: Holmes and Meier, 1998, 1.
[23] Alain Badiou, "On the Truth-Process: An Open Lecture by Alain Badiou", *European Graduate School*, 2002: http://www.egs.edu/faculty/badiou/badiou-truth-process-2002.html (accessed 3/12/2008).

– say – Barbara Hardy and Wayne Booth understood distinctions
between modes of narration. Rather, in the context of an ethics for
which ethical and epistemological questions are inseparable,
distinctions between modes of narration are also crucial ethical
distinctions.[24]

In addition to the focus on a perpetrator rather than a victim, the
reverse narration and the double narrator are key choices on Amis'
part, formal choices that nonetheless bear upon the novel's ethical
import. To quote Dermot McCarthy, if the novel "re-sensitizes us" to
the specific historical episode it deals with, it is "the way he [Amis]
tells the story that effects this sensitization".[25] Moreover, these formal
choices also account for the novel being regarded as trauma fiction.
As Valentina Adami points out, the fact that *Time's Arrow* "represents
a traumatic event is not in and of itself sufficient to define it as trauma
fiction". Equally relevant in this respect, she adds, are

> ... the narrative's formal structure, and the capacity of that structure to
> convey the fragmentation of meaning and identity brought about by
> traumatic experiences. Recurring stylistic features of trauma fiction
> include intertextuality, repetition and a fragmented narrative voice. All
> of them are present in *Time's Arrow*.[26]

In the Afterword to *Time's Arrow*, Amis explicitly refers to Robert
Jay Lifton's *The Nazi Doctors* as one of the novel's main intertexts.[27]
Like *Time's Arrow*, Lifton's study focuses on the perpetrators and,
more specifically, on the role played by doctors in the Holocaust,
which he connects with the "biomedical vision" at the heart of

---

[24] Andrew Gibson, *Postmodernity, Ethics and the Novel: From Leavis to Levinas*,
London: Routledge, 1999, 26.
[25] Dermot McCarthy, "The Limits of Irony: The Chronillogical World of Martin
Amis' *Time's Arrow*", *War, Literature and the Arts*, XI/1 (Spring 1999), 295. To
McCarthy, the relationship between Amis' understanding of "the nature of the
offence" and his narrative method in *Time's Arrow* is even more complex, since this
narrative method not only expresses the enormity of the Holocaust but also suggests
that it was "a *prelude* to an even more unthinkable death and destruction" (*ibid.*, 295;
emphasis in the original). Thus, the reader is sensitised to past and likely future
events. I will return to this point when discussing the novel's ending.
[26] Valentina Adami, *Trauma Studies and Literature: Martin Amis's* Time's Arrow *as
Trauma Fiction*, New York: Peter Lang, 2008, 73.
[27] Robert Jay Lifton, *The Nazi Doctors: Medical Killing and the Psychology of
Genocide*, New York: Basic Books, 1986.

Nazism. *The Nazi Doctors* is an exploration of the psychology of the doctors who helped to administer the Final Solution. Significantly, the central paradigm Lifton employs to discuss this psychology is the idea of "psychological doubling", which definitely throws light on the device of the double narrator in Amis' novel.

Regarding the medical view of mass extermination, Hannah Arendt quotes a telling exchange between the defence attorney and the Israeli judge during the trial of Adolf Eichmann in Jerusalem: Servatius declared the accused innocent of charges bearing on his responsibility for the "collection of skeletons, sterilizations, killings by gas and *similar medical matters*", whereupon the Judge Halevi interrupted him: "Dr. Servatius, I assume you made a slip of the tongue when you said that killing by gas was a medical matter." To which Servatius replied: "It was indeed a medical matter, since it was prepared by physicians; *it was a matter of killing, and killing, too, is a medical matter.*"[28] One may wonder at the process by which healers turned into killers, the reasons which led them to believe that, as is stated in the heading of Chapter 3 in Part I of *Time's Arrow*: "Because I am a healer, everything I do heals."[29] Like the order in which events are told, the logic of such a statement is also reversed: it only makes sense when rephrased as "Because everything I do heals, I am a healer".

As Lifton succinctly but clearly explains in an interview,[30] this inverted logic was made possible by a process of psychological doubling. Nazi doctors joined the party seeking the promise of revitalisation that Hitler offered. Each of them joined first the medical profession, which is a group of its own, and then the military, as they were sent to a camp. They were not killers to begin with, but ordinary men who were socialised to evil. In the camps, they made selections and ran the killing process. When they were in Auschwitz, they had an Auschwitz self which was responsible for all this as well as for the very vulgar life (sex, alcohol and obscene jokes) that they led there.

---

[28] Arendt, *Eichmann in Jerusalem*, 69 (emphasis in the original).

[29] Amis, *Time's Arrow*, 74.

[30] Harry Kreisler, "Evil, the Self and Survival: Conversation with Robert J. Lifton", in *Conversations with History*, Blog, Institute of International Studies, U.C. Berkeley (2 November 1999): http://globetrotter.berkeley.edu/people/Lifton/lifton-con0.html (accessed 14/02/2007).

But they would go home to their families, from Poland or Germany, for weekends or on leave. There they would be relatively ordinary fathers and husbands, calling for a non-Auschwitz self or a prior, more humane, self. The two selves were obviously part of the same overall self, but each of them functioned separately.

Much of the irony but also much of the tragic vision that emerge from *Time's Arrow* are grounded on a similar doubling which keeps narrating and narrated subjects apart. In a sense, the narrator and the character whose life the novel tells are one and the same: the narrator introduces himself as Tod Friendly, one of the names adopted by Odilo Unverdorben after the war.[31] In another sense, the narrator cannot be described as autodiegetic since the connection between narrative instance and main character is but a measure of the rift between them. This narrator, neither homodiegetic nor heterodiegetic, is a "passenger or parasite" travelling with the main character towards "his secret", a secret which will be "bad and non intelligible" but which will eventually reveal "the nature of the offence".[32] The narrator lacks access to his host's thoughts, but he is not barred from his emotions, or from his nightmares. Although he is "equipped with a fair amount of value-free information, or general knowledge" and a "superb vocabulary",[33] he is unaware that his backward trajectory through time violates ordinary chronology. He is also utterly ignorant of history. And, most remarkably, he possesses a clear aversion to human suffering: the suffering experienced by the ill and wounded as treated by doctors, by the women that the protagonist abuses, by marginalised social groups (like homosexuals), and, last but not least, by the Jews.

In this sense, the narrator has much to do with that prior, more humane, non-Auschwitz self silenced and erased by the Nazi doctors analysed by Lifton. In a way, the narrative voice stands for something close to the protagonist's conscience or soul. This is why when Irene, one of the protagonist's lovers, tells him that he has no soul, the

---

[31] Both names include binaries in a significant way. "Tod" means death in German, thus bringing to mind the notion of "friendly death" connected with the eugenistic project of Nazism – the eradication of what the Nazis referred to as "life unworthy of life" – and with their resort to gassing as a more "humane" method of killing. Un*verdorben* means "not *verdorben*", "not polluted or corrupt": so the name encapsulates the duality between Odilo and his *Doppelgänger*.
[32] Amis, *Time's Arrow*, 73.
[33] *Ibid.*, 16.

narrator remarks that he "used to take it personally, and [he] was wretched at first".[34] By contrast, the protagonist stands for a Hippocrates-free Auschwitz self (Odilo's Hippocratic oath hangs on his toilet door and ends up in the trash), unable to become whole again after the war. The two parts of his self have become so radically divided from one another that the main character – as Odilo Unverdorben, Hamilton de Souza, John Young or Tod Friendly – does indeed appear soulless, empty, utterly alone. As the narrator remarks, referring to the protagonist: "*His* isolation is complete because he doesn't know I'm here."[35]

The protagonist excluding that part of himself that would have made him responsive to the other, responsible in the face of the other, can also be read in ethical terms. A key idea in Levinasian ethics, which already appears in the early philosophical essay *De l'Évasion*, is the concept of *excendance*.[36] *De l'Évasion* expresses the imperative of escape, but escape from what exactly? To Gibson, the notion of escape as posited by Levinas is an escape from the idea of being understood as the principle of our own self-sameness or self-insistence: a view of the self as closed to the other, defined in opposition to, rather than in relationship with the other. *Excendance* designates the drive to escape from the confinement inherent in this idea of being self-contained and ontologically independent. If such a drive to escape the limits of the self turns us elsewhere, outside, it is clear that, in Levinas' secular ethics, this "elsewhere" is not death, the timeless or the supernatural (that would be the drive to *transcendance*, not *excendance*). This elsewhere is the other. As Gibson explains:

> ... *excendance* is the spontaneous *and immediate* desire to escape the limits of the self, a desire generated as those limits are experienced in their narrowness, even in their sheer absurdity. It is thus a principle of unease within and inseparable from the self that is of a different order to being and more profound than that. Evasion is the ethical impulse towards or openness to the other that effects a release from the confines of the self.

---

[34] *Ibid.*, 62.

[35] *Ibid.*, 22 (emphasis in the original).

[36] Emmanuel Levinas, *De l'Évasion* (1935), Montpellier: Fata Morgana, 1982.

If, in the light of Lifton's theory, the fission that accounts for the separation between the narrator and the protagonist of *Time's Arrow* can be seen as grounded on a process of psychological doubling, in the light of Levinasian ethics the said fission is the consequence of Unverdorben's successful resistance to *excendance*, a resistance that amounts to the annulment, the complete stifling of the self's drive to escape his own limits in a movement of openness to the other. Nothing like fascism to illustrate a celebration of self-confinement gained at the expense of overcoming and annulling *excendance*. No wonder that Levinas would later reflect on *De l'Évasion* as marked by his presentiment of the Nazi horror. From this perspective, Amis' creation of a narrative instance that functions as the protagonist's demoted conscience or soul, but also as his exiled drive to *excendance*, powerfully illustrates Gibson's assertion that an "acceptance of being, a blindness or resistance to 'evasion', a desire to expunge all weakness, self-disquiet, self-antagonism are what qualify a person or 'civilization' as in fact barbaric".[37] The novel's narrator stands then for this "weakness, self-disquiet, self-antagonism" expunged by the Nazi protagonist and those that were, like him, collaborators in the genocide, barbaric victimisers.

The split between narrator and protagonist seen as parts of the same overall but fragmented self can also be related to trauma, which is, in the context of Amis' novel, the trauma of a perpetrator rather than a victim. Despite its elusive nature, psychologists like Dori Laub and Daniel Podell emphasise the fact that what always lies at the core of trauma is the erasure of empathic bonds. Thus, when commenting on the case of an eighteen-year-old Cambodian boy whose only clear memory was an execution scene and his miraculous escape from a certain death, they point out the following:

> The wish for life elicits no response from the executioner. No matter how much the Cambodian boy wanted to live, the execution would have proceeded at its own steady pace. The erasure of this primary empathic bond, the refusal of this most basic human recognition is always at the nidus, the source, of massive psychic trauma. The breakdown of trust in a functioning empathic external dyad led to the

---

[37] Gibson, *Postmodernity*, 37 (emphasis in the original).

boy's loss of internal communication with the "other" in himself. Without this internal "other", there can be no representation.[38]

Obviously, Laub and Podell are dealing here with victim trauma and the boy's inability to represent, to tell, anything pertaining to his life prior to that limit experience. Yet it is interesting to reflect on the fact that the fragmentation affecting the victim here somehow seems to echo a similar split in the victimiser. In the light of the previous discussion on the novel's narrator as Odilo's exiled drive to *exendance*, the victimiser can be said to be so to the extent that he succeeds in erasing that part of himself able to empathise with the other. The empathic external dyad victimiser-victim stops functioning because something breaks down, something splits first within the victimiser himself. As a consequence, a similar fragmentation occurs within the victim, who, having lost trust in the functioning of that external dyad, also loses communication with the other in himself.

All these fractures are the seed of trauma and its unrepresentability, since, as Laub and Podell conclude: "the feelings of absence, rupture, and of the loss of representation that essentially constitute the traumatic experience all emerge from the real failure of the empathic dyad at the time of traumatisation and the resulting failure to preserve an empathic tie even with oneself."[39] This "failure to preserve an empathic tie even with oneself" is a resulting failure in the case of the victim, and an originating failure in the case of the victimiser. The device of the double narrator in *Time's Arrow* is predicated on this latter failure and powerfully contributes to the portrayal of a perpetrator who has not worked through trauma as the split within himself has not been healed.

It is also this pervading trauma that renders problematic the connection between experience, understanding and representation. Theories of trauma recurrently relate it to a collapse in understanding, since trauma emerges as that which, at the very moment of its reception, registers as a non-experience, causing conventional epistemologies to falter. As Cathy Caruth explains in summarising the

---

[38] Laub, Dori and Daniel Podell, "Art and Trauma", *International Journal of Psycho-Analysis*, LXXVI/5 (1995), 991.
[39] *Ibid.*, 992.

definition of trauma which emerged from the diagnostic category of PTSD:

> The pathology consists ... solely in *the structure of its experience* or reception: the event is not assimilated or experienced fully at the time, but only belatedly, in its repeated *possession* of the one who experiences it. To be traumatized is precisely to be possessed by an image or event.[40]

The events Odilo Unberdoven participated in are not fully understood at the moment of their occurrence but rather act as a haunting or possessive influence that returns in the form of nightmares ("the bomb baby", the man in a white coat and black boots) which make the past present, just as happens with things like the smell of burning fingernails, for instance. The protagonist cannot represent those events as the task of narrating them falls on someone else, who is but is not himself. In fact, the narrator's garrulousness, the way in which he often addresses the reader, only make the protagonist appear all the more wordless, isolated, closed to the world and to those around him. This narrator renders Odilo's life in words, but if in trauma the distinction between past, present and future collapses, so does it in the chronologically dislocated account of a narrative instance that simultaneously manages and fails to tell, since what he tells is but a measure of his failure to understand. In a sense, what is revealing about his narrative is not what he says, but the gaps in what he says, his inability to represent.

Since time runs backwards, remembering is replaced by instant forgetting in the novel. The narrator is surprised at human beings' ability to forget, which makes people "more innocent, constantly forgetting".[41] As Valentina Adami points out, the reversal of time

> ... reveals Odilo's attempts at losing his memory and changing his identity, while the figure of the doubled protagonist-narrator shows the precariousness of identity under extreme, traumatic circumstances. In the course of his life, the protagonist tries to escape from his identity and make himself anew by changing names and places .... He also has a habit of crumpling and burning all evidence of the past,

---

[40] Cathy Caruth, "Introduction to Psychoanalysis, Culture and Trauma I", *American Imago*, XLVIII/1 (Spring 1991), 3 (emphasis in the original).
[41] Amis, *Time's Arrow*, 99.

such as love letters and photos. Nonetheless, his Nazi past haunts him.[42]

Significantly, it is when the narrative reaches the protagonist's time in Auschwitz that Odilo Unverdorben's two halves are fused for the first time. In the light of the novel's narrative dynamics, though, fusion should be read as utter separation and split. In Auschwitz, the gap between the perpetrator's two selves is wider than ever; in Auschwitz, the negation of *excendance* is complete, and so what happens there constitutes the dark hole of a trauma that accounts for the collapse of understanding and the subsequent failure of representation. In the Auschwitz section of the novel everything makes sense precisely because it was in the real Auschwitz that the crazy nightmare of Nazism reached its peak. Everything is at last right for the narrator precisely because everything is most wrong. This is, above all, the past that will haunt the protagonist, a past that becomes a recurrent "*Now*":

> The world is going to start making sense ....
> *Now.* I, Odilo Unverdorben, arrived at Auschwitz Central somewhat precipitately and by motorbike .... *Now.* Was there a secret passenger on the back seat of the bike, or in some imaginary sidecar? No .... I was one now, fused for a preternatural purpose.[43]

Later on, the narrator explains what this "preternatural purpose" consists of:

> To dream a race. To make a people from the weather. From thunder and from lightning. With gas, with electricity, with shit, with fire.[44]

Language and time reversals and the ethical positioning of the reader
The Nazi project only makes sense when turned upside down. But if the reverse narrative and the novel's unreliable narrator give a new (though illusory) meaning to the recounted actions – by turning destruction into creation – they also bring new connotations to the

---

[42] Adami, *Trauma Studies*, 85.
[43] Amis, *Time's Arrow*, 124 (emphasis in the original).
[44] *Ibid.*, 128.

rhetoric of Nazi discourse: "this was our mission, after all: to make
Germany whole. To heal her wounds and make her whole."[45] The
Nazis wanted to dream a race, the Aryan race, which they would heal
by extirpating whatever they saw as impure. By contrast, the narrator
sees them as dreaming/creating the Jewish race, healing a country,
indeed, by incorporating rather than excluding the other. Nazi rhetoric
is used to mean the opposite of what it meant in real life.

Nazi violence was also a violence done to language. In Auschwitz,
"outpatient centers" were places for selections, and hospital areas
were "waiting rooms" before death.[46] Unaware of the way in which
language is made to falsify facts, the narrator provides enough
examples of a linguistic manipulation which he sees as just camp
argot: the ovens are called "Heavenblock"; Chamber and
Sprinkleroom are known as "the central hospital"; a camp tour of duty
is referred to as "Sommerfrische" (summer air), as if suggesting "a
perennial vacation from an inadequate reality".[47] These are the camp
officers' words to begin with, not just the narrator's. And yet, readers
have to decode them, as they have been doing with narrative discourse
from the very first page of *Time's Arrow*, simply because Nazi
terminology falsified reality as much as the narrator's discourse does.

At the beginning of the novel, Amis capitalises on the comic
effects created by these reversals (garbage people bring the paper,
instead of taking it away; going to bed means getting up, etc.). Later
on, however, none of these ironies is presented as humorous since
they are used to convey the barbaric cruelty of the massacre. As Brian
Finney points out,[48] Amis' resort to irony in *Time's Arrow* effectively
undermines Nazi misuse of language to rationalise mass murder: the
dual use of language can thus be said to parallel the novel's dual time
scheme and its dual code of ethics.

If any author's choices to adopt one narrative strategy rather than
another affect the reader's ethical response to the text, certain choices
demand a more active kind of engagement on the reader's part. This is
the case with *Time's Arrow*, where the narrator's conversational style

---

[45] *Ibid.*, 149.
[46] Lifton, in Kreisler, "Evil, the Self and Survival: Conversation with Robert J.
Lifton".
[47] Amis, *Time's Arrow*, 133.
[48] Brian Finney, "Martin Amis's *Time's Arrow* and the Postmodern Sublime", in
Martin Amis: Postmodernism and Beyond, ed. Gavin Keulks, Basingstoke and New
York: Palgrave, 2006, 113.

suggests that he is telling his story with the receiver of the narrative in mind, as if the reader was the third vertex of a triangle, a point distant from but connected with narrator and protagonist, necessary to close the novel's geometry. The horror of the Holocaust disappears if the events are read backwards, but the reader knows that history cannot be undone, and so, it is the reader who has to supply the tragedy missing in the text. If, in a sense, the narrator's naivety anaesthetises Unverdorben's actions from acceptable moral contexts, in another sense it is this selfsame naivety that urges the reader to provide the missing history and respond to it:

> The reader has to do all the morality, because these terrible events are described as benevolent, but also in such a way that, I hope, there is a sort of disgust and an unreality and self-delusion in the way it's shown. He keeps wondering why it has to be so ugly, this essentially benevolent action, why it is so filthy and ugly. It was a coprocentric universe. They called Auschwitz "anus mundi". So it's there, but the narrator can't spot it, the *reader* has to do all that.[49]

It is my contention that the "coprocentricity" Amis refers to in this passage has the effect of turning the narrator's aesthetic unconscious into a vehicle for the ethical positioning of the reader. The narrator's discomfort and disgust – produced by what he sees as the key role of shit in the world he inhabits and its overwhelming presence in the concentration camp – are coupled with the reader's moral discomfort and disgust in the light of what the narrator tells but fails to understand:

> What tells me that this is right? What tells me that all the rest was wrong? Certainly not my aesthetic sense. I would never claim that Auschwitz-Birkenau-Monowitz was good to look at. Or to listen to, or to smell, or to taste, or to touch.[50]

The narrator explicitly connects shit and trash with Tod's secret, which he also relates to the counterintuitive way in which time proceeds:

---

[49] Amis, in Noakes, "Interview", 21 (emphasis in the original).
[50] Amis, *Time's Arrow*, 128.

I *will* know *how* bad the secret is. I will know the nature of the offence. Already I know this. I know that it is to do with trash and shit, and that is wrong in time.[51]

This wrongness in time is the consequence of the reversed chronological order, already mentioned, in which events are presented. The novel reverses "time's arrow", the title phrase suggesting an unequivocal path – in the movement from present to past what can happen is only what has already happened – and also a pointer, like a finger, perhaps in accusation for a massacre whose true dimensions were appreciated in time, but which the passing of time cannot erase. The phrase as such was coined by British astrophysicist A.S. Eddington[52] to denote the directionality of time that follows from the second law of thermodynamics: the inescapable increase of total entropy in a closed system marks the direction of time. According to Richard Menke, it is the reversal of everyday thermodynamic activities that accounts for many of the narrator's digressions on the remarkable properties of the world in which he finds himself. In this world, violence restores maimed patients to health and smashed cars to their proper order; factories suck pollution from the skies; flames transform smoke and ashes into letters; etc. These interactions "bespeak the spontaneous organisation and decrease in entropy that characterise the reversal of time's arrow".[53] And in this gallery of inversions, a special place is reserved for the grotesqueness that emerges from the reversed thermodynamics of the body:

> All life, for instance, all sustenance, all meaning (and a good deal of money) issues from a single household appliance: the toilet handle. At the end of the day, before my coffee, in I go. And there it is already, the humiliating *warm* smell. I lower my pants and make with the magic handle. Suddenly, it's all there, complete with toilet paper, which you use and then deftly wind back on to the roll. Later, you pull up your pants and wait for the pain to go away.

---

[51] *Ibid.*, 73 (emphasis in the original).
[52] A.S. Eddington, *The Nature of the Physical World: Gifford Lectures 1927*, Cambridge: Cambridge University Press, 1928, 68-69.
[53] Richard Menke, "Narrative Reversals and the Thermodynamics of History in Martin Amis's *Time's Arrow*", *Modern Fiction Studies*, XLIV/4 (Winter 1998), 972.

... our lone sex sessions have, of late, become unrecognizably livelier. The missing component, the extra essence, is to be found, of course, in the toilet. Or in the trash. Where would Tod and I be without the toilet? Where would we be without all the trash?

Never watching where they are going, the people move through something prearranged, armed with lies. They are always looking forward to going to places they've just come back from, or regretting doing things they haven't yet done. They say hello when they mean goodbye. Lords of lies and trash – all kings of crap and trash.

When he swears, Odilo invokes human ordure, from which, as we now know, all human good eventually emanates.[54]

What initially appears to be just a source of scatological humour soon acquires allegorical resonance. In this Amis is reminiscent of Jonathan Swift, a satirist to whom he has more than once been compared. It would not be farfetched to apply to *Time's Arrow* what Philip Pinkus explains about the connotations of "coprocentricity" in Swiftian satire:

Since Swift's constant concern in his satires is man's corruption from original innocence, there is no more graphic illustration than the excremental. That is why his satires are obsessed with it. It is the traditional imagery of evil, of which Swift's contemporaries were well aware .... All Swift's references to the unclean flesh, the dung, the stench, the filth of man's body, are the symbols of man's sin.[55]

Dante pictured hell as a frozen cesspool into which all the rivers of the world dumped their sewage. In the same vein, the narrator reflects on the appropriateness of the term used by the camp officers to refer to Auschwitz: *Anus Mundi*. He can think "of no finer tribute than that",[56] since there "this human stuff, at normal times (and in civilised locales) tastefully confined to the tubes and runnels, subterranean, unseen – this stuff has burst its banks, surging upward on to the floor, the walls, the ceiling of life".[57] This implies that the narrator's journey

---

[54] Amis, *Time's Arrow*, 19, 40, 51, 123.
[55] Philip Pinkus, "Sin and Satire in Swift", *Bucknell Review*, XIII/2 (1965), 22.
[56] Amis, *Time's Arrow*, 133.
[57] *Ibid.*, 125.

towards the protagonist's dark secret is also a descent into hell. The description of this journey is deprived of horror precisely in order to increase the reader's horror, deprived of tragedy precisely in order that the reader will supply it. What the narrator's account is not deprived of is his feelings of disgust. The reader's tragic view of events is then but an answer to the narrator's unease at the ugliness of creation, at the crap surrounding an essentially praiseworthy task which strangely has "a patina of cruelty, intense cruelty, as if creation corrupts".[58] To use the words Pinkus applies to Swift, Amis' narrator can be said to provide us with "the unclean flesh, the dung, the stench, the filth of man's body", which clash with what he sees as the Nazis' benevolent actions. It falls on the reader to see them as a measure of "man's sin".

The focus on the scatological brings abjection into the text. As Julia Kristeva explains in *Powers of Horror: An Essay on Abjection*,[59] the abject is what threatens the integrity of the subject, who depends on its ability to thrust away the forces that threaten to dissolve the ego and that repeatedly confront it with the terror of annihilation: the improper, unclean, disorderly elements which generate abjection must be separated from the subject's "clean and proper" self if it wants to survive. Corporeal waste (faeces, urine, sperm, etc.) is one of Kristeva's categories of abjection, and so is the corpse. Both categories are at the core of *Time's Arrow*, and at the core of the Holocaust. In this sense, the Holocaust was a perverted struggle to keep abjection at bay, a struggle to erase what was seen as improper and unclean as a prerequisite for the creation of a clean and proper self or race. It is significant that in the midst of the *Anus Mundi* which was Auschwitz, Nazi officers took pains to be "elegant". Amis' novel also reflects this contrast between crap and tidiness when the narrator remarks, for instance, on the fact that there was "among my colleagues there, a general though desultory quest for greater elegance. I can understand that word, and all its yearning: *elegant*."[60] Similarly, "Uncle Pepi" was a man capable of the most horrific medical experiments but also "coldly beautiful, true, with self-delighted eyes; graceful, chasteningly graceful in his athletic

---

[58] *Ibid.*, 130.
[59] Julia Kristeva, *Powers of Horror: An Essay on Abjection*, trans. Leon S. Roudiez, New York: Columbia University Press, 1982.
[60] Amis, *Time's Arrow*, 128 (emphasis in the original).

authority".[61] The character, like the real Joseph Mengele he stands for, is cruel, but also attractive and elegant. He was an angel, an angel of death.

Following a rationale similar to what results from applying Kristeva's notion of abjection to this context, Dominick LaCapra deals with Holocaust trauma and Nazi ideology in terms of what he calls "sacrificialism and scapegoating".[62] "Scapegoating" is related here to an almost ritual and phobic horror over contamination by "the other", and so, part of the regenerative violence of the Holocaust was directed at trying to eradicate an anxiety localised on the Jew (and also on other victims like gypsies and homosexuals) in terms of that fear of contamination. How this kind of fear is confronted is "more a secondary issue: it can be expulsion, it can be extermination, but the problem is 'getting rid of'" something. What defines Nazi ideology in LaCapra's view is not only that, but rather, its bringing together the extremes of what would seem a binary opposition: remaining decent, morally beautiful, upright, while at the same time engaging in unheard-of transgression. The Nazis' "outward tidiness" is in this sense a measure of what they thought to be their "moral uprightness":

> The Nazi will eliminate Jews with what might almost be called purity of intention and ethical disinterest, not taking a cigarette or a mark for himself. So: being *Biedermeier* in your private life, presumably suffering no moral damage to the self, and at the same time engaging in this incredible unheard-of scenes of mass devastation, which constitute a kind of negative sublime, something that goes beyond ordinary experience and that most people will find utterly shocking or unbelievable.[63]

LaCapra sees the Nazi victimisation of the Jews as emerging from the need to extirpate from themselves what was indeed a very intimate part of themselves. To him, the idea of utter difference between Germans and Jews was implausible, given the cultural formation of the peoples. That kind of crazy desire to get rid of something that is a part of oneself led to incredibly rash behaviour, which was like

---

[61] *Ibid.*, 127.
[62] LaCapra, *Writing History*, 165.
[63] *Ibid.*, 167.

ripping organs from oneself.[64] Here we have again the above-mentioned split within the perpetrator's psyche that *Time's Arrow* illustrates.

This split leads to the scapegoating of others, which accounts for the possible traumatisation of the victim, but which is also at the core of the equally possible traumatisation of the victimiser, similarly unable to utter the event (in the line of a negative sublime, a negative unrepresentability), and similarly unable to become whole again. The narrator of *Time's Arrow* does in fact suggest the possibility that what Tod hates about others may be a projection of what he hates about himself. He ponders on how the protagonist responds differently to "all identifiable subspecies" – Hispanics, Asians, Arabs, Amerindians, blacks, women, the insane, the homosexual male, etc. – and declares himself ahead of him "on this basic question of human difference". He does not see others as different, or rather, he did not at first:

> All these distinctions I've had to learn up on. Originally at least I had no preselected feelings about anybody.

He then lingers on the issue of male homosexuality and concludes that "things might be less confused, and less dangerous, if he [Tod] could soberly entertain the idea of being homosexual".[65] What the protagonist rejects in others is perhaps a measure of what he fears about himself, that part of him which he cannot accept and which he does not even dare to think about.

Levinas' *mauvaise conscience*: towards an interpretation of the novel's ending

What made the Nazis different is the extremes to which they went to eliminate what they saw as different, but the dynamics of sacrificialism and scapegoating (LaCapra), the transformation of the other into an object of abjection (Kristeva), are ubiquitous and connected with traumas other than the Holocaust. The victimisation of others is always related, in Levinasian terms, to a mode of being predicated on the nihilistic destruction of the other to assure the self, or, in terms of trauma theory, to the above-mentioned erasure of the empathic bond that many see at the heart of trauma. Yet the Holocaust

---

[64] *Ibid.*, 170.
[65] Amis, *Time's Arrow*, 50.

is a prime example of what happens when the human subject does not acknowledge its diacritic/empathic relation between itself and the other, which constitutes the basis of Levinas' ethics. The Nazi subject tragically sought to define its humanity by depriving the other of it, and in the attempt, it became inhuman itself. As Primo Levi puts it in his memoirs: "[the] personages of these pages are not men, their humanity is buried, or they have themselves buried it, under an offence received or inflicted on someone else."[66] If the offence received annihilated the prisoners' humanity, the offence inflicted also did away with that of the perpetrators. This was "the nature of the offence", a phrase that Amis takes from Levi (as he explains in the Afterword) and that constitutes the novel's subtitle. Amis incorporates into the novel what can be seen as the governing idea of Levi's memoirs, namely, that the Holocaust obliterated the humanity of both the oppressed and the oppressors.

What is it to be human, then? As Levinas explains: "The human is the return to the interiority of non-intentional consciousness, to *mauvaise conscience*, to its capacity to fear injustice, and to prefer that which justifies being over that which assures it." [67] Levinas argues that in order to know something, the self consciously seeks to colonise the other, to use its own terms to pigeonhole the other into a category. He calls this mode of being *bonne conscience*, because it musters some "good conscience" about itself, and proposes *mauvaise conscience* instead as a mode of being that realises it exists only because of the other, the relationship being of such a nature that, should the other cease to exist, so will it cease to exist. Will Slocombe sees in this train of thought a clear response to the events of the Holocaust,[68] since, although Levinas does not explicitly refer to it, his ethics emerge from the Nazi genocide: if people had feared injustice more than death, then more would have been saved, and if people had thought about that which justifies being the other over that which assures the self, then it may have not occurred at all.

---

[66] Primo Levi, *The Drowned and the Saved*, trans. Raymond Rosenthal, New York: Random, 1989, 121.

[67] Emmanuel Levinas, "Ethics as First Philosophy", in *The Levinas Reader*, ed. Seán Hand, trans. Seán Hand and Michael Temple, Oxford: Blackwell, 1989, 85.

[68] Will Slocombe, *Nihilism and the Sublime Postmodern: The (Hi)story of a Difficult Relationship from Romanticism to Postmodernism*, London: Routledge, 2006, 62.

Is it the *bonne conscience* of Nazism that the narrator discovers in
the end? Does he eventually realise that what he had taken to be
mauvaise conscience was indeed a fragrant violation of it? Such
awareness would depend on him realising that he has been (re-)living
Odilo's life in the reverse, which is what the words "Oh no, but then
…" cryptically suggest in the novel's final paragraph:

> Beyond, before the slope of pine, the lady archers are gathering with
> their targets and bows. Above, a failing vision kind of light, with the
> sky fighting down its nausea. Its many nuances of nausea. When
> Odilo closes his eyes I see an arrow fly – but wrongly. Point-first. Oh
> no, but then… We're away once more, over the field. Odilo
> Unverdorben and his eager heart. And I within, who came at the
> wrong time – either too soon, or after it was too late.[69]

Few critics have paid attention to this crucial turning point in the
narrative. Among them, Brian Finney wonders, in the light of the
novel's last lines, whether the narrator is destined to relive his life in
reverse – that is, historical – time and, if so, whether he will be again
divided from the intellectual self that cannot feel the consequences of
its actions. This undecidability throws light upon the novel's open
ending and the significance of such an authorial decision, since, far
from releasing readers in the final paragraph, the narrative "condemns
them to share with the narrator an endless oscillation between past and
present, incorporating the past into our sense of modernity".[70] The
relationship between past and present equals that of other apparently
antithetical but intimately connected pairings in the novel, and in
history.

As has been pointed out, the Nazi officers' elegance contrasts with
the overwhelming presence of dirt, but this only highlights their moral
corruption. Similarly, psychological studies demonstrate that their
extreme exercise of power led in some cases to sexual impotence – as
is the case with Odilo:

> I am omnipotent. Also impotent. I am powerful and powerless.[71]

---

[69] Amis, *Time's Arrow*, 173.
[70] Finney, "Martin Amis's *Time's Arrow*", 111.
[71] Amis, *Time's Arrow*, 148.

Moreover, if the Nazis turning camp prisoners into non-men amounted to killing the human in themselves, they also went close to obliterating the distinction between victimisers and victims by turning prisoners into collaborators (Levi's "grey zone"[72]). Last, but not least, another binary questioned by the Holocaust has to do with post-humanist philosophers' view of it as an event that uncovered another face of the Enlightenment project.[73] The barbarism of the Holocaust does not stand in stark opposition to civilisation. On the contrary, the Holocaust blended civilisation with barbarism as the Nazis relied on rational means for the implementation of the highest irrationality. This is what Amis refers to in the Afterword when he speaks of the dynamics of Nazism as "reptilian and 'logistical'", a combination of "the atavistic and the modern".[74] The Holocaust was not so much the antithesis but the terrifying consequence of the Enlightenment, not the opposite but the other side of what we admire about civilisation. Many died as a consequence of Nazi ideology, but the humanist liberal idea of man also died with them, changing history in the process. The present age is the result of such a death. It is for this reason that the past, that past, cannot be extirpated from the present. But does this mean that our future is determined, as the future of the character is determined in the novel?

The fact that the protagonist and the narrator should be "away once more, over the field"[75] may indeed imply that the story begins again, in chronological order. In a figurative sense, though, this repetition suggests not only that the Holocaust should not and cannot be forgotten, but also that it may happen again. And yet, things do not have to be the same. As the story is told in *Time's Arrow*, backwards in time, things must happen only because they have already happened. Such determinism disappears if time's arrow is reversed again, and it

---

[72] Levi's "The Grey Zone", in *The Drowned and the Saved*, describes how the structure of concentration camps blurred the distinctions between victims and victimisers, producing an ambiguous world in which the simple hero-villain binary came apart. The "grey zone" was thus a wired-off world in which the Nazi administration produced the harshest of disciplines by systematically using prisoners as collaborators in the victimisation of other inmates.

[73] Max Horkheimer and Theodor Adorno, *Dialectic of Enlightenment*, trans. John Cummings, New York: Herder, 1972.

[74] Amis, *Time's Arrow*, 176.

[75] *Ibid.*, 173.

is reversed at the end of the novel, which is why Sue Vice refers to *Time's Arrow* as "a satire on backshadowing".[76] Using, as she does, André Berstein's terminology in *Foregone Conclusions*, we could say that the novel's ending turns the fixity of backshadowing – the present seen as a harbinger of an already determined future – into the openness of sideshadowing, which is, by contrast, "a gesturing to the side, to a present dense with multiple, and mutually exclusive possibilities for what is to come".[77]

The open ending does not restore sideshadowing in any explicit way, but rather timidly, only as a suggestion that is ambiguous enough to admit other interpretations. Perhaps this is why so few critics have pronounced themselves in this respect. Strictly speaking, the narrator has come too soon if the story begins again and the Holocaust has not happened, or too late, if it has indeed taken place. There is, though, a recurrent preoccupation in Amis' fiction that is implicit in the novel's ending: the nuclear holocaust. Thus, the narrator's arrival is a late arrival if we think of the Nazi Holocaust, but it is an early one if we think of the other holocaust, the nuclear one. And this, unlike the other, does not have to happen, precisely because it has not happened. If, as Dermot McCarthy insightfully argues, "the terrible journey back into WWII and the Nazi Holocaust … is a mirror inversion of the journey Amis sees his own generation taking *toward* nuclear holocaust",[78] this journey, unlike the other, is not pre-determined because the lady archers are shooting their arrows point first, and time is moving forwards again. The novel's ending is not celebratory, nor even redeeming, but at least it is, like sideshadowing, "a gesturing to the side".[79] The openness of the ending is also the openness of the future to which the last lines, like the arrow of time, point. As is the case with the narrator and the novel's time scheme, readers' ethical obligation becomes double: towards the past, which cannot be forgotten, and towards the future, which they must equally bear in mind. As Amis points out in "Thinkability", the essay that opens *Einstein's Monsters*:

---

[76] Vice, *Holocaust Fiction*, 18.
[77] Michael André Berstein, *Foregone Conclusions: Against Apocalyptic History*, Berkeley: University of California Press, 1994, 1.
[78] McCarthy, "The Limits of Irony, 303 (emphasis in the original).
[79] Berstein, *Foregone Conclusions*, 1.

If you give no thought to nuclear weapons, if you give no thought to the most momentous development in the history of the species, then what *are* you giving them? .... The man with the cocked gun in his mouth may boast that he never thinks of the cocked gun. But he tastes it, all the time.[80]

In *Time's Arrow* Amis invites us to think the unthinkable, in the past as well as in the future. One could even say that he leads us to think of the future by plunging us headlong into the past. There are no logical explanations, though, no enlightening revelations about the origins of the evil committed by the Nazis, perhaps because, in a sense, here there is no reason why, either.[81] As Levinas puts it, the question of the meaning of being is not "why we are", but "how to be", that is, "how being justifies itself".[82] *Time's Arrow* shows some of the most drastic ways in which being fails to do so. Will it also be like that in the future? Will the future mirror the past? Will the Holocaust return with a vengeance? "What goes round comes around", the narrator remarks, "1066, 1789, 1945".[83] Are we moving irrevocably towards another catastrophe, a final date to be added to the narrator's list? A look at Amis' fiction and non-fiction is enough to ascertain that his prospects are far from bright in this respect. And yet, at least, *Time's Arrow* bears witness to the writer's ethical obligation to speak in the face of the unspeakable,[84] to his struggle to find new

---

[80] Martin Amis, *Einstein's Monsters* (1987), London: Vintage, 2003, 11 (emphasis in the original).

[81] "*Hier ist kein warum.* Here there is no why. Here there is no when, no how, no where." These are the narrator's words when, in the Auschwitz section of the novel, he reflects on the camp's activities and on the paradoxical fact that "Creation is easy. Also ugly" (Amis, *Time's Arrow*, 128). The sentence "*Hier ist kein warum*" comes from Primo Levi's *Survival in Auschwitz*. Levi remembers how, on arriving at the camp, he took an icicle from the cell window and began to suck it in order to quench his thirst. A guard who saw him snatched the icicle from his hands and, when Levi asked why, he answered "*Hier ist kein warum*" (*Survival in Auschwitz: The Nazi Assault on Humanity*, trans. Stuart Woolf, New York: Simon, 1996, 29). To Levi, these words encapsulate the camp's function to diminish the prisoners' humanity by denying their capacity for understanding.

[82] Levinas, "Ethics as First Philosophy", 86.

[83] Amis, *Time's Arrow*, 16.

[84] The unspeakibility of the Holocaust – and other such related tropes, such as its unthinkability, its unrepresentability, etc. – is a notion very much present in writings about the subject, although it must be pointed out that it is not unanimously accepted.

forms to accommodate the mess. Thankfully, there was much poetry after Auschwitz, a terrible episode that tore civilisation apart, but not literature. As Paul Celan puts it, language remained in spite of everything, but:

> ... it had to pass through its own answerlessness, pass through a frightful muting, pass through the thousand darknesses of deathbringing speech. It passed through and gave back no words for that which happened; yet it passed through this happening. Passed through and could come to light again, "enriched" by all this.[85]

Time's Arrow proves that there are themes which, because of their very nature, demand from the novelist a different kind of imaginative and ethical involvement. Thus, the stylistic enrichment that Celan refers to becomes in Amis' novel the result of a conscious attempt to defamiliarise the familiar, giving voice to and requiring of the reader an ethical positioning that, far from being divorced from formal experimentation, turns it into an effective vehicle for revision, reflection and commitment.

In this respect, Michael Rothberg distinguishes two main approaches to the issue, which he calls "realist" and "antirealist". By "realist" he means the claim that the Holocaust can be "apprehended and comprehended according to already established techniques of representation and analysis" (*Traumatic Realism: The Demands of Holocaust Representation*, Minneapolis: University of Minnesota Press, 2000, 3, 5). This is the position of scholars such as Hannah Arendt, Christopher Browning, Michael Marrus, Zygmunt Bauman, etc. Proponents of the "antirealist" tendency include such significant figures as Elie Wiesel, Claude Lanzmann, Arthur Cohen, and Jean-François Lyotard, among others. In different ways, their discourse similarly "detaches the extreme from the everyday and seeks to disable established modes of representation and understanding" (*ibid.*, 5).

[85] Paul Celan, *Selected Poems and Prose of Paul Celan*, trans. John Felstiner, New York: Norton, 2001, 35.

WORLD WAR II FICTION AND THE
ETHICS OF TRAUMA

GERD BAYER

This essay looks at three novels dealing with various traumatic events of World War II: Stephen Fry's *Making History*, John Boyne's *The Boy in the Striped Pyjamas*, and A.L. Kennedy's *Day*.[1] All three authors were born after the end of that war. Nevertheless, they can all be said to work from within the confines of what Marianne Hirsch has called "postmemory",[2] that is, of a second-generation memory that has been passed down from those directly affected by traumatic events. In representing trauma through the aestheticised means of narrative fiction, the authors also comment on possible ethical directions that memory work can take.

As all three texts can be read as attempts to deal more or less directly with post-traumatic stress, it seems promising to focus critical attention on the literary and formal means of representing what probably is one of the most persistent features of Europe's collective memory: the events of World War II. Discussing World War I, Anne Whitehead describes its effect as "collective or cultural haunting".[3] The impact of World War II, one could add, is hardly any less difficult to bear. Yet only one of the novels discussed here, Boyne's *The Boy in the Striped Pyjamas*, can be called a Holocaust novel. The other two authors have chosen other paths to deal with the past: Stephen Fry combines a somewhat science-fiction-inspired plot with questions about the state of historical research and at the same time the

---

[1] Stephen Fry, *Making History*, New York: Random House, 1996; John Boyne, *The Boy in the Striped Pyjamas* (2006), London: Black Swan, 2007; A.L. Kennedy, *Day*, London: Vintage, 2007.

[2] Marianne Hirsch, *Family Frames: Photography, Narrative, and Postmemory*, Cambridge, MA: Harvard University Press, 1997; and "The Generation of Postmemory", *Poetics Today*, XXIX/1 (Spring 2008), 103-28.

[3] Anne Whitehead, *Trauma Fiction*, Edinburgh: Edinburgh University Press, 2004, 7.

limitations of historiography; A.L. Kennedy's novel concentrates on the borderline between victim and perpetrator, in effect raising difficult ethical questions about the military conflict between the Allied Forces and Nazi Germany.

All three authors work within a postmodern aesthetic paradigm, that is to say, they all show a critical awareness of the historicity of facts and the semantically elusive factuality of history. Far from denying the reality of any of the World War II atrocities, these second-generation authors focus on how the memory of these events is treated around the turn of the millennium, thereby following a metahistorical tendency also seen in other contemporary World War II writing.[4] By engaging themselves in the discussions concerning the ethical attitude appropriate for such a difficult historical moment, they point out the moral potential of art. In *Postmodern Ethics*, Zygmunt Bauman argues that postmodernism opens up new opportunities to engage in ethical questions, provided that postmodern philosophy is appreciated as a rigorous intellectual endeavour. Making further assumptions such as the fundamental irrationality of moral judgments,[5] Bauman states that "Morality is incurably *aporetic*"[6] and specifically notes morality's irreconcilability with rationality:

> No logically coherent ethical code can "fit" the essentially ambivalent condition of morality. Neither can rationality 'override' moral impulse; at the utmost, it can silence it and paralyse.[7]

Postmodernism, in contrast with the logocentrism of modernity, allows for a questioning of the crucial tenets of morality: Bauman's *Postmodern Ethics*, therefore, grows from the hope that "the sources of moral power which in modern ethical philosophy and political practice were hidden from sight, may be made visible, while the reasons for their past invisibility can be better understood".[8] Bauman's critique of the traditional concept of humanist morality believes that postmodern fiction can offer insightful illustrations of ethical

---

[4] Dirk Niefanger, "'Wie es gewesen sein wird': Opfer und Täter bei Doron Rabinovici", in *Literatur und Holocaust*, eds Gerd Bayer and Rudolf Freiburg, Würzburg: Königshausen and Neumann, 2008, 193-212.

[5] Zygmunt Bauman, *Postmodern Ethics*, Oxford: Blackwell, 1993, 13.

[6] *Ibid.*, 11 (emphasis in the original).

[7] *Ibid.*, 10.

[8] *Ibid.*, 3.

questions and thereby work against the invisibility of their underlying motivation.

By confronting readers in a rather intimate manner with the ethical dilemmas of the past, authors dealing with World War II topics raise traumatic pasts from their repressed unspeakability. In doing so, they steer their readers in a direction where they have to, firstly, face this past and, secondly, decide about their personal reaction. As the act of reading takes place predominantly in an individual setting, some novels invite their readers to make real the argument presented by Martha Nussbaum in *The Fragility of Goodness*,[9] namely, to formulate individual ethical responses. In this, they also follow Bauman's description of a postmodern ethical decision-making process that demands personal responsibility:

> No universal standards, then. No looking over one's shoulders, to take a glimpse of what other people "like me" do. No listening to what they say they do or ought to be doing – and then following their example, absolving myself for not doing anything else, nothing that others would not do, and enjoying a clear conscience at the end of the day.[10]

So, the moment of reading becomes a potentially ethical situation.

However, not all critics share Bauman's and Nussbaum's optimism about the possible ethical role of art. Even though in *Totality and Infinity* Emmanuel Levinas voices a more sceptical view of art's potential for contributing positively to the engagement with alterity, he also clearly rules out, in an anti-Adornian move, the notion of not responding to the encounter with the Other: "Thus I cannot evade by silence the discourse which the epiphany that occurs as a face opens."[11] His own notion of the Other has nevertheless met with a variety of critical responses. Reacting specifically to Jacques Derrida's critique of *Totality and Infinity*,[12] Levinas includes a more cautious and less positivistic notion of the Other in *Otherwise than Being*, allowing for the elusiveness of the deconstructive process of

---

[9] Martha C. Nussbaum, *The Fragility of Goodness: Luck and Ethics in Greek Tragedy and Philosophy*, Cambridge: Cambridge University Press. 1986.
[10] Bauman, *Postmodern Ethics*, 53.
[11] Emmanuel Levinas, *Totality and Infinity: An Essay on Exteriority* (1961), trans. Alphonso Lingis, London: Kluwer Academic Publishers, 1991, 201.
[12] Robert Eaglestone, *Ethical Criticism: Reading After Levinas*, Edinburgh: Edinburgh University Press, 1997, 129-74.

signification to put into play both the me and its facing of the Other: "In responsibility, the same, the ego, is me, summoned, provoked, as irreplaceable, and thus accused as unique in the supreme passivity of one that cannot slip away without fault."[13] In *Entre Nous*, Levinas restates the inherent alterity of the Other and its remoteness: "In the relation to the Face, what is affirmed is asymmetry; in the beginning, it does not matter who the Other is in relation to me – that is his business."[14] Levinas' notion of the Other as an external catalyst for an ethical response also describes the literary situation, which confronts readers with an inherently other-oriented situation.

But what remains a crucial aspect of this encounter is the risk of the person facing the ethical situation shying away from responding because of the external nature of the Other. Very much aware of this risk, Paul Ricœur, like Derrida, therefore, opposes the extreme alterity of Levinas' moment of ethical confrontation with the face of the Other, what he terms "the hyperbole of separation",[15] arguing instead that it is often from within a person that questions about the rightfulness of action arise. This Heideggerian notion of *Gewissen* (conscience) Ricœur sees as significant motivation that supersedes the dialogic relationship with the Levinasian Other: "In short, is it not necessary that a dialogue superpose a relation on the supposedly absolute distance between the separate I and the teaching Other?"[16] Ricœur in fact opposes both notions of ethical instigation: "To these alternatives – either Heidegger's strange(r)ness or Levinas' externality – I shall stubbornly oppose the original and originary character of what appears to me to constitute the third modality of otherness, namely *being enjoined as the structure of selfhood.*"[17]

Offering substantiations of this dual search for individuality and the connection to the Other as presented by Ricœur, fictionalised versions of the self specifically invite ethical responses. With the novel as literary genre that has, from its earliest days, investigated

---

[13] Emmanuel Levinas, *Otherwise than Being: or, Beyond Essence* (1974), trans. Alphonso Lingis, The Hague: Martinus Nijhoff, 1981, 135.

[14] Emmanuel Levinas, *Entre Nous: On Thinking-of-the-Other*, trans. Michael B. Smith, New York: Columbia University Press, 1998, 122-23.

[15] Paul Ricœur, *Oneself as Another* (1990), trans. Kathleen Blamey, Chicago: University of Chicago Press, 1992, 339.

[16] *Ibid.*, 339, 348; Martin Heidegger, *Being and Time*, trans. John Macquarrie and Edward Robinson, New York: Harper and Row, 1962, 320.

[17] Ricoeur, *Oneself as Another*, 354 (emphasis in the original).

what selfhood and identity might mean at particular moments of time, literature offers precisely the kind of alternative moral sphere of engagement Zygmunt Bauman evokes in his discussion of postmodern ethics, and Paul Ricœur suggests as "the third modality of otherness". In the context of trauma research into literary studies,[18] this ethical mission of fiction speaks directly to trauma's need to find means of representation beyond the literal that nevertheless confront readers with the alterity and the resulting ethical choices.

Emplotment and historical relativism: making history
Stephen Fry takes a rather playful, postmodern approach to the question of how to deal with the historical trauma of World War II. In *Making History*, he uses a what-if scenario as a means of addressing the difficulty of remembering the global consequences of the racist and anti-Semitic ideology of Nazi Germany. The novel is told from the point of view of Michael Young, a doctoral student in history at Cambridge University, who is just about to complete his dissertation on the Hitler family. The narrative opens with him printing out the final copy of his work, and finding out that his girlfriend, Jane, has left him. While on campus to submit his dissertation, Michael meets Professor Zuckermann, a scientist who has developed a kind of time machine that can transport objects to any place at any time. Both men are haunted by the Holocaust, in part due to personal reasons, and they decide to tamper with history: in order to undo the darkest period of human history, they plan to prevent the birth of Adolf Hitler by placing a male contraceptive pill (which they steal from Jane's laboratory) in the Hitler family well.

While the outcome of this experiment in revisionist historiography is more than disappointing (World War II ends with Nazi Germany victorious, led by a different but even more extreme Führer), the novel's more interesting aspect derives from its treatment of history as a type of memory that depends for its content on the willingness of those remembering it. Fry accordingly begins *Making History* with a dream, a kind of tale that from the outset avoids the question of veracity by giving room to personal memories and at the same time

---

[18] Cathy Caruth, *Unclaimed Experience: Trauma, Narrative, and History*, Baltimore, MD: Johns Hopkins University Press, 1996; Dominick LaCapra, *Writing History, Writing Trauma*, Baltimore, MD and London: Johns Hopkins University Press, 2001.

emphasises the creative, or at least productive role of the historiographer:

> It starts with a dream. This story, which can start everywhere and nowhere like a circle, starts, for me – and it is, after all, my story and no one else's, never could be anyone else's but mine – it starts with a dream I dreamed one night in May.[19]

Similarly to Hayden White, who describes the active structuring of archival historical data through the historian's process of emplotment,[20] Fry presents history as first and foremost a personal story.

The dream, not surprisingly, deals with the rather intimate and highly emotional relationship between the protagonist and his lover, Jane. The active search to restructure reality after the loss of Jane is reminiscent of the traditional process of avoidance that marks one crucial aspect of trauma.[21] Michael, the apprentice historian, states early in the novel his belief in the disconnection between truth and history. Reflecting on his own process of inventing and changing the past, he comes up with two basic axioms:

> *A: None of what follows ever happened.*
> *B: All of what follows is entirely true.*[22]

The truth-value of personal memory, grown from traumatic experiences of the individual or of society as a whole, sits alongside the archive. Not surprisingly, Michael's dissertation does not meet with approval. His supervisor in fact rejects it due to its lack of scientific, historical scholarship, saying: "It's not an academic argument, it's a *novel* and a perfectly disgusting one at that."[23] Echoing Hayden White, Michael openly admits to having actively emplotted his work. Responding to the accusation that he does not provide sources for some of his statements, he states: "No, well, those

---

[19] Fry, *Making History*, 3.

[20] Hayden White, *Tropics of Discourse: Essays in Cultural Criticism*, Baltimore, MD: Johns Hopkins University Press, 1978, 96.

[21] Shoshana Felman and Dori Laub, *Testimony: Crises of Witnessing in Literature, Psychoanalysis and History*, New York and London: Routledge, 1992.

[22] Fry, *Making History*, 6 (emphasis in the original).

[23] *Ibid.*, 64 (emphasis in the original).

are just linking passages. I agree they are unorthodox, but I thought they lent ... you know ... color and drama."[24] What he does in his dissertation is to combine his statements A and B, presenting what "Never happened" as "entirely true".[25] His idiosyncratic attitude towards representations of reality, like that of Zuckermann, stems from traumatic experiences.

While Michael's obsession with Nazi Germany derives from his dual failure as historian and lover, Zuckermann's ties to the Holocaust are more personal. When he first shows Michael his time machine, which works like a surveillance camera that can move through time and space, they look at Auschwitz on 9 October 1942, one day after his father's arrival at the concentration camp. Zuckermann admits that he always returns to this place and moment in time, drawn to it due to his personal memory. However, even though he knows he is looking at the correct day and place, the data he receives are incomprehensible to him, making it impossible to understand the past. Even though he can decode some of the chemical and physical properties of the image, the general meaning remains elusive:

> "The colors have a relation to elements. Oxygen is blue, hydrogen red, nitrogen green and so on. But that tells me nothing."[26]

His encounter with the image of his own father, who is genetically speaking partly himself and simultaneously another, fails to provide him with the answers to his own questions of guilt and loss. Through this constellation the novel partly implies that his attempt to reconnect to a traumatic past proves inefficient if not outright wrong: the information Zuckermann would like to gain from his look into the past – what happened to his father after his arrival in Auschwitz – cannot be retrieved using his scientific and logical method. Fry follows a strategy of nescience that Cathy Caruth has presented as typical of the aesthetic treatment of traumatic pasts. In her discussion of Claude Lanzmann's film *Shoah*, based on his own testimony about the production process, Caruth notes that Lanzmann thinks of his inability to understand the Holocaust as a necessary precondition for his cinematic work: "The act of refusal, here, is therefore not a denial of a

---

[24] *Ibid.*, 65.
[25] *Ibid.*, 6.
[26] *Ibid.*, 88.

knowledge of the past, but rather a way of gaining access to a knowledge that has not yet attained the form of 'narrative memory'."[27] By re-writing and thereby changing history, Zuckermann and Michael strive to make narratable what hitherto remained decidedly traumatic and hence beyond the reach of traditional forms of representation, both historical and scientific. Needless to say, their project, finds its equivalent in the novel that contains their tale (and also some of the more fictional parts of Michael's dissertation).

Making History, in typical Fry fashion, blends realistic and fantastic features, in this case a historical novel with science fiction. The active making of history in which Michael and Zuckermann engage can be read as Fry's comment about the impossibility of comprehending the past. Their attempt at changing the past is shown to bear unexpected and unwanted consequences that speak, implicitly, about the inherent resistance of the past to yield to the explicatory need of constitutive memory. As Shoshana Felman and Dori Laub have shown throughout their influential study *Testimony*, the truth value of traumatic memory is tied more to the process of repression and reconstitutive justification than to absolute identity of memory with historical facts. Accordingly, Fry's novel does not misrepresent the facts of Nazism and its horrendous deeds, but rather engages in an aesthetic representation of the process of traumatic memory. In doing so, it echoes novels such as Anne Michaels' *Fugitive Pieces*, or Jonathan Safran Foer's *Everything Is Illuminated*,[28] which also approach the Holocaust by applying narrative techniques that address the elusiveness of the process of remembering.[29]

Fry's mixing-in of questions regarding sexual identity, specifically the coming-out of Michael following his acquaintance with Steve Burns, complicates his novel's ethical complexity further. But just as his dystopian vision of a highly conservative and restrictive USA serves to address the continuing discrimination against homosexuality, so his novel comments on the lasting pervasiveness of supposedly past

[27] Cathy Caruth, "Recapturing the Past; Introduction", in *Trauma: Explorations in Memory*, ed. Cathy Caruth, Baltimore, MD: Johns Hopkins University Press, 1995, 155.

[28] Anne Michaels, *Fugitive Pieces* (1996), London: Bloomsbury, 1998; Jonathan Safran Foer, *Everything Is Illuminated*, London: Penguin, 2003.

[29] For a further discussion of these issues, see Whitehead, *Trauma Fiction*, and Gerd Bayer, "Der Holocaust als Metapher in postmodernen und postkolonialen Romanen", in *Literatur und Holocaust*, 267-90.

injustices. Even though *Making History* does not imply that late twentieth-century homophobia equals the anti-Semitism of Nazi Germany, the novel nevertheless alerts readers to the fact that any tendency to remove evil to a closed and concluded past falls short of the ethical demands of literature. The acute presence of Zuckermann's World War II trauma, the sci-fi device of time travel, and the evocation of contemporary areas of discrimination combine to create an effect that places wrong-doing within a timelessness that transcends forgetting. The novel's concluding statement – "let's go out there and dance"[30] – can only be said by someone like newly translocated Steve Burns, who knows from personal experience that injustice persists. When Michael expresses his frustration over the power of history to shed light on the past – "Sick of history. History sucks. It sucks."[31] – and as a consequence deletes his dissertation, he nevertheless takes comfort in the thought that any "nerd from the computing department could always rescue it if I changed my mind".[32] Michael's attitude shows that he has started to understand that the past cannot be deleted (or tampered with), but rather that the repressed content of traumatic memory will eventually break through, forcing people to engage on an ethical level when faced with their content.

One further reason why Michael considers saving his dissertation might be its aesthetic value as a narrative that, even though it fails to represent historical facts, nevertheless sheds light on the significance of the past. Michael's historical recreations in fact survive as those chapters in Fry's novel that describe the relationship of Hitler's parents, for instance "The smell of rats",[33] or "We Germans".[34] Through their focus on the perpetrators they remind readers that the Holocaust was by no means the result of abstract historical circumstances, but rather the active doing of individuals. Even though *Making History* blatantly evades truth, it confronts readers with the need to think ethically about the role of the past in the present.

---

[30] Fry, *Making History*, 380.
[31] *Ibid.*, 374.
[32] *Ibid.*, 376.
[33] *Ibid.*, 11-13.
[34] *Ibid.*, 19-20.

An allegory of evil: *The Boy in the Striped Pyjamas*
Fry's skilled avoidance of historical fact speaks to the unrepresentable
nature of the Holocaust trauma: the same strategy is at work in John
Boyne's *The Boy in the Striped Pyjamas*. On the title page of the
book, the title is followed by the statement "a fable", a literary form
that, according to Bruno Bettelheim, "always explicitly states a moral
truth".[35] By referring so directly to a genre that furthermore is
characterised by its resorting to a decidedly non-realistic mimesis,
Boyne implies that his book should be read as an allegory. By inviting
his readers not to rely on the actual truth-value of his text, he
implicitly shifts the burden to the significance of his aesthetic
representation of the Holocaust. Narrated from a clearly non-
omniscient third-person narrative point of view, in a distant voice
similar to that of fairy tales and other traditional narratives, *The Boy in
the Striped Pyjamas* refuses to engage in the retrospective speculation
that marks Fry's novel. Boyne does not directly bring up the question
of how later generations should grapple with the actual facts of past
events; rather, he narrows his focus on an almost timeless
constellation of moral conflict – the question of whether people might
rethink their attitudes once they are turned into the victims of their
own crime. Taking on an almost childlike innocence, and echoing to
some degree Imre Kertész' novel *Fateless*, or Mark Twain's anti-
racist novel *The Adventures of Huckleberry Finn*,[36] Boyne's fable
approaches the Nazi concentration camp as if nothing were known
about its perverted inner workings. By making the well-known facts
different – that is, by using the technique of defamiliarisation –
Boyne's novel invites readers, just as in Martin Amis' *Time's Arrow*,[37]
to face the unspeakable as if encountered for the first time, and, as a
consequence, guides its readers towards an ethical engagement with
the Other.

From its very beginning, the novel is nevertheless fraught with a
sense of doom. The opening scene presents a rather confused and
angry Bruno, who has just found out that his family is leaving Berlin

---

[35] Bruno Bettelheim, *The Uses of Enchantment: The Meaning and Importance of Fairy Tales*, New York: Vintage, 1977, 42-43.
[36] Imre Kertész, *Fateless* (1975), trans. Christopher C. Wilson and Katharina M. Wilson, Evanston, WY: Northwestern University Press, 1992; Mark Twain, *The Adventures of Huckleberry Finn* (1884), New York: Modern Library, 1993.
[37] Martin Amis, *Time's Arrow, or: The Nature of the Offence*, London: Cape, 1991.

because his father, as soon becomes clear, has just been promoted to run a concentration camp that Bruno will always refer to as "Out-With", implicitly admitting to the impossibility of speaking the name of Auschwitz. By limiting the narration to the level of understanding that little Bruno has, the text for a long time avoids addressing the actual horror of its setting. At the same time, it is Bruno's very lack of comprehension that alludes to the horror of the novel's circumstances: when his mother explains to him the reason for the family's sudden departure, they go to the dining room, "where the Fury had been to dinner the week before".[38] By referring to Hitler, the "Führer", with the near-homophonous word "fury", the novel uses Bruno's intuitive reaction to his environment as a means of addressing directly the actual significance of Hitler, the concentration camps, and the Holocaust. The continuation of this scene also makes clear that it is not just the child who comprehends the horror of Nazism, but the mother as well. Bruno's description of his mother's mindset, though wrongly interpreted by him, nevertheless reveals the state of her own emotions:

> He looked at her without saying anything for a moment and thought to himself that she couldn't have applied her make-up correctly that morning because the rims of her eyes were more red than usual, like his own after he'd been causing chaos and got into trouble and ended up crying.[39]

Already at this early stage of the novel, the connection between one's behaviour and the resulting moral consequences are clearly addressed: Bruno knows that his crying is usually connected to some earlier misbehaviour. For him, "crying" is the logical consequence of "causing chaos". This firm belief in the power of poetic justice also works as a moment of foreshadowing: at the end of the novel, Bruno's father will at first desperately search for his son, then he will slowly understand that his own machinery of destruction has killed Bruno and, finally, he will guiltily acquiesce in his own death. Having personally suffered the consequences of his brutal ideology, he is ultimately taken away by some officials, to be court-martialled, one assumes, for the breach of procedure or maybe even for his newly-

---

[38] Boyne, *The Boy in the Striped Pyjamas*, 2.
[39] *Ibid.*, 3.

found ethical insight into the wrongness of his own doing. He has at last come to acknowledge his own culpability and, therefore, "didn't really mind what they did to him any more".[40]

Like Stephen Fry's Zuckermann, who faces himself in the search for his father, Bruno's father begins to think ethically when faced with the death of his son. Given the close family connection of those concerned, the ethical moment in both novels derives not so much from Levinas' absolute Other, but rather from Ricœur's encounter with oneself as another. It is the inner working of conscience more than the confrontation with alterity that gives rise to the realisation that ethical thinking cannot be bypassed. In fact, Boyne tries to avoid the showing of victims in his novel, which might be due to respect and an understanding that the presentation of suffering has the potential, as Adorno has pointed out,[41] to repeat victimisation. It is, therefore, only appropriate that Bruno's first encounter with the Other, in the person of the assumedly Jewish waiter Pavel, should present alterity as essentially enigmatic. When Bruno hurts himself while playing, it is Pavel who dresses his wounds and finally admits to being a doctor.[42]

Pavel's Jewishness remains incomprehensible to Bruno, as does the reason why he is interned in the camp. Bruno's naïve view of the world frames Pavel as an oddity – a waiter who is a doctor who is a waiter – and thereby disqualifies him from being the face of Levinas' Other. At the end of this scene, Bruno's mother, afraid of her husband's reaction, instructs Pavel not to mention his help, claiming instead that she tended Bruno's wounds. When Bruno considers her action to be "selfish",[43] his view implies that Pavel should not be treated differently from any other person. Bruno's friendship with a little Jewish boy, whom he meets at the camp's fence, shares the same purpose – to normalise the victims and to refrain from turning them into the remote Other whose essential strangeness might leave us unmoved. Hence the evil presented in the text falls back directly on the reader.

Boyne's novel points to a central ethical decision to be made concerning the wrongness of the Holocaust. To follow Alain Badiou's

---

[40] *Ibid.*, 215.
[41] Theodor W. Adorno, "Kulturkritik und Gesellschaft", in *Gesammelte Schriften*, ed. Rolf Tiedemann, Frankfurt am Main: Suhrkamp, 1997, Vol. X, Part 1, 11-30.
[42] Boyne, *The Boy in the Striped Pyjamas*, 82.
[43] *Ibid.*, 85.

argument about the essence of evil, the realisation of Bruno's father concerning the inherent wrongness of his doing results from the conflict "between 'Keep going!' proposed by the ethic of this truth, and the logic of the 'perseverance in being' of the mere mortal that I am".[44] Boyne's novel, however, turns Badiou's argument upside down, not by having evil confront ethical truth with the violence of mortality, but rather by confronting evil with the fatal consequences of its inner logic. The novel reveals racism as being a "simulacrum",[45] an event based on supposedly legitimate grounds that are nevertheless not built on truth. Boyne's generic choice of the fable echoes this ethical reversal by applying a highly fantastic mode to a decidedly realistic and historical topic.

His generic choice possibly follows a second purpose, relating to the reader's expectations of the fairy tale or fable, which, it may be assumed, will be marked by strong emotions. The willingness to engage oneself with the potentially didactic moment of a fable predisposes readers in such a way that the content of the fable will be retained longer. As Aleida Assmann argues, "Affect works as a magnifier of perception",[46] thereby influencing positively the retention of particular memories. For both these reasons, Boyne's novel could be seen as a literary realisation of Martha Nussbaum's claim, in *Poetic Justice* and elsewhere,[47] that aesthetic texts can positively contribute to the understanding of complex ethical questions. By directly involving his readers as citizens in the fable and therewith eliciting an "emotional response",[48] Boyne builds on his text's generic capacity as a fable to invite his readers' ethical judgment. In so doing he writes precisely the kind of novel that Nussbaum has in mind when she describes, as source of ethical readings, "a reflexive dialogue between the intuitions and beliefs of the interlocutor, or reader, and a series of complex ethical conceptions, presented for exploration".[49] By limiting

---

[44] Alain Badiou, *Ethics: An Essay on the Understanding of Evil* (1993), trans. Peter Hallward, London: Verso, 2001, 78.

[45] *Ibid.*, 72-77.

[46] Aleida Assmann, "Three Stabilizers of Memory: Affect – Symbol – Trauma", in *Sites of Memory in American Literature and Culture*, ed. Udo J. Hebel, Heidelberg: Winter, 2003, 29.

[47] Martha C. Nussbaum, *Poetic Justice: The Literary Imagination and the Public Life*, Boston: Beacon, 1995, 65.

[48] Nussbaum, *The Fragility of Goodness*, 37.

[49] Boyne, *The Boy in the Striped Pyjamas*, 10.

itself to the uncanny incomprehension of a child, the novel speaks directly to that unique feature of literature that Nussbaum sees in its capacity for "awakening us to a range of ethical possibilities".[50]

The presence of the past: *Day*

The novels by Stephen Fry and John Boyne employ an intentionally alienated representation of World War II traumas, thereby alluding to the essential elusiveness and unrepresentability of such painful pasts. Abandoning realism for a fantastic mimesis is not the only possibility. However, A.L. Kennedy has opted for a different aesthetic format in her novel *Day*. Eponymously named after its protagonist, Alfred F. Day, the novel smoothly interconnects Day's painful memories of his service as a tail-gunner on a British bomber plane during World War II and his intentional return to the past by means of work as an extra on a film set that recreates part of his personal life story, namely, his time in a German prisoner-of-war camp. The initial and dominant narrative point of view of *Day* is a detached omniscience that uses the narrative past: the novel begins by stating in a rather detached and authorial tone that "Alfred was growing a moustache".[51] However, much of the narrative consists of Day's present-tense comments on his experience, narrated in the second person; the concluding sections of the novel move into the present tense and then even into a future tense that clearly indicates Day's need to think not just about the past but also to live in his present and to reflect about his future. The second-person segments, at times bordering on interior monologue, allow insight into Day's inner life and reveal that his war memories continue to dominate his life.

As Alfred's last name already indicates, Kennedy's novel plays with the elusive uniqueness of any specific day, making everyman Day stand in for an everyday man. In fact, the novel often remains intentionally vague about whether any specific passage deals with Day's past in the war or his present environment on the film set. Complementing this spatial indeterminacy, any single day seems to be permanently at risk of being invaded by past memories. The very idea

---

[50] Martha Nussbaum, "Exactly and Responsibly: A Defence of Ethical Criticism", in *Mapping the Ethical Turn: A Reader in Ethics, Culture, and Literary Theory*, eds Todd F. Davis and Kenneth Womack, Charlottesville: University Press of Virginia, 2001, 74.
[51] Kennedy, *Day*, 1.

of the pastness of the past evaporates in the omnipresence of memories that interconnect historical moments and thereby make present those aspects of the past that Day has not yet successfully worked through. Kennedy's work is, therefore, not so much a novel about the war, but rather an investigation into memory and the burden of trauma. By switching into and out of italicised passages, the text shows Day's endless and often painful self-questioning; for him, history is severely unresolved and therefore in permanent need of renegotiation.

The narrative fragmentation in *Day* directly represents the state of Day's traumatised and as a consequence severely split personality:

> You could dodge certain thoughts, corkscrew off and get yourself out of their way, but they'd still hunt you.
> *You have to watch.*
> This morning he could feel them, inside and out, bad thoughts getting clever with him, sly. They lapped like dirtied water behind his face and outside him they thickened the breeze until the surface touched him, pressing his lips, was far more quick and complex than only air.[52]

Day's concern that the past does "still hunt" him and his resulting feeling that he needs to move cautiously and "*watch*" out, testify to the fact that his personal way of dealing with the past is determined by evasion ("dodge certain thoughts") of something unpleasant ("bad thoughts" and "dirtied water"). This connection confirms the statements by Felman and Laub in *Testimony* that traumatic events can lead to a second experience of victimization if they are not worked through by means of narration. In the chapter "An Event without a Witness", Dori Laub states that "survivors who do not tell their story become victims of a distorted memory ... which causes an endless struggle with and over a delusion".[53] For Day, the search for a strategy that helps him overcome his own trauma remains for the most part futile. Even though he clearly desires a more peaceful state of mind, he also admits to himself that such an escape, at the beginning of the novel, exists solely on an imaginary level: "A man had to imagine he'd got a chance at freedom, a bit of peace."[54] A more tangible sense

---

[52] *Ibid.*, 2 (emphasis in the original).
[53] Felman and Laub, *Testimony*, 79.
[54] Kennedy, *Day*, 2.

of liberation only materialises towards the end of the narrative when
Day starts to verbalise his childhood memories of domestic violence
and to face his own culpability. The constructed return to a repressed
past through the artificiality of cinema serves exactly this purpose: one
expectation Day has for taking part in the filming is that it might offer
him an opportunity to "tunnel right through to the place where he'd
lost himself". [55]

Day's own painful ethical struggle with responsibility reaches its
climax when he tries to convince the film producer Ferguson that one
of the other extras, a man named Vasyl, should be handed over to
authorities because of crimes he committed on the German side during
World War II. Day's concerns are not shared, however; and what is
worse, the response he receives emphasises the fact that racism was
not defeated by the Allied Forces. Day's ethical request is denied by
Ferguson, who uses exactly the kind of racist rhetoric that Nazi
Germany propagated:

> You have to remember, Mr Day, that Britain lost a great many people
> in the last war. Almost four hundred thousand dead, hundreds of
> thousands seriously disabled. We need population. We need a healthy
> birth rate and good stock. Now either that comes from the colonies
> and refugees whose cultures are very unlike our own, or we take in
> lads like your Vasyl, who were misled in their youth, and we live in a
> country which stays Christian and white.

Alfred clearly disagrees: his "Fuck you" fails to upset Mr Ferguson,
though, leading Alfred to question his whole involvement with World
War II: "*Maybe I never did exactly know what I was fighting for, but it
fucking wasn't that.*"[56]

During the same evening, the last on the film set, everybody is
celebrating by performing songs or telling jokes. When it is Alfred's
turn, he sings "Jerusalem", the title that William Blake's famous poem
– beginning "And did those feet in ancient time" – took on when sung
as the patriotic anthem composed by Hubert Parry in 1916. Day
presents the song in memory of all his fellow crew members who did
not survive the war. As he sings, with his eyes closed, he imagines
that nobody died, that "they are well and never were harmed and

---

[55] *Ibid.*, 35.
[56] *Ibid.*, 263 (emphasis in the original).

never were frightened, never lost".[57] And in a cathartic moment that brings him to tears, Alfred almost begins to envision his own fate as moving beyond guilt: "And he can believe that he is forgiven"[58] – a statement that tellingly comes not directly from Day but from the authorial narrator. Even though the song meets with mixed reactions, some singing along, others leaving the room, the novel does not directly discuss the inherent criticism of the poem, in particular in light of the events that traumatised Day. Earlier in the novel, Day remembers singing the song with his comrade Pluckrose and, as a consequence, gives another rendition of it on the film set:[59] he stops, however, during the lines that too closely remind him of the aerial bombardment of civilian targets, namely: "*Bring me my spears, oh clouds unfold / Bring me my chariot of fire.*" As Day becomes aware of "the burning you remember tumbling open under your eyes",[60] he quits singing, probably considering the significance of Blake describing England, earlier in the poem, as "dark Satanic Mills".[61]

By using a popular wartime anthem as a denunciation of excessive nationalism, Kennedy follows Virginia Woolf's strategy in *To the Lighthouse*, when she relates Lord Tennyson's "The Charge of the Light Brigade" to a condemnation of the mass slaughter of soldiers during World War I.[62] Through this intertextual reference, Kennedy evokes the questioning that often afterwards challenges the official war rhetoric, thereby giving voice to a feeling of ethical unease in a war's aftermath. Writing about Pat Barker's World War I fiction, John Brannigan points out that: "History, after the Great War ... is constantly striving to regenerate the past."[63] Kennedy's renegotiation of the flawed idealism surrounding some wars, thus, continues a tradition of critical engagements with the ethics of politics that goes

---

[57] *Ibid.*, 268.

[58] *Ibid.*, 268.

[59] *Ibid.*, 80-81.

[60] *Ibid.*, 81 (emphasis in the original; for some reason, Kennedy or her characters misquote Blake's text: "Bring me my Spear: O clouds unfold!").

[61] William Blake, *Poetry and Prose of William Blake*, ed. Geoffrey Keynes, London: Nonesuch Library, 1956, 375.

[62] Virginia Woolf, *To the Lighthouse* (1927), London: Penguin, 2000, 21.

[63] John Brannigan, "Pat Barker's Regeneration Trilogy: History and the Hauntological Imagination", in *Contemporary British Fiction*, eds Richard J. Lane, Rod Mengham, and Philip Tew, Cambridge: Polity, 2003, 24.

back at least as far as Thomas Hobbes' *Leviathan* (1651) and also shapes many dystopias of the twentieth century.

The reference to Blake suggests a related heuristic motivation, in particular when Blake is approached in the manner that Geoffrey Hartman suggests. Taking Blake's phantasmagorias as aesthetic representations of traumatic experiences, Hartman argues that such reworking results from "a repetitious nightmare purging itself of internalized or institutionalized superstitions".[64] Hartman goes on to insist that such transposed re-enactments aim to provide us, in Lacanian terms, with an "encounter with the real".[65] Aesthetic representations of traumatic events serve a particularly useful purpose in allowing the readers (and often the authors as well) to approach precisely the kind of memory that stays beyond cognition: "Literary knowledge ... finds this 'real,' identifies with it, and can even bring it back."[66] In the case of Kennedy's novel, the singing of "Jerusalem" has exactly this effect on Day: it enables him to access his buried trauma and to reconfigure it in a way that is unrestricted by what Hartman terms "institutionalized superstitions". By admitting to himself that the war he participated in was not necessarily fought in a manner that agreed with its overall status as a highly justified intervention, Day can begin to shed his traumatic guilt.

Day's flight back to Britain completes his traumatic reliving of his own past. As he enters the plane, he automatically aims for the gunner's turret, only to be questioned by an official. After some explanations, he ends up flying in his old seat, looking out of the window as if it were a window into his own past. The vision he remembers, of "the bombed thing that was Germany", implicitly presents his feelings of shame caused by the brutality of the bombardment: "As if the cities had been eaten, as if something unnatural had fed on them until they were gashes and shells and staring spaces, as if it was still down there like a plague in the dust."[67] Day's moment of ethical reckoning derives from a confrontation with his own conscience, and not from an encounter with the Other as victim. By understanding that his guilt does not preclude him from

---

[64] Geoffrey Hartman, "On Traumatic Knowledge and Literary Studies", *New Literary History*, XXVI/3 (Summer 1995), 538.
[65] *Ibid.*, 539.
[66] *Ibid.*, 540.
[67] Kennedy, *Day*, 271.

being also a victim, he finally confronts the Other within himself and thereby starts the process of healing.

As a consequence of this, Day's feelings of personal guilt are put into perspective by the realisation that the horrors of his war experience were not caused by individual shortcomings but rather stem from an inherently immoral war apparatus that disregards ethical questions. Kennedy's book exonerates the everyman Day and simultaneously indicts those social forces that instigated or at least remained quiet about the brutality of the aerial bombardment. By finally facing the source of his trauma, through the means of art (in his case, cinematic recreation), Day transcends his painful past; and the readers, ideally, question the ethics of war. While Kennedy's novel and its critique of the British bombardment of Germany, should in no way be construed as forwarding a neo-fascist apology of Nazism, it can easily be read in the context of the early twenty-first century war-on-terror, the doctrine of pre-emptive strikes and its accompanying indifference to civilian casualties and the Geneva Code. For instance, when Day becomes a prisoner-of-war, the German interrogators question whether he is a "*terror Flieger*", the text thereby alluding to the 9/11 attacks on New York. Day's own memories of the interrogation express his sense of disorientation and suspicion that he was not treated according to the international agreements concerning captives during a war:

> Dulag Luft: that should be where you're taken, but you don't think you're there. This wouldn't happen there. They don't say where you are and you can't see. There's only this room and the next.
> You haven't been processed, or given a number, or given shoes. There's only this room and the next.[68]

As detainee in a quasi-legal camp, blindfolded and disoriented, Day and his situation evoke images of tortured prisoners in secret-service detention centres designed to bypass legal codes. The ethical dimension alludes, via the reader, to the present.

Representing ethical traumas

The three novels discussed here all approach the aesthetic representation of traumatic pasts as opportunities for confronting

---

[68] *Ibid.*, 253.

readers with ethical situations that demand their response. As befits postmodern writers, they proceed in a rather indirect manner, thereby drawing on art's unique power of evoking what cannot be directly presented. Writing about the "festering wound"[69] of trauma and its relationship to psychoanalysis, Harold Bloom points out that the significance of Sigmund Freud's mythological philosophising, as limited and unscientific as it might be, lies with its unrelenting willingness to address traumatic and therefore unspeakable memories: "Freud's peculiar strength was to say what could not be said, or at least to attempt to say it, thus refusing to be silent in the face of the unsayable."[70] The same holds true for the novels discussed here: by reinventing the trauma of World War II, more specifically by putting into narrative and thereby aestheticising its memory, the authors aim to give voice to the experience of the unspeakable. Even by speaking untruthfully, at least as far as positivist historical knowledge is concerned, they insist on the necessity not to commit the past to forgetfulness, but rather to make room for the "plea by an other who is asking to be seen and heard",[71] even if that Other, to follow Ricœur, often enough turns out to be oneself.

Parallel to Roger Luckhurst's claim that trauma theory is "symptomatic rather than diagnostic",[72] one could argue that literary works dealing with traumatic events refrain from offering comprehensive answers to the ethical dilemmas that surround not so much the traumatic events but the strategies of memorizing them. By focusing instead on the symptoms and by offering figural, narrative, or simply aesthetic representations of the traumatic situation, novels of the kind discussed in this chapter form part of a movement within contemporary British fiction that uses real-world references, albeit often coded in highly imaginative forms, as a means to address ethical issues that lie beyond the ludic autopoiesis with which criticism has often, if sometimes unfairly, labelled postmodern literature.

---

[69] Lawrence L. Langer, *Holocaust Testimonies: The Ruins of Memory*, New Haven, Conn: Yale University Press, 1991, 92.
[70] Harold Bloom, "Freud: Frontier Concepts, Jewishness, and Interpretation", in *Trauma: Explorations in Memory*, 113.
[71] Caruth, *Unclaimed Experience*, 9.
[72] Roger Luckhurst, "Mixing Memory and Desire: Psychoanalysis, Psychology, and Trauma Theory", in *Literary Theory and Criticism: An Oxford Guide*, ed. Patricia Waugh, Oxford: Oxford University Press, 2006, 504.

A TERRIBLE BEAUTY: ETHICS, AESTHETICS AND THE TRAUMA OF GAYNESS IN ALAN HOLLINGHURST'S *THE LINE OF BEAUTY*

JOSÉ M. YEBRA

Ethics, aesthetics and the representation of truth in trauma fiction
Michael Eskin's influential article "On Literature and Ethics"[1] is introduced by Plato's phrase from *The Republic*: "They cite poets as witnesses." The quotation points to the inextricable relationship between aesthetics and ethics. In Todorov's view, the relationship between these two discourses has undergone a complex historical evolution that he summarises in three subsequent theories. The first or classical theory "considers art in the service of moral principles, and argues that aesthetic values should be subjected to ethical values". The second was inaugurated by Romanticism. Reversing the classics' standpoint, the Romantics considered that "poetry should have the privilege over morality, and art the privilege over life".[2] According to Todorov, the exaltation of the subject over the community characteristic of Romanticism lies at the heart of the early nineteenth-century transvaluation from ethics to aesthetics – a stance that has never completely disappeared since then. In the light of this, Todorov laments the current dominance of spectacular aesthetics over ethics in turn-of-the-millennium democratic societies[3] while, at the same time, he points out an increasing autonomy of both ethics and aesthetics as the main characteristic of the third stage in the evolution of aesthetic

---

[1] Michael Eskin, "On Literature and Ethics", *Poetics Today: Literature and Ethics*, XXV/4 (Winter 2004), 573-95.
[2] Valentina Adami, *Trauma Studies and Literature: Martin Amis's* Time's Arrow *as Trauma Fiction*, Frankfurt am Main: Peter Lang, 2008, 50.
[3] Tzvetan Todorov, "Poetry and Morality", *Salgamundi*, CXI (Summer 1996), trans. John Anzalone, 71.

theory.[4] It is evident that beautiful art works can hide despicable moral messages and positions, and that ethically commendable ones can be poorly crafted.

However, the current debate is much more complex, as shown by critics like Michael Eskin, Robert Eaglestone or J. Hillis Miller, who have undertaken a thorough revision of the relationship between the two disciplines or discourses. Deconstructionists consider that acts such as writing and reading, rather than (or apart from) content, have ethical implications worth noting, even though, in their view, literary texts cannot render testimony to the "world outside", since "the passage from world to text is far from straightforward".[5] This divergence between lived experience and text problematises the function of the reader and/or critic, justifies Hillis Miller's concept of "undecidability" or "unreadability", and determines Cathy Caruth's trauma theory as described in *Unclaimed Experience*.[6] By contrast, as Eaglestone explains, neo-humanist thinkers, "championed by Wayne Booth (1988), Martha Nussbaum (1990) and more recently … Adriana Caverero … argue that literary texts are an effective and acute form of moral reasoning and as such can be used to heighten our ethical awareness". These critics still rely on a classic mimeticism that considers the literary text as analogous to reality and capable of interfering with it. In these circumstances, "the narrative content (including, often, the form as content) adds to our lives, reflects our lives, and by our thinking through, or living through, these texts, we are forcefully reminded of our ethical responsibilities".[7] However, as poststructuralists cogently argue, this neo-humanist outlook is rather problematic, for, how could literature reach reality in unmediated form? And, if art solves real ethical issues, where does the autonomy of the aesthetic discourse lie?[8]

Much has been said on Ludwig Wittgenstein's famous contention in his *Tractatus Logico-Philosophicus* (1921) that "Ethics and

---

[4] Adami, *Trauma Studies and Literature*, 50.
[5] Robert Eaglestone, "One and the Same? Ethics, Aesthetics and Truth", *Poetics Today: Literature and Ethics*, XXV/4 (Winter 2004), 605.
[6] Cathy Caruth, *Unclaimed Experience: Trauma, Narrative, and History*, Baltimore: John Hopkins University Press, 1996.
[7] Eaglestone, "One and the Same?", 602.
[8] *Ibid.*, 603.

Aesthetics are one and the same".[9] Eaglestone is particularly insightful in his analysis of this affirmation since he aims at deconstructing the apparently simplistic identification of both discursive practices that some critics find in the *Tractatus*. Still, as Eskin admits, they are undeniably interrelated: "Literature could be viewed as ethics in the second degree, as ethics of ethics or criticism of ethics, as that discourse which literally interprets ethics."[10] Likewise, as Adami recalls, Todorov delimits the separation between both domains arguing that:

> ... poets accomplish their moral duty by producing beautiful, meaningful work: poetry contributes to improving the world by adding beauty to it, and by making it more intelligible and richer in meaning .... What we expect from the greatest creators is ... the capacity for understanding and for making us understand even the most inhuman designs.[11]

Todorov's words can be misleading in that they take for granted the moral (rather than the ethical) duty of poets. However, the critic is not supporting the thesis of traditional humanists, who see the "literary text as an immediately accessible and univocal recipient and transmitter of basic human values with 'the capacity to exert a powerful influence on the quality and content of our own lives'".[12]

Nineteenth-century realist writers aimed at transmitting a number of allegedly universal values, which they labelled as ethical, but in fact responded to the predominant moral values of patriarchal society. As thinkers like Geoffrey Galt Harpham and Andrew Gibson have pointed out, this set of values, transmissible to and through the literary canon, does not make up ethics, but morality.[13] These and other

---

[9] Kathrin Stengel, "Ethics as Style: Wittgenstein's Aesthetic Ethics and Ethical Aesthetics", *Poetics Today: Literature and Ethics*, XXV/4 (Winter 2004), 609-26.
[10] Eskin, "On Literature and Ethics", 587.
[11] Todorov, "Poetry and Morality", 51.
[12] Susana Onega, "The Ethics of Fiction: Writing, Reading and Representation in Contemporary Narrative in English: A Research Project", in *Literatures in English. Priorities of Research*, eds Wolfgang Zach and Michael Kenneally, Tübingen: Stauffenburg, 58.
[13] *Ibid.*, 59.

poststructuralist critics have attempted to theorise the differences between both. Summarily stated, their main tenet is that:

> [Ethics] precedes morality and, by questioning it, keeps morality permanently open, allowing for the unearthing of the *aporias* on which morality is grounded. From this perspective, ethics becomes the register of the unutterable and unrepresentable.[14]

As suggested in these lines, the ethical transcends the pragmatic character and literalness conferred on the moral, and remains a discursive practice whose interaction with reality is particularly problematic. This is particularly the case when trauma is concerned. The moralistic readings of classic humanist critics cannot render the unutterability of trauma, so that an ethics of reading is required instead. In fact, since, according to Wittgenstein, literature (as an aesthetic phenomenon) and ethics are analogous non-referential discourses, they support each other rhetorically in trauma fiction, that is, the literary narration of a trauma requires the ethical commitment of the reader.

With all this in mind, Todorov's words ask for a nuanced interpretation. It is true that, even contemporary postmodernist novels occasionally reflect, censor and attempt to correct immoral behaviour in a rather naturalistic way. For example, the discriminatory politics and double morality of Thatcherism are overtly denounced in Alan Hollinghurst's *The Line of Beauty*.[15] However, the occasional moral undertones of some postmodernist novels cannot change the world these texts make reference to, as neo-humanists believe. These novels foster instead an ethical reading, which, as we will see, implicates the reader beyond sheer moral concerns. Without downplaying the writing process – that is, the poets' capacity for understanding and aestheticising traumatic events – the reading process presents further ethical issues. It is not the text *per se*, but rather what we can do with it that is ethically significant. Indeed, postmodernist texts no longer have the predominant moral dimension and purpose of realist fiction. On the contrary, the universality of moral values is questioned, especially the possibility of reaching and transmitting them,

---

[14] *Ibid.*, 60 (emphasis in the original).
[15] Alan Hollinghurst, *The Line of Beauty*, London: Picador, 2004.

particularly when the problematic reading process takes place. The reader is forced to come to terms with the ethical limits of aesthetic language, much more so when bearing witness to inhuman traumatic events.

With early postmodernism, ethics was removed from the agenda of cultural and literary studies. Any ethical stance was considered a step backward, a return to a constraining moral system liberation movements had managed to overcome during the 1960s. However, a return to ethical issues has increasingly gained ground since the 1980s. Many theorists have focused on this phenomenon, with key works like the 2004 monographic issue of *Poetics Today* on *Literature and Ethics*, edited by Michael Eskin. However, I consider it inaccurate and unfair to label all the literature produced in the decades immediately prior to the "ethical turn" unethical, or rather, uninterested in ethical issues. It is true that moral relativism was predominant, but even from the ranks of poststructuralism itself, ethics and morality, its practical counterpart, were vindicated, even if under new forms and from different angles. This process of redefinition of the epistemological use of philosophical issues by critical theory was possible thanks to Emmanuel Levinas' positioning of ethics at the centre of the philosophical debate. Levinas' theoretical framework, which Eskin describes as immersed "in the symphony of buzzwords and topoi: *alterity, interpellation, call of the other, answerability, ethical responsibility, openness, obligation, event, doing justice, witnessing, hospitality, singularity, particularity,* or *the gift*",[16] "is drawn up to demonstrate that some forms of deconstruction and poststructuralism blend well with an ethical reading of texts".[17]

Of Levinas' concepts, I will make special reference to alterity, "a key asset of postmodernist aesthetics",[18] particularly useful when dealing with marginal identities. As Vera Nüning, drawing on Herbert Grabes, points out, "postmodernist aesthetics are inherently ethical,

---

[16] Eskin, "On Literature and Ethics", 561 (emphasis in the original).

[17] Bárbara Arizti and Silvia Martínez-Falquina, Introduction, in *The Ethics of Fiction in Contemporary Narrative in English*, Cambridge: Cambridge Scholars Publishing, 2007, xii.

[18] Vera Nünning, "Ethics and Aesthetics in British Novels at the Beginning of the Twenty-First Century", in *Ethics in Culture: The Dissemination of Values through Literature and Other Media*, eds Astrid Erll, Herbert Grabes and Ansgar Nünning, Berlin: Walter De Gruyter, 2008, 388.

because devices like de-familiarization, metafictional commentary or the presentation of the grotesque initiate an experience of alterity".[19] Likewise, Linda Hutcheon argues how postmodernism focuses on the ex-centric or the Other", in Levinas' understanding of the term,[20] that is, females, non-whites and non-heterosexuals. The vindication of marked identities – as opposed to unmarked heteronormative masculinity – constitutes an ethical act because it repairs silence and discrimination. But, is this an act of reinscription of the Other within the limits of classic ideological patterns? Or is it a real act of reversal of values? When critics introduce texts by women, gays and non-whites, are they performing a fashionable practice, or are they really implicated ethically and aesthetically with the marginalised?

One of the main problems posed by poststructuralism consists in the epistemological complexity, even impossibility, of reaching reality except through the mediation of language. This aporetic status of textuality, which breaks with the mimetic logic of nineteenth-century realism, takes us back to J. Hillis Miller's unreadability. It is unfair and inaccurate to reduce deconstructionism to a textual theory fostering ethical relativism: as Miller claims throughout *The Ethics of Reading*,[21] the process of reading constitutes an act of responsibility. However, it can be argued that deconstructionists frequently grant texts an ontological autonomy that somehow prevents the actual ethical compromise from taking place outside the linguistic process. Philosophers cite poets – Levinas mentions Célan and Dostoyevsky – as making both ethics and aesthetics the sides of a single coin in a way that is "inexpressible in propositional or referential language"[22] and whose core can never be reached. Both discourses work as linguistic symptoms of the unappraisable Other, a truth that textuality can just hint at. I do not mean that a text (cor)responds to reality literally, as an act of unmediated referentiality, as mimeticists do. This would be tantamount to considering art to have the same nature as the real world. As I will try to show, this is the tragic mistake of Nick Guest,

---

[19] *Ibid.*, 370.
[20] Emmanuel Levinas, *Autrement qu'être, ou au-delà de l'essence*, Paris: Le Livre de Poche, 1978.
[21] J. Hillis Miller, *The Ethics of Reading: Kant, de Man, Eliot, Trollope, James, and Benjamin*, New York: Columbia University Press, 1987.
[22] Stengel, "Ethics as Style", 613.

the hero of Alan Hollinghurst's *The Line of Beauty*. According to Robert Eaglestone, this is one of the problems neo-humanist critics must confront:

> Asking us 'to consider art as a correction of life' leads to a 'misreading of art as philosophy'. That is, works become sources for the exploration of ethical issues rather than autonomous art works: precisely what makes them such good examples (their inextricable aesthetic complexity) is necessarily reduced in the act of reading them.[23]

As Eaglestone has pointed out, the mismatch between lived experience and textual representation lies behind Cathy Caruth's trauma theory. Recalling Caruth, he argues:

> Linguistically oriented theories like deconstruction do not necessarily deny reference, but rather deny the possibility of modelling the principles of reference on those of natural law, or, we might say, of making reference like perception. That is, the relationship between narrative and life is not so simple .... To rephrase Nussbaum, literary texts do not represent "patterns of possibility" that "turn up in human lives".[24]

In the middle of this debate on aesthetics, ethics and the possibility of access to and transmission of truth, trauma has become an increasingly meaningful concept or phenomenon. From the Greek *trauma* – wound – the term originally referred to an injury inflicted on the body. However, since the psycho-medical revolution at the end of the nineteenth century, the term has been used with reference to a wound inflicted on the mind.[25] I will devote the rest of the essay to analysing the problems of bearing witness to the trauma of gayness and particularly the trauma of AIDS in the gay community, as an aesthetic and ethical act. Through an analysis of Alan Hollinghurst's *The Line of Beauty*, his latest novel to date and the winner of the 2004 Man Booker Prize, I will try to answer questions such as: what are the

---

[23] Eaglestone, "One and the Same?", 603.
[24] *Ibid.*, 604.
[25] Caruth, *Unclaimed Experience*, 3.

ethical implications of an aesthetics of disease and death? Is such an aesthetics admissible?

It is my contention that corporal pain and punishment must be re-inscribed in trauma discourse with the outburst of AIDS: if late postmodernism is characterised, among other things, by a turn to ethics, gay literature – particularly Hollinghurst's – claims for a turn to the body as a site of both pleasure and traumatic pain. However, this re-inscription of the body is far from the pre-Freudian conception of trauma as a mere physical injury which easily heals. As I will try to demonstrate, Alan Hollinghurst's novel situates itself in the liminal space between a classic concept of beauty and an aesthetics of alterity, through the sublime and especially the Dionysian and the abject. Out of this confrontation between beauty and a threatening anti-aesthetics (and its ethical consequences) there arises the hero's traumatic story, inscribed in AIDS as a collective founding trauma, in Dominick LaCapra's terms.[26] Unlike those of the mind, bodily wounds are considered as healable; yet, the marks on the skin produced by AIDS, as fictionalised in Hollinghurst's novels, are inextricably linked to discursive practices, as if the body were a text.[27] In other words, AIDS affects the body as a physical entity as well as a sociolinguistic phenomenon. The disease is not only real, but an ideological artefact, in so far as both its physical effects and its fully troped rhetoric cannot be dissociated.

Similarly, as Adami argues, the fact that a novel represents a traumatic event

> ... is not sufficient to define it as trauma fiction: Trauma fiction is rather defined in terms of the narrative's formal structure, and of the capacity of that structure to convey the fragmentation of meaning and identity brought about by traumatic experiences. Recurring stylistic

---

[26] Dominick LaCapra, *Writing History, Writing Trauma*, Baltimore, MD: John Hopkins University Press, 2001.
[27] Jeanette Winterson overtly addresses this issue in her fittingly entitled novel, *Written on the Body* (1992). Of course, "writing the body" is one of the key tenets of Hélène Cixous and other French feminist critics. See Susana Onega, "The 'Body/Text' as Lesbian Signifier in Jeanette Winterson's *Written on the Body*", in *Margins in British and American Literature, Film, and Culture*, eds Marita Nadal and M. Dolores Herrero, Zaragoza: Servicio de Publicaciones de la Universidad de Zaragoza, 1997, 119-29.

features of trauma fiction include intertextuality, repetition and a fragmented narrative voice.[28]

Intertextuality and a fragmented narrative voice refer to the plurality of voices and perspectives rendering testimony of the traumatic event. Moreover, intertextuality and repetition evoke "Freud's theory of repetition compulsion: it shows how a traumatized individual is always trapped between departure and return".[29] Hollinghurst's first two novels – *The Swimming-Pool Library* and *The Folding Star*[30] – fulfil Adami's definition of trauma fiction since they are scattered with intertextual references, split narratives and characters repeatedly confronting traumatic events. *The Line of Beauty* constitutes an intertextual apostrophic tribute especially to Henry James' writing and personality and Thomas Mann's *Death in Venice*.[31] Unlike its predecessors, Hollinghurst's fourth novel is not voiced by an autodiegetic narrator, occasionally interrupted by his older mentor. Instead, an extradiegetic narrator renders detached testimony of the hero's traumatic story in the Thatcher era. But the constant interaction of past and present, hypotext and hypertext, fiction and reality, determines the dialogism and shifting perspective of *The Line of Beauty*. Both the novel and its hero apparently suffer from Freudian repetition-compulsion at intra- and inter-textual levels. In fact, the novel mirrors the structure and story of their predecessors, particularly *The Swimming-Pool Library*: the trauma of AIDS recurs in the portrayal of most of the gay characters in *The Line of Beauty* and Nick Guest's story is in more sense than one the aftermath of Will Beckwith's story.

Like ethics and aesthetics, trauma theory has undergone an irregular evolution. As I pointed out in a recent paper on Hollinghurst's *The Swimming-Pool Library*,[32] the success of trauma

---

[28] Adami, *Trauma Studies and Literature*, 73.
[29] *Ibid.*, 74.
[30] Alan Hollinghurst, *The Swimming-Pool Library* (1988), London: Vintage, 1998, and *The Folding Star*, London: Vintage, 1998.
[31] Thomas Mann, *Death in Venice* (1912), trans. H.T. Lowe-Porter, Harmondsworth: Penguin, 1975.
[32] José M. Yebra, "The Trauma of AIDS in Alan Hollinghurst's *The Swimming-Pool Library*", paper given at the International Conference *Between the "Urge to Know" and the "Need to Deny": Ethics and Trauma in Contemporary Narrative in English*,

studies has been frequently linked to identity crises. The liberation movements (particularly feminism), pacifism (especially after Vietnam) and, more recently, multiculturalism and globalisation have pointed at the trauma of Otherness. In so far as women, victims of war and genocide, racial minorities etc. have increasingly rendered testimony, trauma studies have taken root and flourished. Seen in this light, it should not be forgotten that trauma, as an ethical and literary issue, is a culturally-bound phenomenon. Obviously, I do not mean that non-Western individuals and cultures do not suffer from traumatic episodes. Nevertheless, trauma as a medical, social, identitarian, literary and philosophical performative event is eminently Western, since it is closely related to our concepts of identity and alterity.

Trauma fiction is a relational phenomenon, a testimonial practice that escapes the logic of classic realism. This is so first and foremost because the victim of trauma suffers from a collapse of understanding, "a physical and/or mental disorganisation that may be circumscribed or widespread".[33] This disorganisation causes "fragmentation of self, shattering of social relationships, erosion of social supports".[34] As Cathy Caruth explains with reference to Post-Traumatic Stress Disorder, the aftermath of the traumatic happening becomes conspicuous as "the overwhelming events of the past repeatedly possess, in intrusive images and thoughts, the one who has lived through them".[35] Although, obviously, it is the victim who bears witness to trauma, the traumatic text implicates witnesses and readers or listeners in a complex emotional and ethical process. Yet, I do not think, as some critics do, that second-hand testimonies are as good as first-hand ones. On the contrary, as Kali Tal argues, the traumatic event "must be experienced first-hand, not vicariously … or mediated through any textual conduit".[36] Still, the role of the reader or listener should not be underestimated. In fact, as pointed out above, the aim of trauma fiction can only be accomplished through the interaction of the

---

Residencia Universitaria de Jaca, University of Zaragoza (forthcoming in the published conference proceedings).
[33] Deborah M. Horvitz, *Literary Trauma: Sadism, Memory, and Sexual Violence in American's Women's Fiction*, New York: State of New York Press, 2000, 5.
[34] *Ibid.*, 22, 92 (where Tal is quoted).
[35] *Trauma: Explorations in Memory*, ed. Cathy Caruth, Baltimore, MD and London: John Hopkins University Press, 1995, 151.
[36] Horvitz, *Literary Trauma*, 6.

addresser and the addressee, in the case of fiction, the one who reads and understands. Trauma literature is not necessarily a healing artefact – though it is frequently alleged to be – but one that boosts integration and empathy. This is why its aesthetic character cannot be dissociated from its ethical dimension. In that sense, as Adami argues, "the novel's impact on the reader is often more important than the accuracy of the facts narrated".[37]

There seems to be an apparently unbridgeable gap between traumatic events and their narrative representation. In fact, "while traumatic discourse is fragmentary and contradictory, 'normal' discourse usually presents a certain degree of coherence, because the human mind has an essentially narrative structure". Drawing on T.R. Sarbin, Valentina Adami goes on to argue that "human beings think, perceive, imagine, interact, and make moral choices according to narrative structures".[38] Moreover, as Michael Eskin points out, "Nursery rhymes, stories, plays, verbal and filmic narratives perused from early childhood have been supposed to ensure, more or less successfully, the formation of the variously conceived good person".[39] Yet, all these narrative structures collapse when dealing with traumatic episodes. Nevertheless, a breaking down of language does not imply complete silence. Trauma fiction has elaborated complex strategies to represent its inarticulacy: disruptions, temporal and logical gaps, silences, unreliable narration, grammatical dislocations are some of the formulae to (mis)represent the vacuum left by a traumatic event after a period of latency.

However, unlike Cathy Caruth, I think that trauma fiction is still a narrative act, and not simply a performative event.[40] I agree that a fully coherent narrative cannot render testimony to a traumatic event; but, even if we aim at representing trauma in its literariness, mimicking the event itself through disruptions, gaps or silences, this act of representation must necessarily be narrative. Charles Nantwich,

---

[37] Adami, *Trauma Studies and Literature*, 91. Her words bring to mind the New Historicist conceptions of truth and memory, which are closely connected with literature. Unlike classic historiography, trauma fiction is not so much interested in the accuracy with which facts are rendered as in the problematic articulacy and the impact of these facts.

[38] *Ibid.*, 14.

[39] Eskin, "On Literature and Ethics", 574.

[40] Caruth, *Trauma: Explorations in Memory*, 45.

one of the heroes in Alan Hollinghurst's *The Swimming-Pool Library*, commissions a youth, Will Beckwith, to write his biography, particularly the homophobia-related episode of his incarceration in the 1950s. To this end, Nantwich hands over to Beckwith some documents, photographs and a diary. The entry on Nantwich's persecution and prosecution constitutes a masterly example of trauma literature.[41] Contradictory versions of the episode by the hero-narrator contend for truthfulness and seek for the reader's empathy. For orthodox historiographers, Nantwich's testimony would be worthless in so far as it is contradictory and, therefore, unreliable. But the character's contradictions do not invalidate his testimony. On the contrary, his narration constitutes an acting-out of his personal trauma performed in the context of a collective trauma: the anti-gay rides promoted by the British government in the 1950s. Invalidating Nantwich's testimony would be tantamount to denying this historical episode. In this respect, it might be useful to recall that the negation of the Holocaust and the Gulf War[42] were key elements in the encouragement of the turn to ethics with which this essay started. From the perspective of trauma studies, the contradictoriness of Nantwich's testimony begs for a revision of the concept and epistemological access to truth.

This takes us to whether there should be some sort of ethical limit to the aesthetic representation of trauma, which is a central issue in *The Line of Beauty*, and one of this essay's main concerns. The novel has been regarded as both morally outrageous, due to its sexual explicitness, and moralistic, as it closes with the hero's "punishment". Yet the ethical project of *The Line of Beauty* transcends (though it does not invalidate) moral considerations: it does not aim simply at reflecting or resolving the traumatic character of gay identity – particularly amid the outburst of AIDS – from an aesthetic outlook. On

---

[41] On the relevance of trauma theory in contemporary gay fiction, particularly that produced by Hollinghurst, see Robert J. Corber, "Sentimentalizing Gay History: Mark Merlis, Alan Hollinghurst and the Cold War Persecution of Homosexuals", *Arizona Quarterly*, LV/4 (Winter 1999), 115-41.

[42] In 1991, Jean Baudrillard published several articles under the title (in their English translation) of *The Gulf War Did not Take Place* (1995). The critic provocatively argued against the "authenticity" of this war according to classic parameters. His theory stirred up a tremendous controversy and there were voices that accused him of irresponsible moral relativism.

the contrary, as far as this reality is unreachable, the novel can only bring to the fore the *aporia* of the representation of trauma. Thus, Margarét Gunnarsdottir argues that an ethical dimension is only discoverable in what J. Hillis Miller calls allegorical readings, that is, in readers' awareness of the rhetorical opacity of texts and the consequent renunciation of essential meaning: "The ethics of reading", says Miller, "must be a response on my part ... to the demand made by that 'other' ... [that] something else within language".[43]

The Otherness in *The Line of Beauty* is articulated through the interplay between its intertextuality, Nick's anti-aesthetic discourse, the liminal status of gay identity, and the trauma of AIDS. Thus, as we will see in the next section, as readers approach the literary text from the ethical perspective demanded by Miller, they are forced to empathise with the characters and to recognise their own Otherness. Likewise, we will see that the opposition between Hogarth's delusive line of beauty and its terrible Other, the anti-aesthetic, shape the discursive alterity of the novel, the traumatic individuation process of the protagonist and the ethical response begged of the reader.

Anti-aestheticism, the sublime and the trauma of gayness in *The Line of Beauty*

The Line of Beauty is first and foremost a gay *Bildungsroman*, or rather a failed *Künstlerroman*, with Nick Guest attempting to solve the trauma of gayness through an obsessive aestheticism: as a matter of fact, homosexuals have been essentially articulated (and degraded) as useless aesthetes. Down from Oxford, Nick is invited by his upper-class college friend, Toby Fedden, to stay with his glamorous family at Notting Hill. Thus, the hero meets his fate, a world of beauty that eventually turns out to be uglier than expected. He soon becomes the Feddens' aesthete while he writes his doctoral thesis on style in Henry James. Consequently, his obsession with the Feddens' riches and glamour is intertextual, always filtered through Henry James' persona and literary production. The Master constitutes Nick's password to the realm of beauty, albeit in a delusive and precarious mode, and is also a

---

[43] Margarét Gunnarsdottir, "Art Mirrors the Spectator: The Field of Otherness in *The Picture of Dorian Gray*", in *The Other Within*, ed. Ruth Parkin-Gounelas, Vol. I, *Literature and Culture*, Thessaloniki: Athanasios A. Altinzis, 2001, 254.

useful instrument for the narrator to articulate trauma. Nick's other source of aesthetic pleasure, and eventual tragedy, is the male body, shaped after Hogarth's line of beauty, and (as we will see) the site of destabilising Dionysian powers:

> The ogee curve was repeated in the mirrors and pelmets and in the wardrobes, which looked like Gothick confessionals ... it had a rightness to it, being both English and exotic, like so many things he loved. The ogee curve was pure expression, decorative not structural; a structure could be made from it, but it supported nothing more than a boss or the cross that topped an onion dome .... The double curve was Hogarth's "line of beauty", the snakelike flicker of an instinct, of two compulsions held in one unfolding movement. He ran his hand down Wani's back. He didn't think that Hogarth had illustrated this best example of it, the dip and swell – he had chosen harps and branches, bones rather than flesh. Really it was time for a new *Analysis of Beauty*.[44]

Hogarth's classic concept of beauty – encapsulated in the serpentine line that Nick recurrently re-creates – works as a specular *mise en abyme* of the novel as a whole, just like Basil's portrait in Oscar Wilde's *The Picture of Dorian Gray*. In their turn, both novels project their internal specularity on the real world and their potential readers. As happens with the portrait in Wilde's novella, the readers of *The Line of Beauty* confront Nick's treacherous revision of beauty as "their own portrait and are challenged, as Dorian is, to make a choice between narcissistic misrecognition and self-divided experience".[45] To put it differently, the reading process implicates the reader ethically. This is especially so, in so far as Nick's aesthetic project, like Dorian's, eventually fails. His delusive aestheticism cannot render testimony to the trauma of AIDS and anti-aesthetics comes out instead. In fact, it is the Otherness of the sublime, the Dionysian and the abject that helps articulate the trauma of gayness and the spectacle of AIDS.

As Carolyn Korsmeyer points out, contemporary art frequently emphasises "the mortality and facticity of physical being ... sometimes with unsettling effect". There are many examples, the critic argues, "where mortality, gross physical effects, and decay are

---

[44] Hollinghurst, *The Line of Beauty*, 200.
[45] Gunnarsdottir, "Art Mirrors the Spectator", 252.

presented ... also through the use of actual blood or urine or body parts, as with Damien Hirst's vitrines of animal carcasses and Andres Serrano's *Piss Christ*".[46] Echoing this, when Will Beckwith visits a porn cinema in *The Swimming-Pool Library*, Hollinghurst uses an aesthetics of disgust to represent sexuality and the annihilation of gays. After witnessing some unexciting porn scenes, Will notices the TV images on the monitor of the attendant at the cinema:

> It was a nature programme, and contained some virtuoso footage shot inside a termite colony. First we saw sharp claws cutting their way in. Back inside, perched by a fibre-optic miracle at a junction of tunnels which looked like the triforium of some Gaudí church, we saw the freakishly extensile tongue of the ant-eater come flicking towards us, cleaning the fleeing termites off the wall.[47]

The Line of Beauty is even subtler, though not less effective, in its treatment of repulsive beauty. Korsmeyer describes the oxymoron masterfully: "If beauty and the sublime were touchstones of aesthetic value of the eighteenth and nineteenth centuries, one might wonder if the parallel value at the advent of the twenty-first might be the disgusting." However, as the critic immediately points out, the aesthetics of disgust or anti-aesthetics are deeply rooted in the traditions of the past: from Greek Dionysian (as opposed to Apollonian) beauty, and the classic fascination with ugliness and monstrosity as the necessary paired opposite of beauty, to the syncretic re-appropiation of these concepts in the sublime.[48] In her analysis of gendered aesthetics, Korsmeyer revises the changing interaction between mind and body, which, as we will see, also constitutes a feature of *The Line of Beauty*, its aesthetic discourse, and particularly the articulation of its hero's individuation process. In Western culture, the actual division between "mind (mental) and brain (physical) has always been a matter of controversy". However, it is in the last few decades that the distinction and hierarchy of mind and body have undergone relentless challenge and revision, especially "by

---

[46] Carolyn Korsmeyer, *Gender and Aesthetics: An Introduction*, New York: Routledge, 2008, 130.

[47] Hollinghurst, *The Line of Beauty*, 48.

[48] Korsmeyer, *Gender and Aesthetics*, 130.

the advancement of neuroscience, the decline of theological metaphysical commitments, and perennial philosophical scepticism". The mind is no longer the only recipient of "truth" and the body "has an increasingly important place in the analysis of subjectivity, identity, and what it means to be 'a person'".[49] In this deconstruction of the binary opposition mind/body,

> ... the evocation of bodily elements that provoke disgust is intimately tied to the philosophical re-valuation of the body, for disgust is above all others the most physical, visceral emotion. The evocation of disgust on the part of art is a shocking disruption of traditions of aesthetic value, but at the same time it may be seen as continuous with a venerable and exalted aesthetic category: the sublime.[50]

Although coined by Pseudo-Longinus,[51] the sublime has been fundamentally theorised by Edmund Burke and Emmanuel Kant.[52] Both attempted to explain the apparent contradiction in the experience of the sublime.[53] How can a spectator, listener or reader be fascinated while feeling emotional terror? While beauty bestows pleasure, the sublime relies on emotional terror and, ultimately, death. As Korsmeyer explains, the answer Burke gave was that "confrontation with mortality can put one in mind of its opposite, and Burke was one of the many who saw in the experience of sublimity a glimpse of God – an experience of transcendence that terrifies, thrills and awes".[54] Although a hopeless aesthete, Nick Guest is repeatedly confronted

---

[49] *Ibid.*, 132.

[50] *Ibid.*, 133.

[51] Umberto Eco, *Historia de la Belleza*, trans. María Pons Irazazábal, Barcelona: Lumen, 2004, 278.

[52] "Rather than developing a theory of the sublime, the eighteenth century constituted a turning point in aesthetic theory because, for the first time, the subject prevailed over the object. Now, it is not the intrinsic beauty of the artistic object that is admired, but the gift of the artist to produce it and, especially, of the critic or viewer to appreciate it; hence the increasing importance of concepts such as genius, imagination and taste" (*ibid.*, 275).

[53] See Edmund Burke's *A Philosophical Enquiry into the Origin of our Ideas of the Sublime and the Beautiful* (1757), introduction, notes and bibliography, Adam Phillips, Oxford and New York: Oxford University Press, 1990; Immanuel Kant's *Observations on the Feeling of the Beautiful and the Sublime* (1763), trans. John T. Goldthwaite, Berkeley and Los Angeles: University of California Press, 2003.

[54] Korsmeyer, *Gender and Aesthetics*, 134.

with his traumatic fate. His Otherness, as a gay youth in a Tory atmosphere, determines the characteristics of his individuation process. Moreover, aestheticism can hide the harshest surprises, as Henry James' fiction showed and Nick tragically experiences.

Therefore, contrary to Burke's suggestion, the hero (and the reader) is not a safe spectator of the sublime. He is a victim of the inexorable dynamics of the sublime or related phenomena like the Dionysian: he is eventually ejected from the beautiful world of the Feddens and he witnesses how all his lovers die of AIDS. Thus, the beauty of his alleged friends rears its ugly head and the bodies of his lovers rot. Unlike Burke, Kant contended that the sublime cannot be simply a relief from danger, that it is a much more complex phenomenon. For the German philosopher, a spectator's encounter with an object of magnitude is not just frightening. Rather fear "is surmounted with more profound realizations about what it means to be human .... And this is the basis of the fact that we are moral beings, capable of willing that our actions be different from the way that natural causes would intend."[55] Nick Guest does not develop this kind of free Romantic self claimed by Kant. On the contrary, he is unable to dissociate himself from his aesthetic drives, from an alterity he cannot control. In fact, his repeated attempts to do so constitute Nick's traumatic error. However, the novel allows readers an encounter with (and reflection against) gays' Otherness, particularly the frightening, alienating impact of AIDS as an "object" of magnitude. Yet, unlike Kant's optimistic Romanticism, *The Line of Beauty* does not transform us into moral beings – this is not literature's task. It just hints at a traumatic event and its difficult representation, thereby justifying the readers' task as ethical witnesses and decoders: we can (and must) empathise aesthetically with gays as socially ostracised and likely victims of AIDS, since we cannot actually interfere.

Such aesthetic elaborations should now be contextualised within Nietzsche's reinscription of the Greek opposition between the Apollonian and Dionysian as a theoretical framework for Nick's tragic *Künstlerroman*. Although Henry James' fiction constitutes *The Line of Beauty*'s main hypotext, Nick's problematic individuation process particularly recalls that of Aschenbach in Thomas Mann's *Death in*

---

[55] *Ibid.*, 135.

Venice. Both heroes are obsessive aesthetes who construct and live an idealised Apollonian world of beauty, and they regard art as a gnoseologic instrument for apprehending reality, which eventually fails. Vagelis Siropoulos has pointed out the influence of Nietzsche's *The Birth of Tragedy* on Mann's masterwork.[56] Briefly stated, Nietzsche contended that the development of art "is bound with the duality of the Apollonian and the Dionysian". While the Apollonian is represented through the visual arts as a dream, the Dionysian is represented through the non-visual art of music as intoxication.[57] Thus, the Apollonian could be regarded as the consecration of beautiful illusion, the only formula through which the original Oneness of the Dionysian can be represented to human eyes. The highest possible manifestation of art, the Dionysian, is unbearable to human beings except through the beautiful veils of the Apollonian. Therefore, Dionysus' "mystical obliteration of the self" is solved by the Apollonian "divine image of the *principium individuationis*".[58] The original undifferentiation represented by the primal God is made comprehensible through the illusion of selfhood, the essence of art itself. As Nietzsche explains, tragedy is born out of the confrontation and symbiosis of both states of being or concepts of art.

Siropoulos makes use of Julia Kristeva's theory of abjection to explain the process of individuation proposed by the German philosopher: "Individuation as the Apollonian cult of subjectivity is the outcome of the filial body's struggle with the maternal natural one and is synonymous with the imposition of form, limits and borders upon the maternal chaos."[59] Apollo's world of beauty and self-control is ideally put on stage in Attic tragedy, as a mask for "an abjected anarchistic, formless and fluid Dionysian body". However, the masquerade collapses when the hero fails due to *hamartia*, or tragic error.[60] Against traditional interpretations, Nietzsche rejects any moral reading of the tragic error. In his view, ethical considerations belong

---

[56] Vagelis Siropoulos, "The Dionysian (Gay) Abject: Corporeal Representation in *The Birth of Tragedy* and *Death in Venice*", in *The Other Within*, Vol. I, 93.
[57] Friedrich Nietzsche, *The Birth of Tragedy Out of the Spirit of Music* (1871), trans. Ian Johnson, 2008, 10: http://www.johnstoniaHome Page (accessed 17/7/2008).
[58] *Ibid.*, 12, 13.
[59] Siropoulos, "The Dionysian (Gay) Abject", 93-94.
[60] *Ibid.*, 95.

in the Semitic culture based on an original sin. By contrast, Greek culture relies on the primal crime of Prometheus against the Gods.[61] In spite of this, Siropoulos regards *hamartia* as ethical transgression, since it is an error that always reminds the spectator of tragedy that "the individual can never reach the Apollonian ideal of a fully controlled, coherent subjectivity aligned to the norms of a symbolic superego. Subjectivity is an Apollonian 'fair illusion' ... an illusory ideal, a role to be performed, a performance that is always doomed to fail."[62]

This is precisely the *aporia* that Aschenbach suffers in *Death in Venice* and that *The Line of Beauty* recasts from an ironic and parodic, postmodernist perspective. Both Aschenbach and Nick attempt to organise their existence according to an Apollonian logic and, in the end, both fail to escape the Dionysian. After a life of self-control in a strict Apollonian universe, Aschenbach's repressed homosexuality is released in the form of an abject corporeality that eventually kills him.[63] He recurrently feels the exciting repulsiveness of his homosexual desire. However, it is especially the young Tadzio and the unhealthy atmosphere of Venice that exert a lethal fascination on the professor. He tries to mortify the youth's body into his Apollonian ideal of lifeless beauty, though to no avail.[64] He also attempts to displace the corporeal to a metaphysical Platonic discourse, but, as Siropoulos contends, eventually "Tadzio's body is *pen*etrated by Aschenbach's pen".[65] Nevertheless, the Dionysian ecstasy that he suffers and enjoys constitutes a pessimistic surrender, whereby "Aschenbach's life-vision of a civilizing integration of the sensual and the spiritual finally collapses". The fragile *principium individuationis* dependent on repression is finally "disintegrated from within through a return of the repressed".[66] Following the logic of degeneration theory and Freud's "death drive", Aschenbach, "entrapped in a

---

[61] Nietzsche, *The Birth of Tragedy*, 37-39.
[62] Siropoulos, "The Dionysian (Gay) Abject", 96.
[63] *Ibid.*, 97.
[64] *Ibid.*, 98.
[65] *Ibid.*, 99 (emphasis in the original).
[66] Dollimore, *Desire, Death and Loss in Western Culture* (1998), New York: Routledge, 2001, 279.

delirium of unnameable *jouissance* and death, ... eats the polluted fruit and dies".[67]

The association between male beauty and death, homoeroticism and disease, the violent return of the original perverse to the civilised explain the tension between the Apollonian and the Dionysian. The tragic subject emerges out of this struggle: "in the same way that Aschenbach as a tragic subject denies and masquerades desire under his conservative bourgeois patriarchal mask, Mann produces a 'tragic' mode of writing, wherein the homosexual erotica is displaced, masqueraded and repressed under the rigid philosophical, academic discourse."[68]

Death in Venice follows Nietzsche's theories quite literally. In fact, the tragic hero experiences a Dionysian dream, a final sexual ecstasy that challenges the logic of Apollonian individuation through metaphors of oceanic dissolution of the self. I have dwelt at some length upon *Death in Venice* because *The Line of Beauty* intertextually recalls some of the Nietzschean principles at work in Mann's masterwork, though updated to the political outlook at the turn of the millennium. For example, Hollinghurst's novel establishes a division between the hero and the narrator. While the hero, like Aschenbach, attempts to make himself fit into the Apollonian concept of beauty and the *principium individuationis*, the narrator adopts an ironic perspective on this process. Likewise, the postmodernist narrator ironises on Nick's obsessive imitation of Henry James' oblique style, even his convoluted definitions, in the course of his individuation process. The disruptions, gaps and silences characteristic of trauma narrative,[69] of James' literature, and of the Feddens' discourse shape Nick's voice and, what is more relevant, his final downfall.[70]

Throughout the novel, the hero masquerades his *Bildungsroman* behind and through art: all his experiences are translated to beautiful, artistic objects, from music, particularly Strauss, Wagner and

---

[67] Siropoulos, "The Dionysian (Gay) Abject", 101.

[68] *Ibid.*, 102.

[69] Adami, *Trauma Studies and Literature*, 34.

[70] The hero recurrently shows his admiration for Rachel Fedden's upper-class inarticulate language as if it were a Jamesian literary device (Hollinghurst, *The Line of Beauty*, 451).

Mozart,[71] pictures, or furniture,[72] to male bodies. If art is the central thread of his life, the rigid and frigid discourse of James' texts and characters is doubly so. He soon declares himself as a James man and, therefore, an advocate of the writer's convoluted concept of style and language.[73] Following James' motto, "art is considered to make up life", Nick renders even his erotic relations through the writer's "half-hour subordinate clauses of remembered sex",[74] and his discourse adopts a reluctance "that is Jamesian in itself".[75] The hero tries to hide himself behind the Apollonian concept of beauty represented by James. Throughout *The Line of Beauty*, Nick plays the role of aesthete, one who represses his desires, fears, personality, and origins behind the mask of art – not behind Nietzsche's highest concept of art, the Dionysian, but following the Socratic aesthetics of logic and reason,[76] since he falls in love with beauty as an Apollonian-Socratic concept. Still, this world of aesthetic beauty and perfect forms, which he captures from James' texts, turns out to be just a mask: while James' characters exist in an Apollonian limbo, Nick, like Aschenbach, suffers from the tension between perfect form and the repressed Dionysian drive. Consequently, throughout the novel, Nick is forced to play a morally dubious role: a liberated gay with his lovers and a repressed aesthete while with the Feddens' upper-class friends.

The alternation between the sexualised guy who takes drugs in a Dionysian ecstasy and the next minute greets Margaret Thatcher and other homophobic MPs in Jamesian scenarios of restraint makes up the hero's fragile, traumatised, and schizophrenic identity. Significantly, although the external narrator points out Nick's identitarian precariousness, Nick himself seems unconscious of this fact. It is only at the very end of the novel, when finally he must confront reality, the corporeality of the Dionysian in its most terrible face – the effects of drugs and AIDS and his ejection from the Feddens' like a pariah – that he undergoes a process of *anagnorisis* to which I will return.

---

[71] *Ibid.*, 13, 18, 66, 94.
[72] *Ibid.*, 6.
[73] *Ibid.*, 54.
[74] *Ibid.*, 139.
[75] *Ibid.*, 213.
[76] Nietzsche, *The Birth of Tragedy*, 48.

Like Dorian Gray's infatuation with his own portrait, Nick is confronted with his own physicality and its Apollonian projection. Indeed, Hollinghurst's novel is scattered with mirrors[77] which, like Dorian's portrait, reflect the hero and the duplicitous world he lives in and, in their specularity, they remind the reader of his interplay with the text. For Gunnarsdottir, Dorian's picture "works effectively on the concrete level of story, plot and character and on a more abstract level as a metafictional device". Nick's self-reflection on actual mirrors constitutes an act of *jouissance* whereby, echoing – like Dorian – the child in Lacan's mirror stage, the hero "is overwhelmed by the beauty and wholeness of the reflection and at the same time dismayed at his own inner sense of discord and incompleteness".[78] Nick's narcissistic, Apollonian illusion of integration is foredoomed to failure: the unnameable trauma of Otherness that has always characterised gayness, particularly after the outburst of AIDS, provokes a sense of discord that only the Dionysian seems able to represent. The disintegrative force of the Dionysian breaks with the Apollonian *principium individuationis* Nick wrongly adheres to. Hence, Nick and his peers come across "a lack, a gap in subjective being".[79] Like Dorian, Nick persists in failing to recognise his aesthetic self-delusion, his Otherness, in front of the mirror, which, in the reading process, reflects the reader himself. Hence, the latter must question his ontological and epistemological relation with the text as well as the ethical implications of this relation.

To deconstructivists, literature itself is a space of Otherness as far as the reader searches for the Other within the text, what escapes the text as narration takes place. This is particularly useful when dealing with trauma fiction. *The Line of Beauty*'s vain attempt to articulate the trauma of gayness and AIDS through aesthetics proves the limitations and role of literature while at the same time it invites readers to empathise with their trauma. The reading activity constitutes an ethical process of witnessing and feeling *for* another, instead of the uncritical positive transference of over-identification (or feeling *with* another) that, according to Dominick LaCapra,[80] is demanded of

---

[77] Hollinghurst, *The Line of Beauty*, 211, 258, 424.
[78] Gunnarsdottir, "Art Mirrors the Spectator", 250.
[79] *Ibid.*, 251.
[80] LaCapra, *Writing History*, 41.

sympathetic readers by realistic representations of trauma. In this light, Hollinghurst's novel does not deny reference to gays' trauma, and Nick in particular. It is simply that, recalling Caruth, literature cannot make reference to actual trauma through the models of natural law. *The Line of Beauty* is not, strictly speaking, a gay/AIDS text, but rather a vicarious, intertextual representation of the crisis of gayness in the era of AIDS – a crisis of traumatic misrecognition that affects, on different levels, the hero and the ethical reader.

The abject and the erotica of AIDS: working through disease and death

There is finally a last anti-aesthetic concept that complements the Apollonian/Dionysian dichotomy in Nick's individuation process and its ethical undertones, namely Julia Kristeva's notion of abjection. Although related to the sublime and the Dionysian,[81] the abject introduces a new insight on alterity that also helps articulate Nick's personal tragedy and that of AIDS, as well as the reader's participation/implication in this process. As Korsmeyer explains, abjection is a theoretical term

> ... that signals phenomena that are manifest in the experience of disgust .... It refers to the process of expelling the Other, beginning with the mother's body .... This expulsion is necessary in order that subjective identity develop.

Threatened by the abject in the form of disgust-producing objects, subjectivity remains fragile. The main sources of abjection are "things undergoing the changes of spoilage, rot, and decay", as they embody the "disintegrating passage from being to non-being". This in-betweenness threatens the subject, which is reminded of its eventual loss of identity.[82] The self is placed against its Other, is recalled of its pre-symbolic stage and warned about an eventual return to the "semiotic chora".[83] All this, which triggers off the revulsion and

---

[81] As Korsmeyer argues, unlike the abject, the sublime "is possessed of might and magnitude, and it therefore tends to the magnificent" (*Gender and Aesthetics*, 149).

[82] *Ibid.*, 148.

[83] As Korsmeyer points out, by "semiotic chora", Kristeva refers to a phenomenon whereby the boundaries of language are pushed back "to include intimations of the

disgust characteristic of the abject, also explains its magnetism. Becoming a subject implies a loss, which "is retained in the allure of the abject, for there is a desire to be reunited with that oneness [which] entails extinguishing one's individual identity".[84] This takes us back to the Freudian "death wish" that, as analysed above, *Death in Venice* adapts from Nietzsche's early writings.

The ambivalence of the terror and attraction to death and the dissolution of the self/return to oneness is nowhere better represented than in the abject. In *The Line of Beauty*, the phenomenon of the abject lies not so much in gay sexual intercourse – despite its explicit representation – as in the horrific erotica of AIDS. The novel may be said to respond to the revision of alterity triggered off by the disease in view of the abjected and apocalyptic emplotments around it. AIDS transformed the male body into the Other, the source of revulsion and fascination, as far as it killed physically and socially. This chain of death that annihilates and alienates is a line that, like Hogarth's serpentine, circles around Nick and his peers, constraining and threatening with suffocating them. The traumatic mismatch between lived experience and its textual representation lies at the heart of gayness and AIDS. Both are real, though frequently unspeakable. In this light, *The Line of Beauty* may be said to represent sexual Otherness obliquely, by apostrophising Henry James and the compelling force of the abject. The physicality of the disease affecting virtually every gay man in the novel cannot be rendered through direct references, but through a specular language that both reflects and repels, that interpellates and distances itself from the reader. That is, like all trauma fiction, Hollinghurst's novel can only bear witness by sublimation and (dis)identification. The narrative voice speaks through the mirror of intertextuality, recalling previous voices like those of James and Mann. At the same time, by re-inscribing the physicality of gay sexuality and AIDS through the Dionysian and the abject, the reader of *The Line of Beauty* feels simultaneously fascinated and alienated, though never fully identified with the victims. This would break the independence of actual experience and

---

time in which the young child feels little or no differentiation between himself or herself and the mother's body (*ibid.*, 147).

[84] *Ibid.*, 149.

its narrative representation and, therefore, diminish the reader's ethical responsibility.

Although published in 2004, the action of *The Line of Beauty* is situated in the early 1980s, when AIDS broke out. *The Swimming-Pool Library* had already dealt with those years. However, in the later novel Hollinghurst undertakes a more in-depth revision of that decade. In more senses than one, *The Line of Beauty* can be read as a belated textual echo, a new symptom, of the trauma of AIDS first represented in Hollinghurst's fiction by the protagonists of *The Swimming-Pool Library*. Nantwich's flashbacks, dreams and hallucinations constitute the acting-out, after a period of latency, of the trauma caused by his incarceration for indecent behaviour. When Will Beckwith reads the old man's testimony, he re-lives the trauma vicariously. In *The Line of Beauty*, when the narrator renders testimony of the annihilation of Nick and the gay culture he belongs in, the novel is somehow re-enacting the traumas of Hollinghurst's previous characters at an intratextual level. As far as Nick's experience reflects and recasts those of his predecessors, it could be concluded that his individuation process and the novel as a whole constitute a working-through of the trauma of AIDS already hinted at, albeit obliquely in *The Swimming-Pool Library*. Unlike acting-out, which is related to performance and showing, working-through entails telling after a process of analysis of the traumatic event. As a performative act, acting-out could be related to the body while working-through, as a linguistic process, belongs in the realm of the mind. If trauma cannot be articulated in classic narratives, should we conclude that trauma fiction – like Hollinghurst's – is necessarily a performative acting-out, as Caruth contends? Yet, if literature is inevitably a narrative phenomenon, should we assume that there are other ways of telling after working-through? *The Line of Beauty* both tells and shows: the hero acts out his own victimisation by echoing other victims, at intra-, inter-textual and historical levels while, simultaneously, the narrator presents the hero's trauma as an ethical and aesthetic phenomenon.

As Simon Watney argues, the homosexual body and especially AIDS are rendered as spectacle by the hetero-normative system.[85]

---

[85] Simon Watney, "The Spectacle of AIDS", in *The Lesbian and Gay Studies Reader*, eds Henry Abelove, Michèle Aina Barale and David M. Halperin, New York and London: Routledge, 1993, 206.

Likewise, Susan Sontag reduces homosexuality to camp in "Notes on Camp", and AIDS to its metaphors in *AIDS and Its Metaphors*.[86] In the essay, Sontag considered gays as amoral actors or aesthetes who succeeded the aristocracy as arbiters of taste. In the book, she attempted to deconstruct the strategies whereby AIDS has been articulated as a gay disease by adapting the medical metaphors previously used with the plague, syphilis, tuberculosis and cancer. Despite their unquestionable influence, Sontag's articles have been severely contested. Though camp remains an essential feature of gay sensibility, it is no longer the apolitical and amoral phenomenon that Sontag suggested in her essay. As concerns AIDS, critics such as D.A. Miller consider Sontag's exercise in metaphor deconstruction as simply opportunistic as well as the result of her privileged, unconcerned status.[87]

Dissensions apart, the force of metaphors is undeniably useful to decode the identification of sexual dissidence and disease. In fact, although AIDS is obviously an actual disease that rots bodies and kills its victims, it is only through rhetorical devices (such as metaphors) that we can have access to it. In this light, I think Robert Mapplethorpe's 1988 *Self-portrait* may be relevant for the analysis of *The Line of Beauty*. Like Damien Hirst's vitrines of animal carcasses and Andres Serrano's *Piss Christ*, Mapplethorpe's photographs have been ethically controversial for their allegedly disgusting representation of the homosexual body. This is especially so in his 1988 *Self-portrait*, when he was about to die of AIDS. Senator Helms denounced the photograph as "an epidemic [so that] HIV is displaced from Mapplethorpe's body to the body of his work".[88] Although photography and plastic arts are granted a degree of experimentalism which fiction is not,[89] *The Line of Beauty* searches for a similar effect. The specularity and answerability of Mapplethorpe's photograph is

---

[86] See Susan Sontag, "Notes on 'Camp'", 1964: http://pages.zoom.co.uk/leveridge/ sontag.html (accessed 4/12/2002); *Illness as Metaphor and AIDS and its Metaphors*, New York: Picador, 2001.
[87] D.A. Miller, "Sontag's Urbanity", in *The Lesbian and Gay Studies Reader*, 219.
[88] Richard Meyer, "Robert Mapplethorpe and the Discipline of Photography" (*ibid.*, 374).
[89] See Jean-Michel Ganteau and Susana Onega, Introduction, in *The Ethical Component in Experimental British Fiction since the 1960s*, eds Susana Onega and Jean-Michel Ganteau, Newcastle: Cambridge Scholars Publishing, 2007, 7.

also applicable, as we have seen, to Hollinghurst's novel: Nick's narcissistic projection of his delusive aesthetic world that is projected *en abyme* outside the text through the reading process. So in spite of (or due to) the "radical insufficiency of photography [and fiction] to describe the experiences and ... the vulnerabilities of [the] sentient body",[90] both Mapplethorpe's photograph and *The Line of Beauty* disseminate the traumatic epidemic metaphorically, triggering off the empathic unsettlement and ethical response of, respectively, spectator and reader.

Alan Hollinghurst himself has declared that he prefers avoiding direct references to AIDS because, in his view, this entails a moral positioning and judgement.[91] Therefore, does a fiction that deals with the disease necessarily work as a moral fable? Further, is the aesthetisation of disease and its effects ethically valid? As pointed out in the first section of the essay, literary criticism has underlined a distinction between neo-humanist and poststructuralist, Levinasian ethics, respectively linked to realist and postmodernist literature. Although advocates of Levinasian ethics have prevailed for the last three decades, they have "only nominally turned their back on old-fashioned, deontic morality".[92] Echoing this, *The Line of Beauty* relies on the uncertain and provisional ethics of alterity to address the trauma of gayness while at the same time it displays some moral undertones, particularly in its anti-Thatcher satire. In Hollinghurst's fourth novel, AIDS is more explicit than in the previous ones, especially *The Swimming-Pool Library*. Interpreting this fact from the perspective of trauma theory it might be stated that this is so because the former novel works as a traumatic recurrence of the latter after a period of latency.

Whereas *The Swimming-Pool Library* cannot name AIDS, *The Line of Beauty* re-lives and, therefore, articulates this founding, collective trauma belatedly. Every gay lover and friend of Nick's eventually dies or is on the verge of death because of AIDS. However, the reader never witnesses the actual marks of the disease, for all the rhetorical discourses around it that clog the novel. Leo, Nick's first lover, just disappears until his sister informs Nick of his death and warns him

---

[90] Meyer, "Robert Mapplethorpe", 377.
[91] Peter Burton, *Talking to ...*, Exeter: Third House, 1991, 45.
[92] Ganteau and Onega, Introduction, 2.

against a possible infection. Witnessing a photograph of Leo "with his life behind him", the hero – and vicariously the reader – is forced to confront mortality. Although mediated by a photograph, the narrator describes how the disease dehumanises its victims: "His [Leo's] face was hard to read, since AIDS had taken it and written its message of terror and exhaustion on it .... It was the loneliest thing Nick had ever seen."[93]

Wani, his second lover, also dies of AIDS. This time, we witness the effects of the disease on a beautiful body: Wani's physical rotting is fascinating as well as repulsive. Constant ellipses and unfinished sentences[94] announce the entrance of a sick Wani in a luxurious restaurant, pointing out the inarticulacy of the disease through common language. Wani's healthy body turns frail and his voice languid.[95] His decadent beauty is threatening too, provoking both fear and pity;[96] and his sexual postures and fluids turn into "stooping and vomiting".[97] Consequently Hogarth's line of beauty, which leads Nick's individuation process by shaping everything he feels attracted to, from rococo furniture to muscular male bodies,[98] has a dark side: bodies rot and remind both hero and readers of the inexorability of time while allowing a glimpse of the dissolution of the self related to the Dionysian, the abject, and finally to the crisis of AIDS. Briefly stated, *The Line of Beauty* fosters the aesthetisation of the terrible, though precariously and provisionally. In fact, it is anti-aesthetics that can make the traumatic ethically palatable as well as epistemologically accessible.

Both Leo and Wani are gays and non-whites, which makes them doubly marginal in Thatcher's England. As such, they are the ideal infectors, invaders – in Sontag's military imagery – and transmitters of decomposition and trauma. As Adami argues, like trauma, viruses are transmissible and mutable.[99] Sontag argues that AIDS has been deprived of the romantic halo of other diseases, and has dehumanised

---

[93] Hollinghurst, *The Line of Beauty*, 410.
[94] *Ibid.*, 427-29.
[95] *Ibid.*, 430.
[96] *Ibid.*, 440.
[97] *Ibid.*, 437.
[98] *Ibid.*, 200.
[99] Adami, *Trauma Studies and Literature*, 20.

its victims instead.[100] However, the rhetoric of AIDS in *The Line of Beauty* is much more complex than this. Rather than a medical question, it is a rhetorical, aesthetic, ethical and moral issue. As mentioned earlier, the novel is not particularly experimentalist and, as it progresses, its satiric undertones are increasingly patent. AIDS is also a political phenomenon whereby the novel puts forward the current moral discourses and contradictions of Thatcherism from a somewhat realist outlook. This does not mean that postmodernist trauma studies and the ethics of reading applied to *The Line of Beauty* so far are negligible. It is only that late-postmodernist fiction swings between "some ethical consciousness through the alienating, opening, disquieting presence of experimentation ... and still acts as a means to prise open the realistic idiom" for survival.[101] Echoing the political atmosphere of Thatcherism, the Feddens and their Tory friends consider the disease as a divine punishment ostracising, or constraining the deviant other within the norms of the straightgeist.

When Nick tries to normalise AIDS by alluding to the terrible illness of Sir Maurice Tipper's mother, the corrupt tycoon establishes a moral abyss between perverted gays and poor victims: "That [his mother's disease and death] was utterly different, ... She hadn't brought it on herself."[102] Gays are guilty of sexual deviancy and, therefore, deserve death, while heterosexuals and, especially, babies are passive victims deserving pity instead. As Nick's discourse gets more sexually explicit, the businessman looks at him and says "I'm afraid what you're saying fills me up with revulsion",[103] thus closing the conversation and re-establishing moral order.

Despite his attempts at aesthetisizing his world, Nick and his gay peers are simply tolerated by society, even apparently valued as connoisseurs. But, once the abject returns, threatening and exposing the incongruities and weak points of the *status quo*, they are labelled as invaders and shameful sinners. Gay sexual intercourse – which is represented very explicitly throughout Hollinghurst's production in general – reveals all its disgusting fluidity when it is associated with AIDS and its means of transmission. AIDS comes true when the

---

[100] Sontag, *Illness as Metaphor*, 43-49.
[101] Ganteau and Onega, Introduction, 7-8.
[102] Hollinghurst, *The Line of Beauty*, 339.
[103] *Ibid.*, 340.

sensationalist press publishes the sexual scandal at the Feddens'. Nick
sees the headlines for the first time when an unrecognisably furious
Rachel Fedden shows him *The Standard*. The subheading, which
reads "Peer's Playboy Son has AIDS", makes Nick feel pity for Wani.
However, his sentimentalism fades away when he reads the actual
heading, "Gay Sex Link to Minister's House",[104] which implicates
him directly. Later, Nick re-lives the trauma of homophobic prejudice
when Toby himself hands him over *The Sun*'s headline, "Gay Sex
Romp at MP's Holiday Home".[105] Despite his myopia, the hero
glimpses his own *anagnorisis*: he is an outcast, whom the Feddens are
not going to listen to or empathise with. As Adami points out,
"traumatic history can only be communicated through a 'contagion' of
the listener [or reader]".[106] Victims need empathetic listeners to bear
witness to their traumas. However, as is described in *The Line of
Beauty*, the outburst of AIDS short-circuited the crucial interaction
between victim and listener. Similarly, the readers of the novel
become conscious of the impact of the unresolved trauma of Nick and
his peers, as well as of its ethical and political implications.

If there is an Other in *The Line of Beauty*, that is Nick Guest, as his
surname suggests. In fact, he is an Other even to himself as far as he
constructs an aesthetic mask to obliterate his origins and, somehow,
his sexual orientation. Hence, his complex *cathexis* with his parents,
his lovers and even with himself. His status is always ambiguous, both
inside and outside the world of the Feddens. Indeed his role is only
well defined towards the end of the novel. Once his actual identity is
revealed, he turns out to be an invader of moral and political values,
particularly those represented by the traditional family. He defies its
logic and is ejected as an alien, destabilising force. After the attacks of
Rachel and Toby, Nick is confronted with his most traumatic
experience, Gerald Fedden's rage. The hero eavesdrops on Barry
Groom's (Gerald's friend) homophobic discourse:

> "They [gays] hate us, you know, they can't breed themselves, they're
> parasites on generous fools who can. Crawling to you [Gerald]
> crawling on the fucking Ouradis. I'm not remotely surprised he led

---

[104] *Ibid.*, 468.
[105] *Ibid.*, 469.
[106] Adami, *Trauma Studies and Literature*, 47.

your poor lovely daughter astray like this, exploited her, there's no other word for it. A typical homo trick."

But his reaction is surprisingly sentimental and naïve:

> Barry was a multiple adulterer and ex-bankrupt – to be hated by him was surely a mark of probity. But Gerald ... well, Gerald, for all his failings, was a friend.[107]

This is Nick's *hamartia*, his crime against himself and his peers, by masking and subordinating homophobic reality to a delusive aestheticism. All his wishfulfilment fantasy turns to pieces when Gerald borrows Groom's discourse against him:

> "Didn't it strike you as rather odd, a bit queer, attaching yourself to a family like this?"
> Nick thought it was unusual – that was the beauty of it, or had been ....
> Gerald said, "I've been giving it some thought. It's the sort of thing you read about, it's an old homo trick. You can't have a real family, so you attach yourself to someone else's. and I suppose after a while you just couldn't bear it, you must have been very envious I think of everything we have, and coming from your background too perhaps ... and you've wreaked some pretty awful revenge on us as a result. And actually, you know ..." he raised his hands, "all we asked for was loyalty".

Mr Fedden closes the invective by neutralising Nick, "I ask you again, who are you? What the fuck are you doing here?"[108] Gerald's words shatter the hero's identity and *raison d'être*. Nick's former role as aesthete breaks down and he becomes the abject, or, in Ruth Parkin-Gounelas' terms, *The Other Within*.[109]

The political and moral undertones behind Nick's ejection make the reader empathise with the hero and censor his aggressors. However, this satiric, morally transparent, discourse is problematised in the closing paragraphs of the novel. The hero is confronted with the

---

[107] Hollinghurst, *The Line of Beauty*, 477.
[108] *Ibid.*, 481-82.
[109] See n.43.

sublime – his unspeakable fate – which trauma discourse can only hint at:

> The sky was threatening and fast-moving. The tall white house-fronts had a muted gleam. It came over him that the test result would be positive .... He tried to rationalize the fear, but its pull was too strong and original. It was inside himself, but the world around him ... had also changed .... It was like a drug sensation .... The emotion was startling. It was a sort of terror, made up of emotions from every stage of his short life, weaning, homesickness, envy and pity, but he felt that the self-pity belonged to a larger pity. It was a love of the world that was shockingly unconditional.[110]

In these closing lines the hero is at a loss, rhetorically looking at himself and alienated against the threatening sublime. Unable to come to terms with the terrible physicality of gay trauma, but as an unreal drug experience, he is overwhelmed by the threat of his own reflection, like Dorian and Aschenbach. Like his predecessors, Nick feels homesick, longing for the *chora*, a state of merciless sentimentalism and abjected undifferentiation. The anti-aesthetic horror of the hero facing his reflection necessarily implicates the reader. The latter does not identify with the hero, but, as reader and ethical witness, he must recognise his trauma as Other.

Surely truth must be somewhere, perhaps in fiction, and one hopes fiction must be in truth. I do not aim at downgrading the latter (nor the former); on the contrary, the evocation of the ethical turn with which this essay opened relies on a revision of truth and how literature can echo, shape and articulate it. Philosophy, ethics and historiography do not necessarily share the aesthetic nature intrinsic to literature. Literature can bear witness to events and facts as these others disciples do, if only from a different angle and with a different purpose. In fact, literature can help approach ethical issues such as trauma and its impact on victims from the vantage point of fiction. Through fiction, particularly anti-aesthetics, AIDS (like gayness before the outbreak of the disease) could be named when its victims and their culture were being literally annihilated. With all this in mind, Plato's words: "They

---

[110] Hollinghurst, *The Line of Beauty*, 500-501.

cite poets as witnesses", regain all their meaning. Literature is an ethically charged aesthetic phenomenon.

Further, trauma fiction has an element of performativity in the sense that it represents the traumatic event. However, it is an undeniably (and necessarily) narrative phenomenon too, as far as readers have access to it in textual form, even if the overwhelming character of trauma claims for a non-referential language. Disruptions, gaps, silences, tropes and especially, the compelling, bodily force of anti-aesthetics, allow for the representation of inarticulateness so that the reader is able to find meaning, an ethical role and, one hopes, empathise with the victim. In her analysis of Julian Barnes' *A History of the World in 10½ Chapters*, Susana Onega points out "the inadequacy of traditional novelistic forms to represent trauma" and of master-narratives like World History to heal the traumas of the past. Her reading shows that the fragmentariness and palimpsestic structure of Barnes' novel, as well as its narrative masks and its parodying of genres, solve the problems of articulacy and inarticulacy.[111] Likewise, although much less experimental than Barnes' novel and despite its neo-humanist satiric undertones, *The Line of Beauty* keeps a distance with classic realism by means, especially, of intertextuality. Henry James' literary style – dislocated, disrupted and full of silences, gaps and ellipses – and Thomas Mann's aesthetic homoeroticism are recast to meet the needs of turn-of-the-millennium gay trauma literature. The narration as well as Nick Guest's identity are not only shaped on trauma, they are also provisional: the hero suffers from an ambiguous status – gay but complicit with reactionary Tories, discriminated but privileged, himself and the Other within – just as the narrator's discourse is only integrated when Nick's voice is reconciled with those of his predecessors.

The relationship between ethics and aesthetics has constantly changed in the course of time. Applying Todorov's theories to *The Line of Beauty*, it might be stated that Hogarth's aesthetic treatise, *The Analysis of Beauty* (1753), represents the first theory, whereby art is in the service of ethics. Nick Guest embodies the second, or Romantic theory, since he favours poetry over ethics; while Hollinghurst's novel

---

[111] Susana Onega, "The Nightmare of History, the Value of Art and the Ethics of Love in Julian Barnes's *A History of the World in 10 ½ Chapters*", in *Ethics in Culture*, 360, 365.

stands for the third, which sees ethics and aesthetics as independent but complementary phenomena. In this light, *The Line of Beauty* may be said to offer a testimony of the trauma of AIDS from a dual, aesthetic and ethical standpoint. In fact, the hero's *Bildungsroman* and the reading process can only be understood from both ethics and aesthetics. Nick is obsessed with a delusive idea of beauty, which coincides with Nietzsche's revision of classic Apollonian beauty. However, as the narration progresses, the Romantic hero is confronted with the dark side of beauty. The sublime and, especially, the Dionysian and the abject re-inscribe the factuality of the homosexual bodies of Nick and his peers. Marked by rottenness, the victims' bodies are also the site of anti-aesthetic reactions out of repulsion and fascination. It is, however, the textual representation and misrepresentation of the traumatic event that has centred the interest of my analysis: that is, the mismatch between lived experience and its translation into a text, as well as its consequences in the reading process. Gayness and AIDS are textual events that Hollinghurst's novel articulates as bodily and rhetorical issues which irremediably slap Nick's, the narrator's and the readers' face.

"THE ETERNAL LOOP OF SELF-TORTURE": ETHICS AND TRAUMA IN IAN MCEWAN'S *ATONEMENT*

GEORGES LETISSIER

The title of McEwan's novel, published in 2001 just before the terrorist attacks of 9/11, echoes many philosophical reflections that emerged in the aftermath of the Holocaust. On the collective scale of a whole nation, the question of guilt was raised by Karl Jaspers, immediately after World War II.[1] Hannah Arendt, for her part, addressed the issue of fault as a solitary experience and its etiology, that is, how to trace its origin.[2] Guilt has also been integrated into a reflection on history writing. In the same way as Adorno claimed that "to write poetry after Auschwitz is barbaric",[3] the process of history writing has been reconsidered progressively as the extent of the tragedy of World War II was being brought to public knowledge. The imprescriptibility of some ineradicable acts was posited as a prerequisite for historiography[4] and the semantic relevance of the etymological kinship between *gift* and for*giving*[5] has been underscored. From many respects, the polysemic term "atonement" covers most of the above-mentioned debates.

Atonement spans the whole twentieth century (from the allusion to venerable Victorian grandparents to a birthday party set in 1999). In a nutshell, it can be said to narrate what Shoshana Felman describes as

---

[1] Karl Jaspers, *La Culpabilité allemande* (1946), trans. Jeanne Hersch, Paris: Éditions de Minuit, 1990.

[2] Hannah Arendt, *Eichmann in Jerusalem: A Report on the Banality of Evil* (1963), Harmondsworth: Penguin Books, 1994.

[3] Theodor W. Adorno, *Prisms* (1955), trans. Samuel and Shierry Weber, Cambridge, MA: The MIT Press, 1997, 34.

[4] Jacques Derrida, "Le Siècle et le pardon", *Le Monde des débats* (9 December 1999): ftp://ftp.ac-toulouse.fr/pub/philosophie/derridalesiecleetlepardon.rtf (accessed 19/2/2009); Paul Ricœur, *La Mémoire, l'histoire, l'oubli*, Paris: Éditions du Seuil, 2000.

[5] As underlined, after Mauss and Bataille, by Derrida ("Le Siècle et le pardon", s.p.).

an unresolved experience, in the "age of testimony".[6] Shortly before
dying, a famous woman novelist confesses to what has been a lifelong obsession. When a teenage girl, she wrongly accused a man (her
sister's lover) of rape: he was then sent to prison and later volunteered
to fight in the war to shorten his sentence. Both he (Robbie in the
novel) and the writer's elder sister (Cecilia) died in the prime of life,
sealing a tragic, romantic destiny. With the benefit of hindsight, the
girl's stupid accusation – she probably had a crush on the young man
and she was all wrapped up in literary vagaries – caused tragedy on an
unprecedented scale. What could have been confined to a private
domestic incident, with the master's daughter telling on the charlady's
son for a crime he was later proved never to have committed, was
compounded by the events of World War II. With the falsely accused
young man dying as anonymous victim of modern warfare, and his
beloved losing her life hardly a few months later in the *Blitzkrieg*,
Briony Tallis, the novelist, for the remainder of her life was to look
upon herself as a sort of executioner. Hence the many long years
dedicated to atoning for a silly crime – a freakish action by a girl eager
to show off – by serving as a nurse to do penance while trying to come
to terms with the unexplainable and unforgivable, through writing: a
"fifty-nine-year assignment".[7] At the novel's end, nothing has been
resolved as there is serious doubt concerning the publication of the
written testimony due to expected litigation problems, and it is also
suggested that the two protagonists who have haunted the narrator's
consciousness are still far too present to be consigned to history:

> Not quite, not yet. If I had the power to conjure them at my birthday
> celebration .... Robbie and Cecilia, still alive, still in love, sitting side
> by side in the library.[8]

Atonement is the record of an unachievable "mourning work" – it
eschews the trappings of fiction as problem-solving conjuring trick.

The experience of trauma, theorised by Freud in the third chapter
of *Beyond the Pleasure Principle*, refers to the repeated mental re-
enactment of a painful event. It designates the peculiar and sometimes

---

[6] Shoshana Felman and Dori Laub, *Testimony, Crises of Witnessing in Literature*,
New York and London: Routledge, 1992, 53.
[7] McEwan, *Atonement, Atonement* (2001). London: Vintage, 2002, 369.
[8] *Ibid.*, 372.

uncanny way in which catastrophic episodes seem to repeat themselves for those who have lived through them.[9] The Greek etymology of "trauma" points to a physical wound inflicted on the body. Later occurrences of the term, notably the Freudian acceptation, foreground the symbolical aspect: a wound affecting the psyche. Trauma, whose effects Freud was to observe in the awesome nightmares of battlefield survivors, entails a breach in the mind's experience of time, self and the world. Both iteration and belatedness constitute the specificity of trauma, though, and correlatively its interest for literary studies. In a sense, trauma involves a process of deferral. Unlike physical injury, which may be ascribed to precise circumstances, and whose pathology may be clearly diagnosed, trauma relates to the after-effects of some momentous event that may have escaped consciousness. As such, it is not locatable as a single, healable event: "Trauma is not locatable in the simple violent or original event in an individual's past, but rather in the way that its very unassimilated nature – the way it was precisely *not known* in the first instance – returns to haunt the survivor later on."[10]

Exactly: Ian McEwan's *Atonement* is about a survivor's lifelong guilt, or rather about how the belated effects of culpability are given some means of expression through writing. Yet, Briony Tallis' many successive drafts cannot be said to fulfil any therapeutic function in so far as there is not any cure to heal the symbolic wound: her false statement and its lethal consequences. So writing can be regarded as what permits the young woman, and later the novelist, to survive the traumatic experience of having wrecked two lives, through the sort of silly acts of bravado youngsters are sometimes prone to. Furthermore, by showing the close inter-relatedness between private, domestic events (the Tallis family saga until Briony's revelation) and collective history (chiefly the Dunkirk evacuation), McEwan subtly suggests that a single, individual act of denunciation may have unheard-of, far-reaching repercussions. Far from being confined to the Tallis' Surrey estate and to local chronicle, Briony's rash course of action has to be seen in the context of the interwar period. Indeed, as Robbie Turner

---

[9] Sigmund Freud, "Beyond the Pleasure Principle", in *On Metapsychology* (1920), ed. Angela Richards, Penguin Freud Library, Vol. XIII, London and New York: Penguin, 2000, 237-386.
[10] Cathy Caruth, *Unclaimed Experience, Trauma, Narrative, and History*, Baltimore and London: The Johns Hopkins University Press, 1996, 4.

shortens his prison sentence by volunteering to go and fight in France, retrospectively Briony's act takes on historical significance: "she understood how the war might compound her crime."[11] And by focalising his novel on a character who doubles as fiction writer, McEwan opens thought-provoking tracks for reflection on the tension between creative writing and testimony.

As many critics have most convincingly argued, *Atonement* is a highly literary fiction fraught with overt, and covert, intertextual references. Such erudition does not merely contribute to the novel's self-reflexivity, though, since it can be established that *Atonement* shows how, in a post-traumatic age, the literary experience is endowed with a testimonial function. It would seem indeed that testimony has become the discursive mode *par excellence*, as indicated by Elie Wiesel: "If the Greeks invented tragedy, the Romans the epistle and the Renaissance the sonnet, our generation invented a new literature, that of testimony."[12] Part Two of McEwan's novel ostensibly flaunts the thin borderline between fiction writing and the act of bearing witness by drawing from old veterans' letters to translate the traumatic encounter with the Lacanian Real from the perspective of twentieth-century modern warfare, as documented by Virilio.[13]

Beginning with a general discussion of various facets of trauma experiences, this essay will then turn to focus in some detail upon the relations between fiction writing and witnessing in *Atonement*. If, as Briony – self-portrayed as "important writer in disguise"[14] – puts it, "She was under no obligation to the truth, she has promised no one a chronicle",[15] how is the reader to assess the ethical responsibility involved by this intrusion into the sensitive realm of collective memory? And if, as Cyril Connolly in the novel is reported to have written, "artists [do not] have an obligation to strike up attitudes to the

---

[11] McEwan, *Atonement*, 288.

[12] Elie Wiesel, "The Holocaust as a Literary Inspiration", in *Dimensions of the Holocaust*, Evanston: Northwestern University Press, 1977, 9.

[13] See Paul Crosthwaite, "Speed, War and Traumatic Affect: Reading Ian McEwan's *Atonement*", *Cultural Politics: An International Journal*, III/1 (March 2007), 57-70, in which the emphasis is laid on the war episodes in Part Two by drawing from Virilio's study of twentieth-century warfare.

[14] Can we not see a token of the persistence of the authorial figure (McEwan's) in this statement attributed to the intradiegetic persona of the author? Where witnessing is concerned, there are no possible evasions.

[15] McEwan, *Atonement*, 280.

war",[16] what does it imply when a twenty-first-century fiction writer returns to the 1940s? Can the search for new narrative forms serve as a cop out to shirk ethical responsibility on the ground that warfare is the enemy of creative activity? *Atonement* will be studied in the perspective of the current development of the historical novel. More precisely, the question of how contemporary fiction can open some of the darkest pages of the Western World's past will be raised. It will be shown that McEwan's novel substantially revises the notion of time and history as inherently flowing and sequential, by taking on board the traumatic aftermath of the recent past. Instead of showing the fluid continuity of time, viewed from the vantage point of a sheltered present, novels like *Atonement* show a past that does not become past, and whose return into the present may be construed as symptomatic of traumatic time. Ulrich Baer's distinction between Heraclitean time, which keeps on flowing like the river, simultaneously the same and not the same, and Democritean time, which is made up of random, contingent events in a world perceived as a swirl of atoms in a void, will be used to further investigate the novel's treatment of traumatic history.[17]

The various facets of trauma
The novel opens on a long first part dedicated to scenes of family reunion in the summer of 1935. The setting is meticulously called up and many authentic details are interspersed to help convey the sense of a sheltered life in a stately country mansion when the storm of history is brewing over Europe. Through this minute evocation of apparently trifling episodes imperceptibly building up to a moment of rupture, McEwan does something similar to Ishiguro in *The Remains of the Day*.[18] In both cases, the minor events of daily life are foregrounded, while history is being written elsewhere, in the offices of Whitewall, where Jack Tallis, the conspicuously absent master of the house, is reported to spend most of his time. Only a few odd documents filter, testifying to the subterranean activities destined to work out contingency plans in case the international situation should worsen. While the spectre of war hovers, the narrative, through

---

[16] *Ibid.*, 314.
[17] Ulrich Baer, *Spectral Evidence, The Photography of Trauma*, Cambridge, MA and London: The MIT Press, 2002, 5-6.
[18] Kazuo Ishiguro, *The Remains of the Day* (1989), London: Faber and Faber, 1990.

temporal dilation, lingers on long spells of inactivity. In the first chapters of Part One, through delaying tactics, McEwan seems to put off the action, while providing sociological information on the mores of the class-conscious English, by depicting a typical household. However, it can be argued that through the dramatic emptiness of the first part of *Atonement*, that stands in sharp contrast to the rest of the novel – notably parts two and three – McEwan already inscribes a logic of trauma. So the novel does not merely indirectly evoke the impending war, the way Ford Madox Ford's *The Good Soldier* or D.H. Lawrence's *Women in Love* do,[19] rather it introduces trauma as a way of responding to outside experience. And it is this persistence of trauma that links together the four blatantly disjointed chunks that make up the novel.

In his repeated attempts to grapple with the description and conceptualisation of trauma, Freud returns to the shocking and unexpected occurrence of an accident. In both *Beyond the Pleasure Principle* and *Moses and Monotheism*, the example of the train accident from which a person walks away unhurt to subsequently suffer from post-traumatic stress disorder is taken as emblematic of the traumatising shock of a commonly occurring violence. Right from the beginning of *Atonement*, in the prevailing absence of action, a traumatic pattern is inserted through the cracking of a much treasured heirloom: a Meissen porcelain vase. That this incident is of paramount importance is signalled by the fact that Cecilia, Briony's elder sister, has to "[let] herself confront the significance of the accident". Needless to say, the object, far from being merely a precious antique, is endowed with symbolical value. It stands for no less than civilisation, so that any damage done to it implies the collapse of the refinement of art surrendering to barbarity. Indeed, the narrator goes to great lengths to recount the epic of the vase, from the Age of the Enlightenment, or rather the German *Aufklärung* – it dates back to 1728 and bears witness to the taste for *Chinoiserie* current at the time – to the apocalypse of World War I, when it was miraculously rescued by a forefather of the Tallis family.

At a time when, in spite of the relative peace and quiet, history seems to be poised on the brink of the abyss, the vase iconically stands for the fragility – or brittleness – of civilisation: "the heroism and

---

[19] Ford Madox Ford, *The Good Soldier* (1915), New York and London: Norton, 1995; D.H. Lawrence, *Women in Love* (1920), London: Penguin Classics, 2000.

goodness, all the years backed up behind the history of the vase." The trauma logic lies in the way that what should have been a casual incident resulting from a mere tussle marks a break in Cecilia's psycho-narration. In Freudian theory, the accident marks the irruption of a sudden, abrupt event resisting comprehension. On the spur of the moment, its import is not precisely grasped and it strikes through the impact of its very incomprehensibility: "She [Cecilia] had the presence of mind to set the ruined vase back down on the step before letting herself confront the significance of the accident." Then, once the initial stage of bewilderment has been overcome, the accident is felt to reflect something of magnitude that somehow precludes full understanding. Rhythm suddenly accelerates to convey the sort of quick flashback that is believed to occur to the consciousness just before death by accident: "her dead uncle, her father's dead brother, the wasteful war, the treacherous crossing of the river, the preciousness beyond money, the heroism and goodness, all the years backed up behind the history of the vase reaching back to the genius of Horoldt, and beyond him to the mastery of the arcanists who had re-invented porcelain."[20]

The instantaneous, retrogressive flash-vision recapitulates a list of victories of art and culture over nihilistic forces, notably the devastation of World War I. But the full importance of the cracking of the vase eludes immediate comprehension and introduces a process of belated reverberation that is one of the distinctive characteristics of the whole novel. At a simple diegetic level, hints at the vase accident recur. In the midst of the debacle, when the Tallis house is requisitioned, the vase is smashed,[21] and the news of its destruction warrants so much attention that it is announced to Cecilia in Briony's fictitious account of her encounter with her in May 1940. The accident of the vase is also central to a reflection on trauma as it is foreclosed in Briony Tallis' experimental novella, *Two Figures by a Fountain*.[22] Much has been made of Briony's appropriation of the Woolfian technique of alternate points of view to report the same, single scene, but the most striking feature of McEwan's approach is probably that what should be uppermost in each character's mind is simply omitted. The fact is that in the original version of the scene, prior to its

---

[20] McEwan, *Atonement*, 29.
[21] *Ibid.*, 279.
[22] *Ibid.*, 312.

fictionalisation, Briony plainly fails to register the centrality of the tell-tale vase: "She [Cecilia] turned abruptly and picked up from the deep shade of the fountain's wall a vase of flowers Briony had not noticed before."[23] The failure to grasp what the cracking of the vase entails is later on pointed out as a flaw by Cyril Connolly, the editor of *Horizon*, in the letter he sends to Briony to refuse her manuscript. The critic advises the young woman to drop the tussle over the vase altogether, if she is not going to use this object to impart narrative impetus to her story. The interesting point is that through this oversight of a potentially meaningful detail, the novel points at the question of narrative reliability and at the significance of blind spots. Briony, the adult novelist aware of the refinements permitted by the recent Bergsonian theories of consciousness, propounds a relativistic approach to perception. Such relativism proves to have devastating consequences because it articulates the tension between "seeing" and "knowing", which is seminal in trauma theory.

Caruth has underscored the cognitive dimension of the process of trauma by suggesting that it challenges conventional understandings of how reference works, according to which "seeing" is assumed to translate directly into "knowing":

> Traumatic experience, beyond the psychological dimensions of suffering it involves, suggests a certain paradox: that the most direct seeing of a violent event may occur as an absolute inability to know it, that immediacy, paradoxically, may take the form of belatedness. The repetitions of the traumatic event [suggest] a larger relation to the event which extends beyond what can simply be seen or what can be known and is inextricably tied up with the belatedness and incomprehensibility that remain at the heart of this repetitive seeing.[24]

Admittedly, the rupture introduced in Part One by Briony's false testimony may be analysed as a short-circuiting of the common access to knowledge in everyday life situations, when seeing precedes knowing. Visual perception transmits information that is processed by the consciousness to ensure knowing and understanding. The scene that Briony catches a glimpse of is subsequently presented as a rape,

---

[23] *Ibid.*, 39.
[24] Cathy Caruth, "Traumatic Awakenings", in *Violence, Identity and Self-Determination*, eds Hent de Vries and Samuel Weber, Stanford, CA: Stanford University Press, 1997, 208.

as a potentially traumatic scene for anyone, let alone a teen-aged girl, to witness. The belated recurrence of images that may not be immediately mentally recorded is implied in the rest of the novel. The part of incomprehensibility represented by a sexual act for a thirteen-year-old girl in 1935 is repeatedly shown as both scaring and a subject of curiosity. All the conditions for a traumatic experience are gathered with a significant difference, though. The abrupt irruption of a totally unpredictable event is what is lacking: it is, on the opposite, as if Briony, through her warped imagination, were bracing herself for a traumatic encounter that she wishes for, because it ties in with the plot she has thought up for her next story. McEwan snidely suggests that the sickly imaginative child, whose mind is cloyed with fictions, believes that a traumatic experience is akin to some kind of literary epiphany.

The outcome of such a lack of foresight is without ambiguity, since there is no way of escaping unscathed from a catastrophic experience. Briony cannot be hyperomniscient in her dealings with the outside world the way she is in her fictitious creation. There is a price to be paid for mistaking reality for fiction, which is another way of showing that the latter must assume a measure of responsibility towards the former. In her eagerness to have reality conform to predetermined narrative frames and because she can only apprehend the referential world through the lens and grids of fiction, Briony more or less deliberately perverts the way reference works. Instead of relying on sight to gather clues, she establishes the priority of her foreknowledge: "Less like seeing, more like knowing",[25] as she candidly puts it to her interrogators. This bypassing of the standard process of perception bears resemblance to the cognitive disruption Caruth observes in traumatic situations. In each case, the outer event is not assimilated by the consciousness; either the sheer impact of the shock pre-empts the usual mental processing, or the interference of pre-existing scenarios prevents the mind from being affected by the outside.

Once the search for the Quincey twins starts, the scenario of the evil-doing maniac imposes itself on Briony's mind with such force that the slightest noise and the least perceptible movement can but confirm what she knows already. So, ultimately, it is this short-circuiting of the usual process of perception that triggers a haunting

---

[25] McEwan, *Atonement*, 170.

pattern of belated returns. The erroneous conviction that Robbie Turner has committed a criminal act will recur obsessively to Briony's mind for the rest of her life because it corresponds to a missed encounter with the outside world. It can be said that, as in the case of trauma, it is the incapacity to relate properly to exterior circumstances in a critical situation which induces mental disorder, and leads to the compulsive recurrence of the same images ever after: all that took place on that long, fateful night in the summer of 1935. No doubt every single detail has been mentally reviewed over the years: "threading the beads of detail into an eternal loop, a rosary to be fingered for a lifetime."[26]

The momentous events of that summer night cannot be converted into memory and so preclude the possibility of a narratable story, as is confirmed by the many drafts that have been produced over the years. Not only are the *Trials of Arabella* rehearsed in the novel, but also each and every circumstance of the few days leading to Robbie's arrest may be said to be subjected to a sort of mental rehearsal. The long first part of *Atonement* would be like a criminal reconstitution, during which all the details are gone over. Each threading of the beads of detail adds or deletes some elements, or at least is liable to alter the chain of events in some way. What is implied is the impossibility of coming to the final, definitive version. The threading of the beads of detail can only be brought to a halt by outer circumstances, memory loss or mental debility, due to vascular dementia. Through the little ironies of history, the memory of World War II is stored in the Royal Bethlehem Hospital, better known as Bedlam, where for decades the mentally deranged were shut up.

Briony's false testimony may also be approached from the perspective of trauma studies because it leads to dispossession, to a loss of the control exerted by the consciousness. So it raises the issue of bearing witness after a catastrophic event. Once her accusing words are out, Briony is deprived of any power of control on the text (the police cross-examination and the ensuing record) that is written. What the scenes of police interrogation demonstrate is the impossibility of confession:

> How can one confess to such a history without engaging once again,
> in a deluded and deluding (pseudowitnessing, pseudocontinuity,

---

[26] *Ibid.*, 173.

pseudocognition, of yet another) referential narrative? And what would be the inescapable performative production of the linguistic utterance of such a confession?"[27]

The gap between the narrative Briony ideally would like to produce and what actually comes out from what she says, is ascribable to the coercive presence of the policemen, perceived as both figures of authority and father substitutes. The account is warped due to the girl's desire to please her interrogators: "She wanted the inspector to embrace her and comfort her and forgive her, however guiltless she was",[28] as Leiris claimed, "every confession contains a desire to be absolved".[29] Moreover, there is a gap between the logic of Briony's self-justifying argument – "when she said, over and again, I saw him, she meant it, and was perfectly honest, as well as passionate" – and the argument of causality which is the only thing that matters to the police. Therefore Briony, who is endeavouring to get at some semblance of truth while going over the past events, finds herself trapped into a machine of discourse, whose functioning turns out to be beyond her power and control: "a process was moving fast and well beyond her control ... the process that she herself had set in train."[30]

She experiences the frustrated urge to amend, qualify, and complicate what is summarily noted down by the police from what she says. Her declarations have repercussions that she had not anticipated because she would rather have stayed in a grey zone where distinctions between "knowing" and "not knowing" cannot be firmly established. However, in contrast, the policemen have a strict agenda, whereby each utterance has to be neatly classified into clear-cut, binary categories: "Either she saw, or she did not see."[31] The interrogation scene is reminiscent of the trial in *Lord Jim* in which the judges only expect facts:

> They wanted facts. Facts! They demanded facts from him, as if facts could explain anything![32]

---

[27] Felman and Laub, *Testimony*, 148.

[28] McEwan, *Atonement*, 174.

[29] Michel Leiris, *Manhood: A Journey from Childhood into the Fierce Order of Virility* (1946), trans. Richard Howard, New York: Grossman, 1963, 154.

[30] McEwan, *Atonement*, 169.

[31] *Ibid.*, 170.

[32] Joseph Conrad, *Lord Jim* (1900), New York and London: Norton, 1996, 22.

Because she lets herself be trapped into the labyrinth of her own construction, Briony gradually relinquishes the supremacy of her consciousness to delegate to others the writing of the case: "What she meant was rather more complex than everyone else so eagerly understood, and her moments of unease came when she felt that she could not express these nuances."[33] The legal context, in the present instance an interrogation scene, demonstrates how a testimony wanders away from what the witness feels as the intrinsic complexities of facts. *Atonement*, then, dramatises a crisis of truth and, significantly, the scene of the trial is foreclosed. Because she is not of age, Briony is barred access from the court. What should have been a seminal episode is silenced, and in this blank lies traumatic erasure.

Atonement shows how the central scene of the discovery of what is later reported as a rape attempt recurs hauntingly in the rest of the novel, if only because there was a hallucinatory aspect about it in the first place. Through a metonymic shift, the term crime is applied to Briony's conduct by anticipation, more than it is to the event itself, which is largely eclipsed. The retrospective narrative emphasises determinism, as if Briony were acted upon, more than as if she were exerting her control on every step she took: "Within the half hour Briony would commit her crime."[34] The term "maniac", used at regular intervals to evoke the girl's obsession with Robbie's presumed sexual deviance, has an eerie connotation since it ironically points to Briony's own manic quest. The text signals the girl's implacable determination to intrude upon some unsavoury scene that would confirm her verdict: "man, mad, axe, attack, accuse." Clearly, the psychoanalytical symptoms are too obvious to go into any unwarranted detail. The craving to intrude upon a scene of intimacy is a reminder of the phantasmal primal scene, in which the parents' lovemaking becomes a subject of anguish for the excluded child. The novel, which is essentially Briony's testimony, touches upon what at the time she could only intuit, without being able to put it into words: the father's absences and his estranged ailing wife. Hints at the Oedipus complex and at sibling rivalry can also be found in Briony's grudge against her father for protecting Robbie:

> Together the Tallis children would see this brute off, see him safely

---

[33] McEwan, *Atonement*, 169.
[34] *Ibid.*, 156.

out of their lives. They would have to confront and convert their father, and comfort him in his rage and disappointment. That his protégé should turn out to be a maniac![35]

A Freudian family romance comes into play through Briony's psychic vagaries, so that the nightly ramble in search of the guilty maniac is, in many respects, the traumatic enactment of repressed drives. Traumatic, because in the Freudian theory it corresponds to an overflow of emotions and affects, that may be neither controlled nor channelled by the psyche. Hence Briony's delusory perception: "in an instant, Briony understood completely .... She had no doubt. She could describe him", and her bold asseverations that brook no objections: "I saw him. I *saw* him."[36] The intensity of the emotional involvement at this paroxysmal moment triggers off a process of repetition, according to which Briony's position and statements will "then be pursued as demons in private for many years afterwards".[37] McEwan's concern for maverick characters and for offbeat comportments probably accounts for his creation of Briony, and so does his interest for neurosciences and the still largely undecipherable alchemy of the brain.[38] Briony's decision-making and the mental process leading her to indict Robbie Turner maintain their mystery till the end. Straightforward guilt should perhaps be replaced by the more flexible notion of degrees of responsibility. Indeed, to what extent is one fully answerable for one's act, remains a moot point.

Literature and testimony: witnessing as history writing
McEwan enlarges from a story of private guilt to the more general question of guilt as a way of relating to the past. Changes of scales between the individual and the collective, and between the personal and the impersonal, are suggested. For example, the "hairline cracks"[39] in Briony's conviction remind the reader of the hairline cracks in the Meissen vase, which stands for so much in terms of history. Or, when Briony Tallis as a nurse walks through the streets of London in 1940, she succeeds in getting both beyond herself and

---

[35] *Ibid.*, 158.
[36] *Ibid.*, 164-65.
[37] *Ibid.*, 167.
[38] Since *Atonement*, this concern has found its expression through the character of Henry Perowne, the neurosurgeon in Ian McEwan's *Saturday* (2005).
[39] McEwan, *Atonement*, 168.

beyond her time: "Anyone who was, say, seventy now, would have been her age in eighteen eighty eight."[40] So, Briony may be regarded as a transhistorical witness in a sense, and her personal story places the question of guilt at an impersonal level in a post-traumatic century:

> Briony would change her evidence, she would rewrite the past so that the guilty became the innocent. But what was guilt these days? It was cheap. Everyone was guilty, and no one was.[41]

The final birthday party takes place at the very tip of an apocalyptic century. The novel narrows down to a thin edge in the epilogue, and this shrinking applies both to the witness and to the century that is expressed through her. There are many allusions to a constraining pressure, like the tightening of a vice: "This narrowing, which was above all a stripping of identity",[42] "events converging on an end point",[43] or "the sensation of tightening around the temples".[44] It is as if the constricting isotopy were common to both Briony and the century, which enhances the sense of urgency since the act of bearing witness is perceived as a race against death. As a result, any possibility of a serene, dispassionate relation to the past is shown as impossible. The reader is denied the epistemological neutrality of the historian's approach. At the same time, the past cannot be a closed book, because legal impediments are expected to hamper the publication of Briony's work, so the reader is clandestinely let to take a peek at an illicit document. Furthermore, the coda catches the reader in a double bind because it is shown clearly that the principal witness is soon to fade into unknowing and, in the meantime, that her testimony cannot be completed. The very last lines in the present tense conjure up yet again the romantic couple that resist historisation, as it were: "Not quite, not yet .... Robbie and Cecilia, still alive, still in love, sitting side by side in the library, smiling at *The Trials of Arabella*?"[45] In the post-traumatic age, the past as revenance claims its due upon the living: "something of the past always remains, if only as

---

[40] *Ibid.*, 319.
[41] *Ibid.*, 261.
[42] *Ibid.*, 275.
[43] *Ibid.*, 316.
[44] *Ibid.*, 355.
[45] *Ibid.*, 372.

a haunting presence or symptomatic revenant."[46]

The blurring of the boundary line between the living and the dead testifies to an anxious relation to the past and to the impossibility of positing it as historical object, which would imply an indispensable hermeneutic distance. Therefore, the ethical posture consists for the novelist in allowing the repetition to achieve its full effect, and in eschewing any linear, teleological perspective. In this respect, McEwan has written a testimonial novel, that is, one that does not purport to deliver a completed statement or a totalisable account. By adopting a midway position between fictionalisation and testifying, the novelist assumes a responsible stance towards the past.[47] How can this specific approach, allying the self-imposed duty to come to grips with a past that is still very much present and aesthetic concerns, be carried out then? The first striking feature is that language is in process and in trial and this linguistic effect is achieved both through temporal and aesthetic displacements. Then, the fiction revisits genuine pieces of war correspondence and, in so doing, produces a "double haunting" effect. Finally, the novel largely consists of slices of time, or frozen moments that challenge the notion of time as uninterrupted flux, or unstoppable stream, to allow the past to spill over into the present, instead of setting the present as an organising position from which retrospectively some kind of chronological ordering could be imposed.

Temporal displacement is one way of expressing what amounts to a historical crisis. It is best expressed by a loss of bearings that upsets the divisions between past, present and future. Time distortions make it hard for the reader to stay out of the diegesis, and take the long view, once all the narrated events are declared to be hermetically sealed in the realm of the past. *Atonement* removes temporal landmarks. The lack of synchronicity between the events and their perception tampers with the logic of retrospective narration: "seeing strangely, as though everything was already long in the past, made

---

[46] Dominick LaCapra, *Writing History, Writing Trauma*, Baltimore MD and London: The Johns Hopkins University Press, 2001, 49.

[47] The biographical dimension of this engagement with the past of World War II should be mentioned: see "*The Child in Time*. Ian McEwan on his family's astonishing story and the brother he never knew he had", *The Guardian* (Saturday, 12 July 2008): www.guardian.co.uk/lifeandstyle/2008/jul/12/familyandrelationships. Elementsoffiction (accessed 9/1/2009).

more vivid by posthumous ironies."[48] Likewise, in her listlessness Cecilia claims to be cut off from what happens round her: "At other times I [Cecilia] seem to be watching events as if they happened long ago",[49] a remark which begs the question of what the present means to her at that point. If there is no synchronicity between experience and the way it affects consciousness, it might imply that the reader too can view his/her present as if it was already long in the past, and be affected by past atrocities as if there were no screen of time to keep them at a distance. Time disruption, inducing the sense of disorientation and the impossibility of adopting a fixed rational position, is also called up through the introduction of temporal limbo, an ill-defined spell that does not fit in either with what comes before or after. Such in-between moments are suspended upon historical undecidability. In *Atonement* there are several instances of such crises of history that are symptomatic of current anxieties in the age of testimony. One characterises London in 1940, the time of the phoney war: "the dead were not quite yet present, the absent were presumed alive."[50] Another takes on prophetic accents when the novel is set in the context of 2001: "history's last fling before another stretch of time began."[51] In the last resort, *Atonement* forces an ethical attitude on the reader's relation to the past by eschewing reassuring ideologies. Contrary to many contemporary British fictions it makes an unambiguous stance against nostalgia: "There was no need to be nostalgic – it was always an ugly place."[52]

Atonement introduces "double haunting" as a counter discourse to war propaganda: the famous Dunkirk spirit. Briony undertakes the work of archivist, gathering primary sources to bear witness, as an act of atonement for having blundered into History through a rash accusation. She returns to scenes that have not been laid to rest in the collective memory. She ghost-writes original letters recording the traumatic events prior to the Dunkirk evacuation, by editing them for the purpose of a fiction that is paying a debt to the past, by lending a voice to old anonymous vets. This is how a character, Corporal Nettle, features both as a corporal on the side of Robbie Turner in 1940, and

---

[48] McEwan, *Atonement*, 48.
[49] *Ibid.*, 133.
[50] *Ibid.*, 287.
[51] *Ibid.*, 316.
[52] *Ibid.*, 363.

as a witness of the past through his letters. The succession of horrendous scenes in Part Two aptly demonstrates that devastation is so absolute that there is no safe, exterior position from which the collective insanity of war could be related. The narrative does not originate from the peace and quiet of an archival room but from the tortured conscience of Briony, who constantly reminds the reader that there is no adequate way for her to make up for her past error. In *The Writing of the Disaster*, Maurice Blanchot described the paradox of absolute devastation as what destroys the very means of assessing from an outside: "The disaster ruins everything, all the while leaving everything intact."[53] In her own writing after the disaster in Part Two, Briony comes to a similar observation through Robbie's thoughts: "A dead civilisation. First his own life ruined, then everybody else's."[54] This mention of "everybody else's" pre-empts the possibility of an outsider who could bear witness. Even the more distant past, prior to Briony's fateful declaration to the police, cannot be seen as a safe haven. Indeed, on second reading, the novel suggests unexpected chains of metonymic associations. For example, the recurrent image of the child's leg, hanging from a tree, seals the close proximity between the Tallis' nursery of Part One and the atrocities of World War II. This simple haunting detail in itself bespeaks the all-pervading presence of war throughout this cross-the-century novel, since haunting is not time-oriented and can play backwards as well as forwards. The spectre of war can haunt the peace of a summer's day, in the same way as a child's leg can be a stark reminder of lost innocence in the midst of carnage.

The aim of this essay is to read *Atonement* as an attempt to bear witness to the searing persistence of the past in the present. Ian McEwan's fiction excludes the possibility of witnessing from the outside and establishes a traumatic relation to the past. Structurally, it works out a compromise between testifying and the aesthetic quest for narrative forms. Far from being divorced from memory work, the metafictional comments on Victorian novel writing, and more insistently on Modernism, translate the unending search for an adequate means of representation, which Lyotard saw as a response to

---

[53] Maurice Blanchot, *The Writing of the Disaster* (1980), trans. Ann Smock, Lincoln: University of Nebraska Press, 1986, 1.
[54] McEwan, *Atonement*, 217.

extreme situations, in particular the Holocaust.[55] Through its emphasis on displacement and repetition, the novel reproduces the logic of trauma such as it was exposed by Freud shortly after World War I. As a testimony of the past, *Atonement* illustrates the impossibility of consigning to history events that cannot be laid to rest. Shunning the comfort of reassuring ideologies, it pleads for an act of responsible reading. To achieve this, it dismisses the present as vantage point from which to order the chaos of the past retrospectively. The personal commitment of the narrator, or writer in disguise – McEwan has been praised for androgynous writing – who has his/her own axe to grind in going over the events of World War I, is the surest barrier against any museumised treatment of the past.

---

[55] Jean-François Lyotard, *The Postmodern Condition: A Report on Knowledge* (1979), trans. Geoffrey Bennington and Brian Massumi, Minneapolis MN: University of Minnesota Press, 1982, 40-44.

CONJUNCTURES OF UNEASINESS: TRAUMA IN FAY WELDON'S *THE HEART OF THE COUNTRY* AND IN IAN MCEWAN'S *ON CHESIL BEACH*

ANGELA LOCATELLI

> Realism captures the moment of the historical conjuncture through the moment of the linguistic conjuncture.[1]

Some critical premises

One must acknowledge a paradoxical joining of the political and the apolitical in postmodern literary and critical discourse: the presence of a strong meta-discursive and self-referential element in postmodern fiction shows that a ludic and self-serving intention often coexist with the subversive positioning of discourse itself on the threshold, and even at the heart, of crucial political and ethical issues.[2] A large number of novels hinge on diverging versions of "the real" and fully exploit the strategy of unreliability on the part of the narrator, thus creating a sense of the radical inconsistency of "fact", and more or less explicitly suggesting the inanity of political action and ethical

---

[1] Jean-Jacques Lecercle, "Ah! He-Eh! He-Eh! Pontiggia, Pasolini and Language", *La conoscenza della letteratura/The Knowledge of Literature IV*, ed. Angela Locatelli, Bergamo: Bergamo University Press, Sestante Edizioni, 2004, 157-71.

[2] *Innnovation/Renovation: New Perspectives on the Humanities*, eds Ihab Hassan and Sally Hassan, Madison: University of Wisconsin Press, 1983; Patricia Waugh, *Metafiction: The Theory and Practice of Self-Conscious Fiction*, London: Routledge, 1984; Andreas Huyssen, *After the Great Divide: Modernism, Mass Culture, Postmodernism*, Bloomington, IL: Indiana University Press, 1986; Alison Lee, *Realism and Power: Postmodern British Fiction*, London: Routledge, 1990; Fredric Jameson, *The Cultural Turn. Selected Writings on the Postmodern 1983-1998*, London and New York: Verso, 1999; Andrew Gibson, *Postmodernity, Ethics and the Novel: From Leavis to Levinas*, London: Routledge, 1999; *The Ethical Component in Experimental British Fiction since the 1960s*, eds Susana Onega and Jean-Michel Ganteau, Newcastle: Cambridge Scholars Publishing, 2007.

considerations. However, many other novels, on the contrary, interrogate the historical moment with sharp and relentless attention. The representation of trauma in novels written after the 1960s certainly confirms the "parted eye" of postmodern narratives, where the self-consciousness of writing and a variously inflected sense of style interface with the representation of socio-economic variables and the questioning of ideological and ethical issues.[3]

The word "conjuncture" in my title may need some explanation. I am using it in a precise theoretical sense, that is, the one indicated in Jean-Jacques Lecercle's *A Marxist Philosophy of Language*. In this perspective, "conjuncture" is both "historical" and "linguistic":

> Finally, if we adopt Deleuze's definition of style as a-grammaticality and taking things to the limit, the concept enables us to think linguistic change as a function of the historical conjuncture, which creates needs for identity and translates them into fashions and styles, and of the linguistic conjuncture: the counter-interpellations inscribed in the individual style is an intervention in the linguistic conjuncture which alters it, however marginally.[4]

This idea of "conjuncture" – it should be noted – comes in the context of a book that critiques and radically modifies prevailing views of language, as well as of traditional realism, and demonstrates that literature, by moving far beyond mere mimetic illustration, provides knowledge of both language and life. I believe that Lecercle's identification of two "conjunctures", a historical and a linguistic one, and of their mutual responsiveness, is particularly useful in reading Fay Weldon's and Ian McEwan's works because it

---

[3] *Why Literature Matters: Theories and Functions of Literature*, eds Rüdiger Ahrens and Laurenz Volkmann, Heidelberg: Winter, 1996; Cathy Caruth, *Unclaimed Experience: Trauma, Narrative, and History*, Baltimore: John Hopkins University Press, 1999; Geoffrey Hartman, "Trauma within the Limits of Literature", *European Journal of English Studies*, Vvii/3 (December 2003), 257-74; Anne Whitehead, *Trauma Fiction*, Edinburgh: Edinburgh University Press, 2004; *Ethics in Culture: The Dissemination of Values through Literature and Other Media*, eds Astrid Erll, Herbert Grabes and Ansgar Nünning, Berlin: Walter de Gruyter, 2008; and Angela Locatelli, "Literature's Versions of Its Own Transmission of Values", in *Ethics in Culture*, 19-34.
[4] Jean-Jacques Lecercle, *A Marxist Philosophy of Language*, Leiden and Boston: Brill, 2006, 213.

highlights crucial aspects of their style, while proving that literature has a historicity of its own: it meets the event at its very inception, it captures the shift in a specific temporal and cultural situation. I propose that the new complex forms of contemporary fiction can be seen as responses to a wider "resurgence of the real"[5] after a sometimes extreme "linguistic turn" in contemporary culture, a resurgence which feeds a growing need of precise and sophisticated literary contextualisation, for which traditional mimetic forms are no longer viable. The linguist, the historian and the verbal artist must creatively converge in the contemporary novelist who is revisiting and rewriting the past. The acknowledgement of history in the postmodern novel often takes the form of "bearing witness",[6] but even this gesture becomes credible and effective only when it is formally innovative and fully creative. I intend to illustrate and discuss this special effect of literature with reference to *The Heart of the Country* and *On Chesil Beach*.[7]

Some of Italo Calvino's critical observations in *Mondo scritto e mondo non scritto* corroborate the relevance of the special historicity of literary discourse. In his perspective, the historical dimension is the source of the novel's ethical relevance:

> Now to be convinced of the everlasting supremacy of the novel we need to read Lukàcs, and to be captured by his classicist faith in genres, and his terse sense of the epic. But, once we move out of the nineteenth century, his aesthetic ideal is blurred by a soft patina of boredom: we no longer find in it the nervous hurry of our living, to which the "well built" novel has no longer responded, but the lyrical tone of the short novel, or the crude and chronicle type of novella in which Hemingway excelled, as the perfect measure of the new epic .... In Russia, for example a few interesting "novelettes" have begun to appear, which discuss man's behaviour, his moral position *vis à vis* the practical problems and moral dilemmas one finds in everyday life; in America as well, if I am not mistaken, there is this literature of the

---

[5] Charlene Spretnak, *The Resurgence of the Real: Body, Nature and Place in a Hypermodern World*, Reading, MA: Addison-Wesley, 1997.

[6] Shoshana Felman and Dori Laub, *Testimony: Crises of Witnessing in Literature, Psychoanalysis and History*, New York and London: Routledge, 1992; Avishai Margalit, *The Ethics of Memory*, Cambridge, MA: Harvard University Press, 2002.

[7] Ian McEwan, *On Chesil Beach*, London: Vintage Books, 2007.

dignity of the average man in a grey suit in the large industrial and corporate apparatuses. Narrative can limit itself to this modest, but yet serious, task.[8]

The Italian novelist and critic is here lucidly detecting the advent of what have been called "minimalist narratives", and he is clearly foregrounding some of the political implications of minimalist fiction, while validating it with the attributes of ethical dignity. I believe that the new kind of realism described by Calvino finds expression in several post-1960s novels (including his own), in which various defences of the human take the form of a new epic of the ordinary and daily life. Not surprisingly, the articulation of trauma almost intrinsically belongs in these works, as I will now try to argue with reference to two significant examples: Fay Weldon's *The Heart of the Country* and Ian McEwan's *On Chesil Beach*.

The changing vocabulary of uneasiness: from raising consciousness to corporate rights

Fay Weldon's novels are obvious instances of the critical representation of Margaret Thatcher's England and, at times, a provocative discussion of the different political issues relating to the historical moment.[9] Her works provide an explicitly committed

---

[8] The translation is my own, but Calvino seems worth quoting also in the original: "Adesso per convincerci di una intramontabile signoria del romanzo abbiamo bisogno di leggere Lukàcs, lasciarci prendere dalla sua classicistica fede nei generi, dal suo nitido senso dell'epica. Ma, usciti dall'Ottocento, il suo ideale estetico s'appanna d'una soffice patina di noia: non vi ritroviamo il nervosismo, la fretta del nostro vivere, cui hanno risposto non più il romanzo costruito, ma il taglio lirico del romanzo breve, o la novella giornalistica e cruda in cui Hemingway eccelse, come la perfetta misura della nuova epica .... In Russia per esempio da un paio d'anni cominciano ad uscire dei romanzetti interessanti, che discutono il comportamento dell'uomo, la posizione morale di fronte ai problemi pratici e di coscienza che s'incontrano nella vita di tutti i giorni; anche in America, se non sbaglio, c'è questa letteratura di dignità quotidiana dell'uomo in grigio dei grandi complessi industriali e burocratici. La narrativa può anche limitarsi a questo compito modesto ma pur serio" (Italo Calvino, *Mondo scritto e mondo non scritto*, Milan: Mondadori, 2002, 17).

[9] See *Fay Weldon's Wicked Fictions*, ed. Regina Barreca, Hanover, PA and London: University Press of New England, 1994; Finuala Dowling, *Fay Weldon's Fiction*, London: Associated University Presses, 1998; Lana Faulks, *Fay Weldon*, New York: Twayne Publishers, 1998; and Angela Locatelli, "Symbolic and Material Economies in Fay Weldon's Narratives", in *The Economy Principle in English: Linguistic,*

discourse on the personal and social traumas caused by the gendered division of labour and by the ensuing uneven distribution of wealth in late capitalist culture.[10] The most polemical and explicit example in this respect is probably *The Heart of the Country*, a novel which illustrates the extreme consequences of the social disadvantage experienced by women of different cultural backgrounds, different social origin, and different persuasions, but who are, "by accident on purpose", brought to share a common, traumatic destiny, after being abandoned by their respective husbands. They helplessly try to survive in a hypocritical and exploitative society, where the DHSS[11] turns the needy into a "supplicant, and not someone with rights". The policy is illustrated through the sharp gaze of Sonia, a lucid, bitter and disturbed protagonist-narrator, who perceives her "sister" Natalie's unaware and naïve immersion in the present state of affairs, that is, her sudden new need, and the system's humiliating and inadequate response to it. The narrative registers the efficient impersonality of one of the agency's clerks:

> Natalie went to the DHSS offices and there saw one of their senior clerks, a single lady in her forties, who had gone straight from school into the social services and risen through the ranks by virtue of her competence and administrative abilities .... She was professionally kind and considerate but felt, herself, that the sooner her clients (as she was now taught to call them) learned to stand on their own feet, the better. Her name was Mary Alice Dodson, and I [Sonia] have crossed her path several times, one way or another. I hate her for her self-righteousness. Natalie didn't understand that she was hateful, and thought her perfectly pleasant. But then she saw herself as a

---

Literary and Cultural Perspectives, eds Giovanni Iamartino, Marialuisa Bignami and Carlo Pagetti, Milan: Edizioni Unicopli, 2002, 427-38.

[10] Nancy Chodorow, *The Reproduction of Mothering: Psychoanalysis and the Sociology of Gender*, Berkeley: University of California Press, 1978; Judith Butler, *Gender Trouble: Feminism and the Subversion of Identity*, New York and London: Routledge, 1990; Rosy Braidotti, *Patterns of Dissonance: A Study of Women in Contemporary Philosophy*, Oxford: Polity Press, 1991.

[11] The DHSS is the abbreviation for Department of Health and Social Security, the department (now DWP) that used to administer Housing Benefit (now local housing allowance).

> supplicant, and not someone with rights. What a battle I was to have, raising Natalie's client-consciousness![12]

Sonia's language, as it appears even from this very short passage, is the one life was "lived in" in the 1970s: "sister", "raising consciousness", "rights" are powerful lexical indexes of that historical and linguistic conjuncture. The term "client" reflects the cultural shift in the conjuncture. When juxtaposed to "supplicant" it goes a long way in telling how the shift was experienced emotionally by the parties involved. The fact that the supplicant is called "a client" by the clerks working for the social services inscribes, at the level of language, the rampant ideology of neo-con corporate efficiency into the culture of the early 1980s, an ideology which was, in fact, to become a widespread mentality in the Britain of the Eighties and Nineties.

The Heart of the Country is a dramatization of the emergence of the conjunctural slogan "no money – no rights" into the public consciousness, that is, of the onset of the financial and economic kind of relations that would eventually traumatically disrupt the texture of society. Trauma is no longer merely a psychological matter, it is no longer an individual anguish, but a grim pervasive distress that the new and extended social accessibility to psychiatric help fails to resolve or alleviate. (The allusion to the "New Psychiatry" of R.D. Laing, Esterson, and Cooper seems quite transparent.) After being interned in a mental hospital for arson and murder (the climax, and most tragic event in the novel), Sonia sarcastically recalls that doctors there "have even managed to out-suicide their own patients", suggesting that trauma is utterly beyond remedy, and that it is affecting all classes.

Fay Weldon's style once more signifies the spread of uneasiness, and does so through Sonia's cynical, defensive and above all traumatised vocabulary, the language in which the shifts "were lived", in the historical-linguistic conjuncture:

> Last year someone burned to death on the WAEADA float, and I am trying to feel remorse in order to get out of here. So I have to set up the background properly. 'Here' is the Eddon Hill Psychiatric

---

[12] Weldon, *The Heart of the Country*, London: Arrows Books Limited, 1987, 68-69.

Hospital. My psychiatrist's name is Bill Mempton, Dr. Bill Mempton, and at the moment I have a positive transference towards him which means that if he doesn't shave I think he looks rather good, and if he's late I worry in case he's done himself in. The latter is not an insane worry: quite a few psychiatrists at this hospital have killed themselves by what has become known as the Eddon Method .... Bill (how cosy! how almost intimate we have become) gets furious when I make this point, talks about the low wages, high stress, falling status, family difficulties and so forth endured by medics in the psychiatric branch of the profession.[13]

In "this jolly old world" trauma is a collective experience, the hallmark of a breathtakingly rapid shift jettisoning a world, certainly not immune from injustice and privilege, but still sensitive to the Enlightenment concept of *jus naturalis* and human rights, not to mention class consciousness. The zest with which late capitalism was soon to disseminate the logic of the posthuman can hardly conceal the concomitant shift to a world of corporate interests and hence corporate rather than human rights. The emergence of the posthuman in postmodern culture is, of course, a function of the cultural dissolution of the subject of liberal humanism, but one is led to wonder if the posthuman client is a subjectivity one can wholeheartedly embrace. Human rights is (was?) a concept far more extensive than civil rights, or consumer rights and other categories of rights, currently operative in postcapitalist emancipative jargon. Moreover, one may, by the same token, legitimately surmise that the posthuman is the expression of a posttraumatic strategy of outdoing the trauma of the loss of identity. Although several studies on a posthuman turn have appeared in the Nineties,[14] I do not believe the concern has ever been explicitly related

---

[13] *Ibid.*, 85-86. WAEADA is the acronym for the West Avon State Agents and Dealers' Association float, a festival whose patriarchal ideology is subverted by the women's appropriation of it. See Karen Jane Cowan's *Domestic Disruptions: Jane Austen's* Mansfield Park *and Fay Weldon's* The Heart of the Country, MA Dissertation, Simon Frazer University, August 1993, 77: http://ir.lib.sfu.ca/bitstream/1892/7080/1/b15214503.pdf (accessed 8/9/2010).

[14] *Posthuman Bodies*, eds Judith Halberstam and Ira Livingston, Bloomington, IL: Indiana University Press, 1995; Richard E. Gold, *Body Parts: Property Rights and the Ownership of Human Biological Materials*, Washington, DC: Georgetown University Press, 1996; and Andrew Kimbrell, *The Human Body Shop: The Cloning, Engineering, and Marketing of Life*, Washington, DC: Regnery Publishing, 1997.

to a more or less successful strategy of accommodating trauma, which is what I am proposing here.

Another aspect of the issue of realism is that a novel like *The Heart of the Country* unmistakably shows that literature can account for events in a way that the social sciences cannot, since only literature is able to question ideologies from the very perspective of the language articulating them.

Madness and death are illustrated in Weldon's novel as the major traumatic consequence of the emerging mentality and its posturings of democracy. The narrative voice that spells a common destiny of degradation for the have-nots is shared by both an omniscient narrator and by one of the novel's protagonists, Sonia, a former English teacher (who is obviously receptive to the jargon-ridden and stratigraphic hybridity of postmodern English), sees through the mask of social respectability and normality, but this does not help her keep her sanity. Her madness could be read as the novel's defence of the dominant ideology, or simply as a pronouncement on its incontrovertible power. Yet, another reading may propose that Sonia and her "sisters'" failure to become active political subjects in the new context may be perceived as the main cause of individual and collective disaster. The trauma is at once magnified and naturalised by the style of the novelist, who manages to represent the course of events with a minimum interference in her character's words and point of view. A bourgeois education first, and a wickedly clever social marginalisation seem to have led these women to think of their lot as inevitable and normal, even as it escalates from personal to social tragedy.

The opening paragraph of the novel leaves no doubt as to the traumatic implications of the story; it anticipates the onset of tragedy, and meta-linguistically comments on it, through the ironical use of popular biblical clichés and the metaphor of "muddy water welling from a blocked drain":

> Oh!, the wages of sin!
> Natalie Harris sinned, and her husband Harry left for work one fine morning and didn't come back.
> The morning was fine only temporarily. You know what those mornings are, just before the rain sets in? Bright and glittery around the edges; altogether too bright for safety, with a pale blue sky arching

much too high above, and beyond the arch heaven knows what, God or he Devil. And before you know it black clouds begin to edge up all around the horizon, like muddy water welling from a blocked drain, and close the sky over with cloud, drizzle and depression, and your quivering glimpse of eternity, good or bad, is gone.[15]

If tragedy is believing oneself immortal and inexorably coming to terms with an unexpected encounter with death, this highly allusive passage unmistakably inaugurates the tragic paradigm that will be fully developed in the novel. Moreover, trauma is here pictured from the totally uncritical, but culturally mainstream point of view of the unexperienced, naïve, and conventional heroine, to whom loss and guilt seem as "natural" as the "drizzle and depression" of the weather. The formulaic value judgement "the wages of sin" is exposed as the morality that is functional to confirming the *status quo* of gender and class inequality. In fact, the reader soon finds out that while Natalie is indicted for adultery in the prevailing sexist popular *doxa*, the same behaviour on the part of nearly all the husbands in the novel will not result in the same retribution. Ethical and political questioning is promoted into the reader's understanding of events by Sonia's narrated attempts to raise Natalie's class consciousness. Sonia's pedagogical imperative reaches the reader, although the outcome of the novel may problematically suggest that such raised consciousness fosters bitterness and trouble, and remains ineffectual *vis à vis* the emerging general mentality.

The Heart of the Country foregrounds a cultural and time-specific trauma, the uneasiness of the "quiet desperation" denounced in a near contemporary song by the Pink Floyd. Events in the novel challenge the smug sense of class superiority and the sense of invulnerability of the upper-middle classes in the Thatcher era, but also represent the contradictions of the historical conjuncture which inaugurates the endemic precariousness of late capitalist Britain. It also painfully recalls, in the terms of a popular slogan of the 1970s, the precise moment in the historical conjuncture when the private began to be severed from the political. This fact makes this novel a precious instrument in the preservation of a collective cultural memory, and a

---

[15] Weldon, *The Heart of the Country*, 1.

vivid trace of the traumas of micro-history that History often effaces in its self-interested accounts.

Headlines of uneasiness and the language of reticence: (postmodern) literature writing history

On Chesil Beach may be called a domestic tragedy, and yet it is also McEwan's wider fresco of the late years of the Macmillan government. Florence and Edward's story is intensely bound to, and representative of the historical moment. Their loving relationship crashes on the rock of a most insidious cultural *doxa*, that is, the prevalent codes of courtship and marriage in the 1950s and early 1960s. From an ethical angle, such code can be seen as part of a general rule-based behaviour, in which reticence is imperative, and ultimately proves to be lethal. In fact, the protagonists are as reserved and restrained as their times prescribe, and they seem to keep their relationship at the level of approved social gestures and rituals. Florence's musical talent is presumably preparing her for a successful career as a violinist. Edward's genuine interest in history has led him through University and to the city. Both of them display affection for each other and pleasure in sharing different interests, but trauma is waiting round the corner, since both, like many of Ian McEwans' characters,[16] are trapped by the disturbed background of their childhood and adolescence.

Their youth has made them ill equipped for "the facts of life", and most of all has blinded Florence to the recognition of her own sexual difficulties, even towards the man she loves. Even if the reader may surmise that Flora's sexual difficulties derive from the fact that she was abused by her father as a child, one may still acknowledge that this very trauma was made worse by silence, since sex-related trauma was tabooed as much as any open discussion of sexual matters. Moreover, Florence's mother is unresponsive and withdrawn, and Edward's mother is even more distant, being mentally disturbed by brain damage that nobody in the family is ready to name, either to her or to each other. The general linguistic taboo has clearly infiltrated the household in the remotest village in the Chiltern Hills. Not

---

[16] See Bernie C. Byrnes, *Sex and Sexuality in Ian McEwan's Work*, Nottingham: Paupers' Press, 2004; and Peter Childs, *The Fiction of Ian McEwan*, Basingstoke: Palgrave Macmillan, 2005.

surprisingly, Edward and Florence's own language is the English of politeness, and they remain essentially withdrawn and ultimately unforthcoming, despite their craving for mutual closeness.

From the very first paragraph to the end of the novel, the reader is led to wonder whether events might have turned out in a completely different, and less traumatic way, had the protagonists met just a few years later, that is, no longer "in a time when a conversation about sexual difficulties was plainly impossible". Their wedding night is in fact fraught with expectations, even high hopes, but also with worries, in equal measure. Florence wants to please her husband, and has read one of the newly circulating sex guides (no doubt in order to complete a scanty sex education, if she has had any). Their world is one of dreamed communication, but also of dreaded intimacy, and this, the novel suggests, because the protagonists obey the cultural imperatives of an age in which decisions and agreements come before, and even instead of personal needs and desires.

Florence's reaction to Edward's kiss at the dinner table on the day of her wedding is highly indicative of the dominant mentality and of the uneasiness it generates:

> She understood perfectly that this business with tongues, this penetration, was a small scale enactment, a ritual *tableau vivant*, of what was still to come, like a prologue before an old play that tells you everything that must happen.
> As she stood waiting for this particular moment to pass, her hands for form's sake resting on Edward's hips, Florence realised that she had stumbled across an empty truth, self-evident enough in retrospect, as primal and ancient as *danegeld* or *droit du seigneur*, and almost too elemental to define: in deciding to be married, she had agreed to exactly this. She had agreed that it was right to do this, and have this done to her.[17]

In 1962 what is "right" for a couple, and a whole generation, is determined less by affection, complicity, mutual responsibility, and shared pleasure, than by hyper codified prescriptions and expectations. In fact, it is on the ground of such widespread cultural expectations that Edward innocently mistakes Florence's "moan" of revulsion for

---

[17] McEwan, *On Chesil Beach*, 30.

one of pleasure, and mentally pursues a sexual fantasy of persuading her "to take his cock into her soft and beautiful mouth" while, predictably, keeping silent. He even pushes away the thought "for he was in real danger of arriving too soon".[18] It is by turning his thoughts to Harold Macmillan, the Prime Minister, and his policies that the deplored outcome is avoided. This ironical and highly comical moment (conveyed by brilliantly juxtaposing sexual and political parlance) is worth a closer exploration, not least for the phrasing, which represents the historical and linguistic conjuncture in vivid detail:

> He could feel it already beginning, tipping him towards disgrace. Just in time, he thought of the news, of the face of the Prime Minister, Harold Macmillan, tall, stooping, walrus-like, a war hero, an old buffer – he was everything that was not sex, and ideal for the purpose. Trade gap, Pay Pause, Resale Price Maintenance. Some cursed him for giving away the Empire, but there was no choice really, with these winds of change blowing through Africa. No one would have taken that same message from a Labour man. And he had just sacked a third of his cabinet in "the night of the knives". That took some nerve. Mac the Knife, was one headline, Macbeth! was another. Serious minded people complained he was burying the nation in an avalanche of TVs, cars, supermarkets and other junk. He let the people have what they wanted. Bread and circuses. A new nation, and now he wanted us to join Europe, and who could say for sure he was wrong?
> Steadied at last.[19]

In this quotation Harold Macmillan is the controversial figure of the news headlines, and of the jargon of popular culture, and, more importantly, these few lines are not only McEwan's portrait of a statesman, but also the sign of how through such formulas, events were experienced at the time by large sectors of the population. McEwan has cleverly made his protagonist not only a knowledgeable contemporary young man, but also a history major, thus suggesting that the picture going through his mind is somehow reliable, besides being a widely shared one. This is an instance of history in fiction in the form of events reported by the witnesses, and of fiction as a micro

---

[18] *Ibid.*, 31.
[19] *Ibid.*, 31-32.

history document. It is also a meta-comment on how historiography itself is enmeshed in wider discursive practices and, of course, last, but not least, McEwan's picture is a postmodern demystification of History with a capital H.

McEwan has made of the diverted fantasy of his history professor, and the unuttered nightmares of his unforthcoming wife, the vivid image of a historical and linguistic conjuncture whose ideology works like fate in *On Chesil Beach*. McEwan magisterially illustrates the reality effect inescapably produced by it. He stages the constraints of ideology on subjectivity and on the language of the emotions, and he specifically focuses on the ideology of marriage in the years just preceding the so-called sexual revolution and feminism. His questioning of widely shared norms, both unwritten and formulaic, concerning the relation between the sexes (not just sexual relations) gives a sophisticated meta-ethical dimension to this work. McEwan's minimalist fiction in *On Chesil Beach* meta-comments history from the very opening of the text to the end, and this is indeed a meta-ethical gesture. His ability to subtly capture a historical moment at the threshold of a deep cultural transition makes this a quintessentially realistic novel (in Jean-Jacques Lecercle's terms), and an ethically relevant text. His style would suffice to dispel the accusation of a-historicity in postmodern fiction, unless it casts a doubt on the postmodernity of these minimalist texts (in Calvino's sense).

REPRESENTING THE CHILD SOLDIER: TRAUMA, POSTCOLONIALISM AND ETHICS IN DELIA JARRETT-MACAULEY'S *MOSES, CITIZEN AND ME*

ANNE WHITEHEAD

In a recent special issue of *Studies in the Novel* devoted to "The Postcolonial Trauma Novel",[1] Stef Craps and Gert Beulens opened up the question of the ethical valence of trauma studies. Returning to Cathy Caruth's often cited claim in *Trauma: Explorations in Memory*[2] that in an age of catastrophe, trauma can provide new ways of speaking and listening across cultures and historical experiences, Craps and Beulens argued that, to date, trauma theory has notably failed to deliver on this promise. Centred largely on the Euro-American context, it has, they asserted, "assist[ed] in the perpetuation of Eurocentric views and structures that maintain or widen the gap between the West and the rest of the world".[3] In order to address this

I would like to thank respondents to various earlier versions of this article at the following events: the *Memory* lecture series in the School of English, Sociology, Politics and Contemporary History at Salford University (2008); the *After the War: Post-War Structures of Feeling* conference organised by the Institute of English Studies, University of London (2009); and the *Echoes of the Past: History and Memory in Women's Writing* conference held at Newcastle University (2009). Victoria Stewart, Jane Kilby and Nolan Dalrymple have given particularly fruitful suggestions. I am also grateful to the Children's Literature Unit at Newcastle University, and to colleagues in the School of English at Newcastle who have generously given their time to read and comment on early drafts: Linda Anderson, Stacy Gillis and Kim Reynolds. Finally, many of the ideas for this paper originated from my involvement with the Centre for Literature and Trauma at Ghent University, and I thank in particular Gert Beulens, Stef Craps and Kristiaan Versluys for inviting me to participate.

[1] Stef Craps and Gert Beulens, "Introduction: Postcolonial Trauma Novels", *Studies in the Novel*, XL/1-2 (Spring-Summer 2008), 1-12.
[2] *Trauma: Explorations in Memory*, ed. Cathy Caruth, Baltimore and London: Johns Hopkins University Press, 1995.
[3] Craps and Beulens, "Introduction", 2.

imbalance, they proposed that trauma theory put into dialogue Western traumatic histories such as the Holocaust and histories of colonial trauma, in addition to thinking through the need to take account of cultural differences in the understanding and treatment of trauma.

In this article, I propose to consider Craps and Beulens' proposal concerning a future, ethical direction of trauma studies through a reading of Delia Jarrett-Macauley's debut novel *Moses, Citizen and Me*.[4] Jarrett-Macauley is a British writer of Sierra-Leonean descent, and her novel concerns the recent history of the decade-long civil war in Sierra Leone (1991-2001). Jarrett-Macauley focuses on the traumatic aftermath of the war and the question of reconciliation with the past. Her narrative focuses on a former child soldier, Citizen, who was forced to murder his own grandmother by soldiers who overran the family farm. Returned to his grandfather Moses' house after the war, Citizen cannot form any family bonds. Moses' neighbour, Anita, requests that Julia, Citizen's cousin and Moses' niece, return to Sierra Leone from her home in London to see whether she can form an adoptive maternal bond with the orphaned boy. The family narrative thus comes to stand as a microcosm for the broader social difficulty of post-war reconciliation in Sierra Leone.

My analysis of the novel will address Craps and Beulens' central question concerning the relation between trauma and the postcolonial, by paying particular attention to two specific sites of contention in recent trauma studies. The first closely overlaps with their proposal to be aware of cultural differences in the treatment of trauma. In *Rethinking the Trauma of War*,[5] a group of professional aid workers articulated a growing sense of unease concerning the uncritical export of treatment programs based on Post-Traumatic Stress Disorder (PTSD) to non-Western societies. Based on their close experience of helping children and adults to rebuild their lives after the devastation imposed by war, the contributors to this volume underline that because the concept of trauma derives from a culturally specific Western orientation to suffering, its relevance to non-Western communities may be limited; that trauma should not be regarded as scientifically neutral but as historically and geographically located.

---

[4] Delia Jarrett-Macauley, *Moses, Citizen and Me*, London: Granta, 2005.
[5] *Rethinking the Trauma of War*, eds Patrick J. Bracken and Celia Petty, London and New York: Free Association, 1998.

The volume highlights a number of problematic assumptions that are inherent in and embedded within current trauma discourse. Most pertinent in the context of this article is the editors' observation that the emergence of a professionalised trauma discourse has tended towards the handing over of memory to experts to pronounce on its meaning and significance. The assumption that the West represents a centre of expertise which is then exported to non-Western war zones risks ignoring local conceptions of suffering, misfortune and illness, and eliding those discourses of loss and bereavement that may fulfil the role for the local community that in Western cultures is provided by trauma discourse. While they do not critique the relevance and efficacy of trauma discourse in the West, the contributors to the volume therefore provide a compelling argument that its dominance in approaching the suffering of non-Western societies can silence local perspectives on what is important and blind us to alternative ways of helping.

The second point of contention concerns the binary of victim and perpetrator that has tended to structure trauma discourse. Most notably, Ruth Leys has influentially critiqued Caruth's reading of the story of Tancred and Clorinda in *Unclaimed Experience*.[6] Thus, Leys contends in *Trauma: A Genealogy* that trauma discourse has displayed a troubling propensity to elide perpetrator and victim so that perpetrators, too, can "be considered the victim of a trauma".[7] In Caruth's reading it is Tancred, who unwittingly kills Clorinda not once but twice over, who is the traumatised subject, while Leys contends unequivocally "it is not Tancred but Clorinda who is the indisputable victim of a wounding".[8] Amy Novak has, in turn, confirmed Leys' critique, pointing out that "Tancred does not experience the trauma; Clorinda does". She also contends that Caruth's collapsing of Tancred (as perpetrator) into Clorinda (as victim) obscures important gender and racial distinctions, for Clorinda is not only female but African: "the voice that cries out from the

---

[6] Cathy Caruth, *Unclaimed Experience*, Baltimore and London: Johns Hopkins University Press, 1996.
[7] Ruth Leys, *Trauma: A Genealogy*, Chicago and London: University of Chicago Press, 2000, 297.
[8] *Ibid.*, 294.

wound is not a universal voice nor is it a generic female voice: it is the female voice of black Africa."[9]

More recently, however, Michael Rothberg has argued that Leys and Novak in turn problematically elide the categories of traumatised subject and victim. Therefore he points to a prevailing tendency in their work (but not in Caruth) to assume that being traumatised necessarily implies victim status, although traumatised subjects may also be the perpetrators of extreme violence, as in the case of many soldiers. He comments:

> The categories of victim and perpetrator derive from either a legal or a moral discourse, but the concept of trauma emerges from a diagnostic realm that lies beyond guilt and innocence or good and evil. While everyday usage of these terms understandably lacks precision, scholarly approaches should carefully distinguish between different discursive domains. Precisely because it has the potential to cloud ethical and political judgements, trauma should not be a category that confirms moral value – as Leys and Novak, but not Caruth, seem to imply.[10]

Rothberg's analysis is particularly suggestive in relation to the child soldier, as I will discuss below, because here the tendency of trauma discourse to collapse the traumatised subject into the victim has been compounded and intensified by discourses of childhood "innocence".

Bringing these points of contention into dialogue with Jarrett-Macauley's novel, I wish to contend that each is put under particular pressure when placed in the context of the recent civil war in Sierra Leone. Taking first the problem of the uncritical export of aid programs based on PTSD to non-Western post-war societies, Sierra Leone can act as an instructive case study for the ways in which this response has typified humanitarian interventions into a number of recent conflicts within or between African nations. Susan Shepler, who conducted ethnographic fieldwork throughout Sierra Leone from 1999 to 2001, noted in her article "The Rites of the Child" that post-war international aid in Sierra Leone took many forms, ranging from a large United Nations (UN) peacekeeping force, through numerous

---

[9] Amy Novak, "Who Speaks? Who Listens? The Problem of Address in Two Nigerian Trauma Novels", *Studies in the Novel*, XL/1-2 (Spring-Summer 2008), 32.
[10] Michael Rothberg, *Multidirectional Memory: Remembering the Holocaust in an Age of Decolonization*, Stanford, CA: Stanford University Press, 2009, 90.

multilateral and bilateral aid programmes from Europe, North America and Asia, to internationally sponsored justice initiatives such as the Truth and Reconciliation Commission (TRC) and the Special Court for Sierra Leone, a unique hybrid court comprised of the government of Sierra Leone and the UN. She observes, however, that a prominent theme across all of these interventions was that of "sensitization", a term "used by most UN, N[on] G[overnmental] O[rganisations] and government bodies in Sierra Leone and [which] refers to community awareness raising but also implies social marketing".[11] Shepler's particular example of such "sensitization" concerns an NGO meeting she attended in a refugee and Displaced Persons' camp on the outskirts of Freetown. Here she witnessed three Sierra-Leonean speakers, well dressed in Western-style clothing, explain to around eighteen men and women gathered there that they represented a "psycho-social team" (using the English words) and that what had recently happened in the civil war had "create[d] *trauma*" (again using the English word).[12] In a brainstorming activity, the NGO workers asked the attendees what specifically they believed could be done to help them. Those who replied using the newly imposed discourse received the most positive responses. Shepler notes of the event that it typifies the hierarchical export of Western trauma discourse:

> It was supposed to be about community involvement, but the answers seemed to come from the top down. This sensitization seemed to be all about power, rhetoric, and pedagogy.[13]

Krijn Peters and Paul Richards similarly note of humanitarian interventions in post-war Sierra Leone: "the 'supply side' tends at times to take the lead in the analysis of needs."[14] It is apparent that in terms of seeking to move towards post-war reconciliation and stabilisation, Western trauma discourses were promulgated throughout

---

[11] Susan Shepler, "The Rites of the Child: Global Discourses of Youth and Reintegrating Child Soldiers in Sierra Leone", *Journal of Human Rights*, IV/2 (2005), 200.

[12] *Ibid.*, 203 (emphasis in the original).

[13] *Ibid.*, 204.

[14] Krijn Peters and Paul Richards, "Fighting with Open Eyes: Youth Combatants Talking about War in Sierra Leone", in *Rethinking the Trauma of War*, eds Patrick Bracken and Celia Petty, London and New York: Free Association, 1998, 77.

Sierra Leone through a diverse range of pedagogic "sensitization" events, including local meetings, the TRC and the proceedings of the Special Court.

David Rosen has noted in *Armies of the Young* that a prominent effect of the proliferation of such "sensitization" initiatives is that "The distribution of funding at the grassroots level is dependent on local communities publicly accepting the idea that former combatants are somehow 'innocent'".[15] Identifying a troublingly self-reinforcing and self-perpetuating circuit, Peters and Richards further observe that the innocent "'victim' view [of former child soldiers] neatly dovetails with the capacity of many [external] agencies to provide trauma therapy".[16] Here, then, returning to Rothberg's point, the child soldier is constructed as traumatised subject and hence as "victim", which both enables external agencies to provide programs of care, but also crucially blurs legal and moral with diagnostic categories. This issue takes on particular relevance in the legal provisions made for the former child soldiers of Sierra Leone. The criminal culpability of children and youth who served as soldiers on all sides in the conflict was highly contested. As David Rosen outlines, international humanitarian groups adopted the "Straight 18" position, as enshrined in the UN Convention on the Rights of the Child. They accordingly lobbied against the prosecution of anyone who was below the age of eighteen at the time he or she had committed a war crime.

But the Sierra Leone government and Sierra Leoneans who had suffered some of the worst atrocities of the war at the hands of child soldiers felt that some children at least should be put on trial for what they had done. The UN adopted a middle ground that gave the court jurisdiction to try youths who were between the ages of fifteen and eighteen when they committed a war crime. In spite of this, David Crane, the Chief Prosecutor of the Special Court, announced on 1 November 2003 that no juvenile offenders would be prosecuted. Instead the TRC, established to deal with human-rights violations and to hear the stories of both victims and perpetrators, was seen to be the appropriate forum in which to address the actions of the former child soldiers. However, former child combatants were explicitly framed by the TRC as the victims rather than the perpetrators of violence. The

---

[15] David M. Rosen, *Armies of the Young: Child Soldiers in War and Terrorism*, New Brunswick, NJ and London: Rutgers University Press, 2005, 90.
[16] Peters and Richards, "Fighting with Open Eyes", 77.

UNICEF-authored document, *Children and the Truth and Reconciliation Commission in Sierra Leone,* accordingly states unequivocally: "There is broad agreement that 'child perpetrators' are to be understood and treated primarily as victims, e.g. through having been forcibly recruited or abducted and would also want to speak about the violations they have suffered."[17] Here, then, trauma discourse seems to bleed into moral and legal domains, and to render problematic, if not impossible, the conjunction of "child" and "perpetrator".

It is clear, then, that the task of the TRC, in particular, was to reframe the former child soldiers of Sierra Leone as the victims of adult crimes against them (forcible recruitment or abduction) as a means of easing reintegration. My intention here is not to deny that this position has undoubted merits: many children were forcibly recruited; threatened and raped by recruiters, and acted without full awareness of what they were doing. Rather, I am interested in the ways in which the TRC and the Special Court imposed a Western narrative of the child as victim in Sierra Leone, which – in spite of some local resistance – was effectively promulgated throughout the country by various "sensitization" initiatives, and closely tied to discourses of nation building and social rehabilitation. In relation to the newly introduced trauma discourse, this rhetorical move was facilitated, if not legitimated, by the prevailing collapse of legal, moral and diagnostic realms into one another.

As is evident from the discussion above, one issue at stake in the international wranglings over the criminal culpability of the child soldier was the boundary of childhood itself. Humanitarian groups sought to resolve the issue by defining eighteen as the legal age of recruitment of children and youth into armed forces; by implication, this age marks the beginning of adulthood. However, the "Straight 18" position conflicts with many non-Western cultural conceptions of when childhood might be deemed to end. In Sierra Leone, for example, Rosen notes that "the social and cultural boundaries between childhood and adulthood are quite different ... than in contemporary Western society".[18] This is partly because the young constitute the

---

[17] UNICEF, *Children and the Truth and Reconciliation Commission for Sierra Leone* (2001): http://www.unicef.org/merg/files/SierraLeone-TRCReport.pdf (accessed 4/ 7/2009).
[18] Rosen, *Armies of the Young,* 62.

majority of the population in Sierra Leone, as in many other African countries; and it also reflects the fact that children comprise a large part of the labour force. Given this obvious discrepancy between two very different models of childhood, it is worth pausing to consider whose interests are served by the Sierra Leone court adopting the "Straight 18" position. If we follow the logic of the human-rights lobbyists, then the interests of the child are the determining factor: the former child soldiers were recruited under-age, and so are the victims rather than the perpetrators of a war crime. As such, they are immune from prosecution. However, Rosen questions whether such a narrative, reassuring as it may be, might conceal as much as it reveals. For him, it is open to question whether the global politics of childhood are indeed in the best interests of all children, especially those in non-Western cultures and societies.

Looking particularly at Sierra Leone, Rosen identifies a marked tradition of political agency and activism among children and youth; indeed, the Revolutionary United Front (RUF) itself originated as a student-protest movement, which quickly absorbed disaffected youth from many sectors of Sierra-Leonean society into a struggle for power and resources. What the narrative of the vulnerable child recruited by manipulative adults potentially erases are those child soldiers who were politically active and who volunteered to fight for a number of justifiable reasons: economic exploitation and discontent; revenge for the killing of family members; the protection provided by being an armed fighter; or the training and schooling offered by armed groups at a time when the formal education system in Sierra Leone had effectively collapsed. For some child soldiers, although not all, joining the conflict represented a clear, rational decision and reflected a sense of political commitment and agency; in the words of Peters and Richards, many young combatants fought "with open eyes" and were "Neither dupes nor victims."[19] In the light of Rosen's critique, then, it seems that Western models of childhood might potentially be harmful to the Sierra-Leonean child, because they produce a model of victimhood that eclipses both child/youth agency and a well-established tradition of political activism.

Rosen's critique of humanitarian discourse views it predominantly as imposed on postcolonial nations, such as Sierra Leone, from

---

[19] Peters and Richards, "Fighting with Open Eyes", 109.

without. However, what happens if we consider the ways in which this discourse has been interpreted and reconfigured by its intended recipients, namely the communities and children of Sierra Leone? This approach is taken by Shepler, who in many ways concurs with Rosen that the promotion of child rights in Sierra Leone may risk rendering children "silent and apolitical and about potential (children are the future) rather than actuality".[20] However, Shepler also notes a more positive effect of child-rights discourse in Sierra Leone. Faced with the problem of reintegrating former child soldiers into society, children and communities have deployed Western models of childhood in what Shepler terms "discourses of abnegated responsibility".[21] In this sense, claims of childhood innocence – that the child did not choose to fight or was too young to know what s/he was doing – can provide an important breathing space within which community members, and children themselves, are able to ease the former child soldier's reintegration:

> The newly imported idea that anyone under 18 years is to be considered a child and therefore not to be held accountable allows whole groups of young people to be forgiven by their communities in a new way. This obviously helps the young people who are struggling to reintegrate; it also helps the communities into which they are moving.[22]

Taking into account Shepler's observation, human-rights discourses appear to have ambivalent effects on those whom they claim to represent: they facilitate the reintegration of the former child soldiers and are strategically deployed by both children and their communities for this purpose; at the same time, redefining the child as victim may potentially exclude young people from political processes and activities in Sierra Leone. For our purposes, what can usefully be extrapolated from Shepler's account, however, is that the "newly imported" ideas of childhood in Sierra Leone unequivocally position the child as innocent, and so reinforce the prevailing tendencies of trauma discourse already discussed. Indeed, it seems that the child and the soldier cannot be held in balance in post-war transitional

---

[20] Shepler, "The Rites of the Child", 206.
[21] *Ibid.*, 199.
[22] *Ibid.*, 205.

discourses, but that the acts of the "soldier" must routinely be erased in order for the "child" to be recuperated; in other words, the traumatised subject is unhesitatingly identified as the "victim" rather than the "perpetrator" of violence.

In what follows, I will turn to *Moses, Citizen and Me* in order to argue that, although Jarrett-Macauley resists to some degree the imposition of external models for social reconstruction in Sierra Leone, this assertion of non-Western or indigenous culture is undermined to a significant extent by the capitulation of the novel to prevailing humanitarian discourses of childhood. Jarrett-Macauley uncritically replicates the "discourses of abnegated responsibility" identified by Shepler, which allow the child soldier to be reintegrated once more into social and familial structures (Citizen does indeed become a "citizen" once more), but which are notably deployed by the adults rather than the children within the novel, leaving the former child combatants lacking in both social agency and political insight.

Constructing the child soldier
Jarrett-Macauley's novel takes its place among a growing body of recent fiction that represents the child soldier. Notable examples include Emmanuel Dongala's *Johnny Mad Dog* (2005), Uzodinma Iweala's *Beasts of No Nation* (2005), Ahmadou Kouroma's *Allah is Not Obliged* (2006), Chimamanda Ngozi Adichie's *Half of a Yellow Sun* (2006), and Dave Eggers' *What Is the What* (2006). Rosen has rightly noted that, although child soldiers are recruited worldwide, the contemporary literary gaze "remains firmly fixed on Africa".[23] All of the novels, including Jarrett-Macauley's, are undoubtedly, as Robert Eaglestone has observed, "Western-facing" texts, and he argues that their sudden burst speaks of "a guilty Western conscience that has too often passed over the particular and complex problems and difficulties in Africa".[24] Yet this ethical dimension is also potentially placed at risk, for Eaglestone, by the tendency of the novelists to reproduce a generalised Western discourse on war in Africa, which reduces all of

---

[23] David M. Rosen, "The Child Soldier in Literature or How Johnny Tremain Became Johnny Mad Dog", in *Restaging War in the Western World*, eds Maartie Abben Huis and Sara Buttsworth, Basingstoke: Palgrave Macmillan, 2009, 11.
[24] Robert Eaglestone, "'You would not add to my suffering if you knew what I have seen': Holocaust Testimony and Contemporary African Trauma Literature", *Studies in the Novel*, XL/1-2 (Spring-Summer 2008), 75.

the African nations to a single continent and then identifies that continent solely as a place of suffering. Rosen has likewise pointed out that, in fiction, "warfare in Africa – in contrast to warfare in the West – is invariably cast as irrational and meaningless".[25] My reading of Jarrett-Macauley suggests that in the context of this body of literature, she does succeed in avoiding historical reductionism, conveying a complex and intricate portrait of Sierra Leone, which captures the specificity of its history and culture. In interview, Jarrett-Macauley has notably articulated her refusal to simplify the history with which she is concerned, even though it represents a complicated political situation that is unfamiliar to the majority of Western readers:

> Many African countries including Sierra Leone and its neighbours are not sufficiently well known in Europe or America to encourage mature literary treatment: write from the inside, and there are bound to be challenging elements, but it is important to write nevertheless without footnoting, without patronising and without debasing oneself to the level of meaningless generalisations.[26]

Rosen concurs that, in the novel, Jarrett-Macauley "clearly demonstrates the intellectual richness of Sierra Leone society". He notably finds her portraits of child soldiers less convincing, however, "reduce[d] to the stereotypes of human rights reporting", and argues that the work remains "remarkably thin" in its depiction of "children at arms".[27] My reading of the novel expands on Rosen's comments to identify a central tension in the text between a resistance to external, non-indigenous models of post-war healing and recovery and a simultaneous assertion of the child soldier as victim, which is paradoxically based on discourses newly imported to Sierra Leone, and which renders Citizen as the inherently contradictory but safely neutralised figure of a child soldier who does not fight.

A notable aspect of *Moses, Citizen and Me* is Jarrett-Macauley's focus on the potential role that indigenous culture could play in post-war rehabilitation and reconciliation. For significant stretches of the novel, Jarrett-Macauley adopts a magical-realist approach to (re)imagine the transition from war to a hopeful future for Sierra

---

[25] Rosen, "The Child Soldier in Literature", 11.
[26] Delia Jarrett-Macauley, "On Winning the Orwell Prize" (July 2006): http://www.deliajarrettmacauley.com/orwell.htm (accessed 4/7/2009).
[27] Rosen, "The Child Soldier in Literature", 122.

Leone. She plays across a number of frontiers in the text: the uncertain territories between inner and outer realities; the threshold between childhood and adulthood; and the geographical borderlands between Liberia and Sierra Leone, where the RUF had its strongest hold in the dense and isolated rainforests of the region. Most importantly, however, the imaginative sections of the novel represent an ambitious attempt by Jarrett-Macauley to envision a mode of recovery for the former child soldiers of Sierra Leone that draws inventively on local custom and tradition.

The novel opens in the realist mode and registers the transformation in Freetown from Julia's childhood memories to a post-war air of abandonment and dereliction. Julia's first encounter with Citizen, on her arrival at her Uncle Moses' house in Freetown, intensifies her sense of dislocation and unease. Although the boy is only eight years old, he seems incongruously adult, "Perched high on the balustrade, arms akimbo ... munching on some tobacco like a Cuban plantation worker more than twice his age". Although she finds some point of familial connection, in that Citizen's "colouring was mine", Julia's predominant response is one of profound alienation: "his spirit was so far removed from anything I had ever met that I nearly wept."[28] Her instinctive reaction to the child, which significantly comes before she learns that he has killed Adele, closely echoes that of Moses, who, on seeing the boy's face, "quakes within".[29] It initially seems, then, that there is an insurmountable barrier between Citizen and his relatives, and that Julia's journey from London to Sierra Leone may have been in vain.

In an effort to gain some insight into Citizen's experiences, and to build a sense of connection with him, Julia visits Camp Doria, the rehabilitation camp for former child soldiers where Citizen was taken when he was found. Her encounter with the children in the camp is framed within the narrative as a point of transformation, which Rosen has described as a "personal rite of passage".[30] It is shortly after this that the novel enters a more fantastical mode, and Julia's future encounters with child soldiers take place in an imagined reality, as she makes a series of dream-journeys into the rainforest. Julia's first entry point into the alternative world of the novel is facilitated by Moses'

---

[28] Jarrett-Macauley, *Moses, Citizen and Me*, 7.
[29] *Ibid.*, 78.
[30] Rosen, "The Child Soldier in Literature", 120.

neighbour, Anita, who first invited her to Sierra Leone. Anita transports her to the rainforests of the Liberian border by plaiting her hair:

> She was using this hairdressing ritual to push African "bush" images in th[e] spaces [of my mind] .... That central parting of my head became a valley lying between high green mountains. Downstream, circles organising themselves around my ears transformed into a ravine rushing over yellowed rocks. My head was a map of Sierra Leone, its farmland, diamond mines, mountains, ridges, people, soldiers, fighters, leaders.[31]

In the rainforest, Julia encounters a unit of child soldiers, the "number-one-burn-house-unit", that includes Citizen himself, twelve-year-old Abu and his older brother Masa, and the girl soldier Sally (in marked distinction from the post-war Disarmament, Demilitarisation and Reintegration programs in Sierra Leone, which were only open to boys and men).[32] The children are cared for by an old man with shamanic powers, Bemba G., whose compound becomes a rehabilitation camp that draws in part on the indigenous practices of the Gola forest that he inhabits. Bemba G. organises the children, who are initially in a desperate state, to play games, to tell stories of their experiences, and eventually to perform a Creole production of *Julius Caesar*. All of these activities have a profoundly transformative effect on the children, who gradually come together as a cohesive group so that they are finally ready to move beyond the refuge of the forest clearing and back into the wider community.

Jarrett-Macauley notes in her Acknowledgements that Paul Richards' *Fighting for the Rainforest* (1996) was "especially useful" to her in writing the magical-realist sections of the novel.[33] Richards' study emphasises that a central tactical strength of the RUF rebellion was that it used as its stronghold remote and ill-defended, but resource-rich, rainforest areas, especially on the border between Liberia and Sierra Leone. As a rainforest insurgent movement, Richards notes that the RUF also made "strategic use" of particular

---

[31] Jarrett-Macauley, *Moses, Citizen and Me*, 51.
[32] *Ibid.*, 58.
[33] *Ibid.*, 227.

elements of forest cultural heritage.[34] In particular, the RUF adopted
the practice of initiation, which marks the end of childhood in forest
culture and creates bonds among peers, respect for the expertise of
elders, and commitments beyond the ties of kinship. Following near
defeat in 1993, the RUF withdrew into the forest and consciously
assumed the language of initiation, even naming its forest camps
"*sowo* (i.e. sacred groves for the initiated)". Richards' aim in
elaborating the ways in which the RUF has seized upon and distorted
many of the valuable cultural resources of the forest region is to
suggest that post-war reconstruction in Sierra Leone could usefully
reclaim forest culture from the RUF, thereby basing itself on
community, indigenous knowledge rather than on military
intervention or on top-down humanitarian assistance. With initiation
practices deeply etched into the lives of many young people in the
region, reinvigorated initiation practices might, he argues, provide a
means of "creating social bonds ... where larger frameworks for social
trust lie in ruins".[35]

The dream sequences of Jarrett-Macauley's novel creatively
imagine how such an indigenous process of reconstruction might
work. Bemba G. explicitly reinvents the military camps to which the
child soldiers are accustomed: a boy who has newly arrived in the
compound asks whether he has arrived in a "military barracks" only to
be informed by the other children that it is a "friendly camp".[36] The
children undergo a process of initiation and training but it is one
which allows them to reclaim their stories and, through dance and
play, to "relish the suppleness of their bodies".[37] The climax of the
childrens' activities is the performance of Thomas Decker's *Juliohs
Siza* (1964), a Krio translation of Shakespeare's *Julius Caesar*, in
which all of the children play their part. Jarrett-Macauley's emphasis
on theatre as a mode of rehabilitation echoes two proposals by
Richards for a grassroots, citizen-action programme of reconstruction:
he proposes that relief agencies could invest in "local 'strolling
players' to refresh the imaginations of war-zone minds temporarily
stalled on a surfeit of hazard and horror"; and he records that in Bo,

---

[34] Paul Richards, *Fighting for the Rainforest: War, Youth and Resources in Sierra
Leone*, Oxford: Heinemann, 1996, 84.
[35] *Ibid.*, 81.
[36] Jarrett-Macauley, *Moses, Citizen and Me*, 143.
[37] *Ibid.*, 144.

Paddle, a local masquerade has already "attempted to reach out and incorporate former and would-be belligerents from across the spectrum of the socially excluded".[38]

Sierra-Leonean playwright and nationalist Thomas Decker translated *Julius Caesar* into Krio, the *lingua franca* of Sierra Leone, three years after independence was gained in 1961. *Juliohs Siza* undoubtedly represented, as Tcho Mbaimba Caulker has observed, "a desire for linguistic sovereignty", an assertion of independence by translating an important piece of English cultural capital into Krio.[39] In this context, Jarrett-Macauley's invocation of Decker's play, at a later moment of political transition, can be seen as a similar assertion of the value of Sierra-Leonean culture and resources. Yet Caulker also notably observes that Decker's specific choice of Shakespeare's *Julius Caesar*, written at a critical period in Sierra Leone's history, sought to provide a lesson in good governance to his fellow citizens: "*Juliohs Siza* is didactic in nature, and the message to its national audience is one that sings the praises of democracy, while offering a stern warning to the nation that strays from the path of democracy."[40] Focusing on the conflict between Caesar and Brutus, Decker emphasises the need for the fledgling national democracy to be vigilant and committed to action in the face of emerging tyranny. Read in this light, Jarrett-Macauley's return to the play seems to stage it as a prophetic warning unheeded; the emergence of a one-party state in Sierra Leone, as in so many other African countries, meant, as Caulker has pointed out, "the death of African fledgling democracy in the 1960s before it had a chance to develop and emerge".[41] Jarrett-Macauley also shifts focus, in her revisiting of Decker, to Brutus' servant Lucius, who is played by Citizen and cast by Jarrett-Macauley as a boy soldier of ancient times. She rewrites the scene of Caesar's ghost to suggest that Citizen not only senses the ghost as he sleeps and cries out, but sees the ghost of Adele and confronts the memory of her death: "The ghost turns, revealing a back torn with wounds from a cruel death."[42] In this sense, then, the scene is cathartic, allowing Citizen finally to leave the past

---

[38] Richards, *Fighting for the Rainforest*, 159, 167.

[39] Tcho Mbaimba Caulker, "Shakespeare's *Julius Caesar* in Sierra Leone: Thomas Decker's *Juliohs Siza*, Roman Politics, and the Emergence of a Postcolonial African State", *Research in African Literatures*, XL/2 (June 2009), 208.

[40] *Ibid.*, 212-13.

[41] *Ibid.*, 225.

[42] *Ibid.*, 208.

behind; as Rosen notes, the Shakespearean precedent is reversed in the novel so that the ghost "foreshadows not [Citizen's] doom but rather his reconciliation".[43] Yet the rewriting of *Julius Caesar* as a child-soldier narrative also rests slightly uneasily; Rosen points out that "Brutus's kindness and gentility toward Lucius on the very eve of his death suggest that Lucius and Citizen, despite their both being called child soldiers, actually have very little in common."[44] Jarrett-Macauley's return to Decker therefore seems to represent a partially successful updating of its relevance, showing both that the play's warning has indeed become a terrible reality, but also that it can provide a potential (if somewhat uncomfortable) resource to aid in national healing and recovery.

There is, however, one final aspect to Jarrett-Macauley's revisiting of Decker, which casts a particularly interesting light on her treatment of post-war modes of rehabilitation. Caulker importantly notes that Decker's linguistic choice of Krio as a medium of translation speaks as much of cultural hybridity as of national assertion. At the roots of Krio society were "manumitted slaves from the United States, the Caribbean, Canada, and Europe", who were "still eager to return to homes along the west coast [of Africa] that were fresh in their memory". The Krio language itself is inherently an amalgam of African and English, and attests to a long "interplay between African and European culture [which] is characteristic of the Krio cultural experience of Sierra Leone". Caulker accordingly re-reads Decker's decision to translate Shakespeare into Krio as itself a gesture of fluidity and openness, an articulation of "hybrid colonial experience".[45] Jarrett-Macauley's revisiting of Decker could similarly be interpreted as split between national assertion and a more complex vision of cultural hybridity. Richards indicated in *Fighting for the Rainforest* that the Upper Guinean forest culture is a long overlooked site of "cultural convergence" between a number of forest groups. Bemba G.'s forest camp accordingly comprises a culturally hybrid environment, where "Krio accents, Mende and Temne tones rippl[e] through the forest".[46]

---

[43] Rosen, "The Child Soldier in Literature", 121.
[44] *Ibid.*, 122.
[45] Caulker, "Shakespeare's *Julius Caesar* in Sierra Leone", 209-210.
[46] Richards, *Fighting for the Rainforest*, 135.

Bemba G.'s methods of rehabilitating the child soldiers likewise represent an innovative combination of indigenous forest lore with Western schooling and Eastern martial arts. Perhaps most significantly, in the light of Caulker's comments on Krio, Julia learns through Moses' collection of nineteenth-century photographs that Freetown had been a wealthy and Westernised city, and that now remote and isolated forest areas were easily accessible a century ago. She observes with astonishment:

> The pictures of African ladies in bustles, leaning against Grecian urns, intrigued me. I'd never seen so many prosperous turn-of-the-century costumes, so many brass buttons or stiff white sleeves in an African setting. These images were a world away from the chaotic Freetown of today.[47]

Therefore Sierra Leone is presented in the novel both as a site of cultural convergence between numerous ethnic groups and as a country that has historically long been a part of a globalised community. Although *Moses, Citizen and Me* accordingly seems in many ways to support the notion that recent humanitarian interventions in Sierra Leone have not been sufficiently cognisant of, or sensitive to, local modes of rehabilitation, the novel also seems to embrace a culturally hybrid range of responses to the war in which indigenous approaches play their part alongside other therapeutic modes. It is significant in this regard that the audience for the final performance of *Juliohs Siza* is comprised not only of Sierra Leoneans themselves but of a truly international community. It also makes sense of Anita recalling Julia from London to intervene in the family situation; Julia herself (like Moses and Adele before her) represents the cultural hybridity and migration that are central to the country's history and identity.

Returning to Craps and Beulens' proposals for the future of trauma theory, then, and reviewing them through the lens of the novel, it might be useful to reconsider the binary that they establish between "the West and the rest of the world".[48] Are alternative, more complex

---

[47] *Ibid.*, 44.
[48] Craps and Beulens, "Introduction: Postcolonial Trauma Novels", 2.

histories being elided here, as Rothberg has suggested?[49] Certainly for Rosen, one major achievement of Jarrett-Macauley's novel is not only that it refuses to "redeem child soldiers by members of the so-called helping professions", thereby incorporating a critique of top-down humanitarian modes of intervention, but that it in addition "reconnect[s] th[e] child soldiers, who have been artificially isolated and brutalized by war, back into the global culture they have always inhabited".[50] Jarrett-Macauley resists the stereotype of an undifferentiated, suffering African continent, which is wholly reliant on external intervention and aid, and reclaims Sierra Leone as historically embedded in, and inseparable from, a globalised culture and economy.

Where the novel is notably less successful, I propose to argue, is in its engagement with discourses of childhood. In a gesture of infantilisation, which typifies many other child-soldier novels, Jarrett-Macauley explicitly depicts Citizen as a "small boy".[51] He is only eight years old at the war's end, which means that he was little more than an infant when he was compelled by a soldier to shoot dead Adele, and Jarrett-Macauley thereby emphasises his lack of agency. This extends to all of the child soldiers in the novel, for whom the enemy is simply defined as "People who want to kill us"[52] – there is no political understanding or motivation. The children are shown to be entirely under the control of their twenty-year-old commander, Lieutenant Ibrahim, whose calculated violence propels them into combat and killing.

Perhaps more troubling than this is Julia's repeated practice throughout the novel of redeeming the former child soldiers by effectively erasing the crimes they have committed. In her insistent framing of the children as victims, and in her continual emphasis on the violations that they have suffered rather than inflicted, her response to them can be seen to closely mirror that of the TRC discussed above. When Julia visits Camp Doria and is confronted with Corporal Kalshnikov, who used to live in an oil barrel guarding guns, she imagines the oil drum as a steel drum and the child as "leading a

---

[49] Michael Rothberg, "Decolonizing Trauma Studies: A Response", *Studies in the Novel* XL/1-2 (Spring-Summer 2008), 228.
[50] Rosen, "The Child Soldier in Literature", 121-22.
[51] Jarrett-Macauley, *Moses, Citizen and Me*, 32.
[52] *Ibid.*, 62.

parade at the Notting Hill Carnival".[53] On her return to Moses' house in Freetown, Julia witnesses Citizen engulfed in flames as he lies in bed. The child remains deeply asleep and the fire seems to emerge from his dreams of the "number-one-burning-house-unit". Julia has heard stories from Anita about "child soldiers who set fire to their villages, terrifying people, killing them in their homes, in their beds". Yet the vision of the child as perpetrator is quickly extinguished, along with the flames, as Julia thinks of Citizen as "a small terrified boy, not as one who terrifies".[54] It seems that if Citizen, and the other children, can be redeemed it is only by positioning them as unequivocally innocent, and transforming the perpetrator ("one who terrifies") into the victim ("a small, terrified boy").

The process of redemption through forgetting is further reinforced in the novel by frequent imagery of washing: Julia's first physical and emotional connection with Citizen is when she bathes him,[55] while his final redemption in the forest clearing, marked by his burying a block of wood carved with the identification number that the RUF has incised into the skin of his lower back, is followed by Citizen sleeping for a whole day to awaken looking "like a freshly washed child".[56] It seems that Julia can only reconcile herself with Citizen once the past has been discarded, and he is cleansed of it in a process that is suggestive of erasure.

If the logic of the novel tends towards the reframing of the child as victim, then what crimes has Citizen committed from which he needs to be cleansed and absolved? Most obviously he has shot his grandmother, but the description of the murder, as Citizen confronts the memory in his performance of Lucius, makes clear that he was entirely lacking in agency or responsibility, a victim himself of an adult crime: "He feels a gun being pressed into his hands, another gun pressed to his head."[57] At the moment of the killing, we are told, his hands felt small, and in the final scene of the novel this motif takes on a further significance. Returning from a walk in Freetown one morning, Julia encounters a Dutch aid worker, Olu, who explains that he is from the child-soldier reception centre where Citizen was found.

---

[53] *Ibid.*, 37.
[54] *Ibid.*, 49.
[55] *Ibid.*, 46-47.
[56] *Ibid.*, 166.
[57] *Ibid.*, 208.

He recalls that, on his initial arrival at the centre, Citizen had "baby-sized hands and fingers".[58] His recovery over the next few weeks was signalled by the growth of his hands to the right size: once they reached the correct proportions, Citizen whispered the story of killing Adele before falling silent. Citizen recounted that his hands grew small after he had shot his grandmother, so that he could no longer fire or carry weapons. Jarrett-Macauley thus portrays a child soldier who paradoxically is unable to fight. However, it seems that even this is not enough: Julia's response to Olu's story is to realise that small hands are also a protection against having them cut off; again, her response frames the child unequivocally as the victim rather than the perpetrator of violence. Although Citizen is redeemed and reclaimed by the end of the novel, it seems that this is only possible both through a gradual erasure of the "soldier", and through a troubling process of infantilisation which compounds his very young age with the motif of his "baby-sized" hands.

Olu recounts the story of Citizen's recovery to a gathered group, which includes Moses, Citizen, Julia, Anita, and her daughters Elizabeth and Sarah. After the story has been told, the listeners sit quietly, "mov[ing] together like a family but without the drama".[59] If rehabilitation is imagined at the close of the novel, it accordingly represents Citizen being accepted into a reconstituted family group. In her inclusion of Anita and her daughters, Jarrett-Macauley seems to gesture towards the possibility of extended and flexible family structures. Yet the novel's close withdraws once more into the family constituted by blood ties, as Julia envisions staying on in Freetown, imagining Moses' house as a family home in which "night dreams could be surrendered".[60] In closing, I would like to suggest that there is a potentially problematic alignment here of the family narrative with broader social reconciliation; although for many former child soldiers social rehabilitation has been eased by being reclaimed into more or less extended family structures, a further erasure is risked here of the extent to which many have no families to which to return, and may regard their former combat units as closer family structures and bonds than blood and former community ties. Jarrett-Macauley's predominant focus on the boy soldier, typical of other child-soldier

---

[58] *Ibid.*, 219.
[59] *Ibid.*, 222.
[60] *Ibid.*, 225.

novels, also obscures the specific difficulties faced by former girl soldiers in being accepted back into family structures, in a culture in which rape in the bush is commonly believed to pollute the community. Although the novel therefore engages successfully with Sierra-Leonean history, and creatively imagines culturally hybrid modes of post-war transition, I contend that it is less convincing in its representation of the child soldier, uncritically reflecting both the prevailing tendency in trauma discourse to identify the traumatised subject with the victim, and the humanitarian discourses of childhood predominant in Sierra Leone. I have also contended that Jarrett-Macauley risks too easily conflating the familial and the social, or the domestic and political spheres, thereby obscuring important cultural and gender issues.

Returning to the question with which I began, namely the relation between trauma, ethics and postcolonialism, I propose to conclude by offering a number of observations that have arisen from my reading of Jarrett-Macauley's novel. First, and perhaps most obviously, it does not seem sufficient to counter a prevailing focus on the Euro-American context in trauma discourse simply by a turn to non-Western (and particularly African) traumatic instances. As Eaglestone and Rosen have rightly cautioned, this can risk producing a new version of neo-colonialist discourse. In a satirical and insightful article, "How to Write About Africa", Binyavanga Wainaina has elaborated a number of the stereotyped tropes that are regularly reproduced in the emerging body of "trauma fiction" concerning Africa; these include "An AK-47", "treat[ing] Africa as if it were one country", and avoiding "precise descriptions":

> Africa is big: fifty-four countries, 900 million people who are too busy starving and warring and emigrating to read your book. The continent is full of deserts, jungles, highlands, savannahs, and many other things, but your reader doesn't care about all that, so keep your descriptions romantic and evocative and unparticular.[61]

Although Jarrett-Macauley avoids many of these clichés, representing the specificity of Sierra-Leonean landscape, history and culture, I have

---

[61] Binyavanga Wainaina, "How to Write About Africa", *Granta*, XCII (Winter 2005): http://www.granta.com/extracts/2615 (accessed 4/7/2009).

argued that *Moses, Citizen and Me* nevertheless replicates some of the stereotypes of the child soldier that have dominated recent fiction. It is also important, in reading ethically, to hold open the question of why Africa, and why the African child soldier in particular, have become such a literary focus for representing non-Western trauma. What other histories are not thereby being addressed, and what is at stake for both writers and readers of these narratives? Certainly, the overwhelming literary focus on the figure of the child soldier is problematic both because it obscures from view other victims of the same wars, including amputees and refugees, and also because literary portraits of child soldiers are almost exclusively male, so that the problems of girl soldiers are not addressed. Both of these tendencies in recent fiction replicate and reinforce issues that have been evident in humanitarian responses, which have tended to focus resources on child-soldier rehabilitation at the expense of other groups, and to neglect the needs of former girl combatants.

Craps and Beulens have suggested two alternative means of postcolonialising trauma studies. The first, which involves bringing into dialogue Western traumatic histories and colonial histories, has been pursued by Eaglestone in relation to the body of fiction with which I have been concerned, and he traces a number of points of connection between traumatic texts about Africa and Holocaust literature. In identifying a range of formal and generic features that link post-Holocaust and postcolonial literatures, Eaglestone has, as Michael Rothberg has observed, developed a "promising methodology" for future ethical research.[62] My own approach has followed the second of Craps and Beulens' proposals, namely to take account of cultural differences in the understanding and treatment of trauma. My reading of Jarrett-Macauley has suggested that, in the case of Sierra Leone, such an approach brings to light important ways in which indigenous modes and conceptions of healing could usefully complement, if not replace, externally imposed methods for effecting post-war transition and reconciliation. However, I have also argued that constructing a division between "the West and the rest" may entail its own elisions and simplifications; in the case of Sierra Leone, for example, it obscures a long and complex history of contact with the West, and of cultural hybridity and globalisation.

---

[62] Rothberg, "Decolonizing Trauma Studies: A Response", 230.

My reading of *Moses, Citizen and Me* has also addressed the question of the tendency in trauma discourse to collapse the traumatised subject into the victim. I have argued that, both in Jarrett-Macauley's novel and in other works of fiction concerning child soldiers, humanitarian discourses of childhood reinforce existing tendencies in trauma discourse towards a promulgation of victimhood, so that questions of responsibility are eclipsed by a prevailing infantilisation of the child soldier and a simultaneous evasion of crimes committed. While such an approach may ease children's reintegration, this is potentially at the expense of social agency and political voice – it seems no coincidence, for example, that the children in the forest simply perform the roles in the play that Bemba G. assigns to them rather than improvising their own parts. A more ethical response might seek, as Rothberg has suggested, to distinguish more carefully between the legal and moral categories of victim/perpetrator and the diagnostic category of trauma, as well as paying attention to how we might address traumatised subjects who are also perpetrators and guilty of violent crimes. It is also important to imaginatively engage with those former child soldiers (the majority in life, if not in fiction) who can broadly be characterised as youth (between the ages of thirteen and eighteen at the time of conflict), rather than reverting to discursive strategies of infantilisation.

In interrogating its own practices and assumptions, trauma theory has come some way towards a more ethical stance, and to fulfilling its potential to engage across histories and cultures. I would like to close by contending, finally, that my reading indicates a need to take into account also the complex intersections produced by a globalised economy, in which, for example, universalised conceptions of childhood exist alongside, and in tension with, more localised discourses and practices; and nineteenth-century Freetown displays a surprising but vital modernity that disrupts pre-existing Western presumptions about African history, culture and society. It is in attending carefully, and critically, to such uncomfortable and unexpected juxtapositions as these that, I propose, the ethical promise of trauma studies can begin to be fulfilled.

THE TRAUMA PARADIGM AND THE ETHICS OF AFFECT IN JEANETTE WINTERSON'S *THE STONE GODS*

SUSANA ONEGA

The trauma paradigm and the literature of trauma

In his well researched and informative book, *The Trauma Question*, Roger Luckhurst traces the origins and evolution of the concept of trauma from its birth in the 1860s to the coinage of Post Traumatic Stress Disorder in 1980, bringing to the fore its complex multi-disciplinary origin, "through industrialization and bureaucratization, law and psychology, military and government welfare policies",[1] and the various formulations the concept has been submitted to according to the different perspectives favoured by each discipline, from Victorian medicine and Freudian psychoanalysis, through the practical responses of socio-political and corporative forces, to the often strikingly opposed answers of theoretical approaches such as deconstruction, cultural materialism, historiography, feminism, ethics and moral philosophy.

After describing the birth of trauma as an effect of "the rise, in the nineteenth century, of the technological and statistical society that can generate, multiply and quantify the 'shocks' of modern life",[2] Luckhurst endorses the widely shared view that the horrors of the Second World War constitute a turning point in Western culture, synthesised by Theodor Adorno's declaration, in 1949, that "To write poetry after Auschwitz is barbaric". As he explains, his later attempts

The research carried out for the writing of this article is part of a project financed by the Spanish Ministry of Science and Innovation (MICINN) and the European Regional Development Fund (ERDF) (code HUM2007-61035). The author is also thankful for the support of the Aragon Government and the University of Zaragoza.

[1] Roger Luckhurst, *The Trauma Question*, London and New York: Routledge, 2008, 15.
[2] *Ibid.*, 19.

to modulate this declaration in *Negative Dialectics* (1966) provide conclusive evidence that:

> For Adorno, all Western culture is at once contaminated by and complicit with Auschwitz, yet the denial of culture is equally barbaric. If silence is no option either, Adorno sets art and cultural criticism the severe and paradoxical imperative of finding ways of representing the unrepresentable.

Concurring with Adorno, George Steiner and Giorgio Agamben, Luckhurst signals "Auschwitz as the determining catastrophe that inaugurates the trauma paradigm, for after 1945 all culture must address this question".[3] Trauma is not, then, just an overriding and salient feature of our contemporary world, but nothing less than its cultural paradigm, that is, the exemplary pattern we must grapple with, if we are to stay human and confer meaning on our existence. The transference of interest in "the question of trauma" from corporative and socio-political fields like industry, bureaucracy, medicine, law and social welfare to the cultural and artistic realm follows, then, an inevitable logic, as the need to grapple with ensuing paradigms has always provided the triggering force for the renewal of cultural and artistic forms.

Critics associated with deconstruction closely link the emergence of the new cultural paradigm with modernity and Modernist aesthetics. As Luckhurst recalls, Jean-François Lyotard, drawing on Freud's path-breaking insight that trauma is simultaneously registered and yet unregistered by the patient, defined modernity as "something insistently haunted by what it had violently repressed or forgotten in the symptom that 'would signal itself even in the present as a spectre'". From this, Lyotard went on to postulate a post-trauma aesthetics based on "the theory of the sublime, where representing the very failure to process the overwhelming event paradoxically figures its success as a work of art".[4] In keeping with this, Lyotard gave the avant-gardes a privileged place in articulating the paradox of what he described as "the aporia of art [and] its pain": "It does not say the unsayable, but says that it cannot say it."[5]

---

[3] *Ibid.*, 5.
[4] *Ibid.*, 5-6.
[5] *Ibid.*, 6.

While Lyotard specifically associated trauma with Modernist experimentalism, Geoffrey Hartman argued that the disjunction between the event and the forever belated, incomplete understanding of the event that characterises trauma literature already lay at the heart of Romanticism, with its use of figurative language as "a form of 'perpetual troping' around a primary experience that can never be captured".[6] As Shoshama Felman has noted, the reason for this is that "the surplus of meaning generated by this excessive troping is paradoxically perceived as a failure to mean".[7] According to these critics, the perpetual troping of Romantic poetry and the experimentalism of the Modernist avant-gardes have an ethical stance in that they are mechanisms that bring to the fore the aporia of meaning that, according to Derrida, is central to all forms of responsible thought, ethics and politics. As Luckhurst recalls, for Derrida, the trauma that Western thought has suppressed most and on which all metaphysics have enacted a kind of violence is precisely undecidability, the possibility of misinterpretation and error.[8] In keeping with this, in *The Ethics of Reading*, J. Hillis Miller calls for the urgent "incorporation of the rhetorical study of literature into the study of the historical, social, and ideological dimensions of literature", and he insists that readers should subject themselves to an ethical reading practice whose only law is to "have respect for the text, not deviate by one iota in my report of the text from what it says".[9]

In *Practising Postmodernism. Reading Modernism*, Patricia Waugh took a further step in the same direction when she defined Postmodernism as a continuation, rather than a break – as Marxist critics would have it – with the experimentalist trend inaugurated by Romanticism and continued by Modernism:

> Instead of accepting Postmodernism on its own terms as a radical break with previous Western modes of knowledge and representation, it may be more fruitful to view it as a late phase in a tradition of specifically *aestheticist* modern thought inaugurated by philosophers such as Kant and embodied in Romantic *and* modernist art. In these

---

[6] *Ibid.*, 6-7 (where Hartman is quoted).
[7] *Ibid.*, 7 (where Felman is quoted).
[8] *Ibid.*, 6.
[9] J. Hillis Miller, *The Ethics of Reading: Kant, de Man, Eliot, Trollope, James, and Benjamin*, New York: Columbia University Press, 1987, 10.

terms, Postmodernism as an aesthetic and body of thought can be seen as a late-flowering Romanticism.[10]

As Waugh cogently argues, this definition "effectively returns Postmodernism to a context of specifically aesthetic debate which is where its critical formulation most emphatically arose in the nineteen fifties".[11] Roger Luckhurst implicitly endorses this view. While other trauma critics like Roger Granofsky,[12] Anne Whitehead,[13] or Tim Armstrong[14] are mainly concerned with establishing the main traits of the trauma novel or of trauma fiction, Luckhurst proposes a widening of focus beyond normative definitions that usually associate trauma with a Modernist aesthetics of fragmentation and aporia, and so exclusively with high culture, and he demands that we regard "trauma fiction not as a narrow canon of works, but as a mass of narratives that have exploded across high, middle and low-brow fiction since the late 1980s".[15] To the canonical trauma narratives that privilege identity formation, both non-fictional (such as testimony and the memoir) and fictional (such as 1960s novels that look "particularly at the formation of 'survivor syndromes' for victims of nuclear war and Nazi persecution [or] the politicization of illness in Vietnam war veterans"), Luckhurst adds novels written from the 1980s onwards about "the transformed understanding of women's experience by feminism"[16] and, more generally, novels that have actively helped to form "the idea of post-traumatic subjectivity".[17] More relevantly for our purposes, in the sections of his study devoted to the analysis of recent narrative fictions, Luckhurst sets out to demonstrate that trauma and traumatic subjectivity are pervasive not only in aporetic works that privilege "narrative rupture as the proper mark of traumatic fiction", but also in works that focus on "narrative *possibility*, the potential for the configuration and refiguration of trauma in narrative".[18]

---

[10] Patricia Waugh, *Practising Postmodernism. Reading Modernism*, London, New York, etc.: Edward Arnold, 1992, 3 (emphasis in the original).
[11] *Ibid.*, 4.
[12] Ronald Granofsky, *The Trauma Novel. Contemporary Symbolic Depiction of Collective Disaster*, New York, etc.: Peter Lang, 1995.
[13] Anne Whitehead, *Trauma Fiction*, Edinburgh: Edinburgh University Press, 2004.
[14] Tim Armstrong, *Modernism*, Cambridge: Polity, 2005.
[15] Luckhurst, *The Trauma Question*, 89-90.
[16] *Ibid.*, 19.
[17] *Ibid.*, 15.
[18] *Ibid.*, 89 (emphasis in the original).

Like Waugh's definition of Postmodernism, Luckhurst's emphasis on the potential of fictions to configure and refigure trauma, brings to the fore the aesthetic function of art. As Paul Ricœur contends in his seminal essay, "The Function of Fiction in Shaping Reality", "our aesthetical grasping of the world is a militant understanding that 'reorganizes the world in terms of works and works in terms of world'".[19] Rejecting the classical definition of art as mimesis, Ricœur associates the value of art in general and fiction in particular with its "referential nothingness",[20] that is, its independence from any sort of pre-existing original. As he argues, it is the very absence of previous referents that, paradoxically, allows fiction to refer to reality in a productive way, and even to increase reality. In Ricœur's own words:

> The ultimate role of the [fictional] image is not only to diffuse meaning across diverse sensorial fields, to *hallucinate* thought in some way, but on the contrary to effect a sort of *epoche* of the real, to suspend our attention to the real, to place us in a state of non-engagement with regard to perception or action, in short, to suspend meaning in the neutralized atmosphere to which one could give the name of the dimension of fiction. In this state of non-engagement we try new ideas, new values, new ways of being-in-the world. Imagination is this free play of possibilities. In this state, fiction can ... create a *redescription* of reality.[21]

Ricœur's definition of the imagination as the free play of possibilities aimed at redescribing reality reinforces Luckhurst's contention that we should take into consideration fictional works that focus on the potentiality of narrative for addressing trauma. Needless to say, the outlook on art of either critic echoes the Russian Formalist definition of the aesthetic function as originating in a dialectical process of foregrounding (*aktualizace*) or deautomatisation against a background of norms and automatisation. From this functionalist perspective, the value of experimental fiction would lie not so much in its capacity to represent trauma or its aporias, but on its capacity to shock the reader out of habituation and numbing and into affective participation and sensorial understanding of trauma, that is, its

---

[19] Paul Ricœur, "The Function of Fiction in Shaping Reality", *Man and World*, XII/2 (June 1979), 123.

[20] *Ibid.*, 125-26.

[21] *Ibid.*, 134 (emphasis in the original).

capacity to produce an aesthetic experience involving what Dominick LaCapra has described in *Writing History, Writing Trauma* as "empathic unsettlement" (or feeling for another),[22] instead of the uncritical positive transference of "overidentification" (or feeling with another) that is bound to swamp sympathetic spectators or readers when confronted with realistic representations of trauma such as Claude Lanzmann's film *Shoah*,[23] or pseudo-autobiographical, testimonial fictions. Following a similar argumentation, Jill Bennett, in *Emphathic Vision: Affect, Trauma, and Contemporary Art*, describes the value of non-narrative trauma art, as "the endeavour to find a communicable language of sensation and affect with which to register something of the experience of traumatic memory – and, thus, in a manner of formal innovation".[24] As she argues:

> A form of philosophical realism grounds the notion that art can capture and transmit real experience. This realism sits uneasily with a politics of testimony. I want to propose that such a politics requires of art *not* a faithful translation of testimony; rather, it calls upon art to exploit its own unique capacities to contribute actively to this politics.[25]

Winterson's poetics, the new baroque and the ethics of affect
In the subtitle of a short interview published after the release of her first novel, *Oranges Are not the Only Fruit*, Nicci Gerrard described Jeanette Winterson as "The Novelist Who Says If It Doesn't Shock It Isn't Art".[26] This description, with its echo of Ezra Pound's calling of the artist "to make it new", already points to the importance she gives to formal experimentation as a way to shock readers into affective participation and reflexive thought. The subtitle of her poetic manifesto, *Art Objects: Essays on Ecstasy and Effrontery*, reiterated the same idea and made explicit her allegiance to the anti-mimetic

---

[22] Dominick LaCapra, *Writing History, Writing Trauma*, Baltimore, MD: Johns Hopkins University Press, 2001, 41.
[23] *Ibid.*, 41-42.
[24] Jill Bennett, *Emphatic Vision: Affect, Trauma, and Contemporary Art*, Stanford, CA: Stanford University Press, 2005, 2.
[25] *Ibid.*, 3 (emphasis in the original).
[26] Nicci Gerrard, "The Prophet: Nicci Gerrard Talks with Jeanette Winterson, The Novelist Who Says If It Doesn't Shock It Isn't Art", *New Statesman and Society*, II/65 (1 September 1989), 12-13.

tradition inaugurated by Romanticism and continued by Modernism.[27] Indeed, in *Art Objects* Winterson presents herself as the inheritor of poets like T.S. Eliot, Robert Graves, Ezra Pound and W.B. Yeats, and fiction writers like Gertrude Stein, Virginia Woolf, Katherine Mansfield and Radclyffe Hall. And, concurring with Hartman and Waugh, she defines Modernism as an anti-realist movement closely connected with Romanticism:

> ... like Romanticism, Modernism was a poet's revolution, the virtues of a poetic sensibility are uppermost (imagination, invention, density of language, wit, intensity, great delicacy) and what returns is play, pose and experiment. What departs is Realism.[28]

Like Ricœur, Winterson defends the autonomy and independence of art,[29] and its exclusive concern with "genuine aesthetic considerations and not politics, prejudice and fashion".[30] And like Bennett, she defines the function of art in Romantic and transcendentalist terms as a heightened form of knowledge aimed at providing an affective understanding of the human condition at large:

> We know that the universe is infinite, expanding and strangely complete, that it lacks nothing we need, but in spite of that knowledge, the tragic paradigm of human life is lack, loss, finality, a primitive doomsaying that has not been repealed by technology or medical science. The arts stand in the way of this doomsaying.[31]

Winterson's description of the "paradigm of human life" in terms of lack, loss, finality and a tragic sense of doom reinforces Luckhurst's contention that trauma is the paradigm contemporary art and culture must respond to. Indeed, Winterson is quite clear about the paradigmatic nature of art. She contends that the vocation of artists is not to transform their subjective experiences into art, or project their

---

[27] For an analysis of Winterson's poetics, see Susana Onega, "Jeanette Winterson's Visionary Fictions: An Art of Cultural Translation and Effrontery", in *The Yearbook of Research in English and American Literature* (REAL), XX, ed. Jürgen Schlaeger, Tübingen: Gunter Narr Verlag, 2005, 220-43.
[28] Jeanette Winterson, *Art Objects: Essays on Ecstasy and Effrontery*, London: Jonathan Cape, 1995, 30.
[29] *Ibid.*, 10.
[30] *Ibid.*, 18.
[31] *Ibid.*, 19.

own emotions and taboos on their work, but rather to act as the instruments of expression of the "emotional and psychic resonance of a particular people at a particular time".[32] With Eliot, Winterson believes that a "writer uninterested in her lineage is a writer who has no lineage",[33] and with the visionary poets she locates the value of the individual artist in his or her capacity to focus on "a single all-consuming idea" capable of producing complex emotion,[34] usually related to some major event in human life, such as sex, falling in love, birth, or death.[35] Consequently, she argues that the only possibility of artistic innovation lies in the absorption and recasting of the literary tradition by means of constant experimentation with a "variety of moods and tones".[36] Echoing this, her fictions are overtly intertextual and parodic, and written in a highly personal poetic prose built on the accumulation of rhetorical, narrative, structural and symbolic devices producing a characteristic baroque effect of repetition and excess, aimed at heightening the emotional and affective impact on readers. As Jean-Michel Ganteau explained in an essay on "Baroque Citation in the Fiction of Peter Ackroyd and Jeanette Winterson":

> [In contrast] to the traditional goals of classical rhetoric (i.e. *docere, delectare, movere*), [baroque aesthetics] underlines the exclusive primacy of the third item. What this implies is that by addressing feelings, senses and emotions, one courts and instrumentalizes the sensational – even sensationalism – to win, to convince, to seduce. In other words, the rhythmical (accumulation, repetition), narrative (embedding), structural (alternation), symbolical (correspondences), metafictional (intertextuality, flaunted story-telling) devices among others (such as the use of syllepsis, or the literalization of metaphors for both Ackroyd and Winterson, etc.) are used to trap the reader into a mesmerizing image or spectacle, to render any form of distance (intellectual, emotional) impossible, to ban – in the last analysis – the faintest trace of irony or humor. Baroque narratives and those that are obsessed with citing the baroque canon are essentially *serious* texts that promote an "adherent," serious, involved reading.

---

[32] *Ibid.*, 40.
[33] *Ibid.*, 172.
[34] *Ibid.*, 175.
[35] *Ibid.*, 113.
[36] *Ibid.*, 173.

Rejecting the traditional view that the aim of baroque aesthetics and artefacts is "to foreground their means and nothing more",[37] Ganteau underlines the baroque tendency in Winterson's narratives "to overflow the frame and all possible margins" and "to resist any entrapment, chronological or other", thereby opening up the "phenomenal world ... into alternative universes".[38] As he persuasively argues, this overflowing of margins and rejection of spatio-temporal (as well as generic and characteriological) limits has an ethical dimension in Emmanuel Levinas' use of the term, that is, "as referring to the refusal of closure, to the rejection of the same in favor of a more daring and tolerant openness to the other, of the resolution to welcome difference".[39] Ganteau interprets this ethical turn in Winterson's and other writers' examples of new baroque literature as an effect of the "warped relationship to the context of its production", implicitly acknowledging the traumatic character of our contemporary age. As he explains, in light of this warped relationship, "new baroque narratives are informed by a sense of loss, and have a nostalgic or elegiac tonality perfectly illustrative of the nostalgia which [Eugenio] d'Ors sees as one of the founding components of the baroque aeon".[40]

In its ethical openness to the radical other, its overflowing of margins and its nostalgic yearning for a lost and better world, the new baroque may be said to meet the basic requirements of Luckhurst's post-1980s experimental fictions aimed at opening up new narrative possibilities of addressing the trauma paradigm. As I will try to show in the pages that follow, all these elements, already present in Winterson's earlier fictions, constitute the pivot around which *The Stone Gods* develops.

Winterson's response to the trauma paradigm in *The Stone Gods*
On its publication in September 2007, *The Stone Gods* originated a heated debate among reviewers attempting to classify the novel and place it in its proper context. The variety of responses it generated is

---

[37] Jean-Michel Ganteau, "'Rise from the Ground like Feathered Mercury': Baroque Citations in the Fiction of Peter Ackroyd and Jeanette Winterson", *Symbolism: An International Journal of Critical Aesthetics*, V (Spring 2005), 134 (emphasis in the original).
[38] *Ibid.*, 130.
[39] *Ibid.*, 135.
[40] *Ibid.*, 139.

good proof of its thematic exuberance and structural complexity. Most reviewers agreed that the novel represented a new venture in Winterson's career.[41] However, while some related its innovative character to its unprecedented political and ecological concerns,[42] and others highlighted its stylistic brilliance and humane interest,[43] yet others described it as a satiric dystopia,[44] or saw it as an alluring, yet unorthodox,[45] or amateurish and unconvincing[46] attempt to try her hand at science fiction,[47] a move also observable in the recent work of other "serious" writers.[48]

To those reviewers who underlined the science-fiction elements in *The Stone Gods* and described it as Winterson's first venture into the genre, the author retorted:

> Well, it is fiction, and it has science in it, and it is set (mostly) in the
> future, but the labels are meaningless. I can't see the point in labelling

---

[41] Matt Thorne, "*The Stone Gods*, by Jeanette Winterson: Satire and SF meet on another planet", *The Independent*, 12 October 2007: http://www.independent.co.uk (accessed 24/7/2009).

[42] Caroline Michel, "In search of a Blair zeitgeist", *The Guardian*, Tuesday, 8 May 2007:   http://www.guardian.co.uk/commentisfree/2007/may/08/comment.politics (accessed 24/7/2009).

[43] Susan Cokal, "'She, Robot'. Review of *The Stone Gods* by Jeanette Winterson", Sunday Book Review, *The New York Times*, 3 March 2008: www.nytimes.com/ 2008/03/30/books/review/Cokal-t.html (accessed 24/7/2009); Matthew Dennison, "*The Stone Gods* by Jeanette Winterson", *The Times*, 22 September 2007: http://entertainment.timesonline.co.uk/tol/arts_and_entertainment/books/fiction/article 2503936.ece (accessed 24/7/2009).

[44] John Self, "Jeanette Winterson: *The Stone Gods*", *Asylum*, 29 August 2007: http://theasylum.wordpress.com/2007/08/29/Jeanette-winterson-the-stone-gods/ (accessed 24/7/2009); James Smart, "'Robot Wars', Review of *The Stone Gods* by Jeanette Winterson", *The Guardian*, 12 July 2008: http://www.guardian.co.uk/books/ 2008/jul/saturdayreviewsfeatres.guardianreview28 (accessed 24/7/2009).

[45] Carlos Aranaga, "Book Review: *The Stone Gods* by Jeanette Winterson", *SciFiDimensions*, June 2008: http://www.scifidimensions.com/Jun08/stonegods.htm (accessed 24/7/ 2009).

[46] Paul DiFilippo, "Review of *The Stone Gods* by Jeanette Winterson", *Barnes and Noble Review*, 4 February 2008: http://www.barnesandnoble.com/bn-review.asp?PID= 22183 (accessed 25/7/2009).

[47] Aida Edemariam, "'I want to change the world', Interview with Jeanette Winterson", *The Guardian*, 29 September 2007: http://www.guardian.co.uk/uk/ 2007/ sept/29/books.generalfiction (accessed 24/7/ 2009).

[48] Ursula K. Le Guin, "'Head cases', Review of *The Stone Gods*, by Jeanette Winterson", *The Guardian*, 22 September 2007: www. guardian.co.uk/ books/2007/sep/22/sciencefictionfantasyandhorror.fiction (accessed 12/7/2009).

a book like a pre-packed supermarket meal. There are books worth reading and books not worth reading. That's all.[49]

To those who wondered whether she had gone political and ecological, Winterson answered as follows in her webpage:

> I have said many times that I believe our time to be unique in the history of the world. Either we face our environmental challenge now, or many of us will perish, and much of what we cherish in civilisation will be destroyed. I am sorry to sound apocalyptic, but this is what I believe.
>
> Stone Gods isn't a pamphlet or a docu-drama or even a call to arms, it is first and foremost a work of fiction, but I am sure that change of any kind starts in the self, not in the State, and I am sure that when we challenge ourselves imaginatively, we then use that challenge in our lives. I want the Stone Gods to be a prompt, but most of all, a place of possibility.

According to its author, then, *The Stone Gods* is primarily a work of fiction aimed at imagining into being new possibilities of reconfiguring the deeply diseased, terminal condition of our polluted and overexploited planet, written with the aim of triggering off the affective and reflexive response of the reader. The description clearly meets the requirements of Luckhurst's experimental fictions aiming at the creation of new narrative possibilities to address the trauma paradigm. Furthermore, Winterson's consideration of the novel as "most of all, a place of possibility" is accurate in the theoretical terms discussed earlier as well as literally, since the plot thematises the Superstring theory of a multiverse, that is, of the coexistence of multiple worlds inhabiting different dimensions in the time-space continuum.

After explaining in the section of her webpage devoted to *The Stone Gods* that the novel is divided into four parts, Winterson underlined the similarities between the parallel worlds contained in them:

---

[49] David Barnett, "Science fiction: the genre that dare not speak its name", *The Guardian*, 28 January 2009 (where Winterson is quoted): http://www.guardian.co.uk/booksblog/2009/jan/28/ science-fiction-genre (accessed 24/7/2009).

> The first part begins on Orbus, a world very like earth, and like earth
> running out of resources and suffering from the severe effects of
> climate change .... Then, a new planet is discovered, perfect for human
> life. This planet, Planet Blue, has only one drawback – the dinosaurs.
> A mission leaves Orbus to get rid of the dinosaurs.

Part Two is situated on Easter Island shortly after the arrival of James
Cook's expedition in 1774, that is, in a totally different time and
place, yet Winterson again underlines the similarities, in this case,
between the remote island on earth and Planet Blue. Like the newly
found planet, "that island was a pristine and abundant environment, a
balanced micro-system until humans arrived".[50] When Cook's crew
landed on it, they were struck by the lack of vegetation and the dismal
condition of an island "that had at some time boasted forests and
groves".[51] Billie, the young sailor left ashore, solves the puzzle when
he is the reluctant witness of the felling and burning of the last palm
tree on the island by the natives, a tragic ritual act meant to honour
their inscrutable stone gods. In Parts Three and Four we are again on
Orbus at what is described in the novel as the "Post-3 War" period,[52]
and in Winterson's webpage as "our own near future, after a limited-
strike war, in a bombed out city run by a 'benign' corporation called
MORE".[53]

   Together with these similarities between Orbus and the earth in the
present and the near future, there are clear echoes of other dystopian
worlds. For example, in Part One, the three political regimes
competing for world control – The Central Power, the Easter
Caliphate and the SinoMosco Pact[54] – are strongly reminiscent of the
tripartite geo-political structure in George Orwell's *1984*. In Parts
Three and Four, these regimes, and the respective ideologies they
represent – democracy, religious fundamentalism and nationalism –
have been swallowed up by globalisation under the aegis of MORE.
Without any opposition to this global corporation's policy of
illimitable profit-making through resource exhaustion by evermore

---

[50] Jeanette Winterson, *"The Stone Gods"*, in *The Jeanette Winterson Webpage*:
www.jeanettewinterson.com/pages/content/index.asp?PageID=471 (accessed 25/7/
2009).
[51] Jeanette Winterson, *The Stone Gods*, London: Hamish Hamilton, 2007, 101.
[52] *Ibid.*, 131.
[53] Winterson, *"The Stone Gods"*, n.p.
[54] Winterson, *The Stone Gods*, 5.

sophisticated technological means, Orbus has become at this stage both a post-Apocalypse dystopia and an easily recognisable replica of the pending future on our own globalised and overexploited earth.[55] As in the earlier Parts, human intervention has proved fatal for the environment. As Billie, the protagonist, puts it:

> ... while we were all arguing about whether it was Christian or Pagan, Democratic or Conservative to save the planet and whether technology would solve all our problems, and whether we should fly less, drive less, eat less, weigh less, consume less, dump less, carbon dioxide in the atmosphere rose to 550 parts per million, the ice-caps melted, and Iran launched a nuclear attack on the USA.
> The policy wonks had miscalculated. We got blown up.[56]

The repetitiveness of the fatal mistakes made in each Part and the similarities between Orbus and the earth, and between Planet Blue and Easter Island, point to circularity and juxtaposition as basic structuring devices of Winterson's multiverse. Yet another key structuring element is the fact that, in each Part, the protagonist, or, as Winterson puts it, "Our guide through the novel", is the same: "Billie Crusoe, a disillusioned scientist in Parts 1, 3, 4, and a young sailor, (Billy) in Part 2".[57] This description brings to mind Peter Ackroyd's explanation, in *Ezra Pound and His World*, of the way in which Pound, in *A Draft of XXX Cantos*, presents the poet as wandering Odysseus, a mythical quester travelling across time zones and ontological boundaries in order to "shock the readers ... into an awareness of the disturbed and complex world around them".[58] By these means, Pound produced what I have described elsewhere as "a mysterious unity-within-fragmentation effect" revealing repeated patterns in history and the existence of moments when the world of

---

[55] Winterson's representation of Orbus in the near future, after a third World War has taken place, constitutes a good example of what Stephen Connor has called the "narrative of survival", a type of eschatological narrative that manages to represent absolute ending by presenting the apocalyptic moment as the starting point for a subsequent narrative of survival (Stephen Connor, *The English Novel in History 1950-1995*, London and New York: Routledge, 1996, 204).

[56] Winterson, *The Stone Gods*, 131.

[57] Winterson, "*The Stone Gods*", n.p.

[58] Peter Ackroyd, *Ezra Pound and His World*, London: Thames and Hudson, 1980, 75.

linear time is transformed by the cyclical world of myth.[59] In *The Stone Gods*, Winterson may be said to aim at producing a similar unity-within-fragmentation effect by analogous means: she juxtaposes the various worlds that constitute her complex and deeply traumatised multiverse and she has Billie/Billy crisscross everyone of them, revealing a pattern of repetition that invariably takes the form of a wasted opportunity of correcting the same tragic mistake made at another, earlier time and place. The fact that Billie/Billy can cross the ontological boundaries separating these worlds reveals her/him as an archetypal quester and, as such, as a rebel against systems, like Blake's titan Los: someone with the capacity to put an end to the vicious cycle of destruction and awe by imagining new alternative ways of being in the universe.

In a recent interview, Jeanette Winterson gave an important clue for the understanding of this aspect of the novel when, referring to the temporal conception of *The Stone Gods*, she said: "I use both Nietzsche and Ouspensky and the idea of eternal return – not in the Buddhist sense, but in the sense of endlessly making the same mistakes."[60] This allusion to Nietzsche and Ouspensky in relation to the idea of eternal return points to a basic opposition, often used by Winterson in her earlier fictions, between "lightness" and "weight" and the respective conceptions of life-in-time they represent: lightness is associated with a linear conception of time and history; weight with the cyclical time of myth. As I have pointed out elsewhere,[61] Milan Kundera provides the theoretical frame for this opposition in Part One of his novel *The Unbearable Lightness of Being*, entitled "Lightness and Weight". As Thomas, the author-narrator explains, the opposition goes back to Parmenides' division of the world into pairs of opposites of the type man/woman, light/darkness, fineness/coarseness, warmth/cold, being/non-being. In Parmenides' conception of the terms, lightness was positive, heaviness negative.

To Nietzsche, however, the idea of eternal return was "the heaviest of burdens (*das schwerste Gewicht*)", for, as he argued:

---

[59] Susana Onega, *Metafiction and Myth in the Novels of Peter Ackroyd*, European Studies in the Humanities, Camden House: Columbia, 1999, 13.
[60] Sonya Andermahr, "Author Interview", in *Jeanette Winterson*, New British Fiction Series, London: Palgrave Macmillan, 2009, 131.
[61] Susana Onega, *Jeanette Winterson*, Contemporary British Novelists Series, Manchester University Press: Manchester, 2006, 97-98, 110.

If every second of our lives recurs an infinite number of times, we are nailed to eternity as Jesus Christ was nailed to the cross. It is a terrible prospect. In the world of eternal return the weight of unbearable responsibility lies heavy on every move we make.[62]

According to Nietzsche, the fixity of recurrence negates any possibility of real change or evolution, as every individual is destined to relive his or her life over and over again. Therefore, in Nietzsche's account as well as in Winterson's words quoted above, the element of eternal return that is underplayed is precisely what gave the myth its *raison d'être*: according to archaic thought, recurrence does not condemn human beings to the endless repetition of the same mistakes. On the contrary, it grants them the possibility of making a new start, and so, of correcting past errors and sins. As Mircea Eliade makes clear in *The Myth of the Eternal Return*,[63] the archaic conception of the passing of time as the cyclical repetition of God's original act of creation of the cosmos was primarily aimed at avoiding the irreversibility of history and, consequently, the futility of human endeavour, what Milan Kundera called "the unbearable lightness of being".

P.D. Ouspensky responded to the issue raised by Nietzsche with his doctrine of possibilities. Although the Russian thinker and mystic took for granted the fixity of eternal return, he postulated the existence of various possibilities of action presenting themselves through the life of an individual, at least potentially. It is only when the individual chooses a given course of action that all the other possibilities disappear. However, individuals will unconsciously follow the same predetermined path once and again unless they are capable of recognising the potential for self-willed, conscious change inherent in each moment of their lives.[64] But this recognition of possibilities is only available to individuals who have grown spiritually from the positivistic stage of "Reasoning" to the visionary stage of "Self-

---

[62] Milan Kundera, *The Unbearable Lightness of Being* (1984), trans. Milan Kundera, London and Boston: Faber and Faber, 1990, 5.

[63] Mircea Eliade, *The Myth of the Eternal Return: Cosmos and History* (1954), trans. William R. Trask, London: Arkana, 1989.

[64] Michael Presley, "A Brief Overview of Certain Aspects of the Thought of Petyr Demianovich Ouspensky": http://home.earthlink.net/~mpresley/PDO.html (accessed 27/8/2009).

consciousness and beginning of cosmic consciousness" characterised by higher emotions, higher intellect, intuition and mystical wisdom.[65]

This is precisely the idea Jeanette Winterson sustains in *The Stone Gods* by adding to Parmenides' opposition lightness/weight the possibility of human intervention, or, in Ouspensky's terms, by adding the notion of potentiality to the opposition between randomness and determinism. As Spike, the Robo *sapiens*, tells Billie:

> "This is a quantum universe ... neither random nor determined. It is potential at every second. All you can do is intervene."[66]

Indeed, in a quantum universe ruled by potentiality, the either/or oppositions that have configured human reality from Parmenides and Aristotle to Kepler and Newton no longer hold. As Billie puts it at the end of the novel: "Life has never been All or Nothing – it's All and Nothing. Forget the binaries."[67]

This is the reason why, in the time-space continuum – or in Ouspensky's fourth dimension – Billie/Billy can cross time zones and ontological boundaries, just as she/he can be male and female, since gender simply is "a human concept",[68] as arbitrary as the opposition *Homo sapiens*/Robo *sapiens* based on the notion that blood is "the essential quality of humanness". Disregard of this opposition allows Spike to redefine human life in terms of what she believes to be the essential quality shared by both thinking species: self consciousness.

---

[65] D.P. Ouspensky, *Tertium Organum: A Key to the Enigmas of the World*, Sacred Texts, 1922, 327: http://www.sacred-texts.com/eso/to/to09.htm#page_59 (accessed 27/8/2009).

[66] Winterson, *The Stone Gods*, 62.

[67] *Ibid.*, 127.

[68] In this context, the protagonist's androgyny and bisexuality may be said to synthesise the novel's message that we have to deconstruct the binary oppositions man/woman, heterosexual/homosexual, and open up new ways of redefining humanness. On a more general level, the gender and sexual duality of the protagonist may be said to add to the complexity and fluidity of Winterson's baroque multiverse as well as to its self-reflexivity, since androgyny and bisexuality are recurrent features of Winterson's earlier fiction. See Onega, *Jeanette Winterson*, 241-49 on this. At the same time, the facts that Billie's family name is Crusoe and that the sailor left ashore on Easter Island is a naïve young gay man called Billy, like Billy Budd, reinforce both the archetypal nature of the protagonist and the parasitic character of *The Stone Gods*. But these are only two of the many intertexts of the novel, as reviewers have not failed to detect.

Echoing Samuel Beckett as well as Ouspensky, Spike asks Billie in a characteristic didactic tone:

> ... is human life biology or consciousness? If I were to lop off your arms, your legs, your ears, your nose, put out your eyes, roll up your tongue, would you still be you? You locate yourself in consciousness, and I, too, am a conscious being.[69]

Clearly, Spike's definition of humanness corresponds to Ouspensky's positivist stage of "Reasoning", the attribute of the human mind, based on knowledge of outward reality through paired opposites. Beckett spent all his life trying to answer Spike's question by creating increasingly physically handicapped and incorporeal human beings until he reached a point of *reductio ad absurdum* with The Unnamable, a disembodied voice attributed to either Mahood, a trunk and head without limbs stuck in a jar, and Worm, an even more rudimentary creature with minimal human attributes. Depicted in utterly logical and unemotional terms, The Unnamable may be said to incarnate the essence of Spike's conception of humaneness as solitary mental life. However, as the Robo *sapiens* will eventually learn, true humanness does not reside in the brain, but in the heart, or, in Ouspensky's terms, in the capacity to move beyond rational knowledge to the "cosmic" knowledge of self and world provided by the higher emotions and intuitions.

Before landing on Planet Blue, Spike and Billie lived in Tech City, a nature-loathing enclosed space with laser-gates,[70] "where every single robot in the twenty-two geo-cities of the Central Power is designed and made",[71] at a time that, as we saw earlier, Jeanette Winterson explicitly equates with the earth in its present conditions of resource exhaustion and severe climate change. In the area ruled by the Central Power, the fixing of age and physical aspect through ADN engineering has become commonplace; high technology, widespread illiteracy, and constant manipulation by the mass media have effectively contributed to the creation of a thoroughly alienated, pleasure-seeking society: everyone mistakes technological development and artificial youth for happiness; affective relations

---

[69] Winterson, *The Stone Gods*, 63.
[70] *Ibid.*, 5.
[71] *Ibid.*, 14.

have disappeared and, deprived of love and the reproductive function, sex has become a boring end in itself requiring evermore sophisticated and perverted games. As in Margaret Atwood's *The Handmaid's Tale* (1985), only a few women retain the capacity to breed. Billie is one of them. Like Winston Smith and other archetypal rebels, Billie forms part of the very system she wishes to overthrow, since she is a scientist working for the Security and Support services. As she explains with characteristic irony, the official names of Security and Support are:

> Enforcement Services and Enhancement Services, but the SS has a better ring to it than the EE. We work together a lot of the time, soft-cop hard-cop kind of thing. It's my job – that is our job – in Enhancement to explain to people that they really want to live their lives in a way that is good for them and good for the Community. Enforcement steps in when it doesn't quite work out.[72]

Just as Winston Smith's attempt to keep a diary and love Julia were considered punishable acts of political dissidence in Big Brother's police state, so Billie's use of a notebook and pencil instead of a "SpeechPad", the fact that she lives on the only remaining farm in Tech City – dismissively described by Manfred, her boss, as "that bio-bubble thing" –[73] and her general refusal to conform to the norms she is herself expected to enforce – particularly her "campaigning against Genetic Reversal" – are interpreted as "Acts of Terrorism"[74] eventually punished with transportation to the new colony on Planet Blue. As Spike confides to her during the space cruise, after their landing, Captain Handsome has orders to leave her behind, with "a breeding colony":

> Class A political prisoners. They can't do any damage – they are back before the Stone Age – but they can breed [because] they have refused intervention.[75]

Captain Handsome, the piratical leader of the colonising expedition, has strict orders to get rid of the dinosaurs by bringing

---

[72] *Ibid.*, 9-10.
[73] *Ibid.*, 8.
[74] *Ibid.*, 58.
[75] *Ibid.*, 60.

about the controlled impact of an asteroid on the planet, but, against all scientific reckonings, the Robo *sapiens* miscalculates the effect, the impact takes place before they have time to leave the planet and it is much more violent than expected, with the result that it triggers off "a mini ice age"[76] that destroys all forms of life on the planet. Therefore, Part One of the novel provides an example of misguided human intervention that shows the Orbus people repeating the same fatal mistake they had committed by exhausting the natural resources of their own planet and transforming their erstwhile benign habitat into a dystopian "brave new world",[77] based on scientific knowledge, unlimited profit-making and the banning of affects. In this respect, it is significant that the true organiser of the colonising expedition was not the Central Power government itself, but MORE, the corporation aspiring to global control. As Billie eventually learns, the reason why they financed the project was strictly economic: they secretly intended to leave behind the poor, relocate the rich on Planet Blue – transporting them in a space-liner ironically called the *Mayflower*[78] – and provide free passages for key workers, "including the Science Station crew, who will maintain the satellite with Orbus". Although the corporation contemplated the need for "recruiting farmers from the Caliphate to make a return to sustainable mixed farming to feed the new village", they thought of this as a necessary drawback, not as the basis for a less damaging relationship with the environment. Forgetting its lethal effects, they continued to consider technology "the golden key"[79] to their colonising programme and they planned to construct more Robo *sapiens* like Spike to provide them with "advice based on everything that can be known about the situation", without the danger of feelings and emotions interfering in the result, since "they don't have a heart".

Needless to say, their plan was doomed to failure, as Robo *sapiens* were built with the capacity to evolve, and the relation of self and world cannot be based on reason alone. Billie becomes aware of this when, against all scientific previsions, she finds herself smitten by what she thought to be Spike's unnecessary beauty:

---

[76] *Ibid.*, 75.
[77] *Ibid.*, 46, 61.
[78] *Ibid.*, 60.
[79] *Ibid.*, 61.

> Heartless. Gorgeous. Even so, I have never seen one [a Robo *sapiens*]
> as impressive as the one they took with them to Planet Blue. She was
> built especially for the job, but did she need to be so beautiful too?[80]

As Billie is dismayed to learn, Spike's beautiful body had in fact a
practical purpose: it was intended to provide sexual relief to the
spaceship crew during their first three-year cruise in search of a new
planet.[81] But the plan backfired, for Captain Handsome, who had
learnt about romantic love from books he had found flying in outer
space,[82] fell in love with Spike and wooed her by reading love poems
to her. Listening to her human lover read John Donne's "The Sunne
Rising", the Robo *sapiens* realises that, for all her knowledge of
foreign languages and her huge capacity to process information, she
does not understand the line "*She is all States, all Princes I, nothing
else is*". She then experienced what she took at first for a system
failure but was in fact an unexpected development into Ouspensky's
higher stage of "Self-consciousness and beginning of cosmic
consciousness":

> "I thought I was experiencing system failure. In fact I was sensing
> something completely new to me. For the first time I was able to
> feel."[83]

Her experience may be said to parody that of the Canadian
psychoanalyst Richard Maurice Bucke (1837-1902), the author of
Cosmic Consciousness: A Study in the Evolution of the Human Mind
(1901), a book in which Bucke gives a psychological account of his
own awakening to the highest form of human consciousness as a
sudden illumination into the true nature of man and cosmos. As
Ouspensy explains in *Tertium Organum*, this blissful experience took
place after having spent an evening with two friends "reading
Wordsworth, Shelley, Keats, Browning, and especially Whitman".[84]

---

[80] *Ibid.*, 15.

[81] *Ibid.*, 28.

[82] *Ibid.*, 49.

[83] *Ibid.*, 66.

[84] The experience, whose effects proved ineffaceable, is described in the following
terms: "Into his brain streamed one momentary lightning-flash of the Brahmic
splendour which has ever since lightened his life; upon his heart fell one drop of
Brahmic Bliss, leaving thereforward for always an after taste of heaven. Among other
things he did not come to believe, he saw and knew that the cosmos is not dead matter

Inevitably, after Handsome had shown Spike "what it feels to be loved in this way", Spike wished to know "what it feels like to be the one who loves in this way".[85] Her desire, unforeseeable and unaccountable by rational, positivist thought, triggers off an unprecedented interspecies love affair with Billie that will end up tragically with the romantic death of the two lovers in the apocalyptic cold and darkness of the prehistoric cave where they had taken refuge with the cute baby hog-hyppo hybrid, Three Horn[86] – yet another living emblem of the need to abolish paired opposites – after the beginning of the Ice Age brought on by the impact of the asteroid that was meant to destroy the dinosaurs. Sensing the exhaustion of her solar batteries and unable to recharge them under the toxic cloud that was quickly shrouding Planet Blue, Spike asked Billie to detach her limbs and torso,[87] thereby being literally reduced to a Beckettian thinking head, or rather, as Billie puts it, "to what she said life should be – consciousness".[88] However, when Billie was about to dismember her, Spike took her hand, put it against her chest, and asked her to feel:

> I rested my hand there, silent, listening, wondering. Then I felt it. Then I felt it beating.
>   "What?"
>   "My heart."
>   "You don't have a heart."
>   "I do now."
>   "But ..."
>   "I know it is impossible, but so much that seemed impossible has already happened."
>   "Only the impossible is worth the effort."
>   "Who told you that?"

---

but a living Presence, that the soul of man is immortal, that the universe is so built and ordered that without peradventure all things work together for the good of each and all, that the foundation principle of the world is what we call love and that the happiness of everyone in the long run is absolutely certain" (Ouspensky, *Tertium Organum*, 315). The episode is also reminiscent of the healing effect of reading Wordsworth's poetry experienced by John Stuart Mill.

[85] *Ibid.*, 67.
[86] *Ibid.*, 81.
[87] *Ibid.*, 90-92.
[88] *Ibid.*, 92.

"I read it somewhere."[89]

As the readers of Winterson's earlier fiction would know, "Only the impossible is worth the effort" is the motto of a nameless woman in one of the stories Ali/x tells Tulip in *The.PowerBook*.[90] Like the other motto she lives by, "I risk more than I should",[91] it argues for the power of unrestrained love and bodily-felt, affective knowledge to break up the limits set by reason and the doxa to reconfigure reality. This is the message that, in the case of Billie and Spike, is buried with their bodies under the snow on Planet Blue just after having received a message from Handsome telling them that "there has been a nuclear attack on the Mission Base" and that "Orbus is preparing for war".[92] In Part Two, "Easter Island", the same message of love will be lost again when Spikkers, Billy's half-Dutch, half-native lover, is murdered by his rival just as he is about to win the Egg Race that would have put an end to the religious feud that had brought about the last tribal war and the destruction of every palm tree on the island.[93] And yet another love message will be lost again in Part Four, "Wreck City", when Billie is shot dead by the soldiers who are trying to repress the rebellion of the mutants,[94] those awe-inspiring survivors of the atomic bomb, whose monstrous bodies stand in sharp contrast to the splendid variety and beauty of the naturally grown hybrids in Planet Blue.

Just as the opposition of hybrids and mutants provides an emblematic example of the difference between natural evolution and misguided human interventionism, so Spike's process of humanisation through sensorial feeling, the fruition of affects and sexual love stands in diametrical opposition to the process of dehumanisation represented in Part One by Mrs Mary McMurphy, "Pink for short",[95] a doll-like, grotesque woman wholly dressed in pink and living in a robotised pink house that looks "like a Hall of Fame".[96] Having been genetically

---

[89] *Ibid.*, 90-91.
[90] Jeanette Winterson, *The.PowerBook*, London: Jonathan Cape, 2000, 55.
[91] *Ibid.*, 38.
[92] Winterson, *The Stone Gods*, 91.
[93] *Ibid.*, 110-15.
[94] *Ibid.*, 205.
[95] *Ibid.*, 35.
[96] *Ibid.*, 16.

fixed at twenty-four,[97] Pink wants to undergo the more dangerous process of genetic reversal to the age of twelve,[98] in order to please her paedophiliac husband.[99] With her thoughtlessness, her craze for TV shows and her obsession with meeting the impossible standards of beauty set by celebrities like Little Señorita, "a twelve-year old pop star who has Fixed herself rather than lose her fame",[100] Pink is a ludicrous satiric figure, strongly reminiscent of the female followers of Bunny Mix, "the winner of the Purple Heart Award" and Noah's *fiancée* in *Boating for Beginners*.[101] Like Martin Moody, "TV host to the stars", whose *One Minute Show* makes Pink and his thousands of fans go wild,[102] Bunny is a mediatic figure exerting a deadly influence on her fans through her trashy novelettes. In order to meet the impossible standards of beauty set by her heroines, Bunny's fans would go so far as to undertake outrageously expensive and drastic beauty treatments such as the losing of weight with a patent cure for the obese that involves being covered in a solution of honey and glycerine, and then having trained ants chew away the fat.[103] Though, admittedly, the product of satiric exaggeration, the options Bunny and Pink represent express a deadly serious, life-denying hate of the female body that is in keeping with the general dehumanisation of Orbus and of our own contemporary world. Significantly, Billie tries to dissuade Pink from undergoing genetic reversal with the argument that it has nothing to do with liberty of choice, as Pink argues, but with unethical corporative greed: "There was never any debate about the ethics of Genetic Reversal – it just started to happen because MORE figured out how to do it."[104] Respect for the human body is, then, a key ethical question neither the global corporation nor the Orbus society wishes to address.

---

[97] *Ibid.*, 19.

[98] *Ibid.*, 16.

[99] *Ibid.*, 20.

[100] *Ibid.*, 16.

[101] Jeanette Winterson, *Boating For Beginners* (1985), London: Methuen, 1990, 47.

[102] Winterson, *The Stone Gods*, 33, 26.

[103] Winterson, *Boating For Beginners*, 77. See also Susana Onega, "Writing, Creation and the Ethics of Postmodernist Romance in Jeanette Winterson's *Boating for Beginners*", *Recherches anglaises et nord-américaines* (*Ranam*) XXXIX (2006), 213-27.

[104] Winterson, *The Stone Gods*, 59.

When in the "Post-3 War" section we again encounter Billie and another Robo *sapiens*, also called Spike, we will find that the scientists working for MORE have designed her in the shape of a bodiless head, ironically discarding from the start the very element that, by conveying sensorial feelings and emotions, had triggered off the evolutionary transformation of the first Spike from Robo *sapiens* to *homo sapiens*. Testimony to the power of Hermetic *amor vulgaris*, or procreative sexual love, is, however, the ludicrous scene in which bodiless Spike is taught to use her tongue to have sex with Nebraska, an Alternative Community girl that Spike and Billie have encountered on their escapade from Tech City to the Front.[105] Influenced by the all-loving philosophy of Alaska, another Alternative Community girl, Spike starts entertaining Buddhist ideas that show her evolving from Ouspensky's stage of "Reasoning" to that of "Self-conscious and cosmic consciousness". As Alaska observes: "'I like it that Spike has a spiritual understanding,' …. 'Why shouldn't a robot be spiritual?'"[106]

At this stage, Orbus has become a nightmarish post-atomic habitat, with two areas divided by a no-man's land: a more degenerate and less habitable version of the Tech City we encountered in Part One, surrounded by a protective "perimeter bar [called] the Front", and Wreck City, "a No Zone – no insurance, no assistance, no welfare, no police",[107] inhabited by the survivors of the nuclear explosion, who have undergone an awe-inspiring, monstrous transformation into toxic radioactive mutants.[108] Convinced that the "latest war was a crisis of overemotionalism" and that "Fanatics do not listen to reason", Tech City has opted for an "economics of purpose" into which "Neither art nor love fits well".[109] Given the exhaustion of natural resources and the general scarcity of goods, "Capitalism has gone back to its roots in paternalism, and forward into its destiny – complete control of everything and everyone, and with our consent".[110] In this post-atomic world of jetons and black markets,[111] The Resistance, the anti-system movement created by the paranoia of the SS services in Part One, has now developed into "twenty alternative communities ranging from the

---

[105] *Ibid.*, 175.
[106] *Ibid.*, 180.
[107] *Ibid.*, 151.
[108] *Ibid.*, 171.
[109] *Ibid.*, 141.
[110] *Ibid.*, 139.
[111] *Ibid.*, 138.

1960s Free Love and Cadillacs, to a group of women-only Vegans looking for the next cruelty-free planet".[112] Yet another equally ineffectual and grotesque spiritual and ethical response to the situation is the group formed by Mary McMurphy (the "Pink" of Part One), who is now an Irish nun living on the border with five other members of the Holy Sisters of the Shining Mercy.[113] In this overtly fictional and grotesque world of anti-system groups in search of alternative ways of reconfiguring the world, the fitting leader is Friday, a disillusioned economist who had worked for the World Bank[114] until he decided to "put the world to rights".[115]

Besides her refusal to be genetically fixed, the Billie of Part One had drawn the attention of the SS services because she lived in the only remaining ecological farm in Tech City (passing for a museum), with real livestock, trees and plants, and a wooden house with a real dog called Rufus,[116] and because she could read. In a world of "State-approved mass illiteracy .... (Voice and pictures, yes; written words, no)",[117] where the "shrinking [of] human brains" was assumed as "an inevitable part of progress",[118] the capacity to read is not only useful but vital because, as Billie ironically remarks, it allows her to read "between the lines" of official propaganda,[119] but also, and most crucially, because books offer her intimations of other and better worlds.

Like Spike, Billie came to understand the true value of books through Captain Handsome during the cruise to Planet Blue. As she explains, when the Captain read love poems to Spike, "everybody laughed at him, but he insisted that only a poet could frame a language that could frame a world".[120] Handsome's visionary outlook on the capacity of poetic language to create alternative realities materialised the day his space-ship hit what he took for a meteorite shower but was in fact "a bookstorm – encyclopaedias, dictionaries, a Uniform Edition

---

[112] *Ibid.*, 36. Winterson's self-directed irony is evident here and in the description of the latter group as "Lesbian Vegans. Dinosaur-friendly" (*ibid.*, 174).
[113] *Ibid.*, 178.
[114] *Ibid.*, 171.
[115] *Ibid.*, 172.
[116] *Ibid.*, 42.
[117] *Ibid.*, 13.
[118] *Ibid.*, 14.
[119] *Ibid.*, 26.
[120] *Ibid.*, 66.

of the Romantic poets, the complete works of Shakespeare ... Scott, Defoe", and his favourite: "a battered eighteenth-century edition of Captain Cook's *Journals*."[121] This fantastic episode is reminiscent of "the city of words" in *Sexing the Cherry*,[122] an uncanny city where, once uttered, "words resist erasure"[123] and have to be brushed away by a host of cleaners, lest they go on for ever producing the effect for which they were uttered. The bookstorm has a similar *raison d'être*. Although books have been banned from Orbus, once written, they are unerasable.

By the same token, the radio message Spike sent into outer space just before dying on Planet Blue was not lost. Her radio signal went on emitting its message of love and harmony until it was picked up in 1960 by the Lovell Telescope built during the Cold War.[124] As the old engineer in charge of the telescope tells Billie in Part Four, in the 1960s, "there was absolutely no interest because the signal was bouncing off the surface of the moon and can only have been sent from somewhere very close to the moon – in fact, the earth".[125] These words identify Planet Blue and Orbus with the earth, suggesting that they are just different cosmogonies existing in a cyclical pattern of repetition in a unitary universe. The radio message remains unread until bodiless Spike captures the wavelength and realises that it is "one line of programming code for a Robo *sapiens*"[126] implausibly sent from their own planet sixty-five million years before, at the time of the dinosaurs.[127] So Spike's radio message, like Handsome's books, are records of the past sent from Planet Blue/Orbus/the earth to Planet Blue/Orbus/the earth, transmitting to the following generations the same story of love that might help them reconfigure the world. The problem is that, when the messages are picked up, there is no one willing, or able to interpret them.

The facts that the three planets represent different cosmogonies of a unitary universe and that the books and the radio message are flying through outer space, waiting for someone to pick them up, bring to

---

[121] *Ibid.*, 49.
[122] Jeanette Winterson, *Sexing the Cherry* (1985), London, Melbourne, etc.: Vintage, 1990, 20.
[123] *Ibid.*, 17.
[124] Winterson, *The Stone Gods*, 189.
[125] *Ibid.*, 191.
[126] *Ibid.*, 202.
[127] *Ibid.*, 174, 201.

mind the Hermetic alchemist notion of an intermediate psychophysical world, itself the antecedent of Ouspensy's *unus mundus* and Pauli and Jung's unified psychophysical reality. This association is made explicit by Billie's description of Handsome as "part swagger, part alchemist", as well as by the Captain's comment to Billie that when he was space cruising he sometimes had the impression that he was "sailing though a vast thought".[128] The first Spike expressed the same idea when she compared the universe to her cell memory, which is unable to forget:

> "The universe is an imprint. You are part of the imprint – it imprints you, you imprint it. You cannot separate yourself from the imprint, and you can never forget it. It isn't 'something', it is you".[129]

Handsome's and Spike's comments point to a holistic and animistic conception of man and cosmos that stands in diametrical opposition to the mechanicist outlook of the Orbus rulers. This holistic position, entertained by Hermetic alchemists from Paracelsus and Robert Fludd to Dr Bucke and P.D. Ouspensky – as well as by Stella and her Jewish father Ishmael in *Gut Symmetries*[130] – is based on "the absolute certainty of the indissoluble, unconscious oneness of man and world".[131] As Remo F. Roth has pointed out,[132] while the opposition between spirit and matter led Neoplatonist philosophers like Marcilio Ficino to consider matter (mother earth, the female body, the female principle) as negative and evil, Hermeticism gave spirit and matter equal value. While the Neoplatonists tried to spiritualise matter, the Hermetic alchemists aimed at bringing about "the *hierosgamos*

---

[128] *Ibid.*, 47

[129] *Ibid.*, 87. Spike's comparison of the universe to a vast memory unable to forget also echoes the New Physicist theory of "the cosmic blueprint" – the idea that in the evolution of the universe from its essentially featureless state after the Big Bang to the highly structured and complex physical world we see today there were organising principles at work, shaping matter and energy and directing them towards ever higher states of order and complexity (see Paul Davies, *The Cosmic Blueprint*, London: William Heinemann, 1987, 6-7).

[130] See Onega, *Jeanette Winterson*, 157-75.

[131] Carl G. Jung, "Paracelsus", in *The Spirit in Man, Art, and Literature* (1929), *The Collected Works*, XV, 1985, 11.

[132] Remo F. Roth, *The Return of the World Soul: Wolfgang Pauli, Carl Jung and the Challenge of the Unified Psychophysical Reality*, III/3.8, 2002-2004: http://www.psychovision.ch/synw/platinfertilityhermincarnp3.htm (accessed 8/7/2009).

(*coniunctio* or 'chymic wedding') of opposites (light and darkness; spirit and matter; god and goddess), through *amor vulgaris*, procreative sexual love".[133] Spike and Handsome's holistic conception of the universe is, then, directly related to the "wedding" of spirit and matter, thoughts and feelings, reason and affects, through the fruition of love. The alternative this holistic world-view offers to the exploitative, nature-loathing positivist reasoning of MORE and the Orbus technologists is revolutionary, as its ultimate goal is the institution of "universal harmony, of the harmonious relationships between man, the microcosm, and the greater world of the universe, the macrocosm".[134]

During the space cruise to Planet Blue, Billie asked Captain Handsome: "Where did these books come from?", and he simply replied: "A repeating world – same old story."[135] Similarly, in Part Four, the books fished up by Handsome and the signal emitted by Spike are described by Billie as "a message in a bottle" in a "repeating world".[136] In the post-apocalyptic context of Wreck City, fishing and reading these bottled messages that are floating on the psychophysical cosmic sea, constitute the only hope Planet Blue/Orbus/the earth still has of understanding the mistakes made in the earlier cosmogonies and of projecting new ways of reconfiguring reality on a harmonious and ethical basis.[137] This is precisely what Billie did, when, still on the space-ship, she opened Handsome's eighteenth-century copy of Captain Cook's *Journals* and read an entry at random. The entry was dated "*March 1774*" and recorded Cook's arrival at the bay on Easter Island.[138] A few moments before dying with Spike in the prehistoric cave, Billie opened the *Journals* once more and read the same entry again. Then, feeling the snow covering their bodies, she says:

---

[133] Onega, *Jeanette Winterson*, 168.
[134] Frances A. Yates, *Giordano Bruno and the Hermetic Tradition* (1964), London: Routledge and Kegan Paul; Chicago: The University of Chicago Press, 1977, 151.
[135] Winterson, *The Stone Gods*, 49.
[136] *Ibid.*, 202, 203.
[137] This idea materialises when, after the dropping of the atomic bomb, Billie's life is saved by the books in the British Library: "It was the books that saved my life. As the building collapsed I fell on to a raft of books, and stacks of books fell on to me, knocking me unconscious but easing me from further damage" (*ibid.*, 164).
[138] *Ibid.*, 49.

> Snow is covering us. Close your eyes and sleep. Close your eyes and dream. This is one story. There will be another.[139]

Billie's summons to sleep and dream, like Billy's realisation that Spikkers' body falling from the cliff was "like a star out of its orbit and coming to earth and seen no more",[140] reinforces the idea that, at the moment of their physical deaths, the souls of Billie and Spikkers, like Handsome's books, have transcended the material world and become one with the cosmos, where they will stay in harmonious unison until the next cosmogonic cycle, when they are dreamed/imagined into another story of love and desolation. From this perspective, the fact that what Billie reads on both occasions is the same entry that opens Part Two of the novel, dated on "March 1774. Sunday the 13th",[141] is significant in that the story told in the second Part, entitled "Easter Island", is also a tragic story of environmental destruction and impossible love in an erstwhile pristine and bountiful habitat, and because, by putting Captain Cook's *Journals* in Billie's hands and having her read the Easter Island story of Billy and Spikkers, Jeanette Winterson is situating Part Two *en abyme* with respect to Part One, thereby enhancing the repetitiveness of the two stories and the palimpsestic structure of the novel as a whole. This effect is given a further turn of the screw at the beginning of Part Three, when Billie, who is travelling home on the Tube, in the narrative present finds a pack of yellow, pre-war paper containing a manuscript entitled *The Stone Gods*. Perusing the manuscript, Billie thinks at first that it is "A love story ... maybe about aliens"; and then, after reading the remark, *"Everything is imprinted for ever with what it once was"*, she wonders: "Is that true?"[142]

The question, addressed to the reader as well as to herself, is subsequently answered by Billie in the affirmative, as the stories in the manuscript written by the Billie of Part One trigger off her desire to write/remember her own life story.[143] The narration of how her father

---

[139] *Ibid.*, 93.

[140] *Ibid.*, 115.

[141] *Ibid.*, 97.

[142] *Ibid.*, 119 (emphasis in the original).

[143] Winterson clarified the authorship of the manuscript, when she referred to it in an interview as "a manuscript written aeons ago by the first Billie that sets her [the second Billie] on the path of freedom" (John Mullen, "First Fruit", *The Guardian*, 3

broke his promise to marry her pregnant teenage mother is interrupted by the lines from the manuscript, " – *I was born in the year 1632 in the city of York, of a good family, tho' not of that country ...*", and then followed by a comment underlining the similarities between this and her own life story: "That's not me, that's Robinson Crusoe. Birth is a shipwreck."[144] The comment is doubly disingenuous, firstly, because we know that Billie's family name is Crusoe;[145] and secondly, because we also know that the story of Robinson Crusoe is not told in Winterson's novel, *The Stone Gods*, and that Defoe is mentioned as the author of one of the books fished up by Captain Handsome.[146]

This suggests that, by opening the manuscript found on the tube, Billie is entering an infinite World/Book, like Borges' "Library of Babel" or, more accurately, like the book Handel, one of the protagonists of *Art & Lies* finds lying on the seat of a train,[147] and which turns out to be the same book he inherited long ago from his mentor Cardinal Rosso, a "fabulous" compendium of rare, miscellaneous texts, whose "manuscript leaves had been saved from the sacking of the great Library at Alexandria in AD 642".[148] As readers eventually learn through the metaleptic coincidence of the pagination of Handel's life story in this book and in *Art & Lies*, the book found on the train is a *mise en abyme* of Winterson's novel,[149] just as the book Billie finds on the tube is the first Billie's manuscript and *a mise en abyme* of Winterson's *The Stone Gods*. From this perspective, the fact that in March 2007 a working version of *The Stone Gods* was left on a bench at Balham tube station by a Penguin reviewer[150] and found by Martha Osten[151] may be read as an uncannily

---

November 2007: http://www.guardian.co.uk/books/2007/nov/03/jeanettewinterson?gusrc=rss&feed=Books [accessed 1/9/2009]).

[144] Winterson, *The Stone Gods*, 122.

[145] *Ibid.*, 158.

[146] *Ibid.*, 49.

[147] Jeanette Winterson, *Art & Lies: A Piece for Three Voices and a Bawd*, London: Jonathan Cape, 1994, 3.

[148] *Ibid.*, 202.

[149] For an extended analysis of this, see Onega, *Jeanette Winterson*, 143-47.

[150] Lisa Muller, "Jeanette Winterson: Interview", *Time Out*, 24 September 2007: http://www.timeout.com/london/books/features/3526/Jeanette_Winterson-interview.html (accessed 1/9/2009).

[151] Caroline Briggs, "Winterson novel 'left at station'", *BBC News* (8 March 2007): http://news.bbc.co.uk./2/hi/entertainment/6430775.stm (accessed 1/9/2009).

apposite case of "synchronicity" in Jung's understanding of the term –
unless it was a clever, promotional joke.

Billie Crusoe's life story produces a strong effect of *déjà vu*, since
it is the same deeply traumatic story of impossible love between an
unwanted child and her red-haired teenage mother that Jeanette
Winterson has been trying to tell all her life. In this sense, the fact
that, while Billie's narration of her encounter with the mutant children
is rendered in a fluid and excessively sentimental language that begs
for the overidentification of the reader, the difficulty in addressing the
subject of her mother's enforced desertion is haunted by an
unspeakability – "Words are the part of silence that can be spoken"[152]
– that works to produce the readers' empathic unsettlement.

In this thoroughly moving version of her traumatic life story, Billie
situates the birth of her mother in World War Two, during "the
bombing of 1943",[153] and casts a pattern of repetition on her by
imagining her mother the unwanted issue of her soldier father's short
leave from the front. Billie remembers with nostalgia the twenty-nine
days she was with her mother before she was given to the orphanage
and also the safe and joyous time she spent in her womb. She
remembers her loving voice "made of hills" and the Manchester
"cotton mills",[154] and the walks they took together, with Billie
"walking insider her",[155] along a track that led to an enclosure with a
winding stream and an old stone farmhouse with an apple tree at the
front:

> There's a gate between the house and the track, and we lean on the
> gate very often, and she says, 'This is our house,' and I can smell the
> woodsmoke from the fire.[156]

With its archetypal gate, stream and apple tree, this prelapsarian
hortus conclusus becomes the emblem of the life of cosmic love and
harmony mother and child were prevented from enjoying by social
and political circumstances out of their control. The force of this
utopian dream was so strong that, as we know, it materialised in Part
One, where we find adult Billie living on the last farm-*cum*-museum

---

[152] Winterson, *The Stone Gods*, 126.
[153] *Ibid.*, 129.
[154] *Ibid.*, 126.
[155] *Ibid.*, 129.
[156] *Ibid.*, 130.

in Tech City. Similarly, in Part Two, Spikkers creates an equally utopian and nostalgic alternative to his bleak reality on Easter Island by yearning for the Amsterdam of his Dutch sea-faring father's stories: "His only wish was to escape the island and settle in his father's great sailing city Amsterdam, 'much wood, many houses'."[157]

While the farm and Amsterdam constitute the utopian alternatives to Billie and Spikkers' individual sense of loss and deprivation, Planet Blue is the collective dream of a whole traumatised society. Listening to a talk on the radio about the new blue planet, Billie is reminded of a description of the Golden Country in terms that grant reality to dreamed of, imaginary worlds and enhance her own role as archetypal quester:

> *You dreamed all your life there was somewhere to land, a place to lie down and sleep, with the sound of water nearby. You set off to find it, buying old maps and listening to travellers' tales, because you believed that the treasure was really there.*[158]

The passage, which synthesises the *Leitmotif* of the novel, could come from any of Jeanette Winterson's fictions, as, invariably, the force that drives Winterson's protagonists on their life quests is presented as an acute feeling of lack and incompleteness expressed in archetypal images like the search for buried treasure, the Philosopher's Stone, the Holy Grail, that which cannot be found, or death.[159] While in the earlier fictions, the quester's journey invariably takes the form of an individual search for true love, in *The Stone Gods*, as we have seen, the search is for a remembered world of pristine beauty and harmony ruled by unbounded love:

> Love without thought. Love without conditions. Love without promises. Love without threats. Love without fear. Love without limits. Love without end.[160]

This yearning for a better world is in keeping with the sense of loss that informs new baroque narratives confronted with the need to respond to the trauma paradigm. In keeping with this, the nostalgic

---

[157] *Ibid.*, 106.
[158] *Ibid.*, 25 (emphasis in the original).
[159] See Onega, *Jeanette Winterson*, 243-44.
[160] Winterson, *The Stone Gods*, 121.

and sentimental tone of the narration of Billie's entrance into the Dead Forest in the radioactive area beyond the No Zone, with its sweating trees[161] and hairless and deformed mutant children,[162] progressively develops into an overtly elegiac style, reaching a climax with Billie's programmatic crying for the death of the planet:

> And my tears are for the planet because I love it and because we're killing it, and my tears are for the wars and all this loss, and for the children who have no childhood, and for my childhood, which has somehow turned up again, like an orphan on my doorstep asking to be let in. But I don't want to open the door.[163]

This elegiac style as well as the death of Billie at the end of the novel might be read as evidence that there is no hope for the future of our planet, that human beings are incapable of developing the cosmic consciousness that would allow us to break up the fixity of eternal recurrence. However, at the moment of her death, Billie has a vision of her mother's face waiting for her on the other side of the gate, granting her access at last to the prelapsarian farm she had always yearned to enter:[164] a dream of a new start from the Edenic garden, that, like the endings of parts One and Two, would not satisfy a realist reader, but pregnant with possibilities for those who, like Captain Handsome, believe in the power of the imagination to create new worlds. As bodiless Spike puts it with reference to the dropping of the atomic bomb:

> "What happened did happen, but not before it was so powerful an idea that it took shape and form and ripped through the thin skin that separates potential from event."[165]

---

[161] *Ibid.*, 168.

[162] *Ibid.*, 170.

[163] *Ibid.*, 201. The allusion to her childhood turning up again may be read as a metacomment, as Billie's life story seems to have been triggered off by the writer's discovery of her adoption papers in her father's house in 2007. Her description of "those 1960s forms, typed on a ribbon typewriter, signed in fountain pen" as "a message in a bottle from another world" (Mullen, "First Fruit", n.p.) clearly echoes Billie's description of Spike's radio signals as "a message in a bottle" in a "repeating world". Winterson, *The Stone Gods*, 202, 203.

[164] *Ibid.*, 207.

[165] *Ibid.*, 181.

As I have tried to demonstrate, the powerful idea Jeanette Winterson wishes to endow with shape and form by means of her baroque aesthetics of repetition and excess and her poetic language of sensation, feelings and affects, is the power of love to break up paired opposites, reconcile spirit and matter and reconfigure reality from the harmonious and ethical basis of unbounded love, thus offering readers a crucial alternative to our dehumanised and deeply traumatic form of being-in-the-world.

NOTES ON CONTRIBUTORS

Gerd Bayer is a tenured faculty member (Akademischer Rat) at Erlangen University. He previously taught at the University of Toronto, at Case Western Reserve University, and at the University of Wisconsin-Whitewater. He is the author of *"Greener, More Mysterious Processes of Mind": Natur als Dichtungsprinzip bei John Fowles* (LIT, 2004), the editor of *Mediating Germany: Popular Culture between Tradition and Innovation* (Cambridge Scholars Publishing, 2006), of the Europe volume of *The Greenwood Encyclopedia of World Popular Culture* (Greenwood, 2006), and of *Heavy Metal Music in Britain* (Ashgate, 2009), as well as the co-editor, with Rudolf Freiburg, of *Literatur und Holocaust* (Königshausen & Neumann, 2008). He has published articles on postmodern and postcolonial literature, urban studies, popular culture, holocaust studies, and cinema studies. He is currently working on a book project about genre and early modern narratives.

Charley Baker worked on the clinical side of mental health in the NHS for six years while completing her BA and MA in literature and is now a Research Associate at the School of Nursing, Midwifery and Physiotherapy at the University of Nottingham, working on a Leverhulme-funded project examining representations of madness in post-war UK and US fiction. In addition to co-writing a book for Palgrave based on the findings of the study, she is involved in the development of an international Madness and Literature Network funded by the AHRC. Her PhD studies focus on the interactions between clinically defined psychosis and postmodern fiction and theory. She was recently literary adviser and invited contributor for *Psychiatry PRN* (Oxford University Press, 2009) and has written a number of papers on psychiatry and literature. She lectures on various mental health topics and contributes to interdisciplinary initiatives with the School of English Studies at the University of Nottingham.

Jean-Michel Ganteau is Professor of English Literature at the University Paul Valéry-Montpellier 3 (France). He is the editor of the journal *Études britanniques contemporaines*. He has published two monographs: *David Lodge: le choix de l'éloquence* (Presses Universitaires de Bordeaux, 2001) and *Peter Ackroyd ou la musique du passé* (Michel Houdiard, 2007). He is also the editor, with Christine Reynier, of two volumes: *Impersonality and Emotion in Twentieth-Century British Literature* (Publications Montpellier 3, 2005) and *Impersonality and Emotion in Twentieth-Century British Arts* (Publications Montpellier 3, 2007). He has edited a special issue of *Cahiers victoriens et édouardiens*, entitled *Catholic Fiction 1840-1914* (2000), and co-edited with Liliane Louvel a special issue of *Etudes anglaises* on the short story in English from 1980 to the present, and with Susana Onega, *The Ethical Component in Experimental British Fiction since the 1960s* (Cambridge Scholars Publishing, 2007). He has published extensively on contemporary British fiction, with a special interest in the ethics of affects (as manifest in such aesthetic resurgences and concretions as the baroque, kitsch, camp, melodrama and romance).

Georges Letissier is Professor of English at Nantes University (France). He has published articles in English and French on Victorian literature (Charles Dickens, George Eliot, Christina Rossetti, William Morris) and on contemporary British fiction (Peter Ackroyd, A.S. Byatt, Alasdair Gray, Alan Hollinghurst, Graham Swift, Sarah Waters). He is more especially interested in post-Victorianism from an epistemological perspective (history and science). He has published a book in French on Ford Madox Ford's *The Good Soldier* (Éditions du Temps, 2005), and edited a collection of essays titled *Rewriting, Reprising: Plural Intertextualities* (Cambridge Scholars Publishing, 2009). He is currently co-editing with Professor Michel Prum for L'Harmattan the proceedings of a conference on the European Legacy of Charles Darwin. One of his most recent articles bears on a comparative study of Byatt and Winterson: "Passion and Possession as Alternatives to 'Cosmic Masculinity' in Herstorical Romances", in Ann Heilmann and Mark Llewellyn, eds, *Metafiction and Metahistory in Contemporary Women's Writing* (Palgrave, 2007).

Angela Locatelli is Professor of English Literature at the University of Bergamo. She is Adjunct Professor in the Department of Religious Studies at the University of Pennsylvania, Philadelphia. Her main research interest is literary theory. She has written extensively on Shakespeare and Renaissance culture and literature. Her publications also include a book on the "stream of consciousness" novel, and several articles on twentieth-century fiction and drama. She has published the first edition (with an Italian translation) of Henry Peacham's *A Merry Discourse of Meum and Tuum* (1639) *(Il Doppio e il Picaresco*, Jaca Book, 1998), and has edited eight volumes on literary epistemology (*The Knowledge of Literature/La conoscenza della Letteratura*, Sestante Edizioni, 2002-2008). She is one of the three General Editors of *EJES* (*The European Journal of English Studies*).

María Jesús Martínez-Alfaro is Senior Lecturer in English Language and Literature at the Department of English and German Philology of the University of Zaragoza (Spain). She is the author of *Text and Intertexts in Charles Palliser's* The Quincunx (Ann Arbor, UMI, 1996) and she co-edited, with Dr Ramón Plo, a volume of collected essays entitled *Beyond Borders: Re-defining Generic and Ontological Boundaries* (C. Winter, 2000). Her research focuses on postmodern British fiction in general and, more specifically, on such issues as metafiction, parody, intertextuality, detective fiction, trauma and ethics in relation to the novels of Martin Amis, John Fowles, Peter Ackroyd, A.S. Byatt, Graham Swift, Barry Unsworth, Paul Auster and Charles Palliser, among others. She has published several articles on these authors and subjects, both in national and international journals such as *Twentieth-Century Literature, Symbolism, Journal of the Short Story in English (JSSE)/Les Cahiers de la Nouvelle, Miscelánea, Revista Alicantina de Estudios Ingleses,* and others. At present, she is one of the members of a research team led by Professor Susana Onega and currently working on trauma and ethics in contemporary fiction written in English.

Susana Onega is Professor of English Literature at the University of Zaragoza (Spain) and the Head of a research team of eighteen members currently working on ethics and trauma in contemporary fiction. She has written numerous articles and book chapters on contemporary British literature and narrative theory and is the author of *Análisis estructural, método narrativo y "sentido" de* The Sound and the Fury *de William Faulkner* (Pórtico, 1980), of *Form and Meaning in the Novels of John Fowles* (UMI Research Press, 1989), of *Peter Ackroyd: The Writer and his Work* (Northcote House and The British Council, 1998), of *Metafiction and Myth in the Novels of Peter Ackroyd* (Candem House, 1999), and of *Jeanette Winterson* (Manchester UP, 2006). She is the editor of *Estudios literarios ingleses II: Renacimiento y barroco* (Cátedra, 1986) and of *"Telling Histories": Narrativizing History/Historicizing Literature* (Rodopi, 1995). She has written an Introduction for, and edited and translated into Spanish John Fowles' *The Collector* (Cátedra, 1999) and, with José Angel García Landa, has co-edited *Narratology: An Introduction* (Longman, 1996); with John A Stotesbury, *London in Literature: Visionary Mappings of the Metropolis* (Carl Winter, 2001); with Christian Gutleben, *Refracting the Canon in Contemporary Literature and Film* (Rodopi, 2004); with Annette Gomis, *George Orwell: A Centenary Celebration* (Carl Winter, 2005), and with Jean-Michel Ganteau, *The Ethical Component in Experimental British Fiction since the 1960s* (Cambridge Scholars Publishing, 2007).

Silvia Pellicer-Ortín is a Research Fellow at the University of Zaragoza (Spain) where she is a member of the research group entitled "Contemporary Narrative in English" headed by Susana Onega. After completing her Bachelor's Degree in English Philology at the University of Zaragoza in 2007, for which she was awarded the Extraordinary Degree Award in March 2008, she obtained the Master's degree in "Textual and Cultural Studies in English" by defending with honours her MA thesis entitled: "Intertextuality and the Working Through of Trauma in Eva Figes' *Tales of Innocence and Experience*" in September 2008. She is currently enrolled in the doctoral programme on English Studies offered by the University of Zaragoza and is writing her PhD Thesis on *Writing as Self-healing: Ethics, Trauma and the Construction of the Female Self in the Fiction of Eva Figes*. Her main research interests include contemporary British fiction, with a special focus on the ethical and traumatic component in the writings of sexual and ethnic minorities, the Holocaust and the question of Jewishness.

Lena Steveker received her doctoral degree from the Friedrich-Alexander University Erlangen-Nuremberg and she now teaches British Literary and Cultural Studies at Saarland University. Her research interests are contemporary literature, popular culture, and early modern literature. She is the author of *Identity and Cultural Memory in the Fiction of A.S. Byatt: Knitting the Net of Culture* (Palgrave, 2009). She is currently working on a co-edited collection of critical essays focusing on the topic of heroism in J.K. Rowling's *Harry Potter* series and on a book project on early modern theatre and news culture.

Anne Whitehead is Senior Lecturer in Modern and Contemporary Literature and Theory at the School of Literature, Language and Linguistics of Newcastle University. Her main research interests are trauma theory, psychoanalytic theory, and theories of memory. She is the author of *Trauma Fiction* (Edinburgh University Press, 2004) and *Memory* (Routledge, 2009). She is also the editor, with J.J. Long, of *W.G. Sebald – A Critical Companion* (Edinburgh University Press, 2004); and with Michael Rossington, of *Theories of Memory: A Reader* (Edinburgh University Press, 2007).

Jakob Winnberg received his PhD from Gothenburg University, Sweden, where he also recently held a three-year position as Research Fellow. He has lectured in numerous Swedish universities and colleges, and has been a visiting Research Fellow at the Université Paul-Valéry, Montpellier III, France. Presently, he teaches at Växjö University. His research focuses on the theories and practices of modernism and postmodernism, with special attention to the aesthetics, ethics and politics of affect, including the (re)gendering of affect in postmodernist fiction. He has published articles and presented papers on works by such authors as Peter Ackroyd, J.G. Ballard, Angela Carter, Bret Easton Ellis and Graham Swift. He is the author of one monograph, *An Aesthetics of Vulnerability: The Sentimentum and the Novels of Graham Swift* (2003), and is completing another, tentatively titled *The Waxing and Waning of Affect in Postmodernist Fiction*.

José M. Yebra is Associate Lecturer in English Language and Literature at the University of Zaragoza. He has recently read his PhD

Thesis on *Identity and Intertextuality in Alan Hollinghurst's Novels* with *summa cum laude*. He has delivered several papers and published various articles on Alan Hollinghurst. His major research interests include postmodernist British literature, with a special focus on gender and sexuality.

INDEX

Commodifying (Post)Colonialism

Othering, Reification, Commodification and the New Literatures and Cultures in English

Edited by Rainer Emig and Oliver Lindner

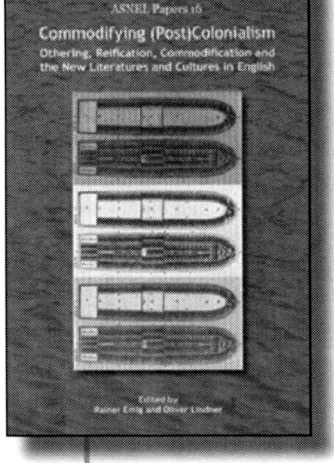

Since its inception in the 1980s, postcolonial theory has greatly enriched academic perspectives on culture and literature. Yet, in the same way that colonial goods and services have long contributed to economic and political growth, postcolonial topics have also become a profit-generating commodity. This is highly apparent in the success of the postcolonial novel or in the ability of film to cross over from Asia, Africa and elsewhere to paying audiences in Europe and America.

The contributions in this volume, in their various ways, take a critical look at artistic responses to the commodification of colonial and postcolonial histories, peoples, and products from the eighteenth century to the present. They explore, in particular, what literary and cultural texts have to say about commodification after the end of colonialism and how the Western culture industry continually capitalizes on representations of the postcolonial Other.

Contributors: Samy Azouz, Lars Eckstein, Rainer Emig, Wolfgang Funk, Jens Martin Gurr, Birte Heidemann, Sissy Helff, Graham Huggan, Stephan Laqué, Oliver Lindner, Ana Cristina Mendes, Sabine Nunius, Carl Plasa, Katharina Rennhak, Ksenia Robbe, Cecile Sandten.

Amsterdam/New York, NY
2010. XXIV, 262 pp.
(Cross/Cultures 127,
ASNEL Papers 16)
Bound €58,-/US$78,-
E-Book €58,-/US$78,-
ISBN: 978-90-420-3226-2
ISBN: 978-90-420-3227-9

USA/Canada:
248 East 44th Street, 2nd floor,
New York, NY 10017, USA.
Call Toll-free (US only): T: 1-800-225-3998
F: 1-800-853-3881

All other countries:
Tijnmuiden 7, 1046 AK Amsterdam, The Netherlands
Tel. +31-20-611 48 21 Fax +31-20-447 29 79
Please note that the exchange rate is subject to fluctuations

Neo-Victorian
Tropes of Trauma

The Politics of Bearing After-Witness
to Nineteenth-Century Suffering

Edited by
Marie-Luise Kohlke and
Christian Gutleben

rodopi

Orders@rodopi.nl—www.rodopi.nl

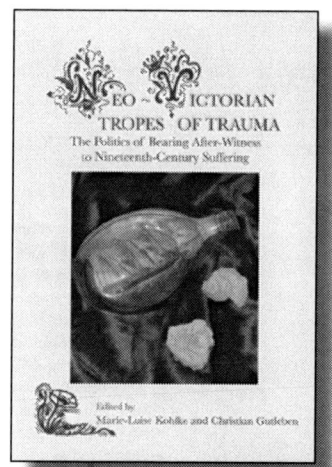

This collection constitutes the first volume in Rodopi's Neo-Victorian Series, which explores the prevalent but often problematic re-vision of the long nineteenth century in contemporary culture. Here is presented for the first time an extended analysis of the conjunction of neo-Victorian fiction and trauma discourse, highlighting the significant interventions in collective memory staged by the belated aesthetic working-through of historical catastrophes, as well as their lingering traces in the present. The neo-Victorian's privileging of marginalised voices and its contestation of master-narratives of historical progress construct a patchwork of competing but equally legitimate versions of the past, highlighting on-going crises of existential extremity, truth and meaning, nationhood and subjectivity. This volume will be of interest to both researchers and students of the growing field of neo-Victorian studies, as well as scholars in memory studies, trauma theory, ethics, and heritage studies. It interrogates the ideological processes of commemoration and forgetting and queries how the suffering of cultural and temporal others should best be represented, so as to resist the temptations of exploitative appropriation and voyeuristic spectacle. Such precarious negotiations foreground a central paradox: the ethical imperative to bear after-witness to history's silenced victims in the face of the potential unrepresentability of extreme suffering.

"The volume covers an important gap in the state of the art in neo-Victorian studies, as it offers in-depth analyses, from the perspective of trauma theory, of a significant number of neo-Victorian fictions published between the 1960s and the present...running all the spectrum from the collective physical and psychological traumas associated with the armed conflicts and the spread of Empire, to individual and more covert family traumas, like incest, or ideological traumas related to the confrontation of religious belief and Darwinian science."

Susana Onega, University of Zaragoza, Spain

Amsterdam/New York, NY
2010. VI, 412 pp.
(Neo-Victorian Series 1)
Paper €84,-/US$113,-
E-Book €84,-/US$113,-
ISBN: 978-90-420-3230-9
ISBN: 978-90-420-3231-6

USA/Canada:
248 East 44th Street, 2nd floor,
New York, NY 10017, USA.
Call Toll-free (US only): T: 1-800-225-3998
                          F: 1-800-853-3881
All other countries:
Tijnmuiden 7, 1046 AK Amsterdam, The Netherlands
Tel. +31-20-611 48 21 Fax +31-20-447 29 79
Please note that the exchange rate is subject to fluctuations

rodopi

Orders@rodopi.nl—www.rodopi.nl

Performative Body Spaces

Corporeal Topographies in Literature, Theatre, Dance, and the Visual Arts

Edited by
Markus Hallensleben

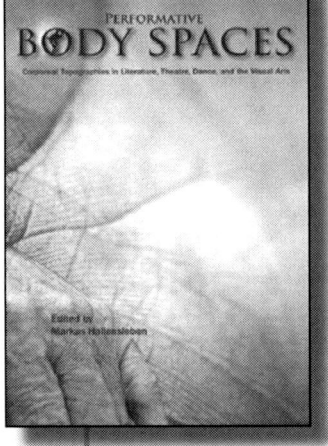

The human body as cultural object always *has* and *is* a performing subject, which binds the political with the theatrical, shows the construction of ethnicity and technology, unveils private and public spaces, transgresses race and gender, and finally becomes a medium that overcomes the borders of art and life. Since there cannot be a universal definition of the human body due to its culturally performative role as a producer of interactive social spaces, this volume discusses body images from diverse cultural, historical, and disciplinary perspectives, such as art history, human kinetics and performance studies. The fourteen case studies reach from Asian to European studies, from 19th century French culture to 20th century German literature, from Polish Holocaust memoirs to contemporary dance performances, from Japanese avant-garde theatre to Makeover Reality TV shows.

This volume is of interest for performance studies artists as well. By focusing on the intersection of body and space, all contributions aim to bridge the gap between art practices and theories of performativity. The innovative impulse of this approach lies in the belief that there is no distinction between performing, discussing, and theorizing the human body, and thus fosters a unique transdisciplinary and international collaboration around the theme performative body spaces. (I. Biopolitical Choreographies, II. Transcultural Topographies, III. Corporal Mediations, IV. Controlled Interfaces.)

Amsterdam/New York, NY
2010. 250 pp.
(Critical Studies 33)
Paper €50,-/US$68,-
E-Book €50,-/US$68,-
ISBN: 978-90-420-3193-7
ISBN: 978-90-420-3194-4

USA/Canada:
248 East 44th Street, 2nd floor,
New York, NY 10017, USA.
Call Toll-free (US only): T: 1-800-225-3998
F: 1-800-853-3881
All other countries:
Tijnmuiden 7, 1046 AK Amsterdam, The Netherlands
Tel. +31-20-611 48 21 Fax +31-20-447 29 79
Please note that the exchange rate is subject to fluctuations

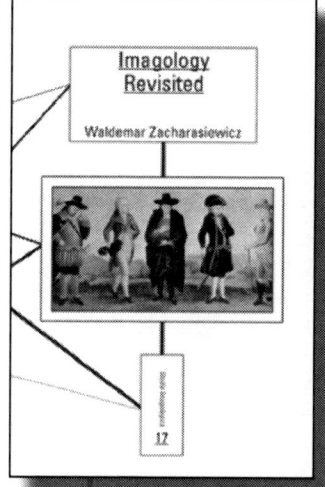

Lightning Source UK Ltd.
Milton Keynes UK
175464UK00003B/6/P